Art by Akiko Kawano
Story by Aki Shikimi

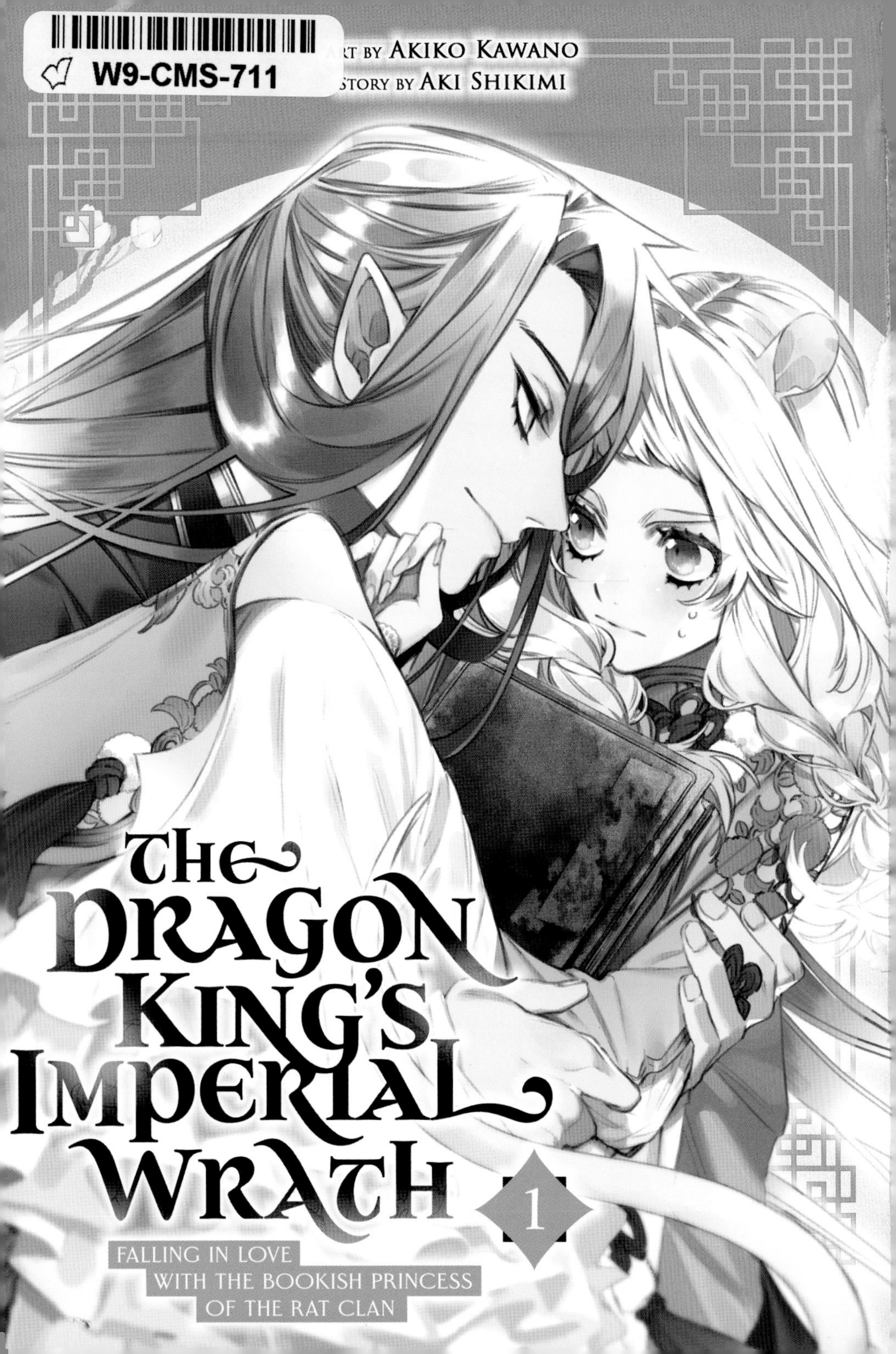

The Dragon King's Imperial Wrath

1

Falling in Love with the Bookish Princess of the Rat Clan

The Dragon King's Imperial Wrath

◆

Contents

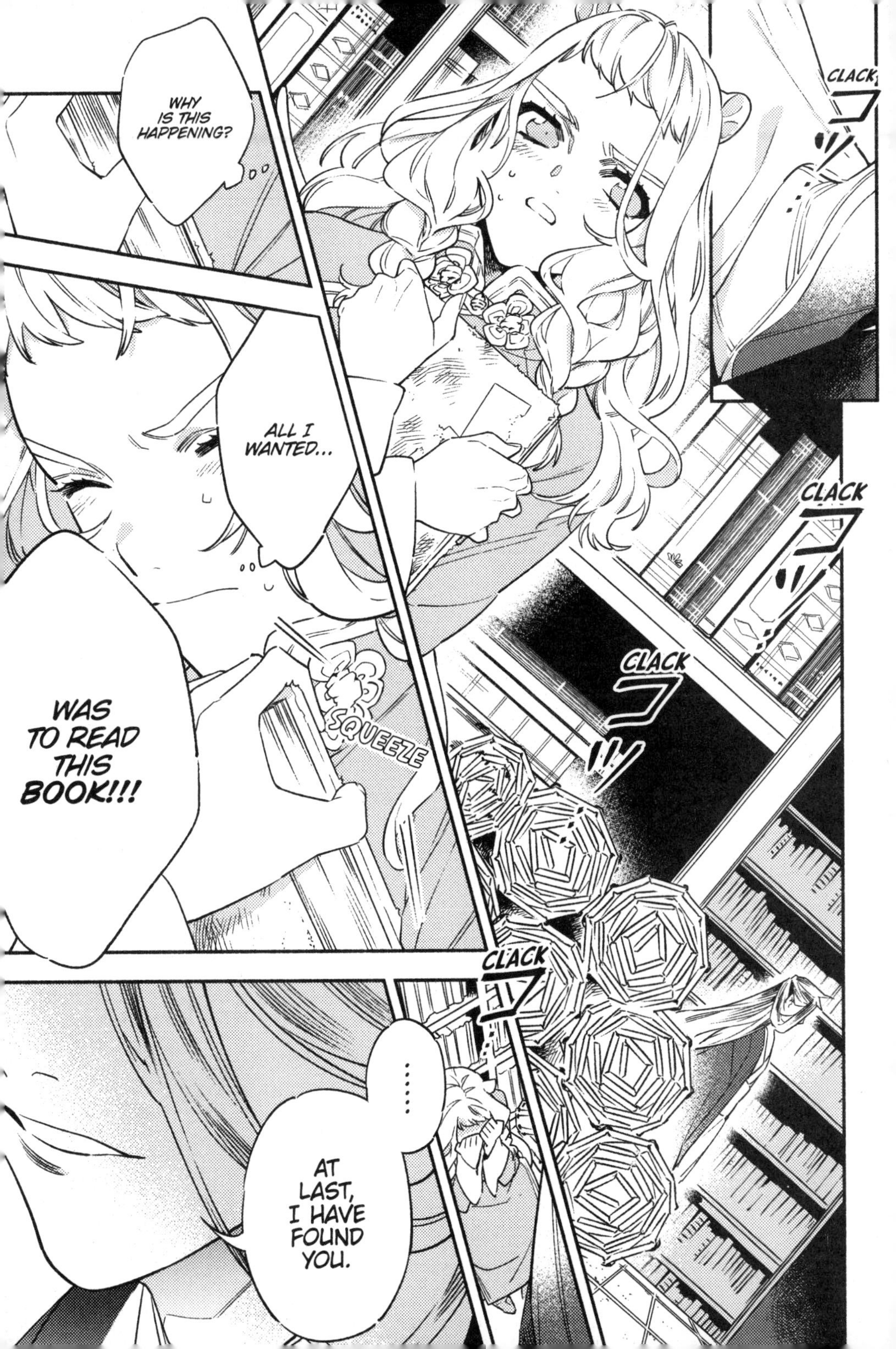
CLACK
CLACK
CLACK
CLACK
WHY IS THIS HAPPENING?
ALL I WANTED...
SQUEEZE
WAS TO READ THIS BOOK!!!
......
AT LAST, I HAVE FOUND YOU.

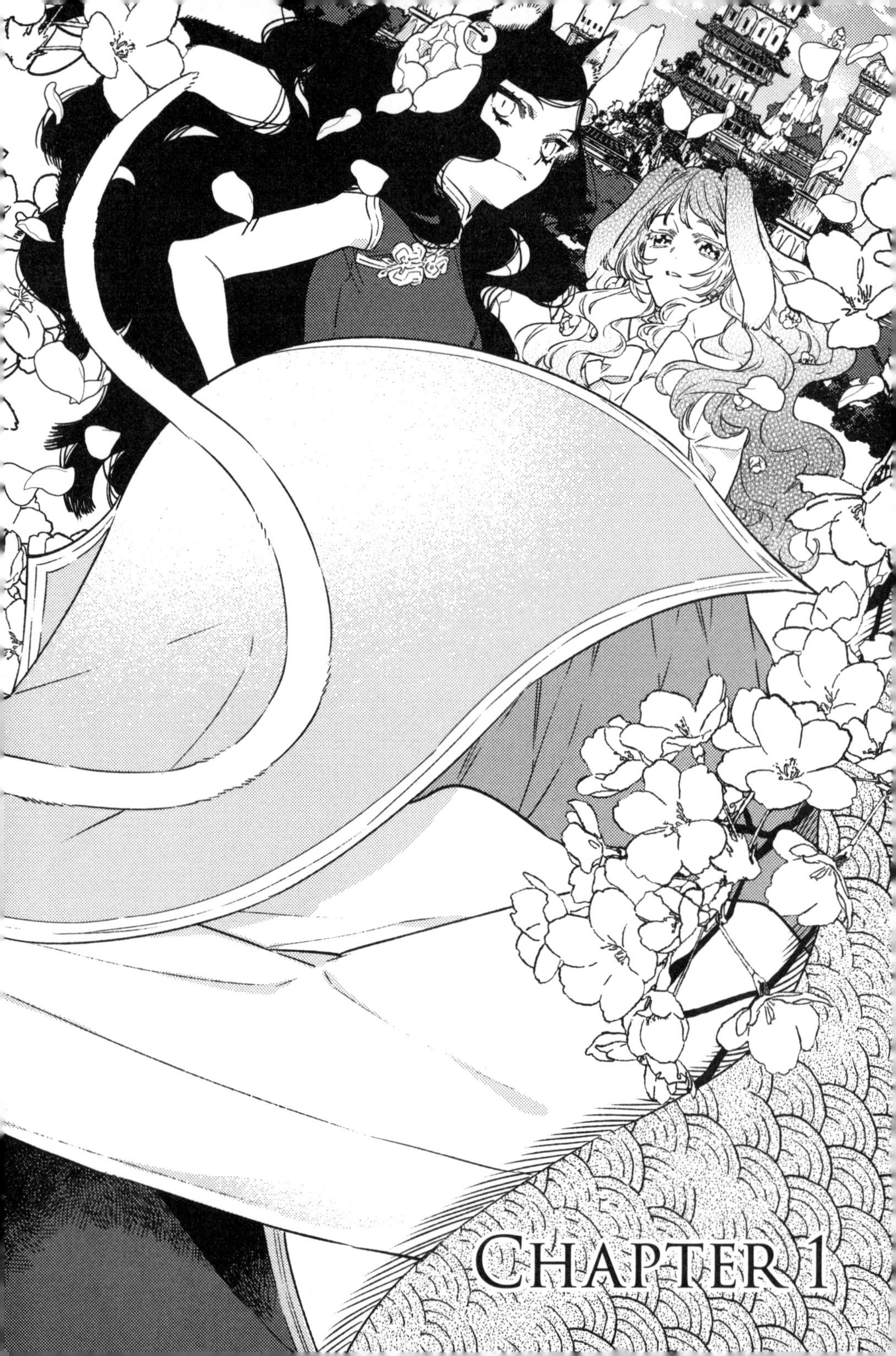
CHAPTER 1

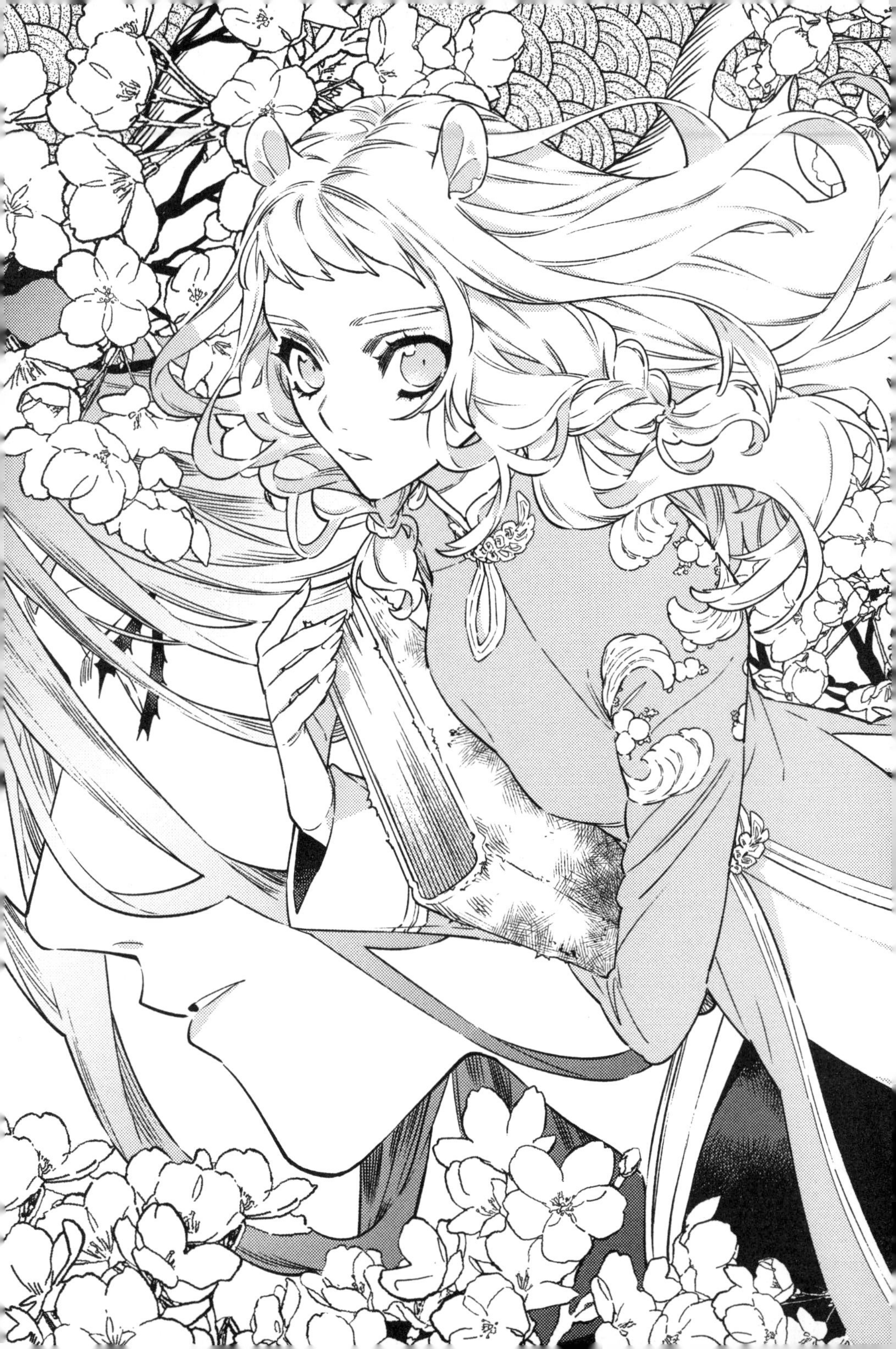

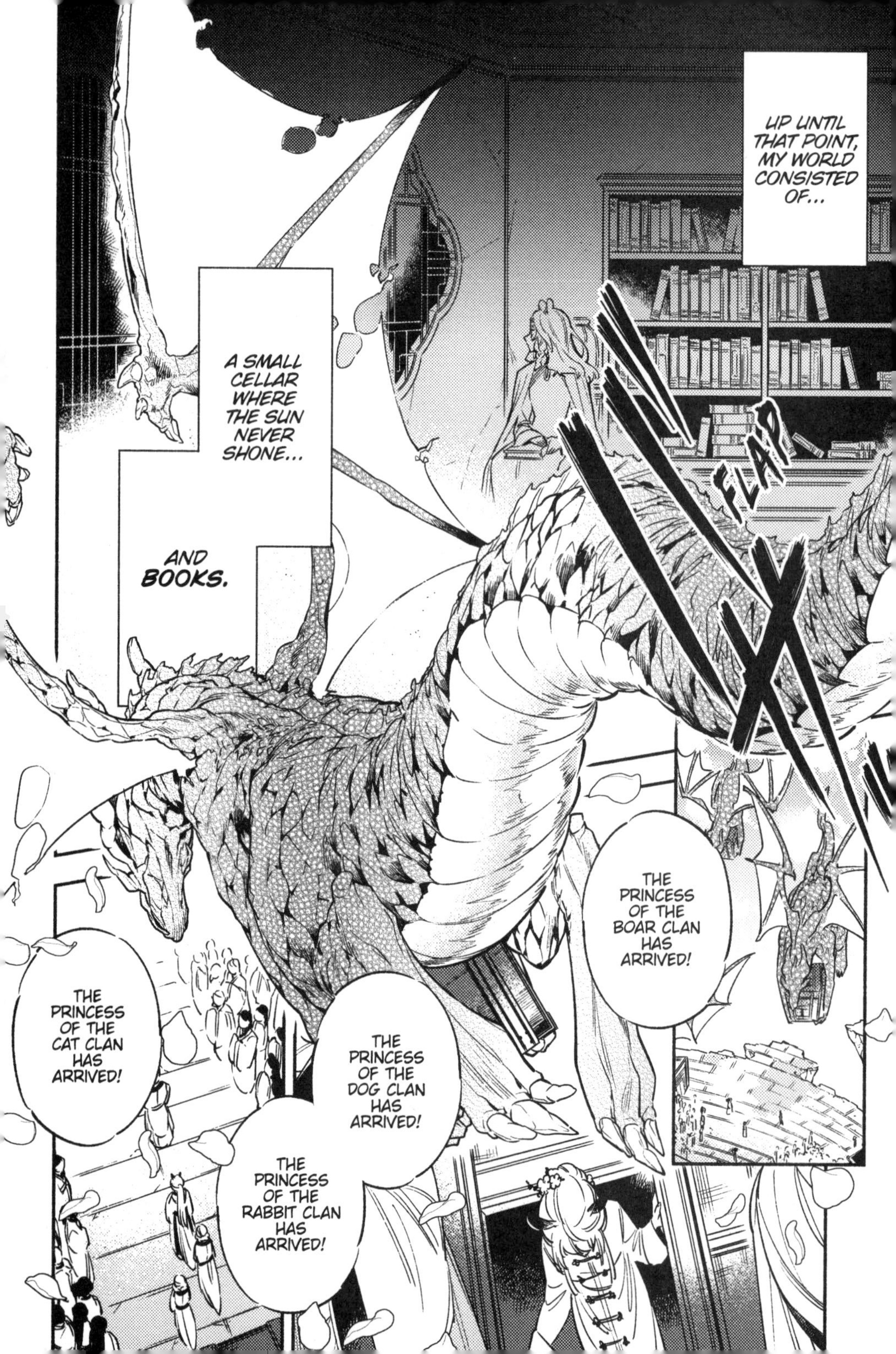
UP UNTIL THAT POINT, MY WORLD CONSISTED OF...
A SMALL CELLAR WHERE THE SUN NEVER SHONE...
AND BOOKS.
FLAP
THE PRINCESS OF THE BOAR CLAN HAS ARRIVED!
THE PRINCESS OF THE DOG CLAN HAS ARRIVED!
THE PRINCESS OF THE CAT CLAN HAS ARRIVED!
THE PRINCESS OF THE RABBIT CLAN HAS ARRIVED!

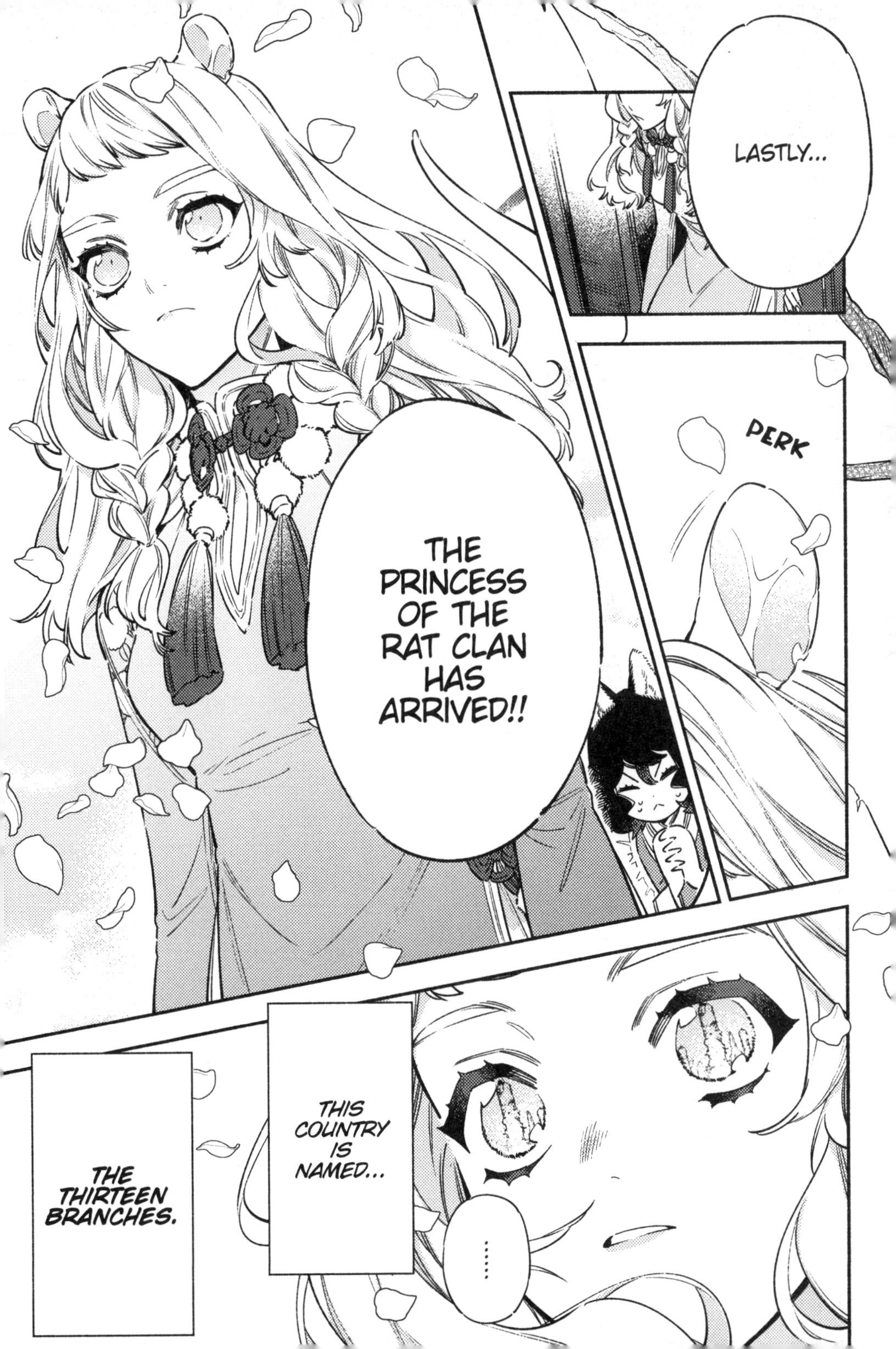
LASTLY...
PERK
THE PRINCESS OF THE RAT CLAN HAS ARRIVED!!
......
THIS COUNTRY IS NAMED...
THE THIRTEEN BRANCHES.

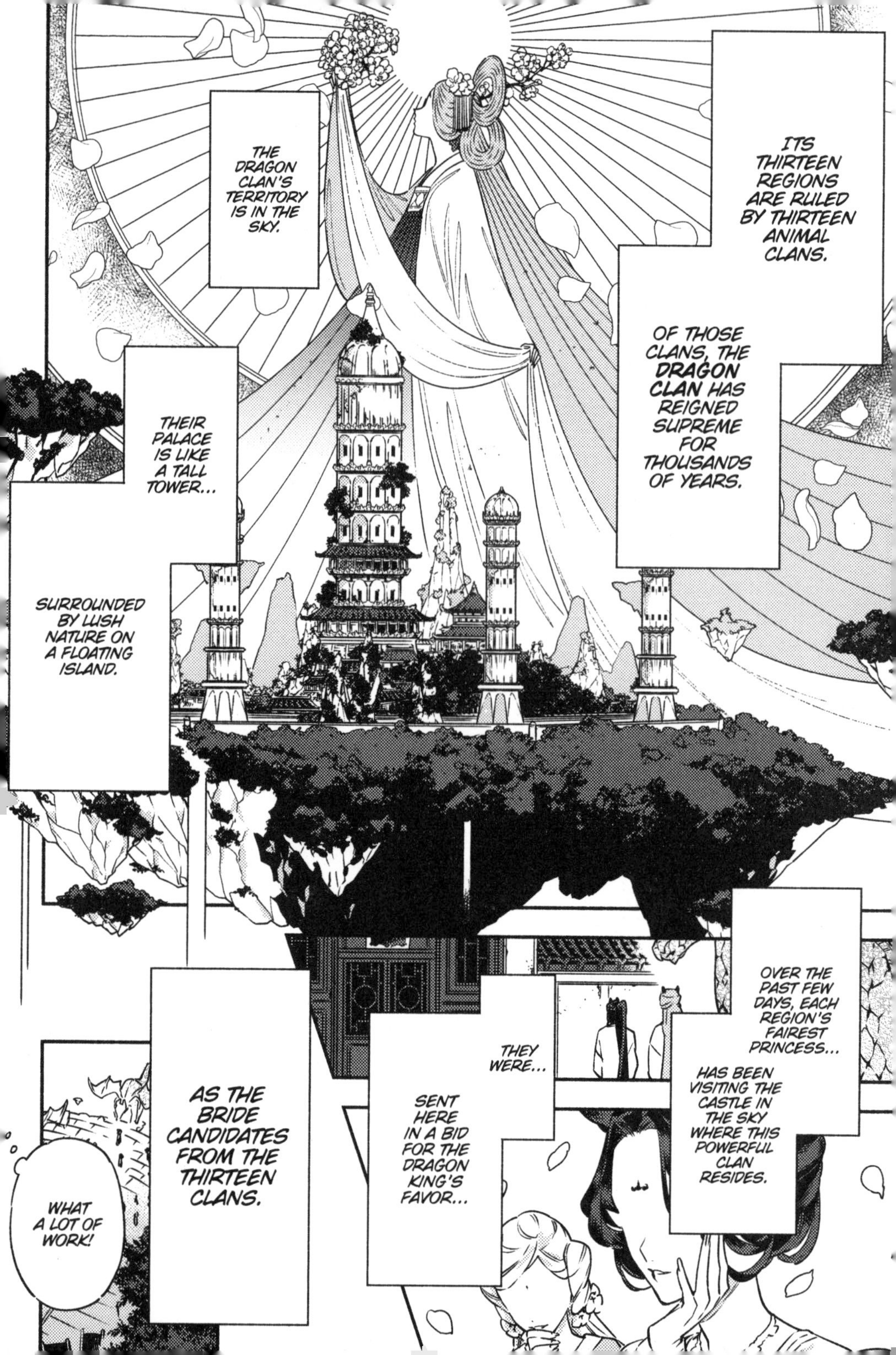
ITS THIRTEEN REGIONS ARE RULED BY THIRTEEN ANIMAL CLANS.
OF THOSE CLANS, THE **DRAGON CLAN** HAS REIGNED SUPREME FOR THOUSANDS OF YEARS.
THE DRAGON CLAN'S TERRITORY IS IN THE SKY.
THEIR PALACE IS LIKE A TALL TOWER...
SURROUNDED BY LUSH NATURE ON A FLOATING ISLAND.
OVER THE PAST FEW DAYS, EACH REGION'S FAIREST PRINCESS...
HAS BEEN VISITING THE CASTLE IN THE SKY WHERE THIS POWERFUL CLAN RESIDES.
THEY WERE...
SENT HERE IN A BID FOR THE DRAGON KING'S FAVOR...
AS THE BRIDE CANDIDATES FROM THE THIRTEEN CLANS.
WHAT A LOT OF WORK!

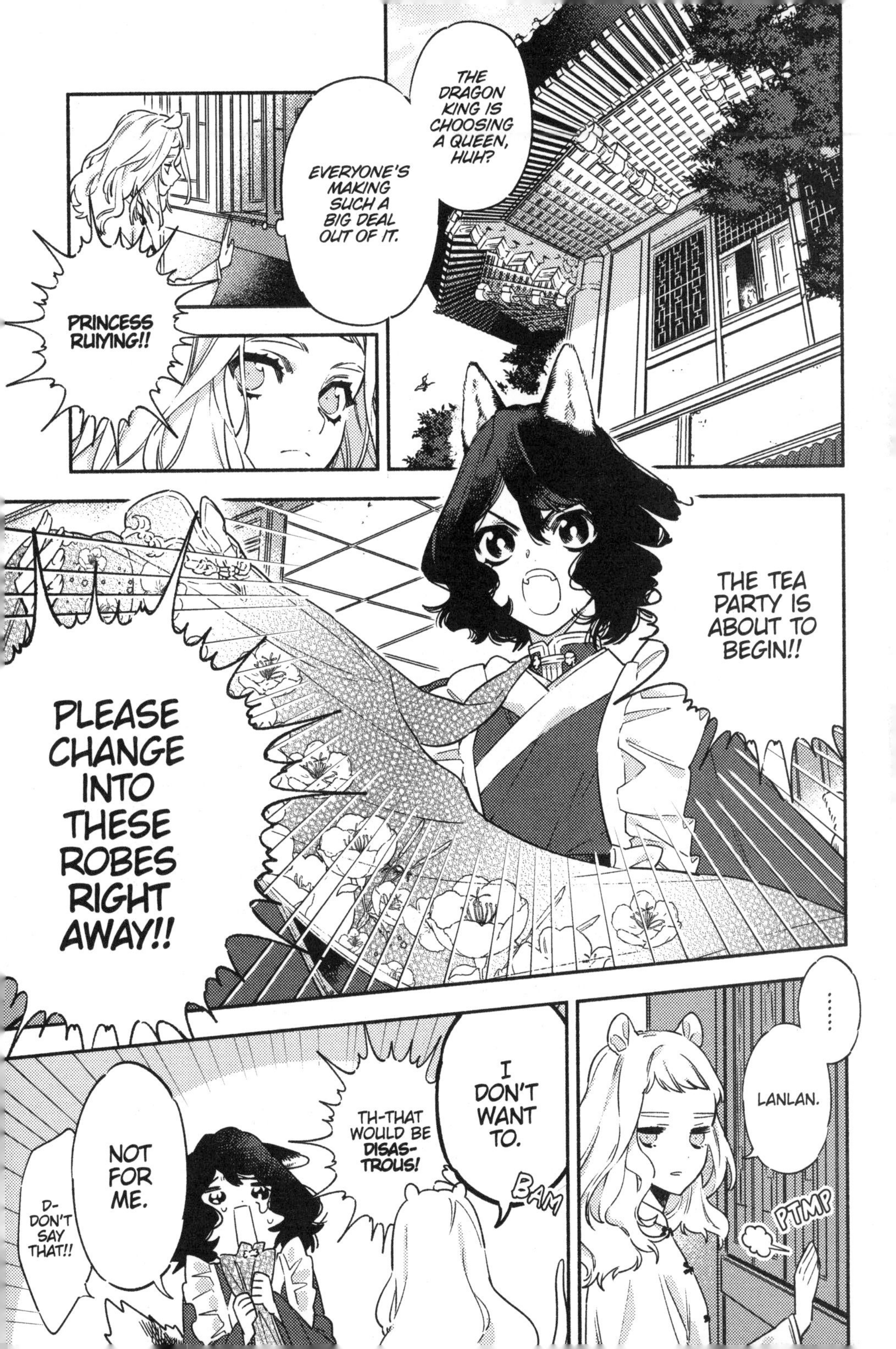
THE DRAGON KING IS CHOOSING A QUEEN, HUH?
EVERYONE'S MAKING SUCH A BIG DEAL OUT OF IT.
PRINCESS RUIYING!!
THE TEA PARTY IS ABOUT TO BEGIN!!
PLEASE CHANGE INTO THESE ROBES RIGHT AWAY!!
......
LANLAN.
PTMP
I DON'T WANT TO.
BAM
TH-THAT WOULD BE DISAS-TROUS!
NOT FOR ME.
D-DON'T SAY THAT!!

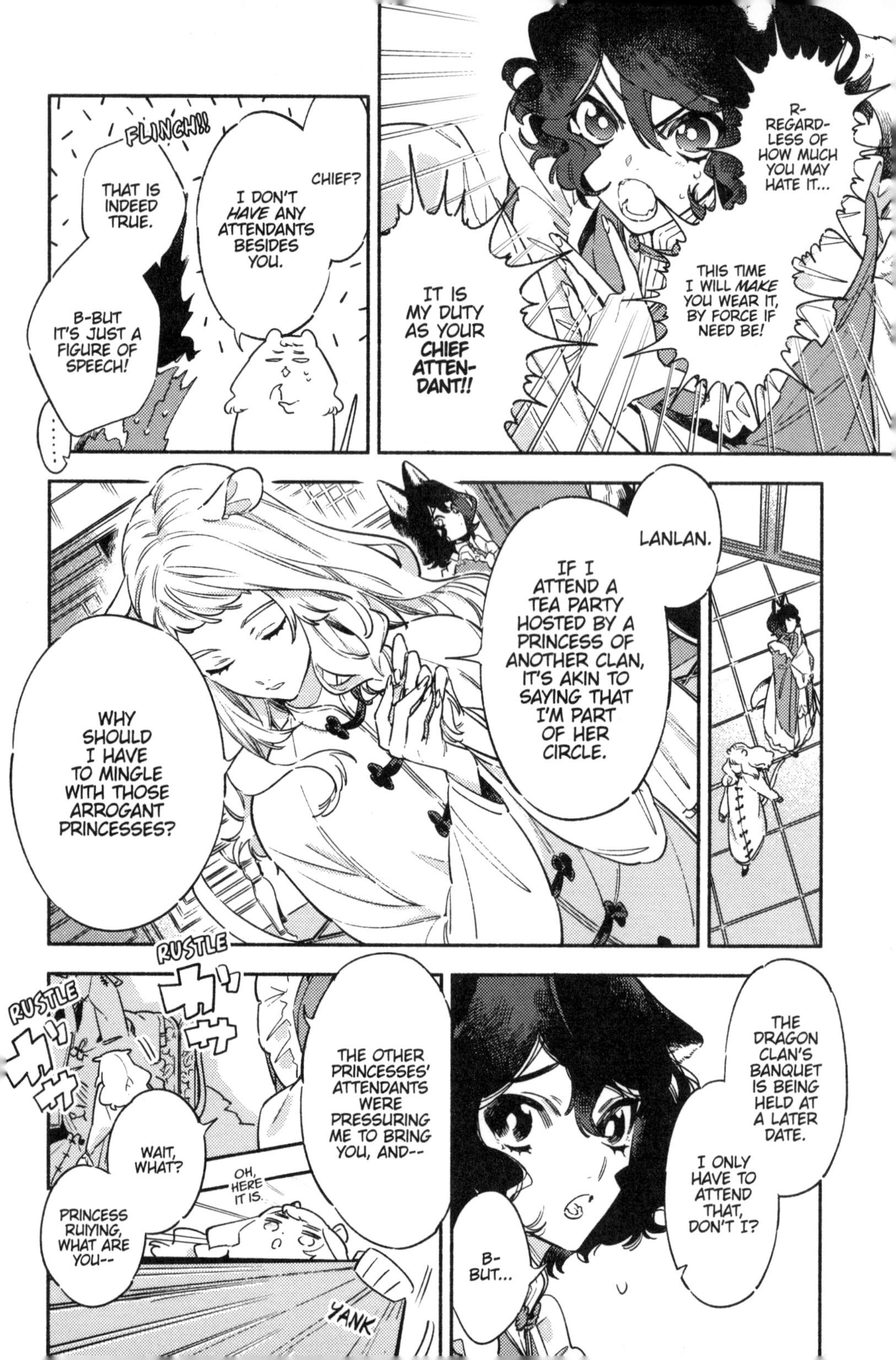
R-REGARDLESS OF HOW MUCH YOU MAY HATE IT...
THIS TIME I WILL *MAKE* YOU WEAR IT, BY FORCE IF NEED BE!
IT IS MY DUTY AS YOUR **CHIEF ATTENDANT!!**
CHIEF?
I DON'T *HAVE* ANY ATTENDANTS BESIDES YOU.
FLINCH!!
THAT IS INDEED TRUE.
B-BUT IT'S JUST A FIGURE OF SPEECH!
......
LANLAN.
IF I ATTEND A TEA PARTY HOSTED BY A PRINCESS OF ANOTHER CLAN, IT'S AKIN TO SAYING THAT I'M PART OF HER CIRCLE.
WHY SHOULD I HAVE TO MINGLE WITH THOSE ARROGANT PRINCESSES?
THE DRAGON CLAN'S BANQUET IS BEING HELD AT A LATER DATE.
I ONLY HAVE TO ATTEND THAT, DON'T I?
B-BUT...
THE OTHER PRINCESSES' ATTENDANTS WERE PRESSURING ME TO BRING YOU, AND--
RUSTLE
RUSTLE
WAIT, WHAT?
OH, HERE IT IS.
PRINCESS RUIYING, WHAT ARE YOU--
YANK

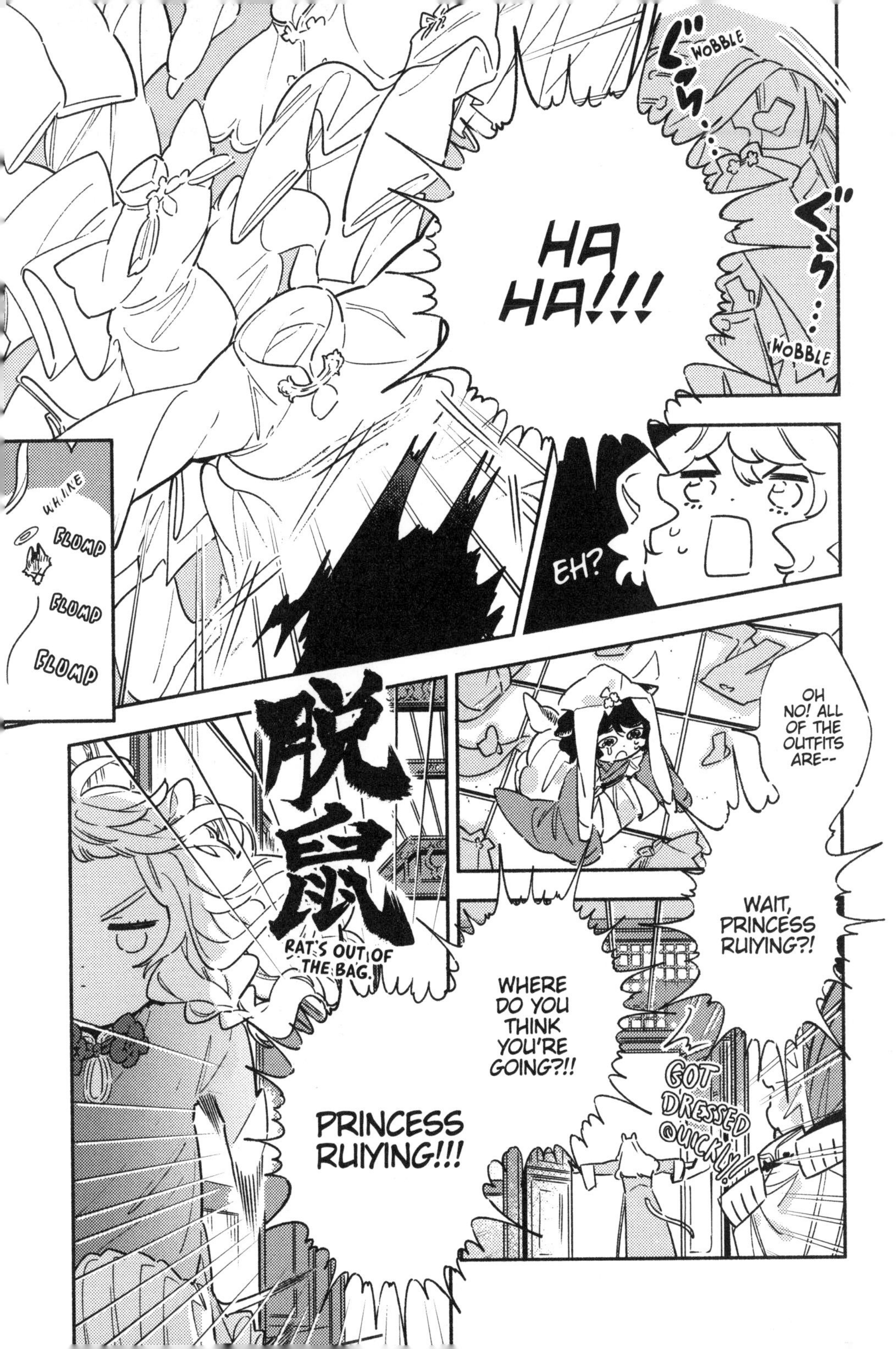
WOBBLE
HA HA!!!
WOBBLE
EH?
WHINE
FLUMP
FLUMP
FLUMP
OH NO! ALL OF THE OUTFITS ARE--
WAIT, PRINCESS RUIYING?!
GOT DRESSED QUICKLY!!
WHERE DO YOU THINK YOU'RE GOING?!!
PRINCESS RUIYING!!!
脱鼠
RAT'S OUT OF THE BAG.

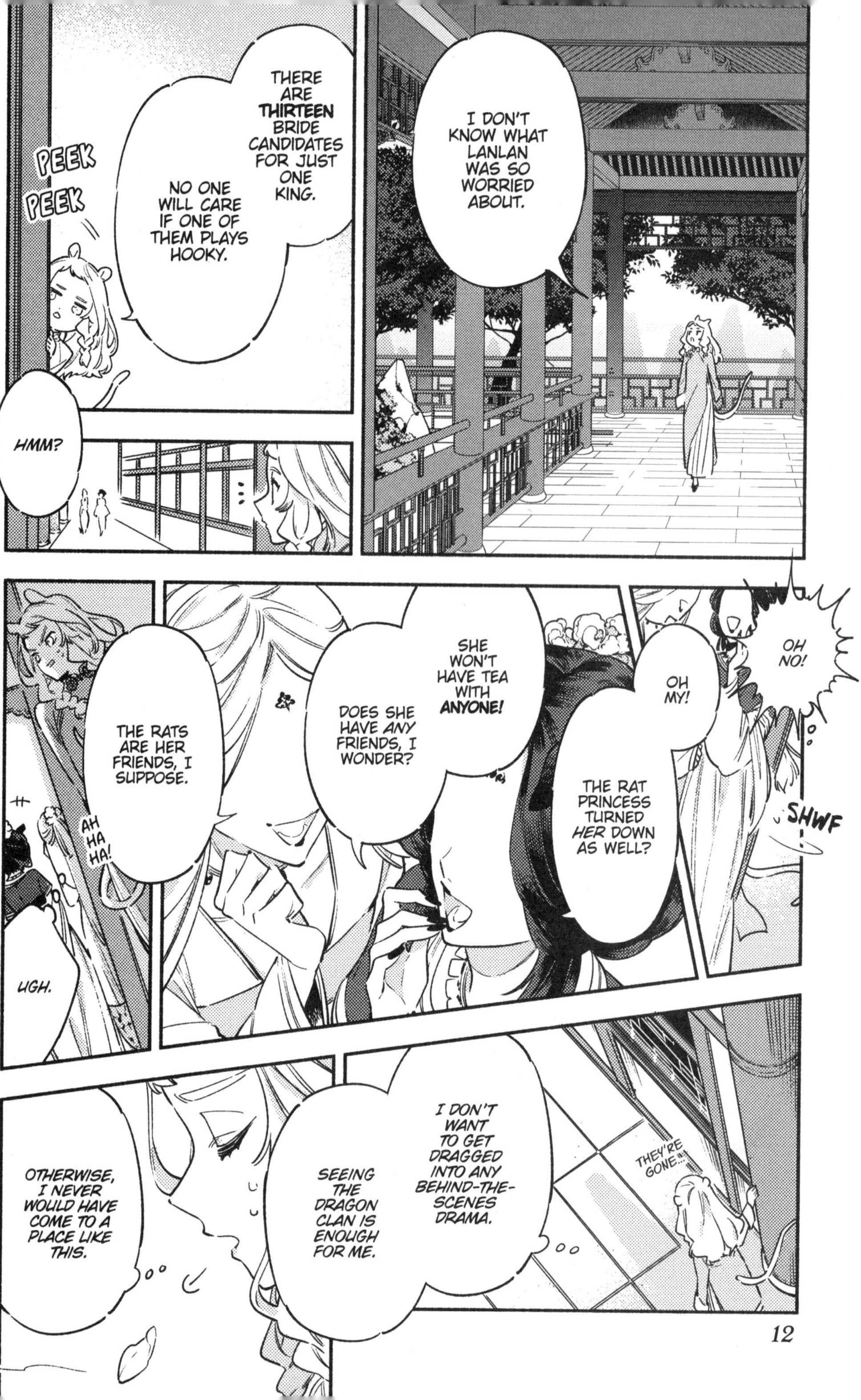
I DON'T KNOW WHAT LANLAN WAS SO WORRIED ABOUT.
THERE ARE **THIRTEEN** BRIDE CANDIDATES FOR JUST ONE KING.
NO ONE WILL CARE IF ONE OF THEM PLAYS HOOKY.
PEEK
PEEK
HMM?
...
OH NO!
SHWF
OH MY!
THE RAT PRINCESS TURNED *HER* DOWN AS WELL?
SHE WON'T HAVE TEA WITH **ANYONE!**
DOES SHE HAVE *ANY* FRIENDS, I WONDER?
THE RATS ARE HER FRIENDS, I SUPPOSE.
AH HA HA!
UGH.
THEY'RE GONE...
I DON'T WANT TO GET DRAGGED INTO ANY BEHIND-THE-SCENES DRAMA.
SEEING THE DRAGON CLAN IS ENOUGH FOR ME.
OTHERWISE, I NEVER WOULD HAVE COME TO A PLACE LIKE THIS.

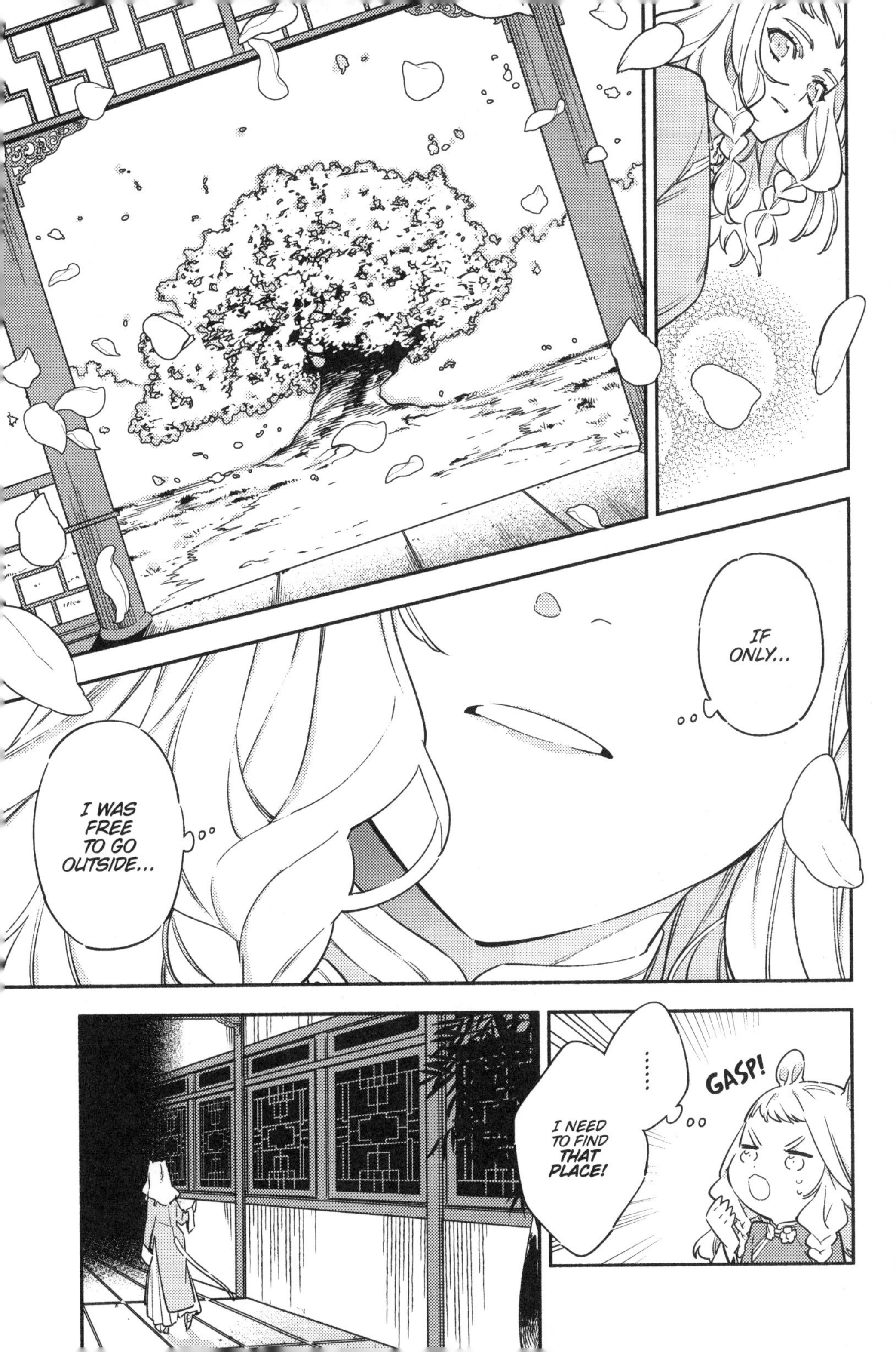
IF ONLY...
I WAS FREE TO GO OUTSIDE...
GASP!
......
I NEED TO FIND THAT PLACE!

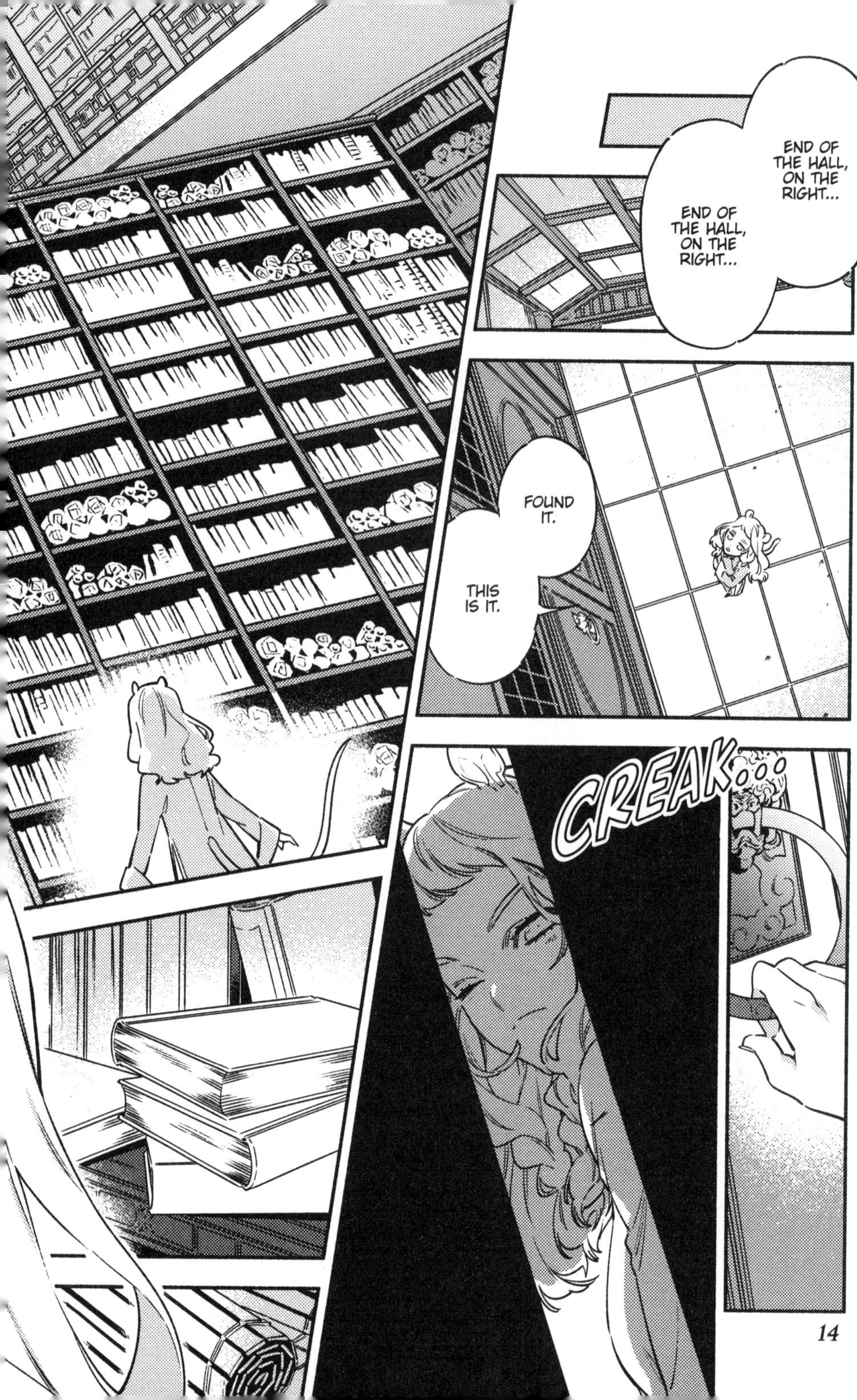
END OF THE HALL, ON THE RIGHT...
END OF THE HALL, ON THE RIGHT...
FOUND IT.
THIS IS IT.
CREAK...

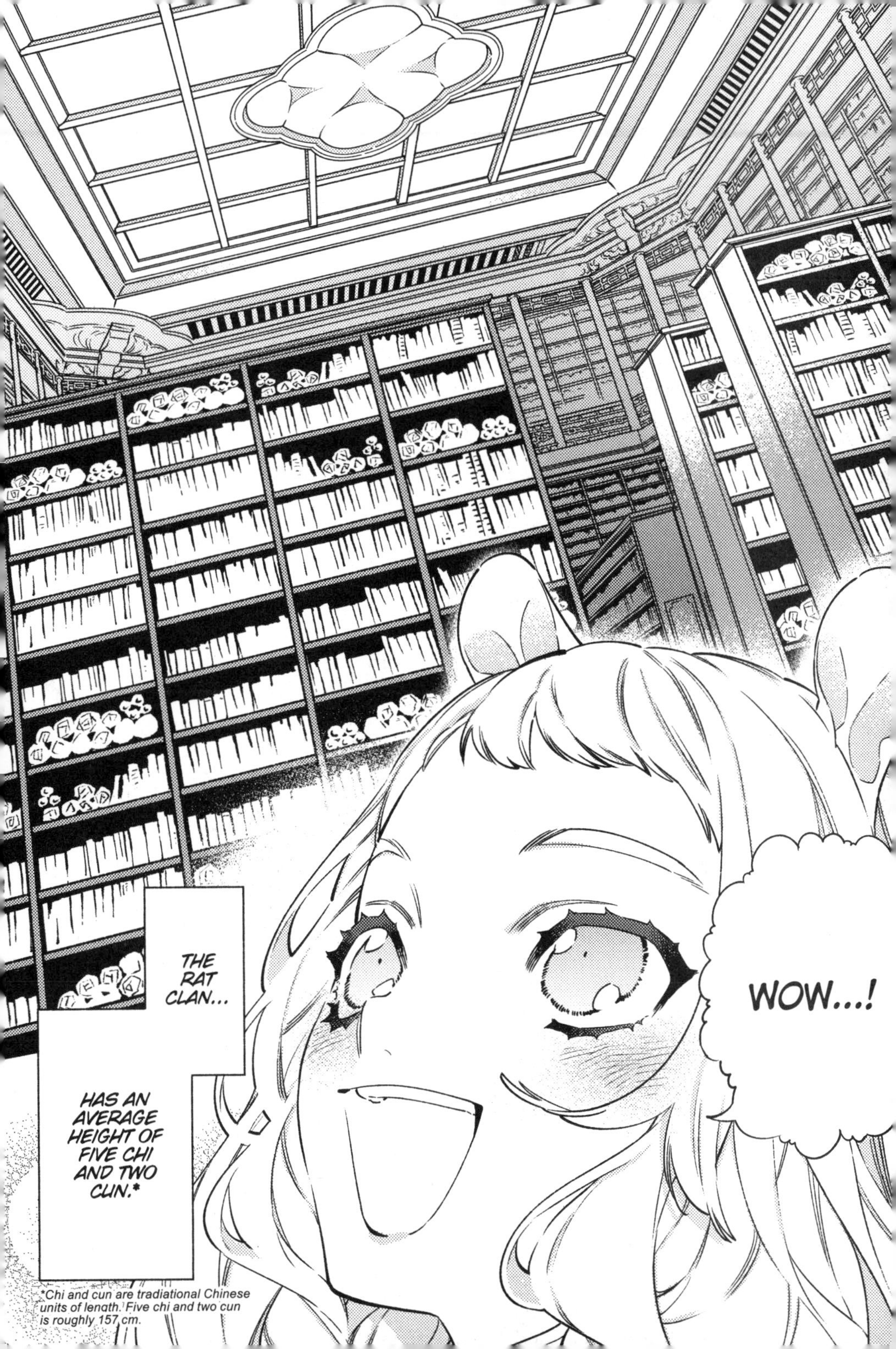
WOW...!
THE RAT CLAN...
HAS AN AVERAGE HEIGHT OF FIVE CHI AND TWO CUN.*
*Chi and cun are tradiational Chinese units of length. Five chi and two cun is roughly 157 cm.

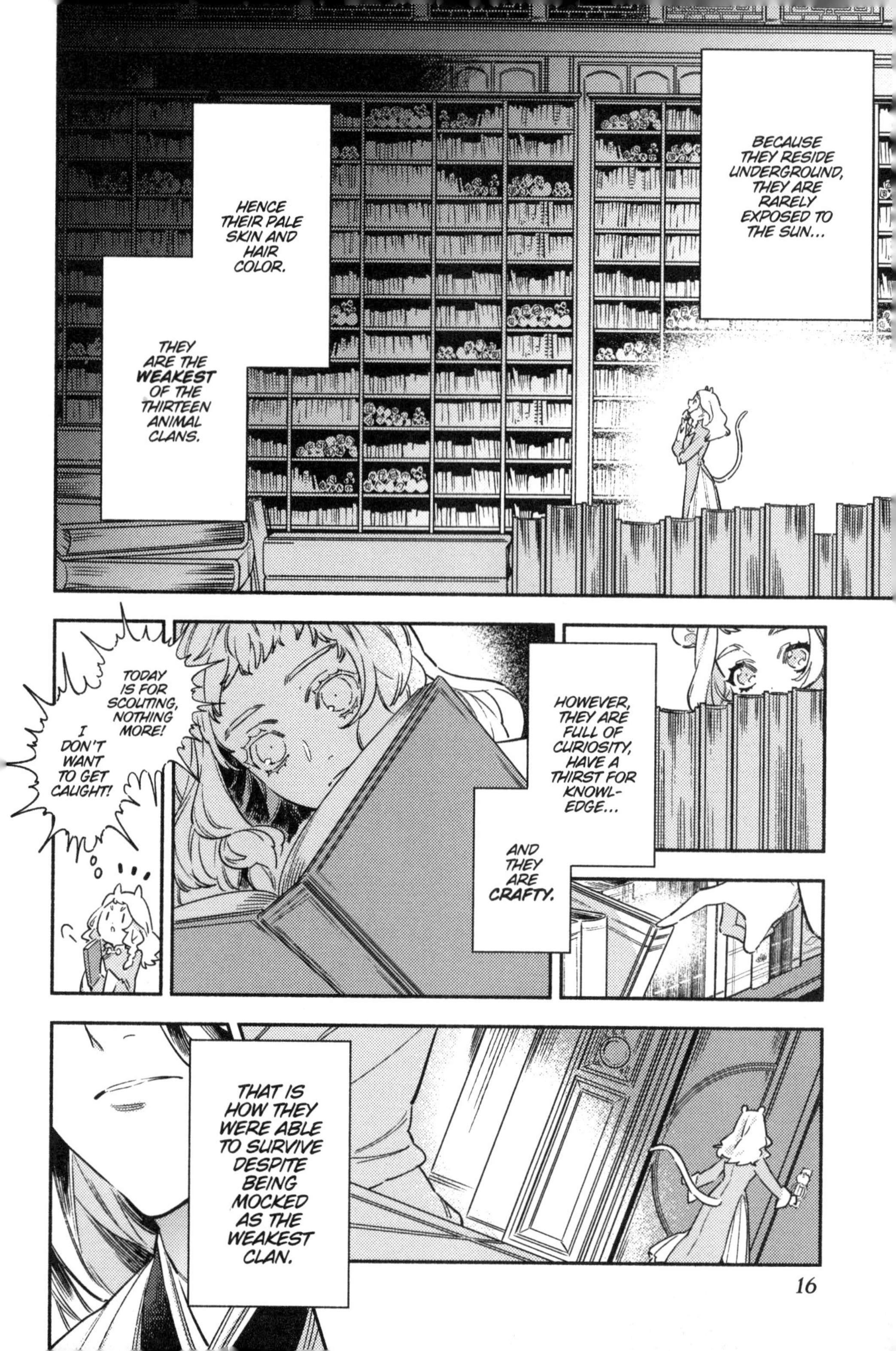
BECAUSE THEY RESIDE UNDERGROUND, THEY ARE RARELY EXPOSED TO THE SUN...
HENCE THEIR PALE SKIN AND HAIR COLOR.
THEY ARE THE **WEAKEST** OF THE THIRTEEN ANIMAL CLANS.
HOWEVER, THEY ARE FULL OF CURIOSITY, HAVE A THIRST FOR KNOWL-EDGE...
AND THEY ARE **CRAFTY.**
TODAY IS FOR SCOUTING, NOTHING MORE!
I DON'T WANT TO GET CAUGHT!
THAT IS HOW THEY WERE ABLE TO SURVIVE DESPITE BEING MOCKED AS THE WEAKEST CLAN.

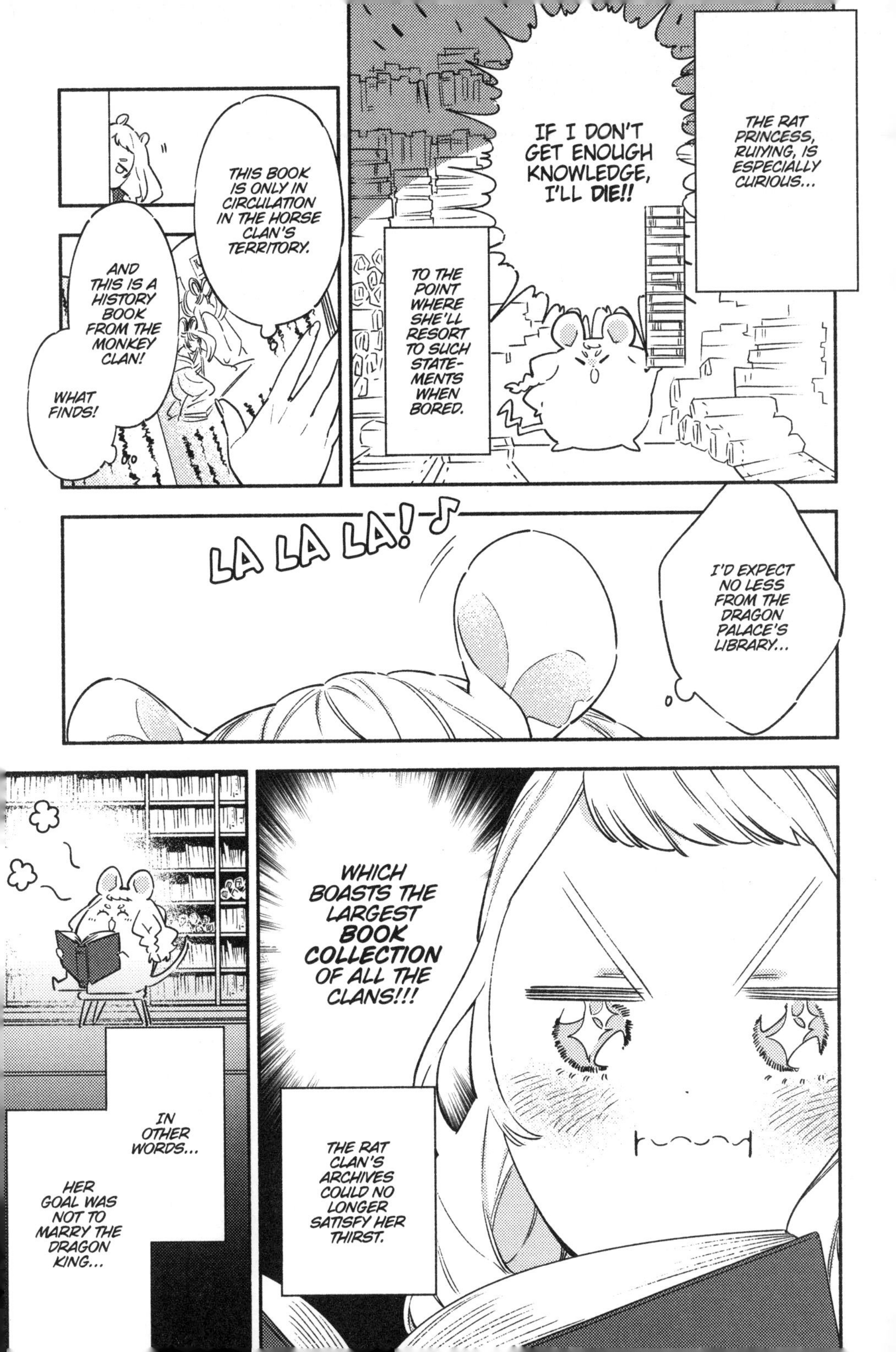
THE RAT PRINCESS, RUIYING, IS ESPECIALLY CURIOUS...
IF I DON'T GET ENOUGH KNOWLEDGE, I'LL DIE!!
TO THE POINT WHERE SHE'LL RESORT TO SUCH STATEMENTS WHEN BORED.
THIS BOOK IS ONLY IN CIRCULATION IN THE HORSE CLAN'S TERRITORY.
AND THIS IS A HISTORY BOOK FROM THE MONKEY CLAN!
WHAT FINDS!
I'D EXPECT NO LESS FROM THE DRAGON PALACE'S LIBRARY...
LA LA LA!
WHICH BOASTS THE LARGEST BOOK COLLECTION OF ALL THE CLANS!!!
THE RAT CLAN'S ARCHIVES COULD NO LONGER SATISFY HER THIRST.
IN OTHER WORDS...
HER GOAL WAS NOT TO MARRY THE DRAGON KING...

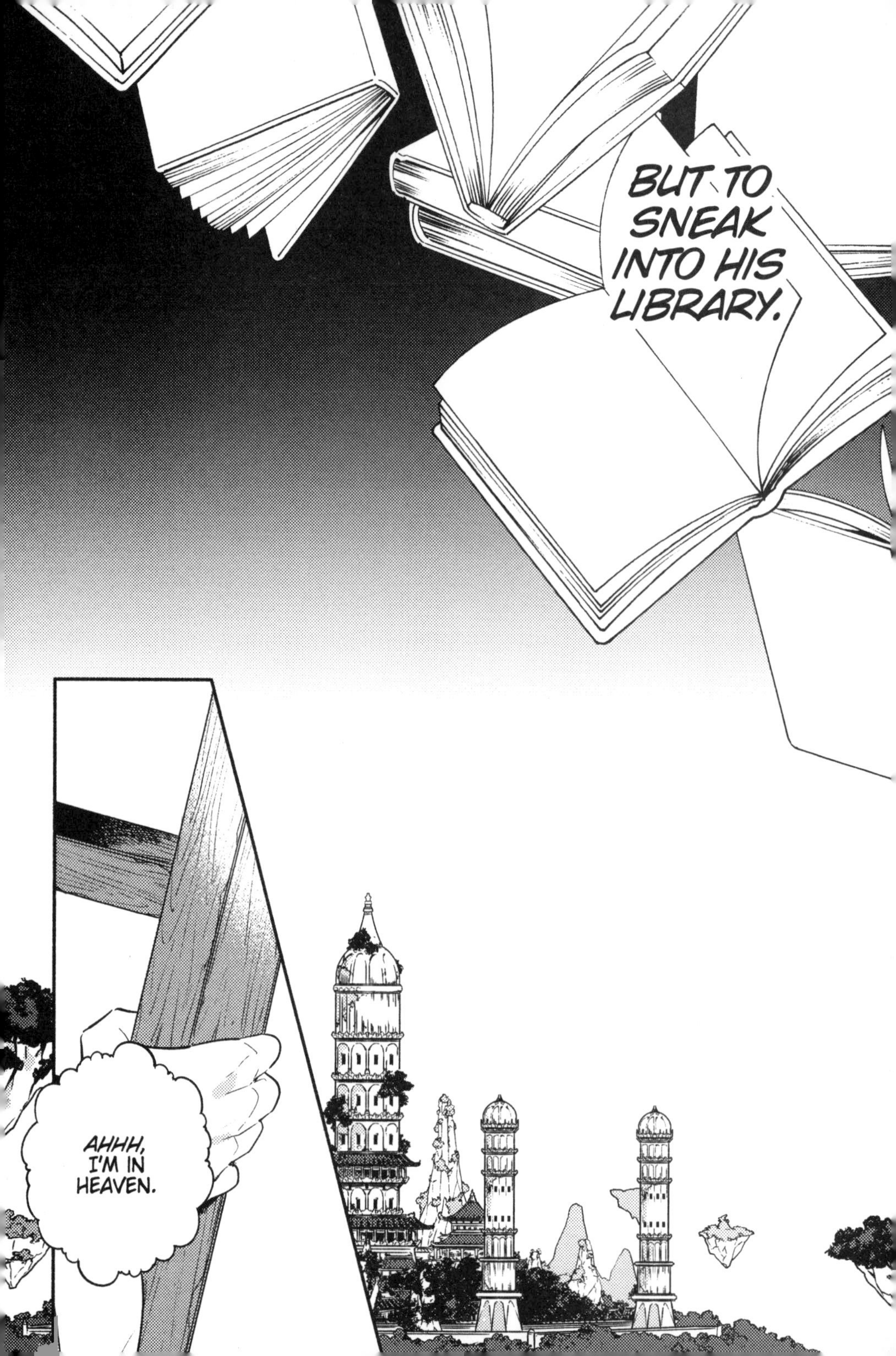
BUT TO SNEAK INTO HIS LIBRARY.
AHHH, I'M IN HEAVEN.

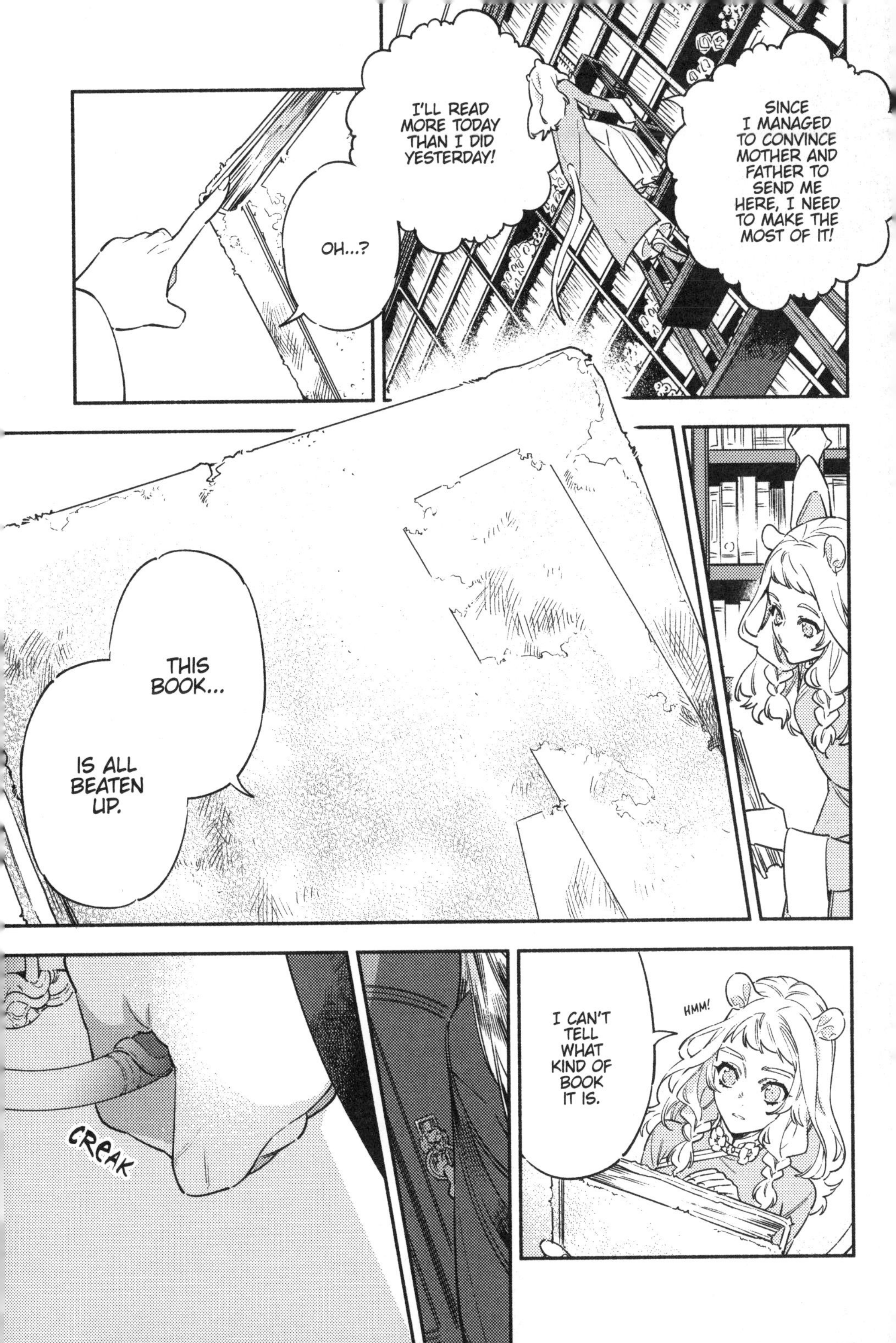
SINCE I MANAGED TO CONVINCE MOTHER AND FATHER TO SEND ME HERE, I NEED TO MAKE THE MOST OF IT!
I'LL READ MORE TODAY THAN I DID YESTERDAY!
OH...?
THIS BOOK...
IS ALL BEATEN UP.
HMM!
I CAN'T TELL WHAT KIND OF BOOK IT IS.
CREAK

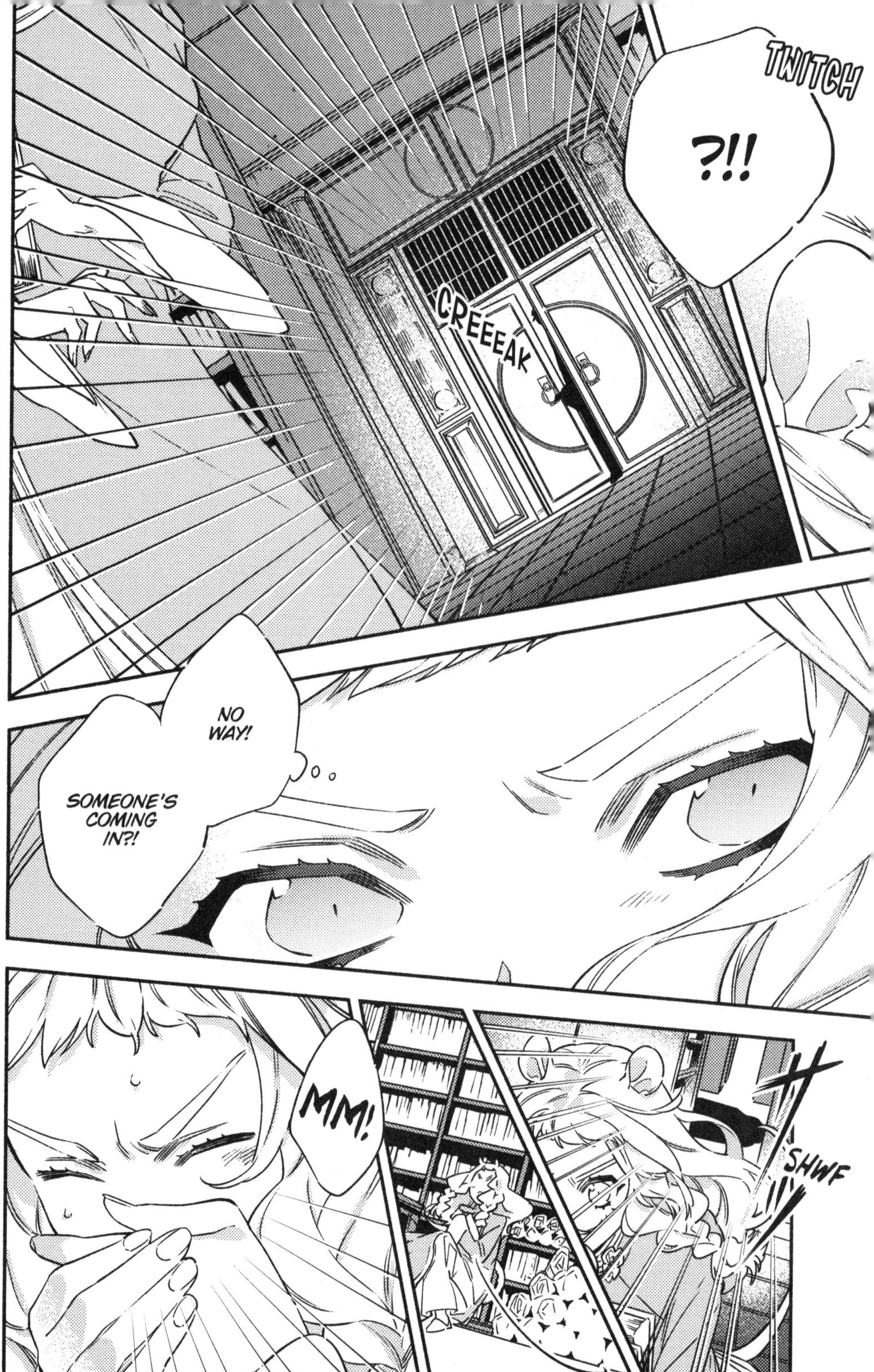
TWITCH
?!!
CREEEAK
NO WAY!
SOMEONE'S COMING IN?!
SHWF
MM!

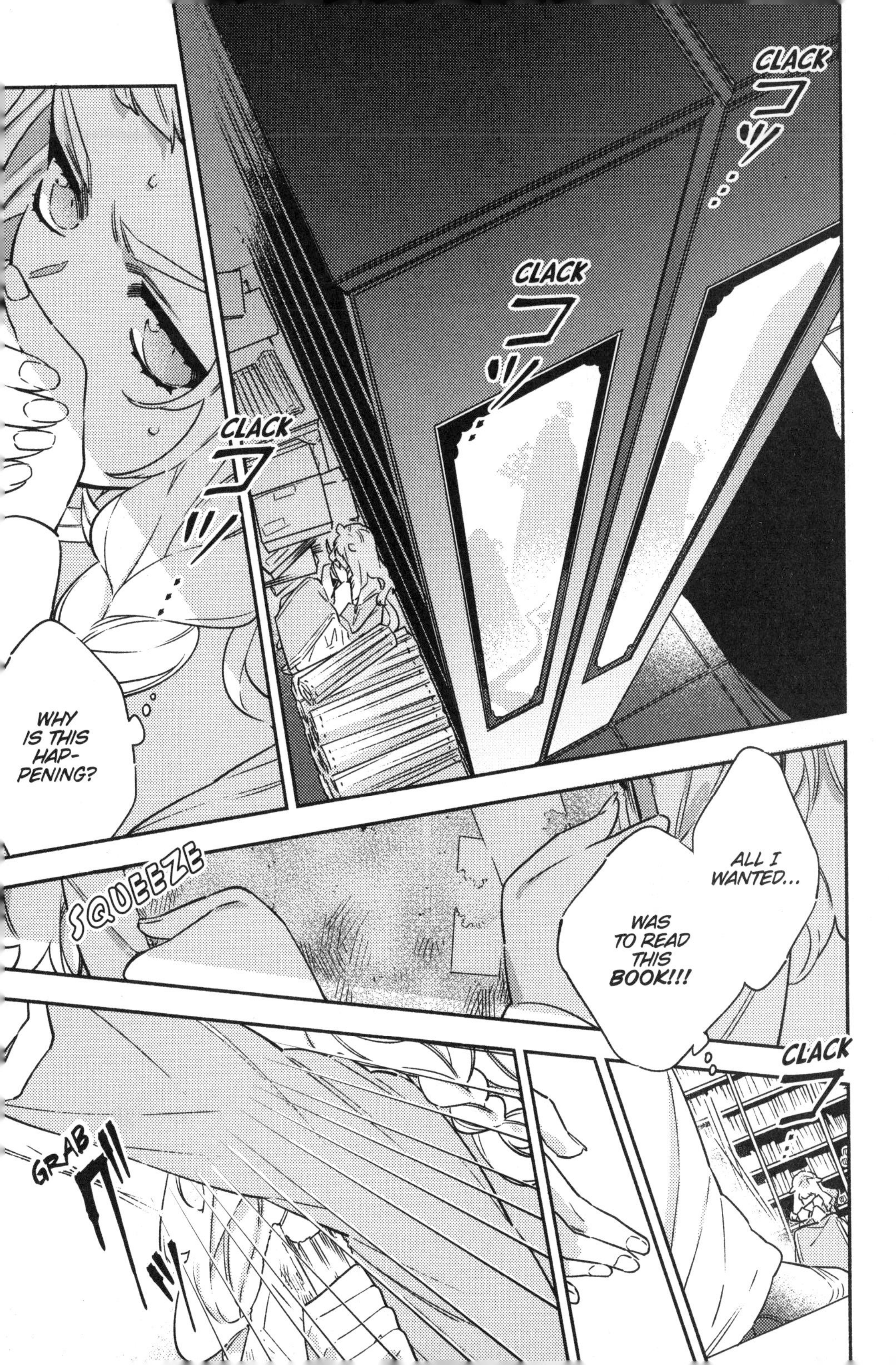
CLACK
コッ…
CLACK
コッ…
CLACK
コッ…
WHY IS THIS HAPPENING?
ALL I WANTED...
WAS TO READ THIS BOOK!!!
SQUEEZE
CLACK
コ…
GRAB

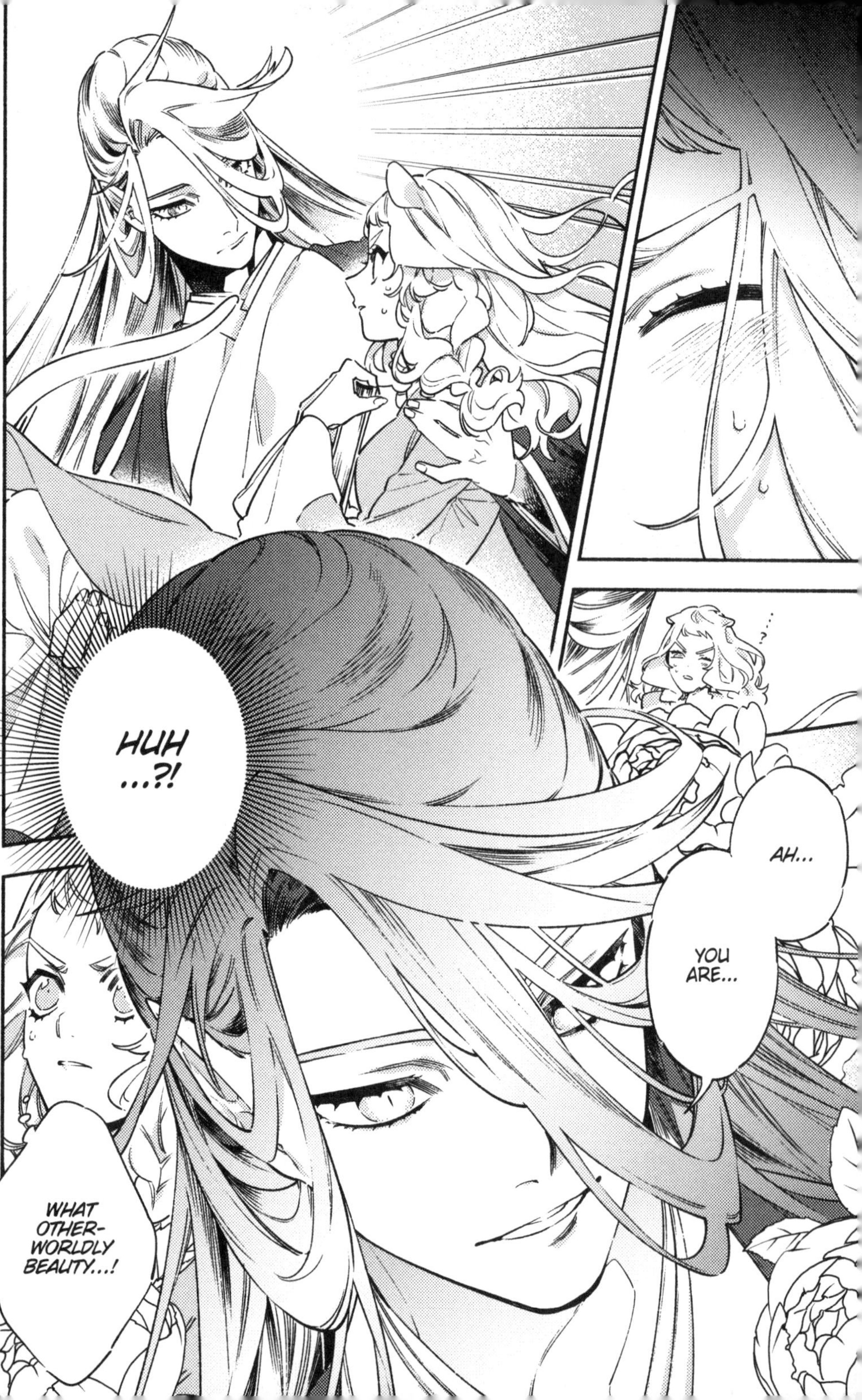
HUH ...?!
AH...
YOU ARE...
WHAT OTHER-WORLDLY BEAUTY...!

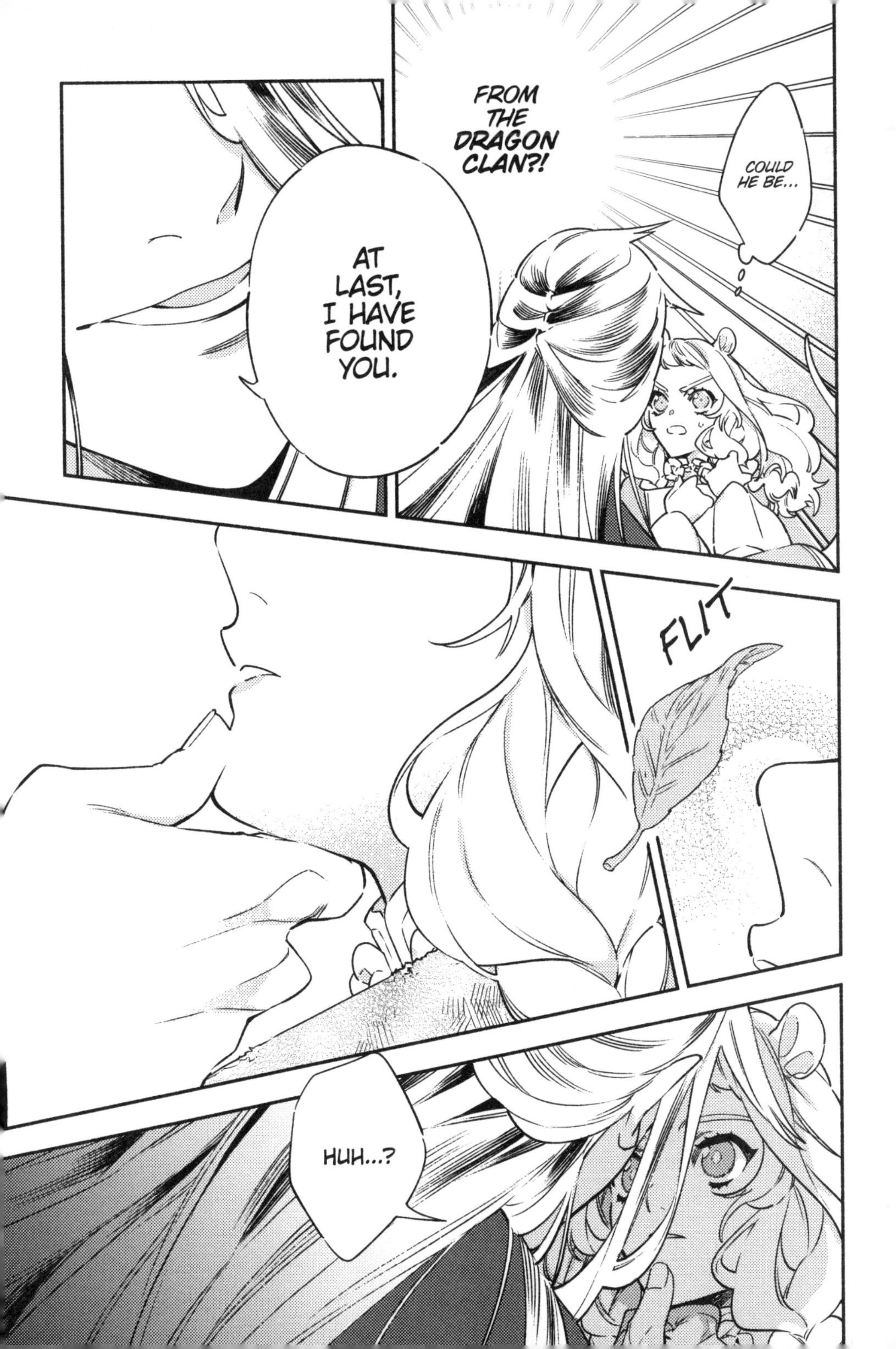
COULD HE BE...
FROM THE DRAGON CLAN?!
AT LAST, I HAVE FOUND YOU.
FLIT
HUH...?

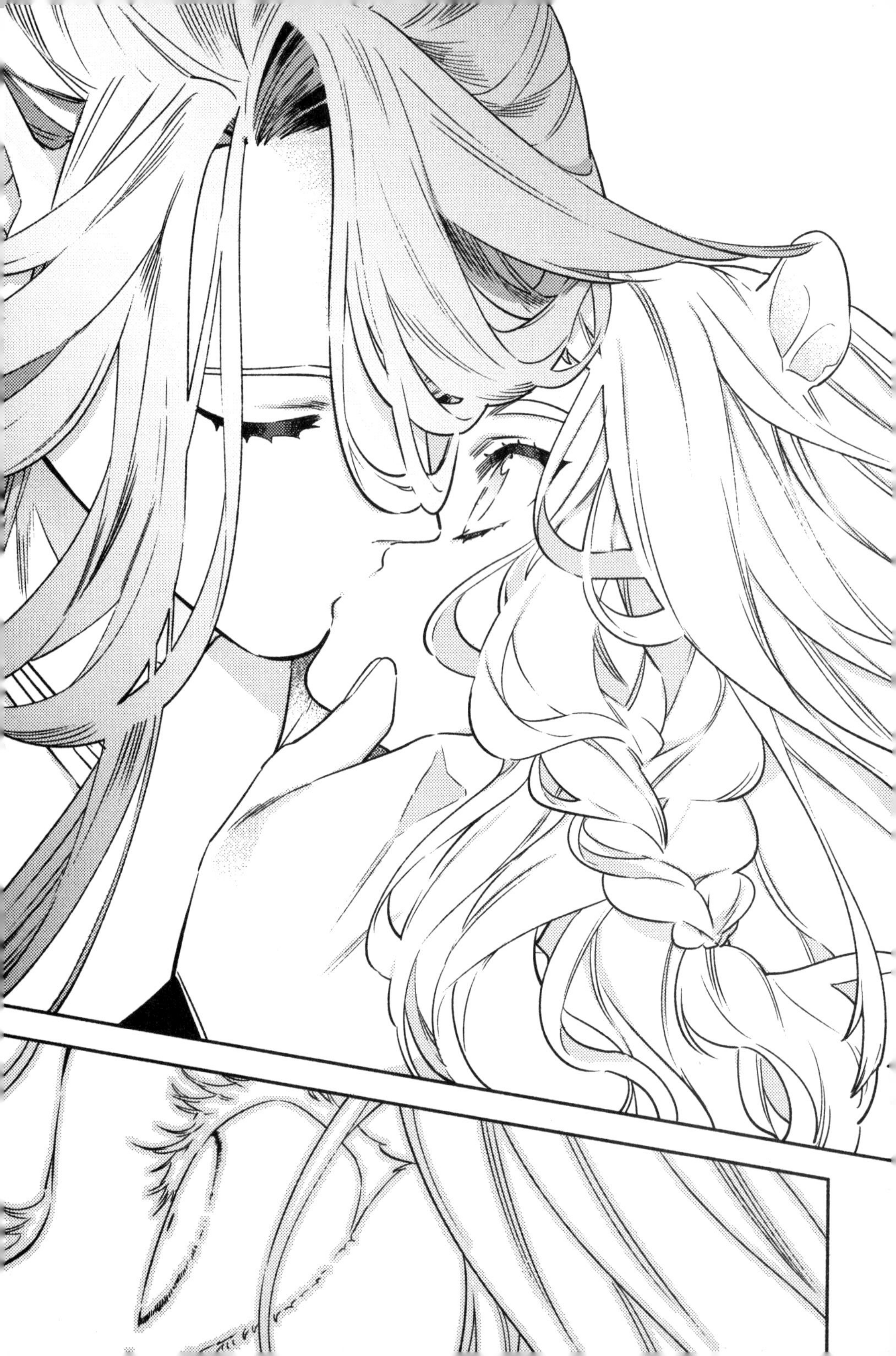

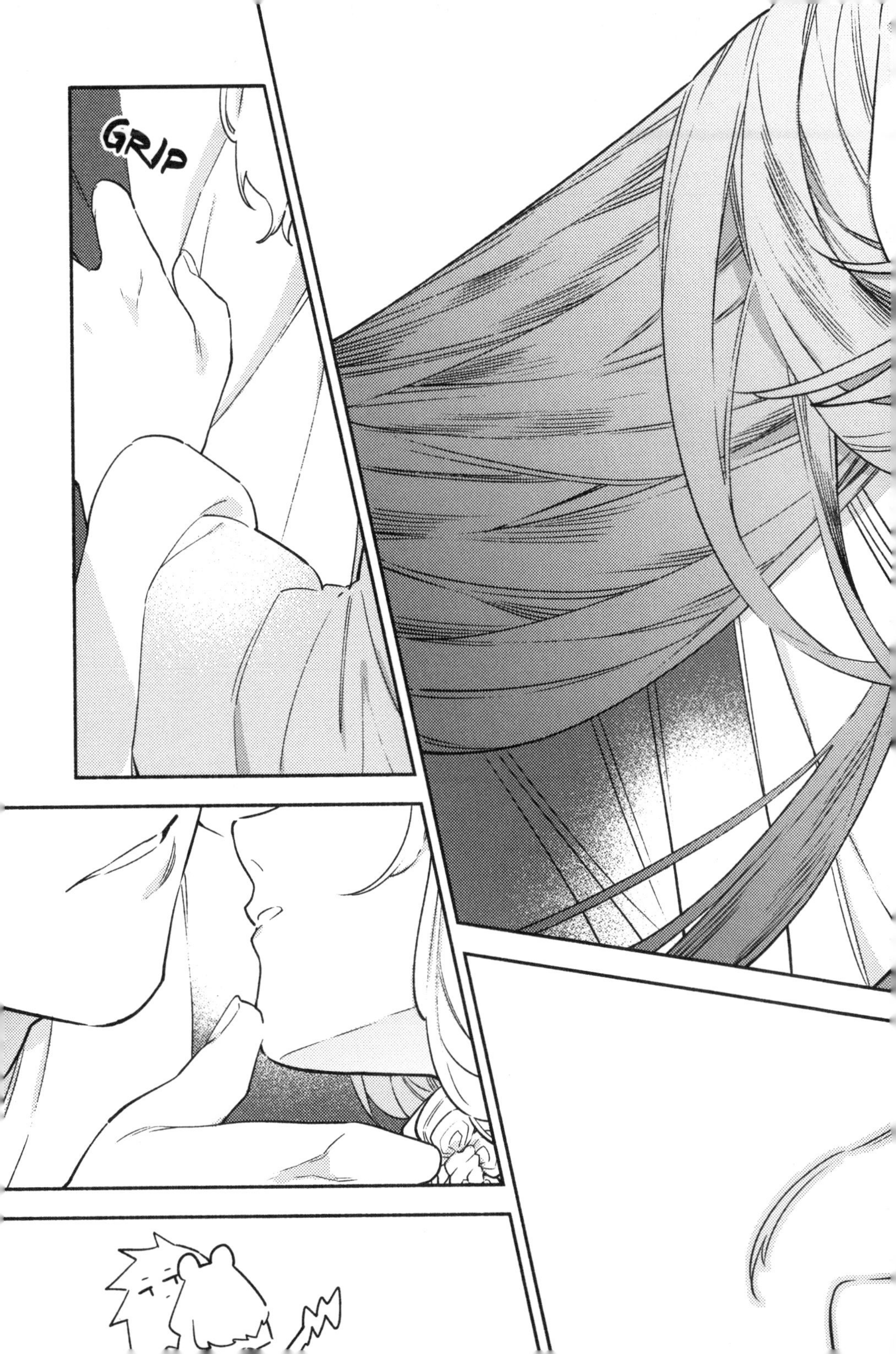
GRIP

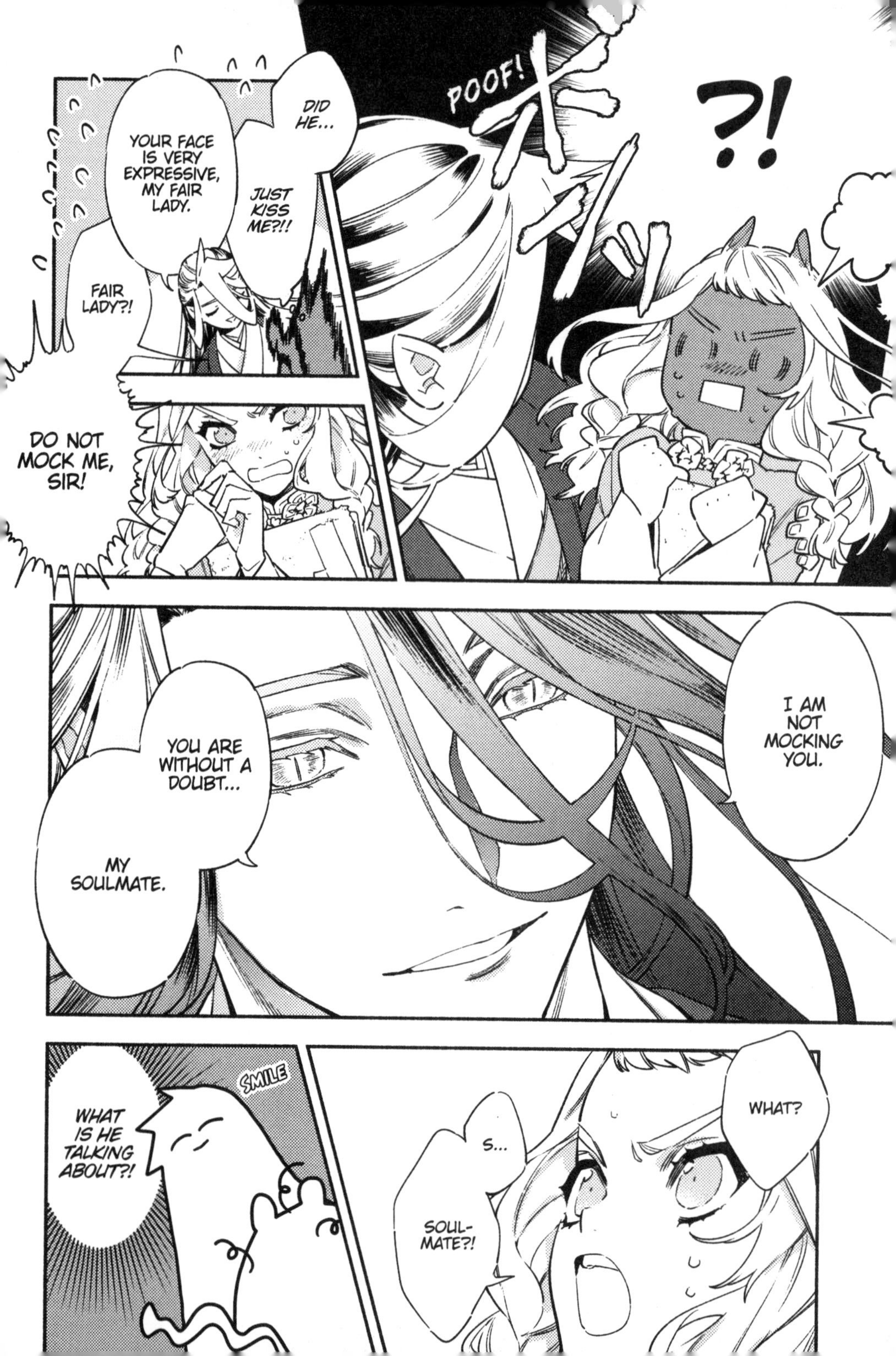
POOF!
?!
DID HE...
JUST KISS ME?!!
YOUR FACE IS VERY EXPRESSIVE, MY FAIR LADY.
FAIR LADY?!
DO NOT MOCK ME, SIR!
I AM NOT MOCKING YOU.
YOU ARE WITHOUT A DOUBT...
MY SOULMATE.
WHAT?
S...
SOUL-MATE?!
SMILE
WHAT IS HE TALKING ABOUT?!

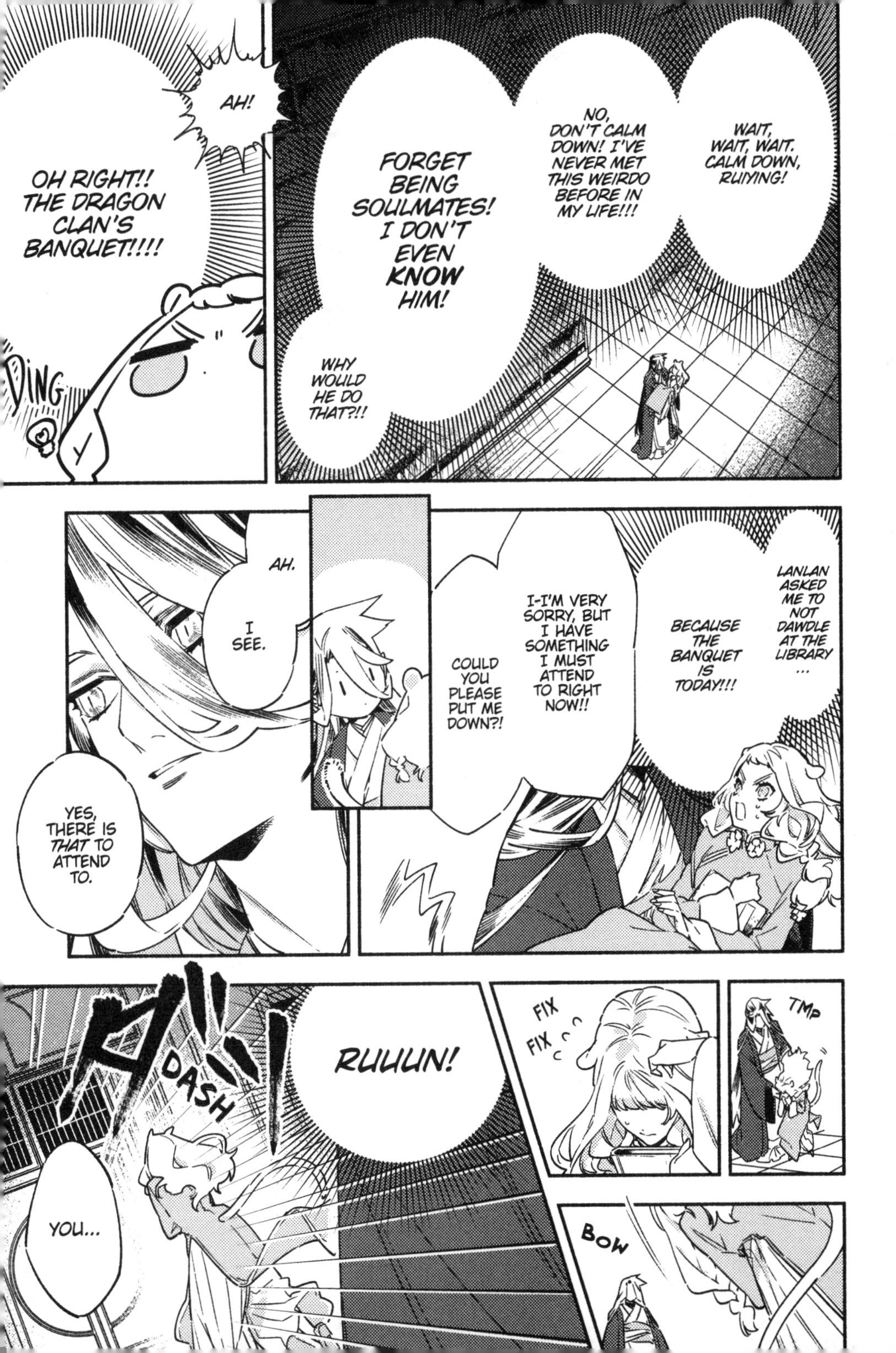

WAIT, WAIT, WAIT. CALM DOWN, RUIYING!
NO, DON'T CALM DOWN! I'VE NEVER MET THIS WEIRDO BEFORE IN MY LIFE!!!
FORGET BEING SOULMATES! I DON'T EVEN **KNOW** HIM!
WHY WOULD HE DO THAT?!!
AH!
OH RIGHT!! THE DRAGON CLAN'S BANQUET!!!!
DING
LANLAN ASKED ME TO NOT DAWDLE AT THE LIBRARY...
BECAUSE THE BANQUET IS TODAY!!!
I-I'M VERY SORRY, BUT I HAVE SOMETHING I MUST ATTEND TO RIGHT NOW!!
COULD YOU PLEASE PUT ME DOWN?!
AH.
I SEE.
YES, THERE IS *THAT* TO ATTEND TO.
TMP
FIX
FIX
BOW
RUUUN!
DASH
YOU...

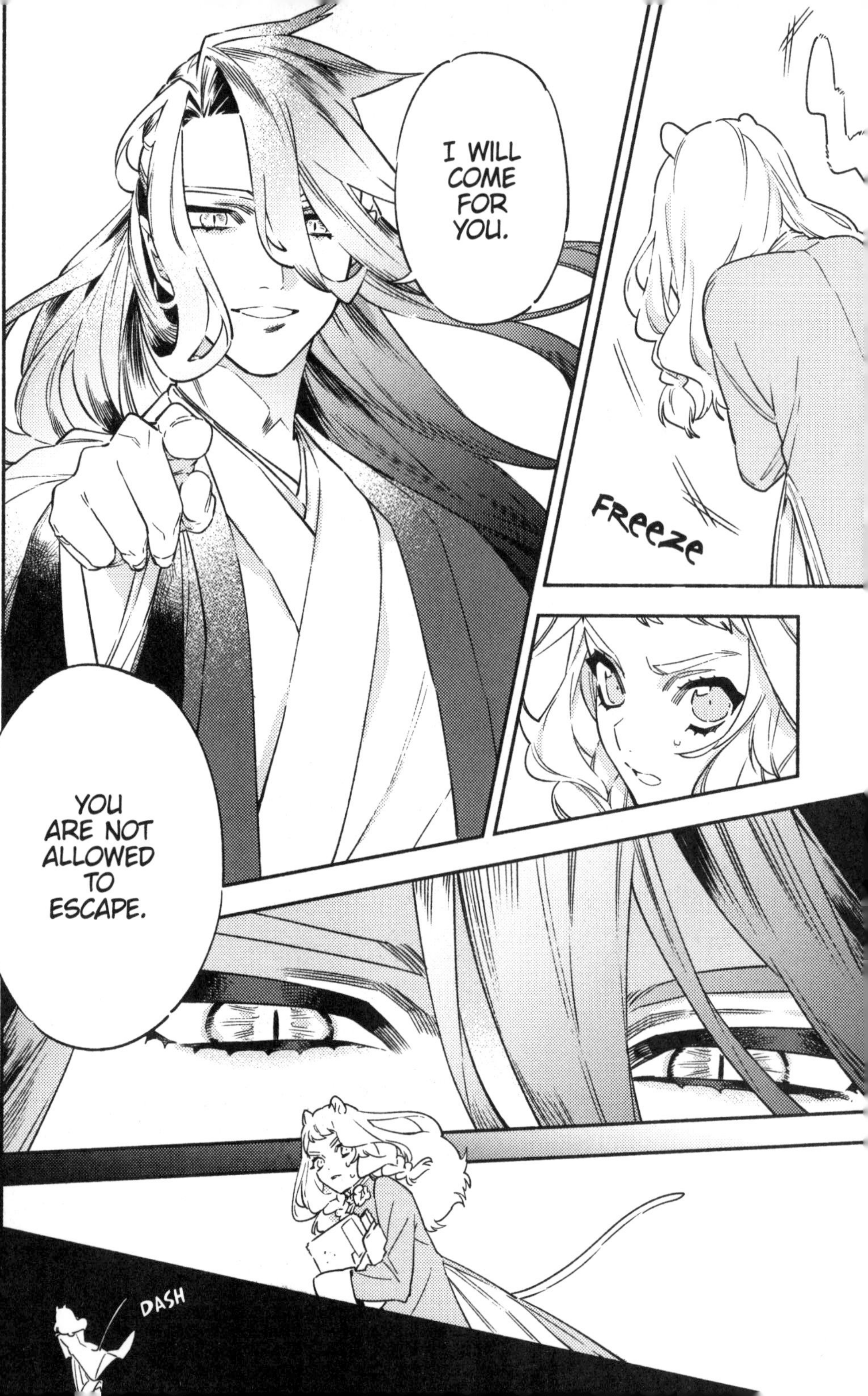
Freeze
I WILL COME FOR YOU.
YOU ARE NOT ALLOWED TO ESCAPE.
DASH

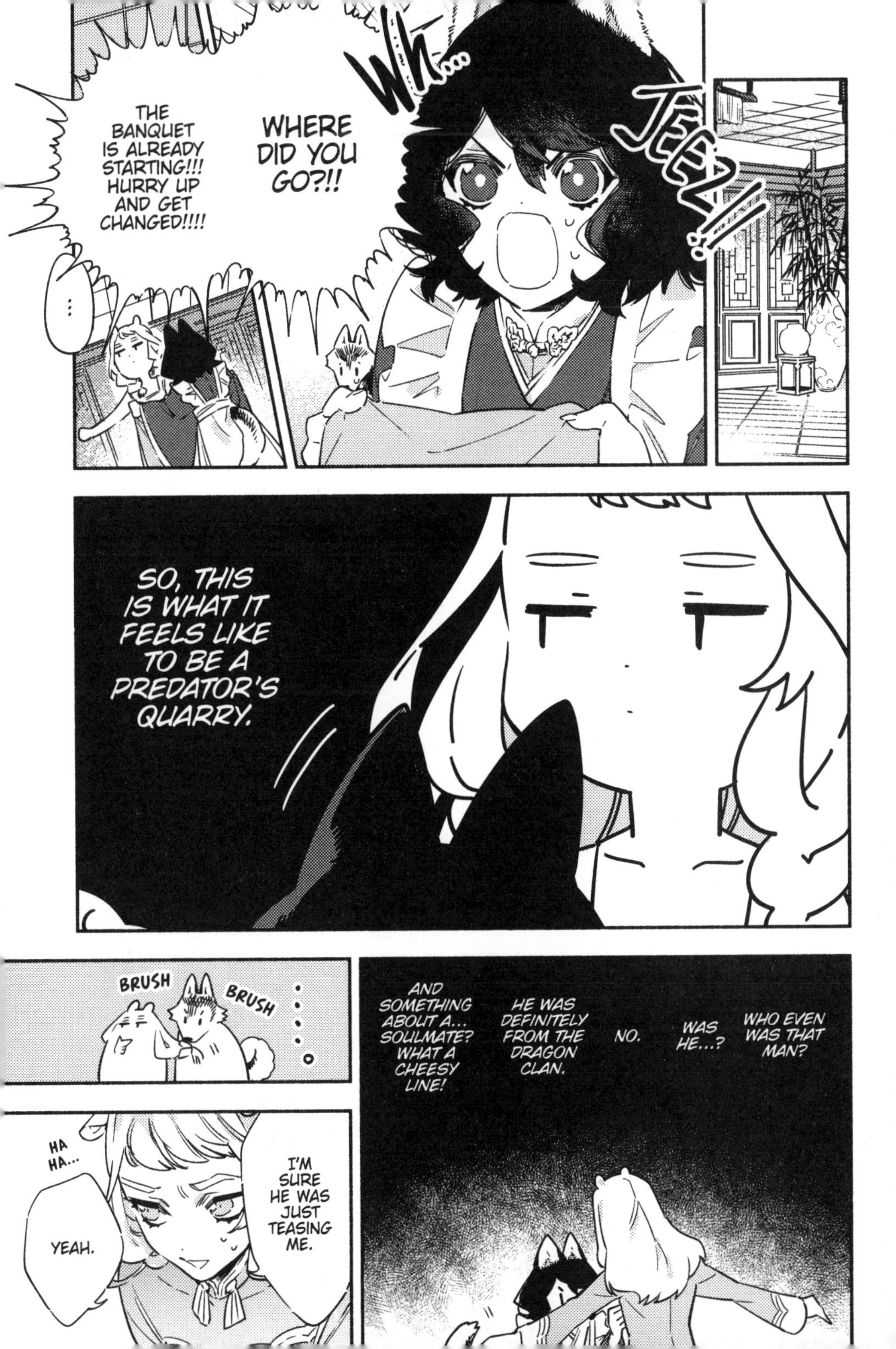
JEEZ!!
WH...
WHERE DID YOU GO?!!
THE BANQUET IS ALREADY STARTING!!! HURRY UP AND GET CHANGED!!!!
...
SO, THIS IS WHAT IT FEELS LIKE TO BE A PREDATOR'S QUARRY.
WHO EVEN WAS THAT MAN?
WAS HE...?
NO.
HE WAS DEFINITELY FROM THE DRAGON CLAN.
AND SOMETHING ABOUT A... SOULMATE? WHAT A CHEESY LINE!
BRUSH
BRUSH
.....
I'M SURE HE WAS JUST TEASING ME.
HA HA...
YEAH.

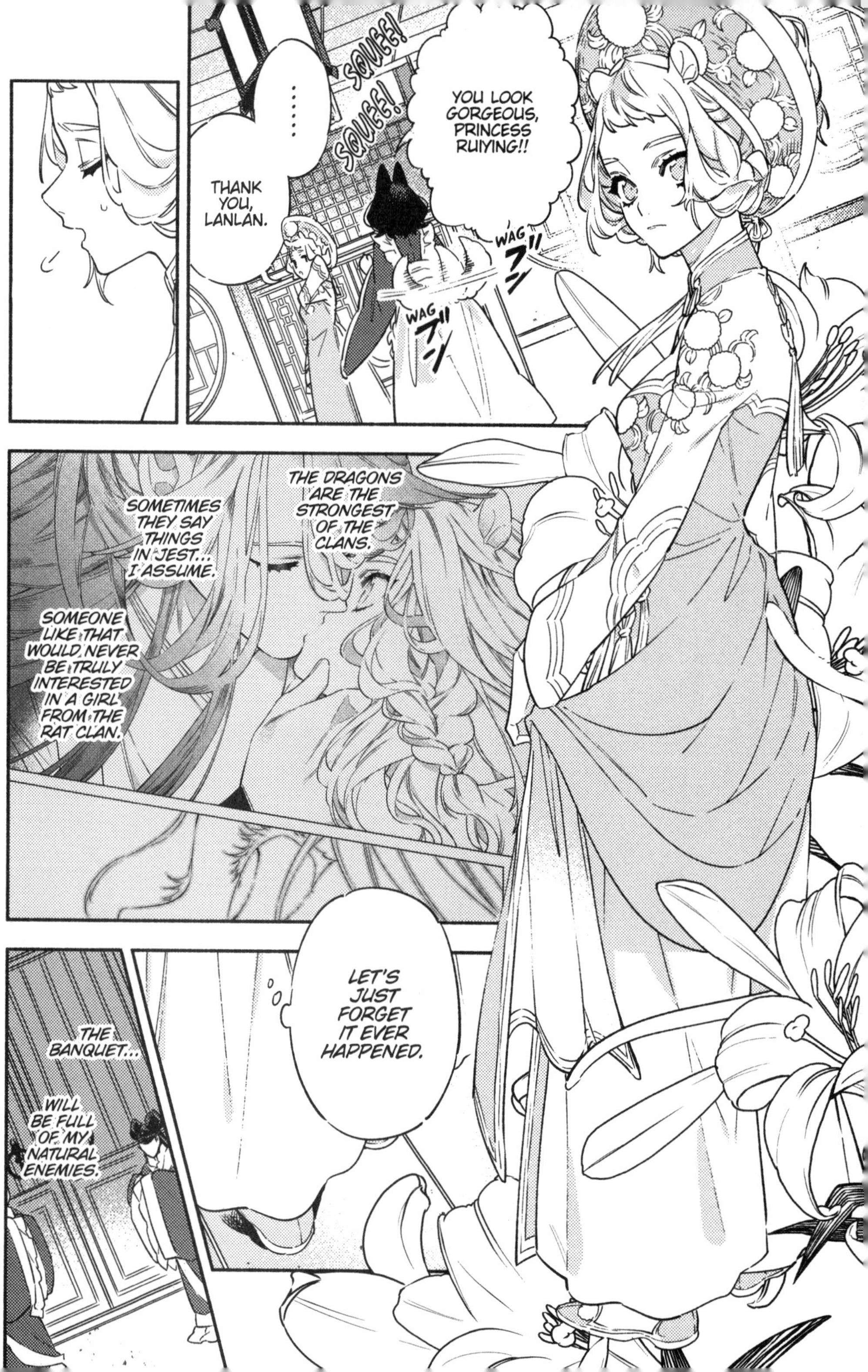
YOU LOOK GORGEOUS, PRINCESS RUIYING!!
WAG
WAG
SQUEE!
SQUEE!
......
THANK YOU, LANLAN.
THE DRAGONS ARE THE STRONGEST OF THE CLANS.
SOMETIMES THEY SAY THINGS IN JEST... I ASSUME.
SOMEONE LIKE THAT WOULD NEVER BE TRULY INTERESTED IN A GIRL FROM THE RAT CLAN.
LET'S JUST FORGET IT EVER HAPPENED.
THE BANQUET...
WILL BE FULL OF MY NATURAL ENEMIES.

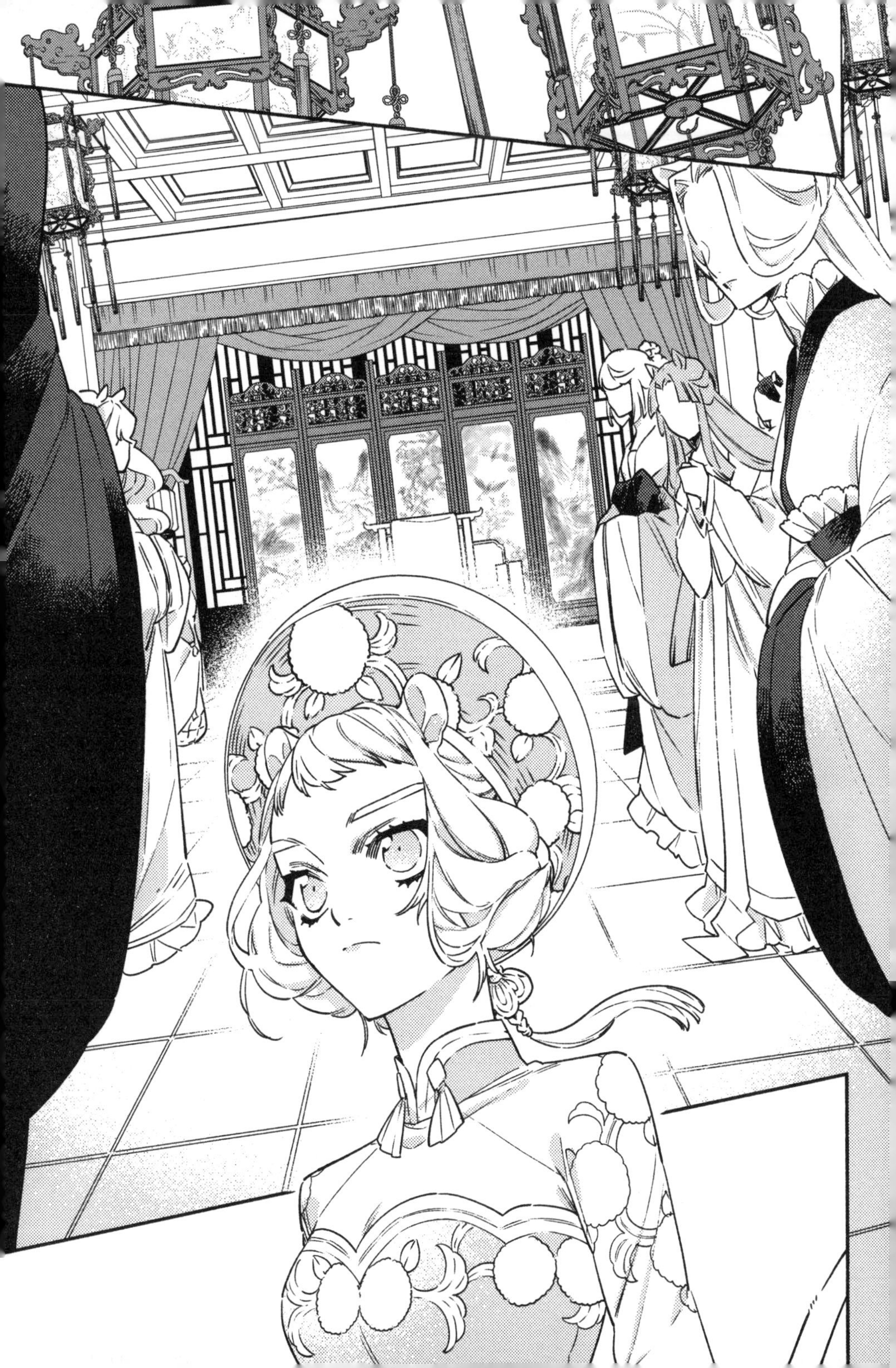

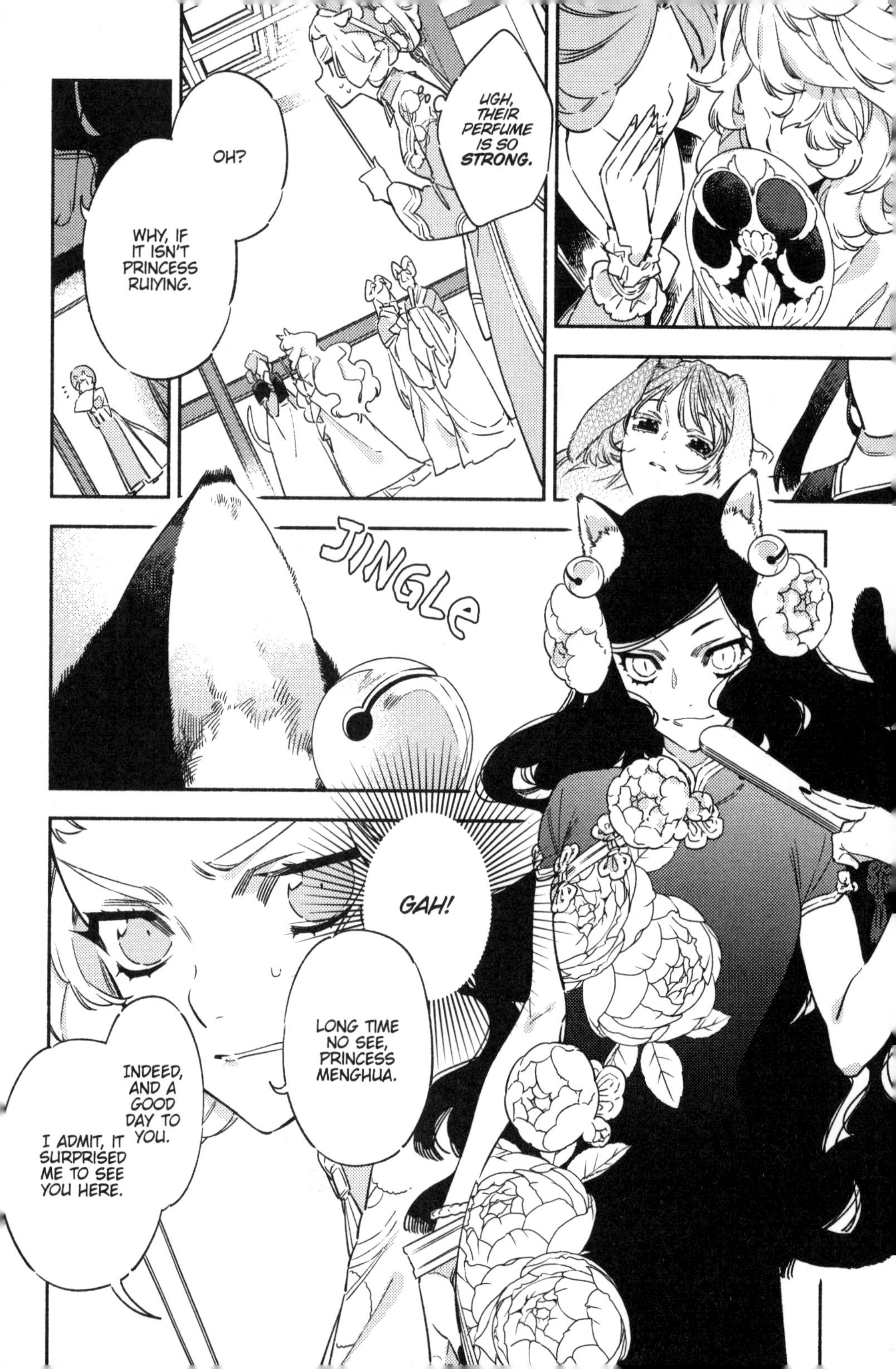
UGH, THEIR PERFUME IS SO STRONG.
OH?
WHY, IF IT ISN'T PRINCESS RUIYING.
JINGLE
GAH!
LONG TIME NO SEE, PRINCESS MENGHUA.
INDEED, AND A GOOD DAY TO YOU.
I ADMIT, IT SURPRISED ME TO SEE YOU HERE.

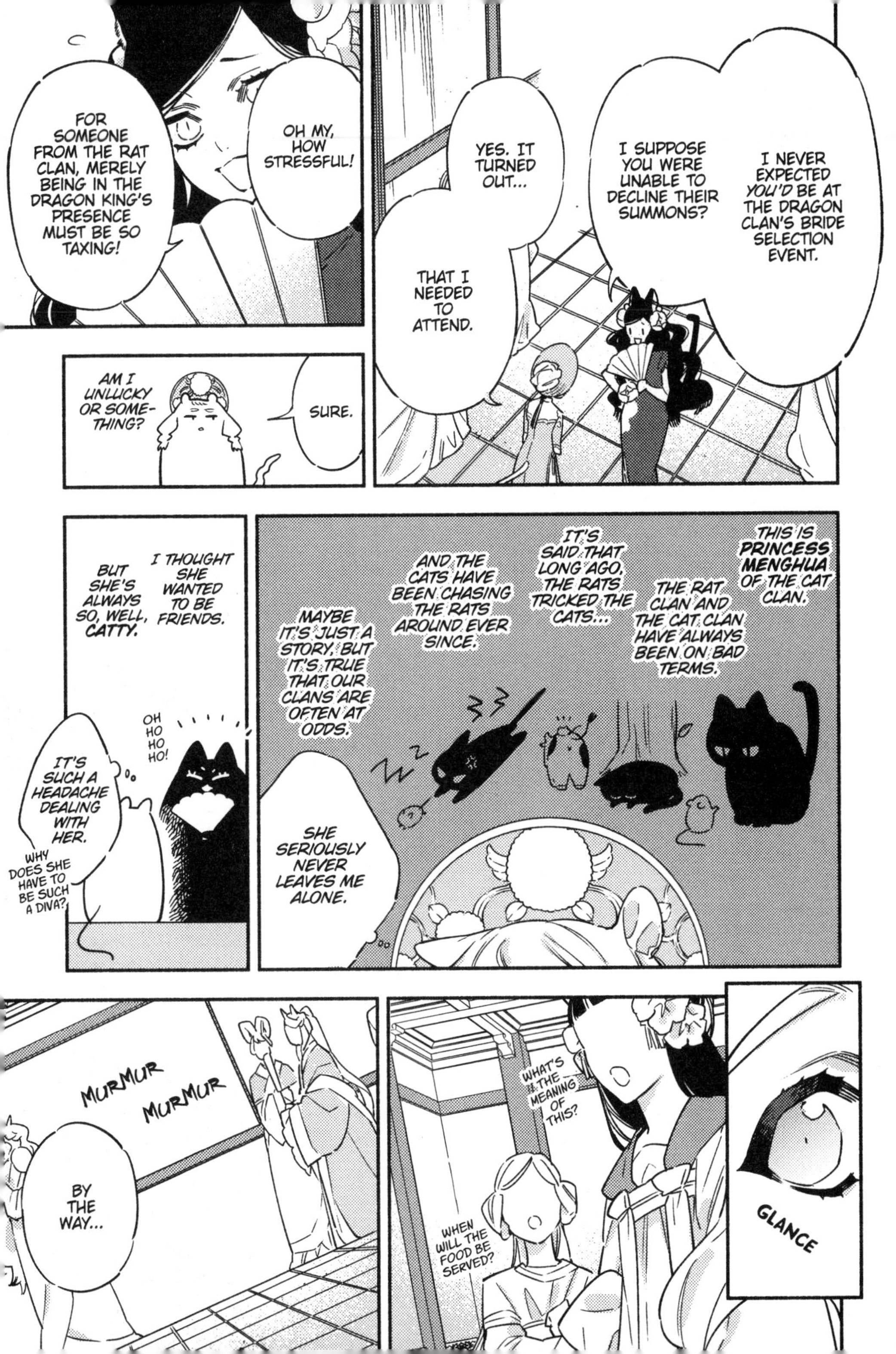

I NEVER EXPECTED *YOU'D* BE AT THE DRAGON CLAN'S BRIDE SELECTION EVENT.
I SUPPOSE YOU WERE UNABLE TO DECLINE THEIR SUMMONS?
YES. IT TURNED OUT...
THAT I NEEDED TO ATTEND.
OH MY, HOW STRESSFUL!
FOR SOMEONE FROM THE RAT CLAN, MERELY BEING IN THE DRAGON KING'S PRESENCE MUST BE SO TAXING!
SURE.
AM I UNLUCKY OR SOME-THING?
THIS IS **PRINCESS MENGHUA** OF THE CAT CLAN.
THE RAT CLAN AND THE CAT CLAN HAVE ALWAYS BEEN ON BAD TERMS.
IT'S SAID THAT LONG AGO, THE RATS TRICKED THE CATS...
AND THE CATS HAVE BEEN CHASING THE RATS AROUND EVER SINCE.
MAYBE IT'S JUST A STORY, BUT IT'S TRUE THAT OUR CLANS ARE OFTEN AT ODDS.
SHE SERIOUSLY NEVER LEAVES ME ALONE.
I THOUGHT SHE WANTED TO BE FRIENDS.
BUT SHE'S ALWAYS SO, WELL, **CATTY.**
OH HO HO HO!
IT'S SUCH A HEADACHE DEALING WITH HER.
WHY DOES SHE HAVE TO BE SUCH A DIVA?
GLANCE
WHAT'S THE MEANING OF THIS?
WHEN WILL THE FOOD BE SERVED?
MURMUR
MURMUR
BY THE WAY...

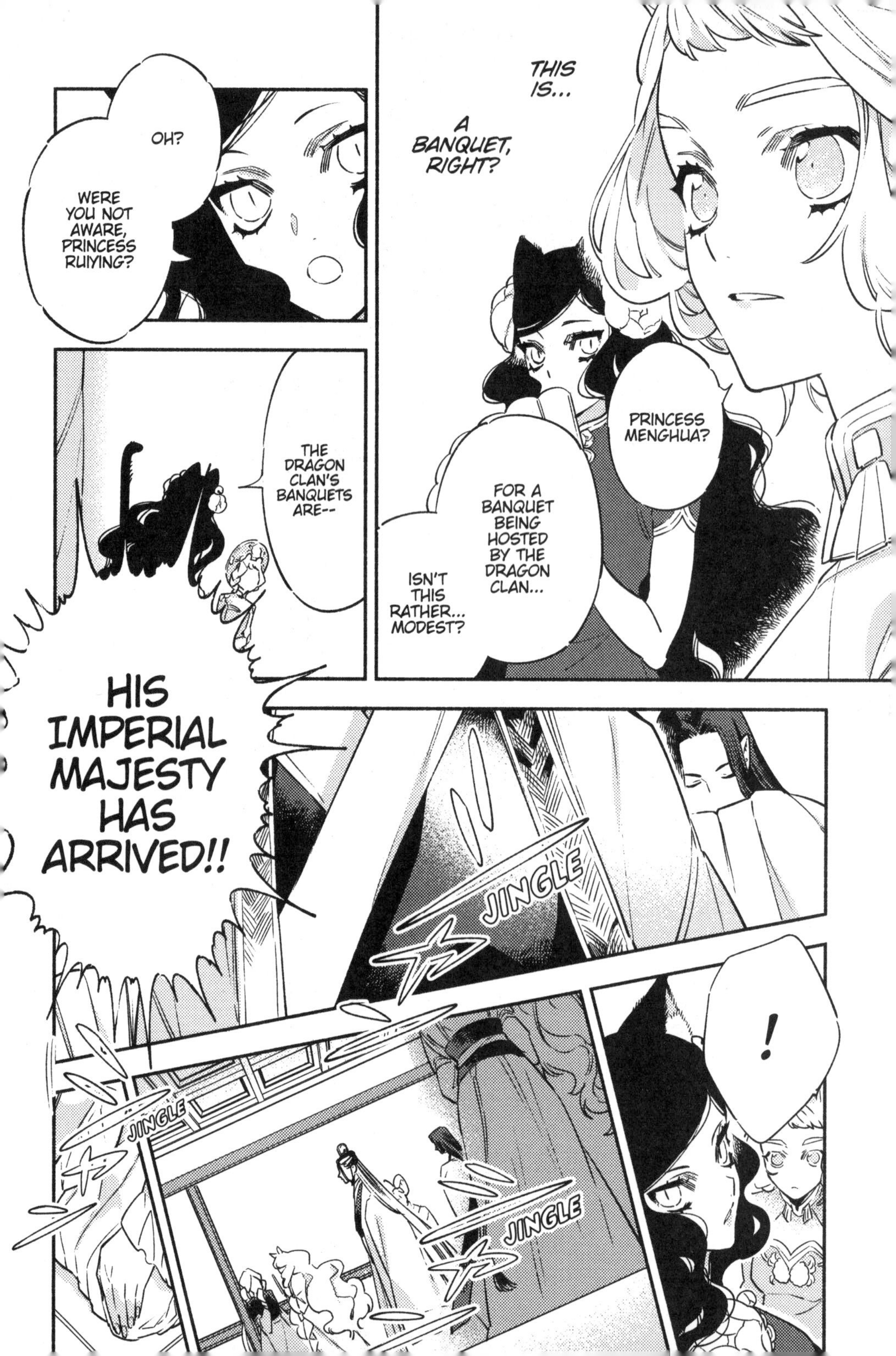
THIS IS...
A BANQUET, RIGHT?
PRINCESS MENGHUA?
FOR A BANQUET BEING HOSTED BY THE DRAGON CLAN... ISN'T THIS RATHER... MODEST?
OH?
WERE YOU NOT AWARE, PRINCESS RUIYING?
THE DRAGON CLAN'S BANQUETS ARE--
HIS IMPERIAL MAJESTY HAS ARRIVED!!
JINGLE
!
JINGLE
JINGLE

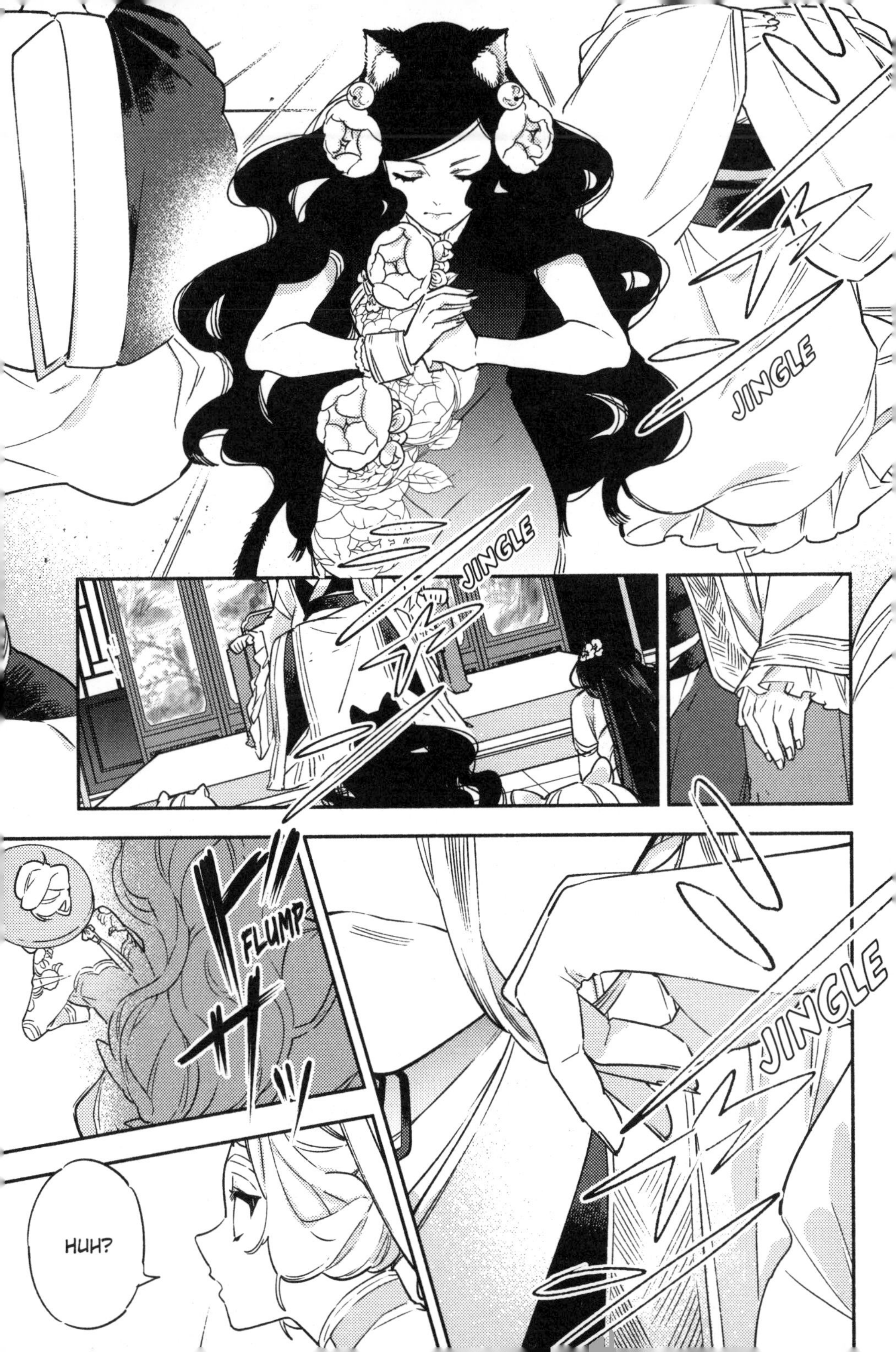
JINGLE
JINGLE
JINGLE
FLUMP
HUH?

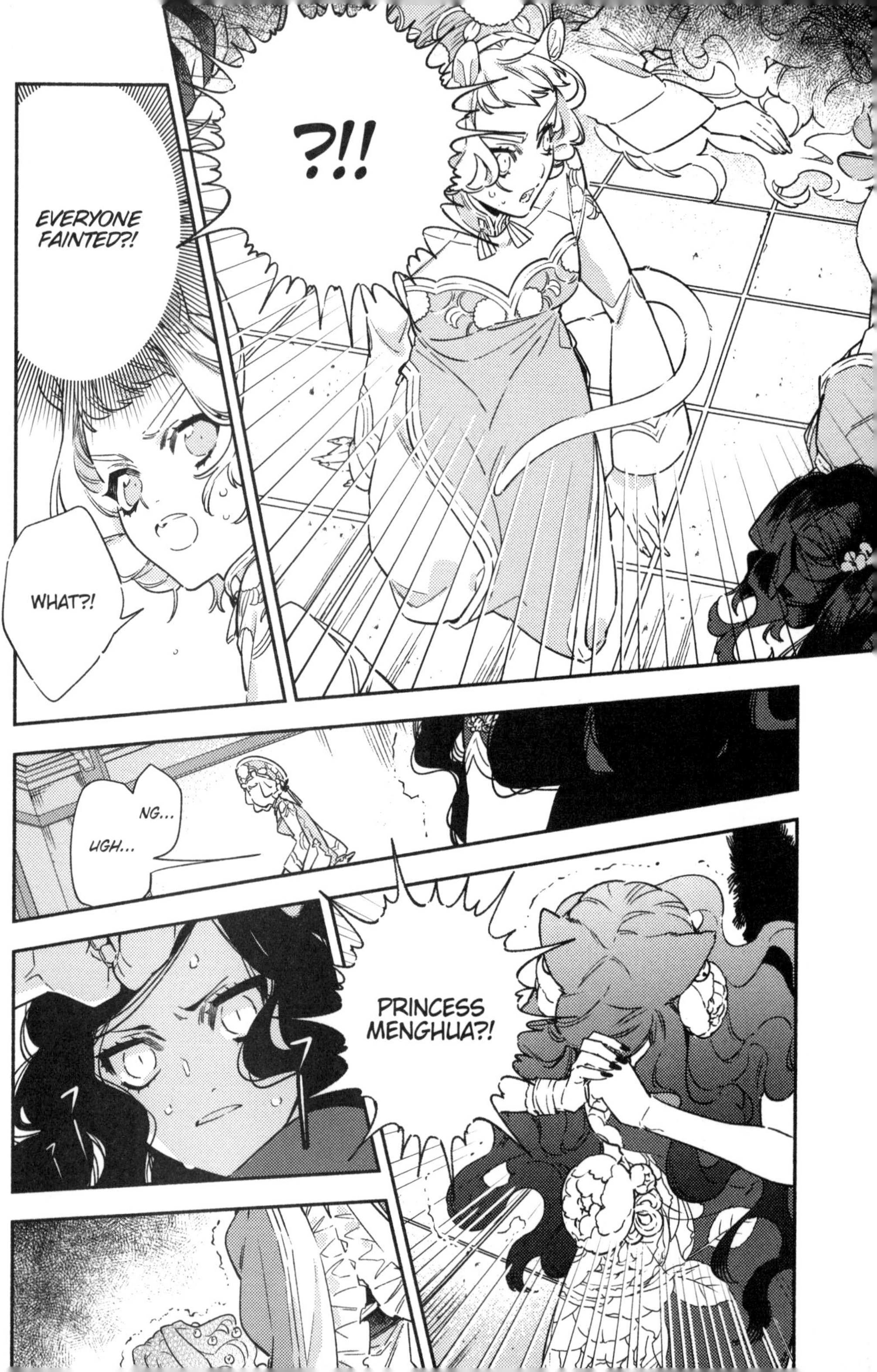
?!!
EVERYONE FAINTED?!
WHAT?!
NG...
UGH...
PRINCESS MENGHUA?!

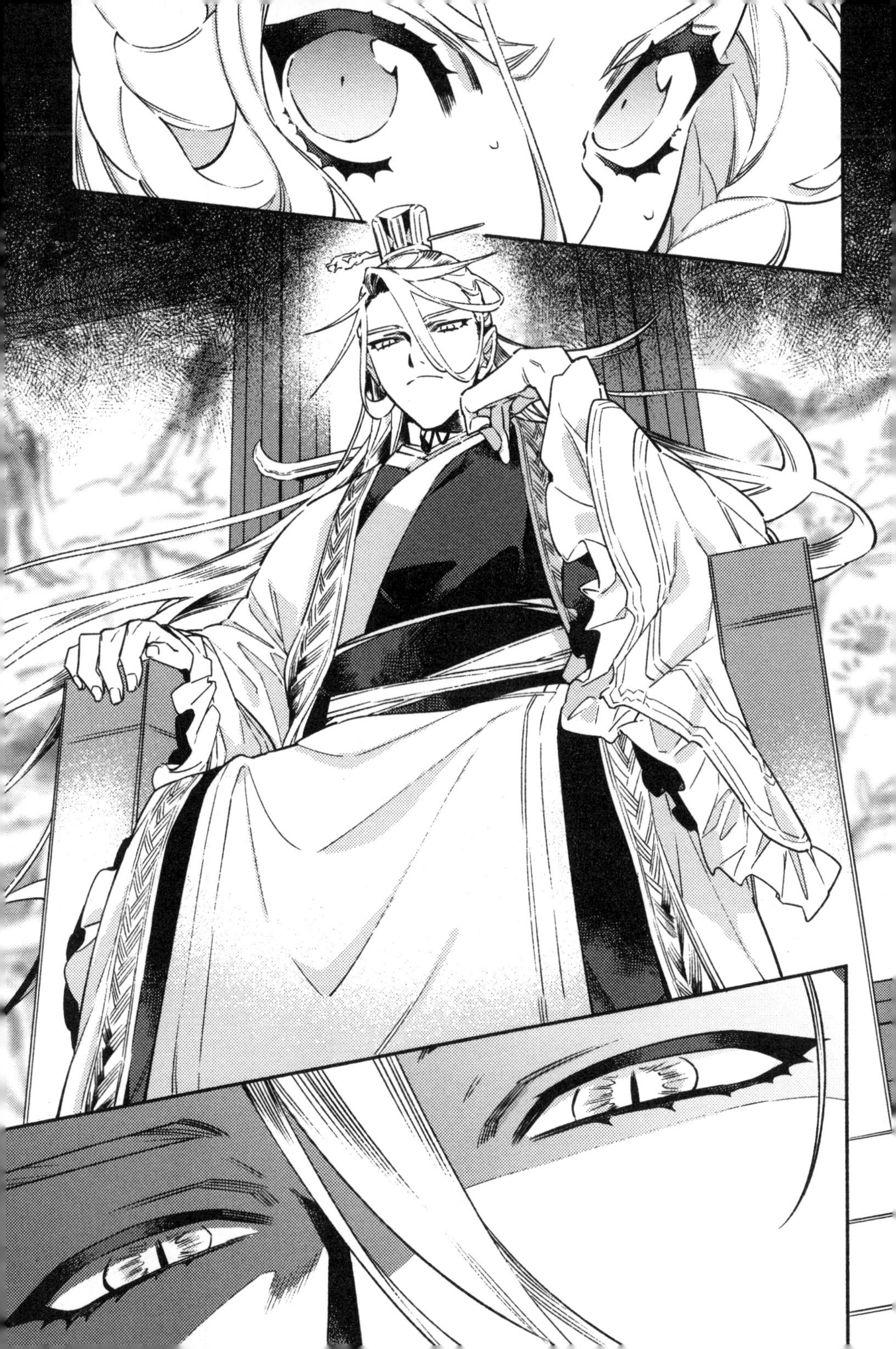

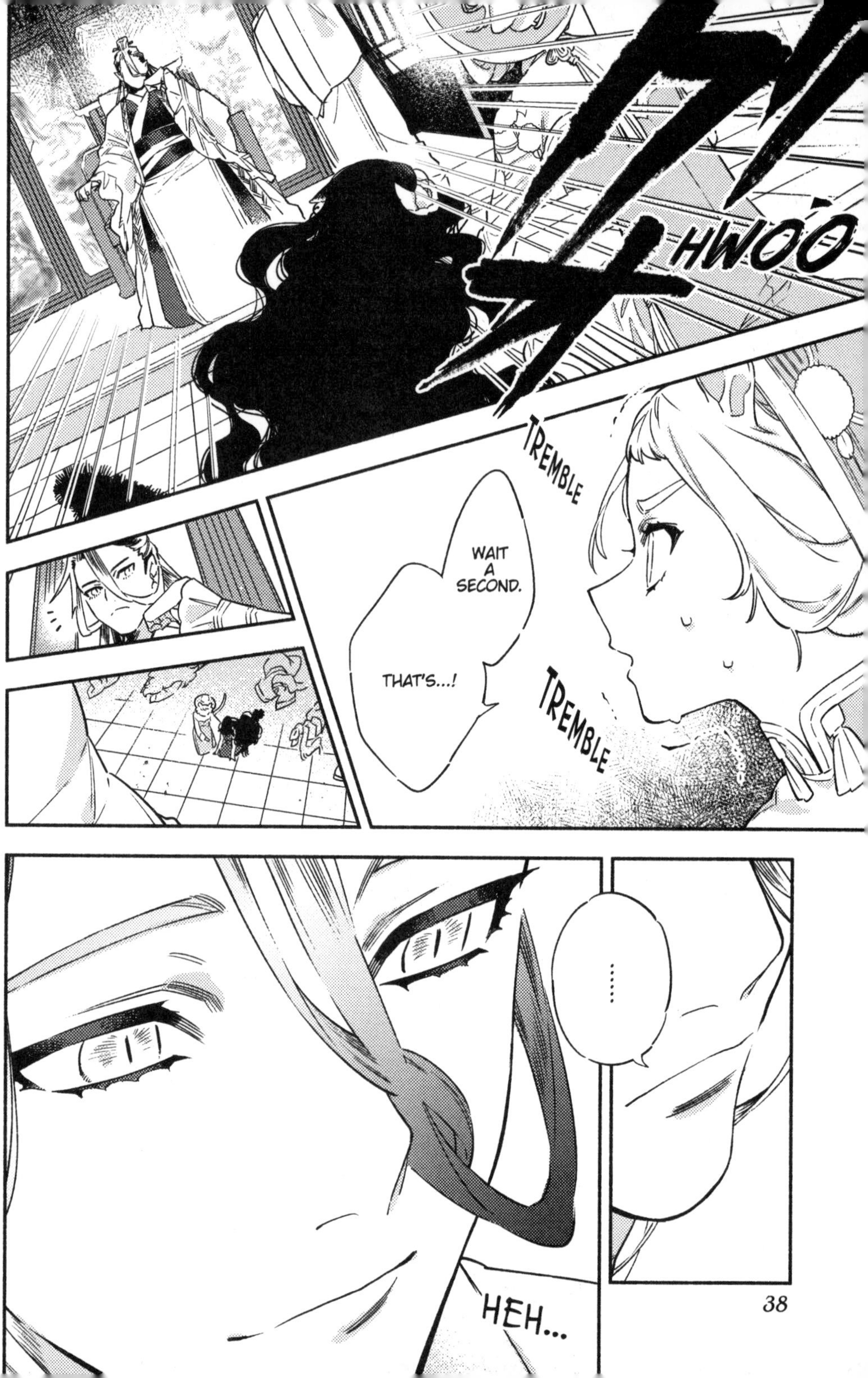

HWOO
TREMBLE
WAIT A SECOND.
THAT'S...!
TREMBLE
......
HEH...

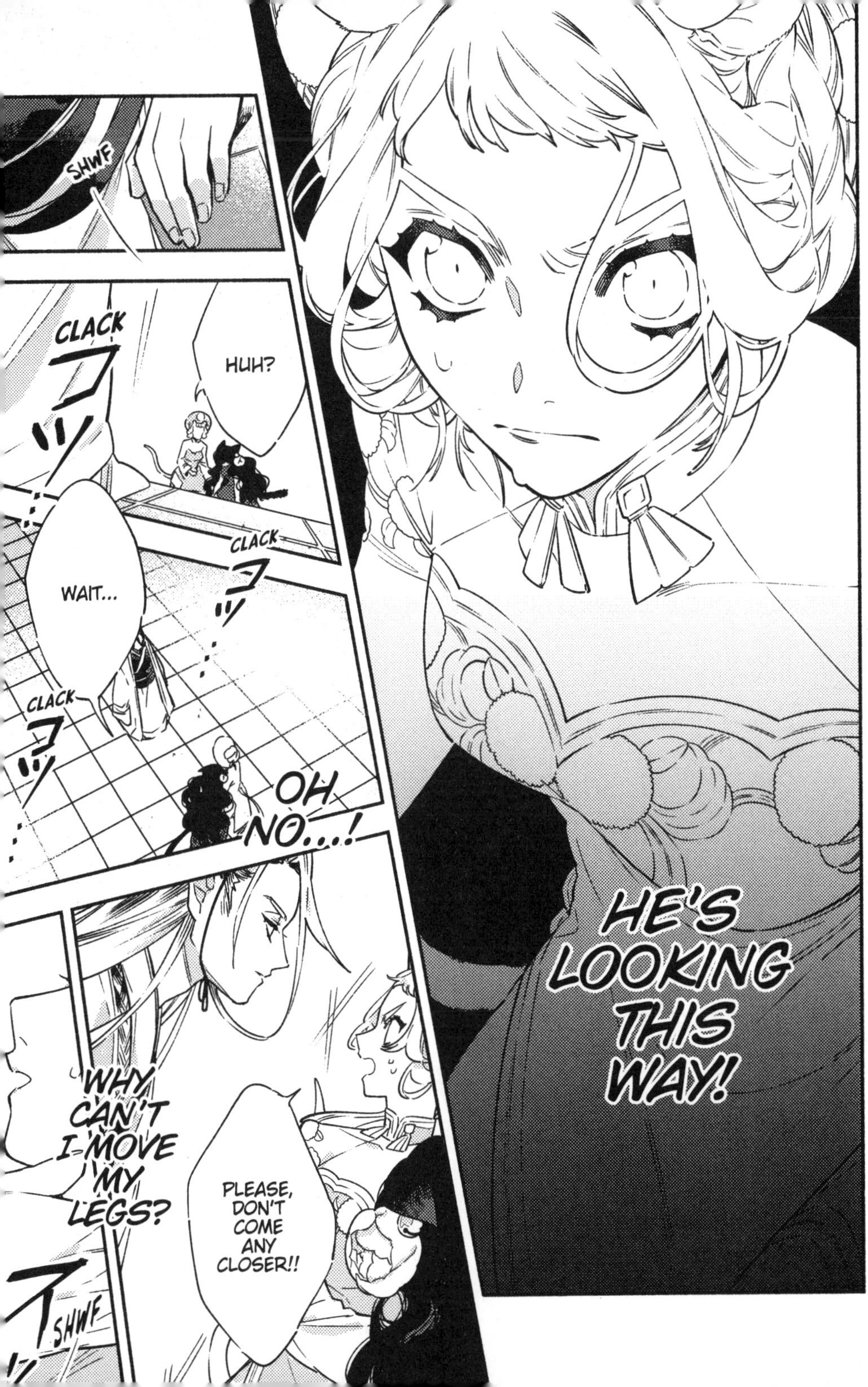

HE'S LOOKING THIS WAY!
SHWF
CLACK
HUH?
CLACK
WAIT...
CLACK
OH NO...!
PLEASE, DON'T COME ANY CLOSER!!
WHY CAN'T I MOVE MY LEGS?
SHWF

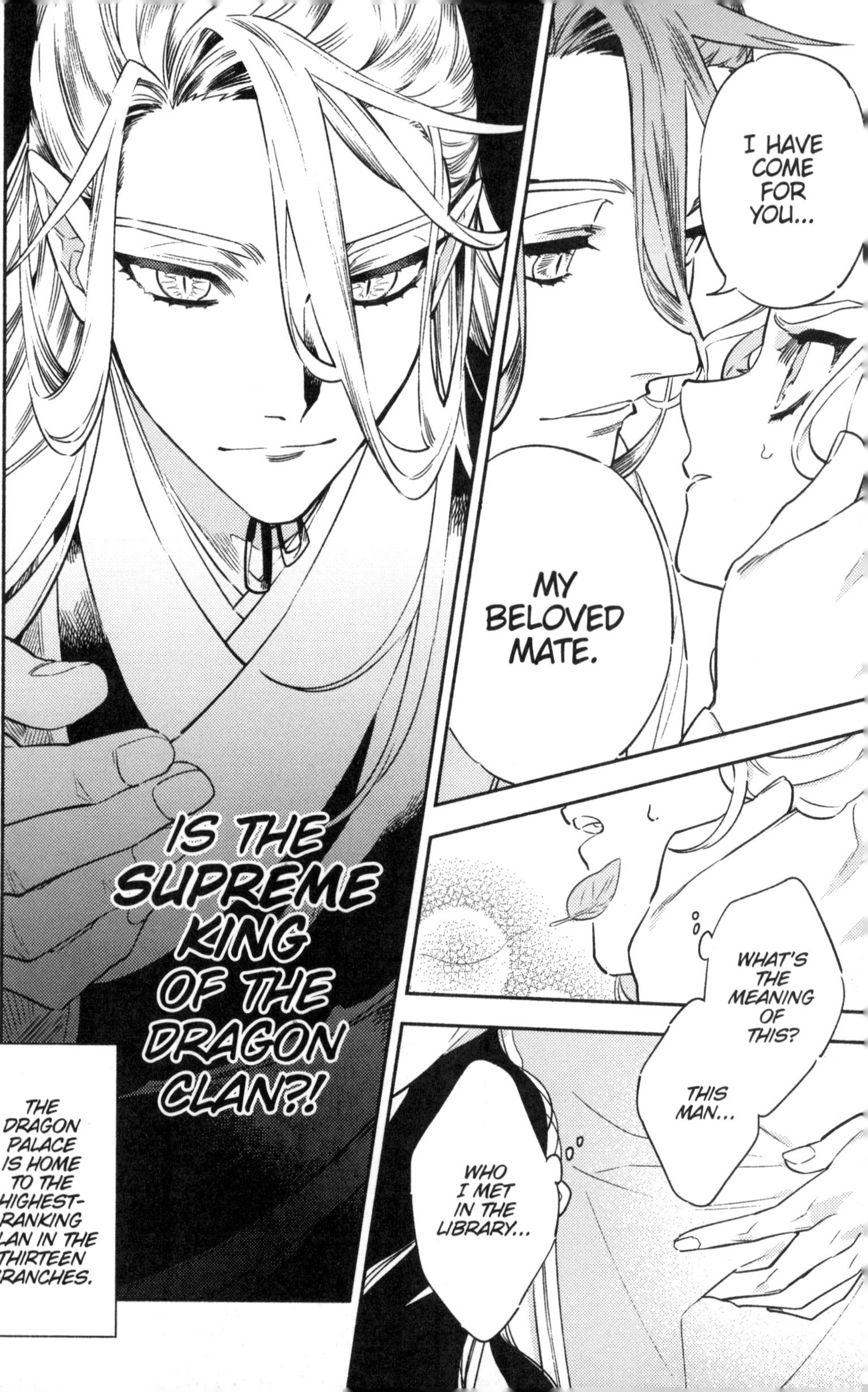
I HAVE COME FOR YOU...
MY BELOVED MATE.
WHAT'S THE MEANING OF THIS?
THIS MAN...
WHO I MET IN THE LIBRARY...
IS THE SUPREME KING OF THE DRAGON CLAN?!
THE DRAGON PALACE IS HOME TO THE HIGHEST-RANKING CLAN IN THE THIRTEEN BRANCHES.

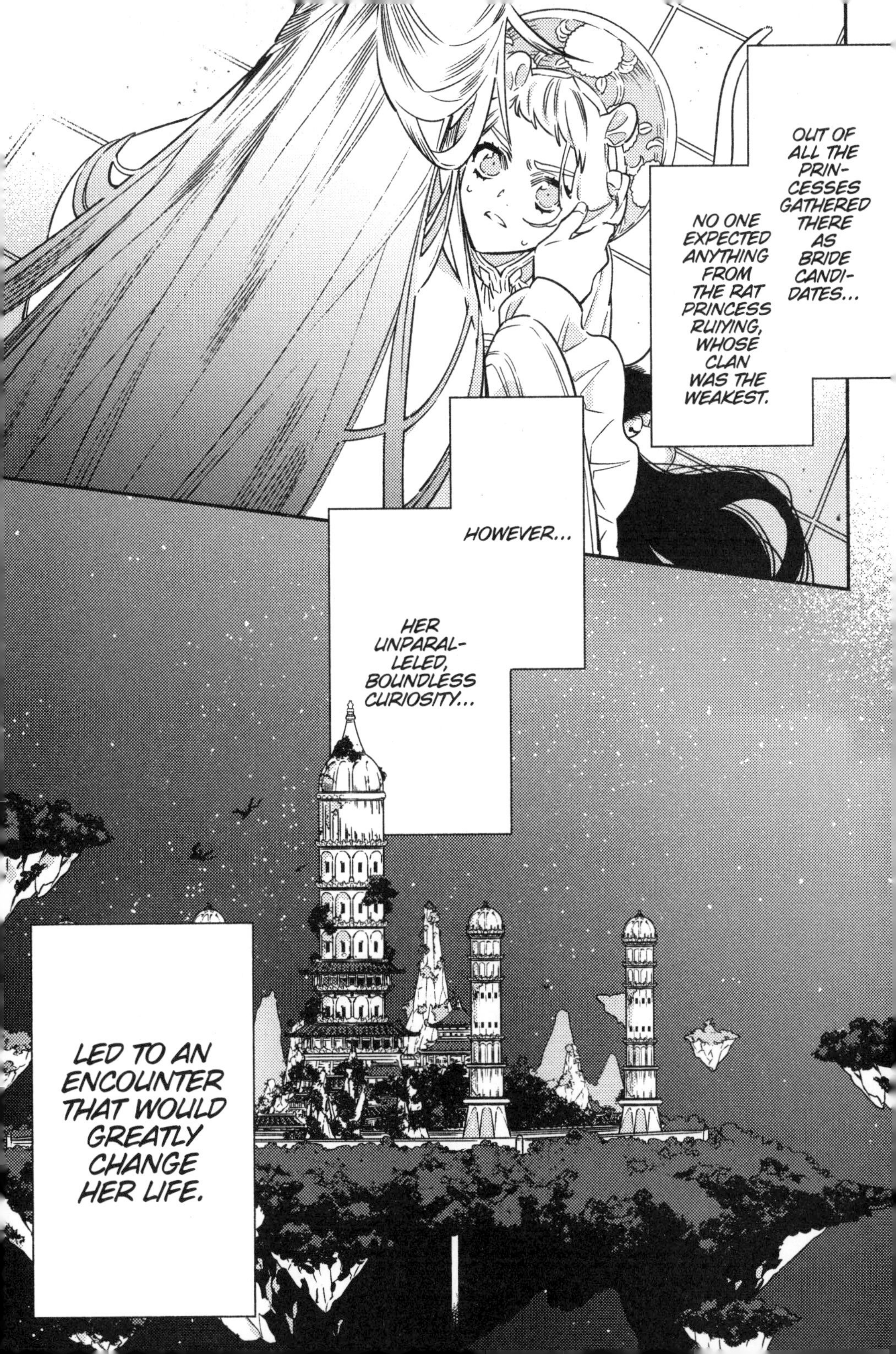
OUT OF ALL THE PRINCESSES GATHERED THERE AS BRIDE CANDIDATES...
NO ONE EXPECTED ANYTHING FROM THE RAT PRINCESS RUIYING, WHOSE CLAN WAS THE WEAKEST.
HOWEVER...
HER UNPARALLELED, BOUNDLESS CURIOSITY...
LED TO AN ENCOUNTER THAT WOULD GREATLY CHANGE HER LIFE.

THE DRAGON KING'S IMPERIAL WRATH

FALLING IN LOVE
WITH THE BOOKISH PRINCESS
OF THE RAT CLAN

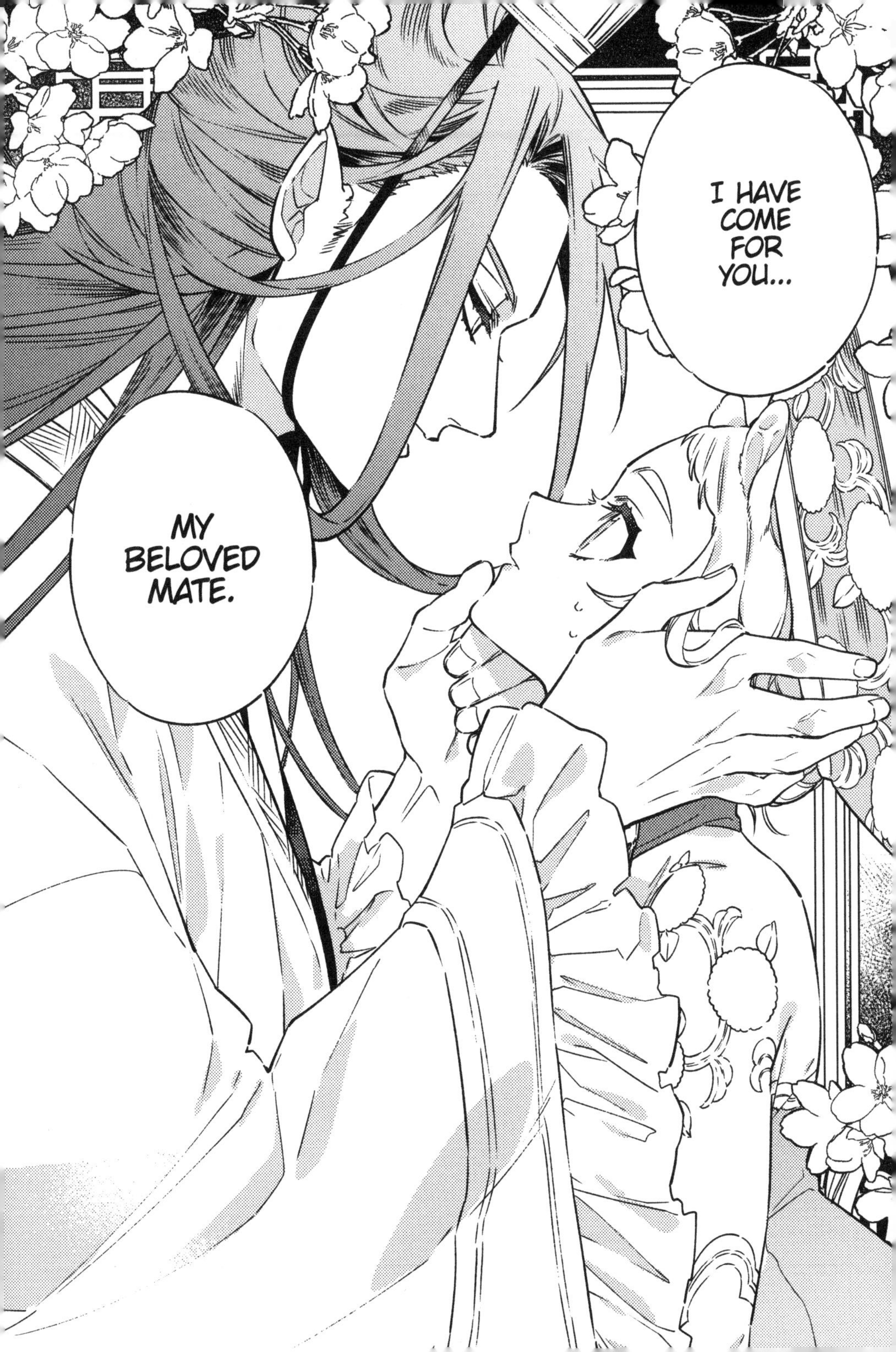
I HAVE COME FOR YOU...
MY BELOVED MATE.

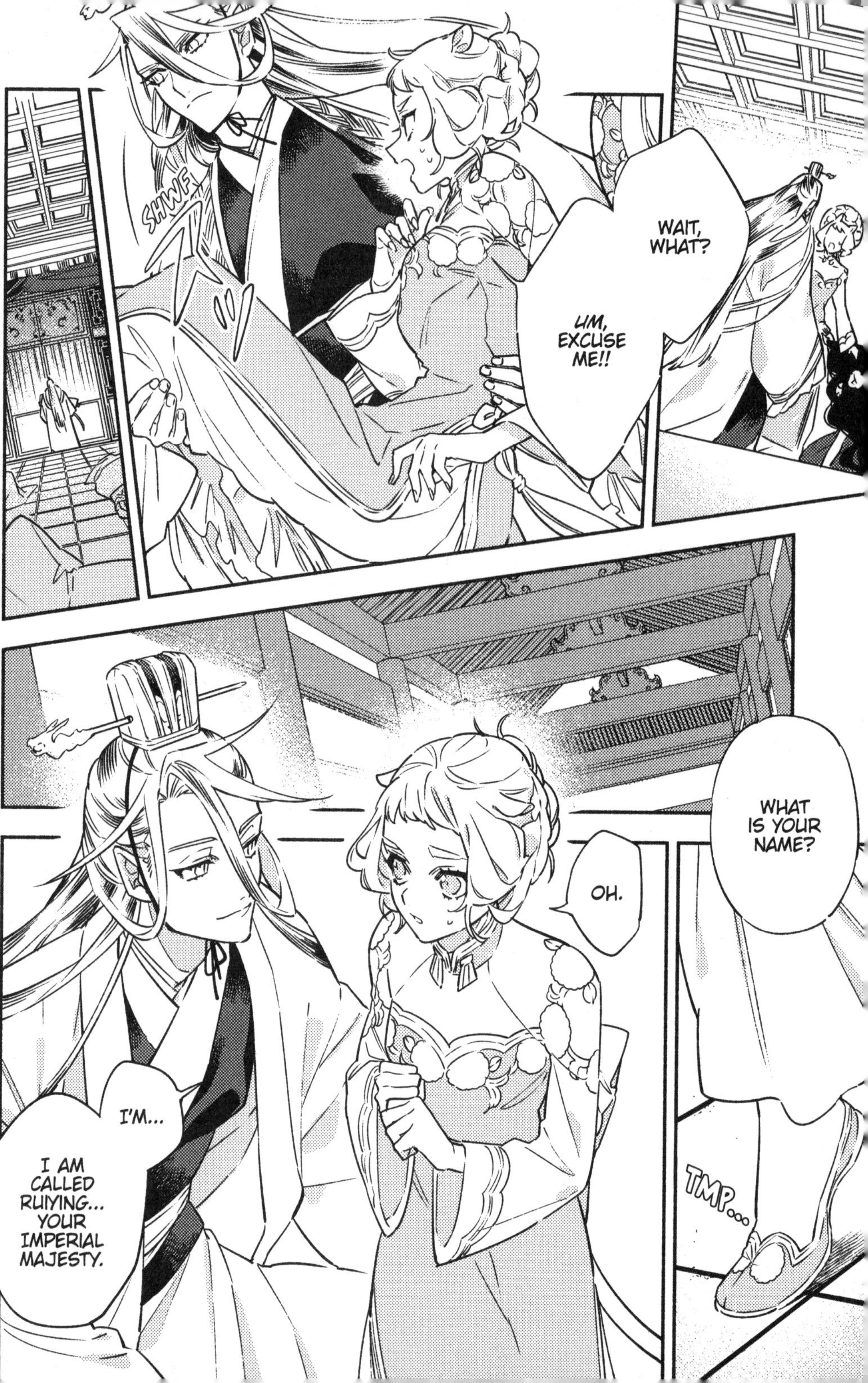
WAIT, WHAT?
UM, EXCUSE ME!!
SHWF
WHAT IS YOUR NAME?
TMP...
OH.
I'M...
I AM CALLED RUIYING... YOUR IMPERIAL MAJESTY.

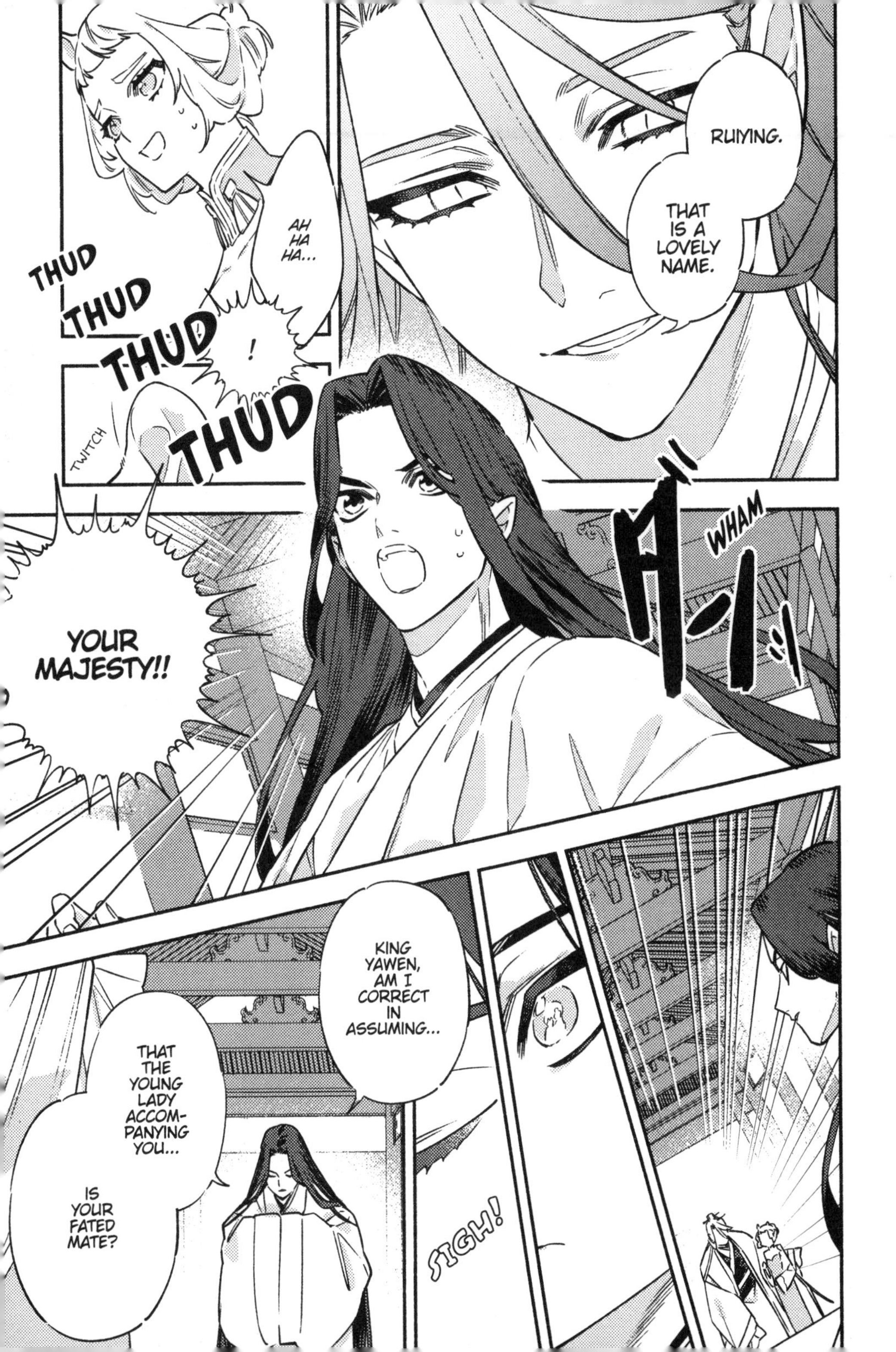
RUIYING.
THAT IS A LOVELY NAME.
AH HA HA...
THUD THUD THUD THUD
!
TWITCH
WHAM
YOUR MAJESTY!!
KING YAWEN, AM I CORRECT IN ASSUMING...
THAT THE YOUNG LADY ACCOMPANYING YOU...
IS YOUR FATED MATE?
SIGH!

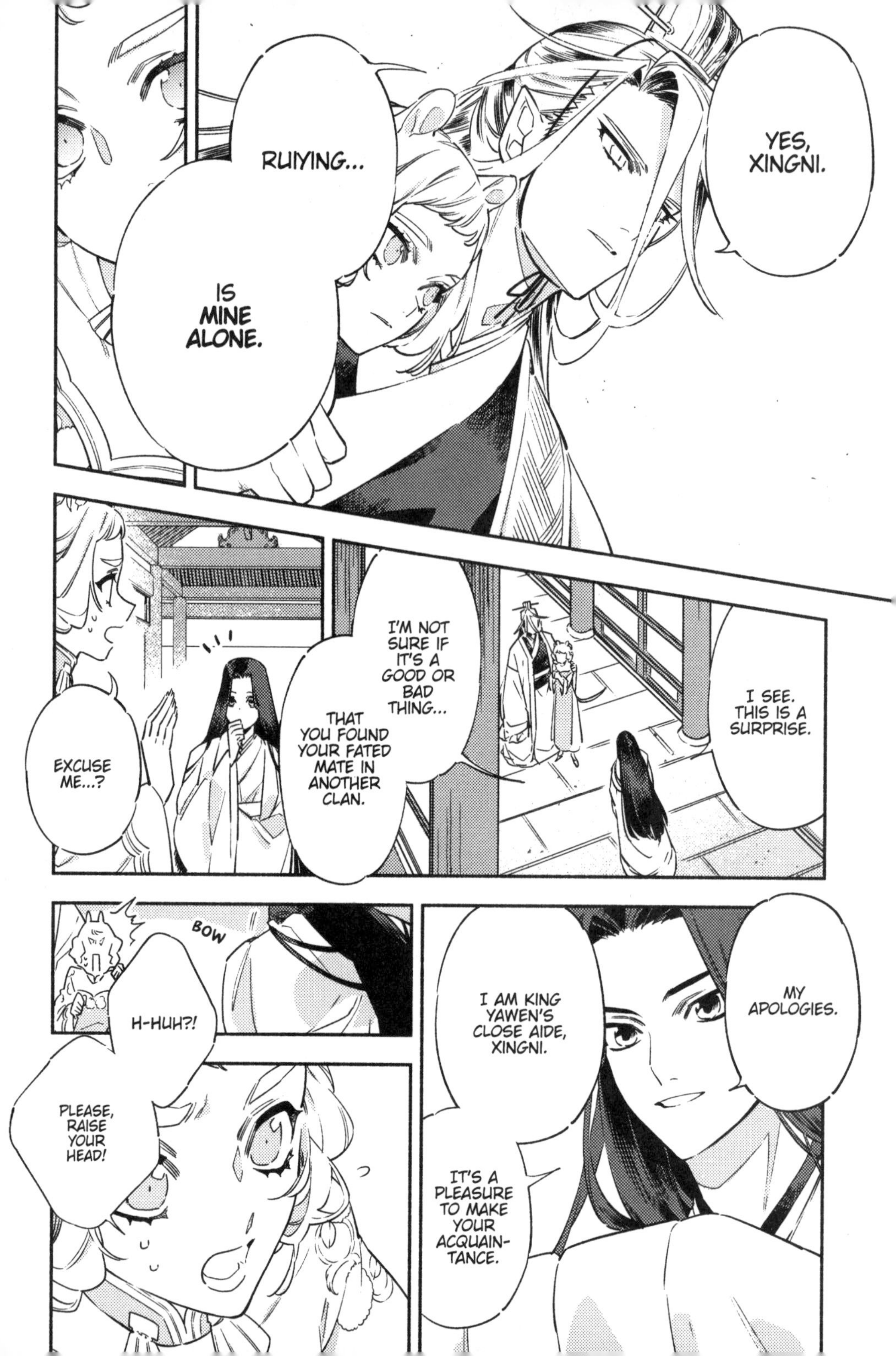
YES, XINGNI.
RUIYING...
IS MINE ALONE.
I SEE. THIS IS A SURPRISE.
I'M NOT SURE IF IT'S A GOOD OR BAD THING...
THAT YOU FOUND YOUR FATED MATE IN ANOTHER CLAN.
EXCUSE ME...?
MY APOLOGIES.
I AM KING YAWEN'S CLOSE AIDE, XINGNI.
IT'S A PLEASURE TO MAKE YOUR ACQUAINTANCE.
BOW
H-HUH?!
PLEASE, RAISE YOUR HEAD!

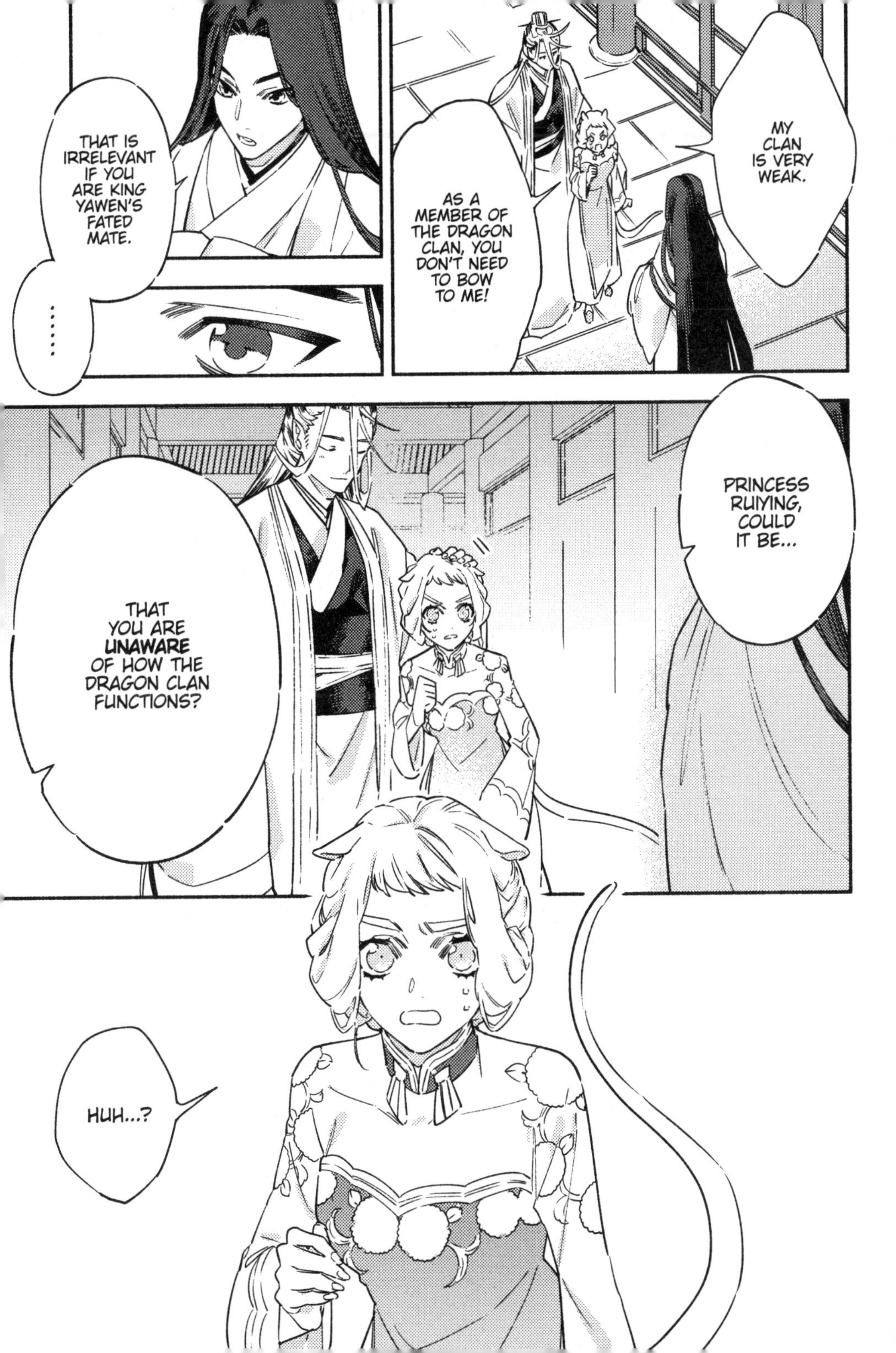
MY CLAN IS VERY WEAK.
AS A MEMBER OF THE DRAGON CLAN, YOU DON'T NEED TO BOW TO ME!
THAT IS IRRELEVANT IF YOU ARE KING YAWEN'S FATED MATE.
......
PRINCESS RUIYING, COULD IT BE...
THAT YOU ARE **UNAWARE** OF HOW THE DRAGON CLAN FUNCTIONS?
HUH...?

CHAPTER 2

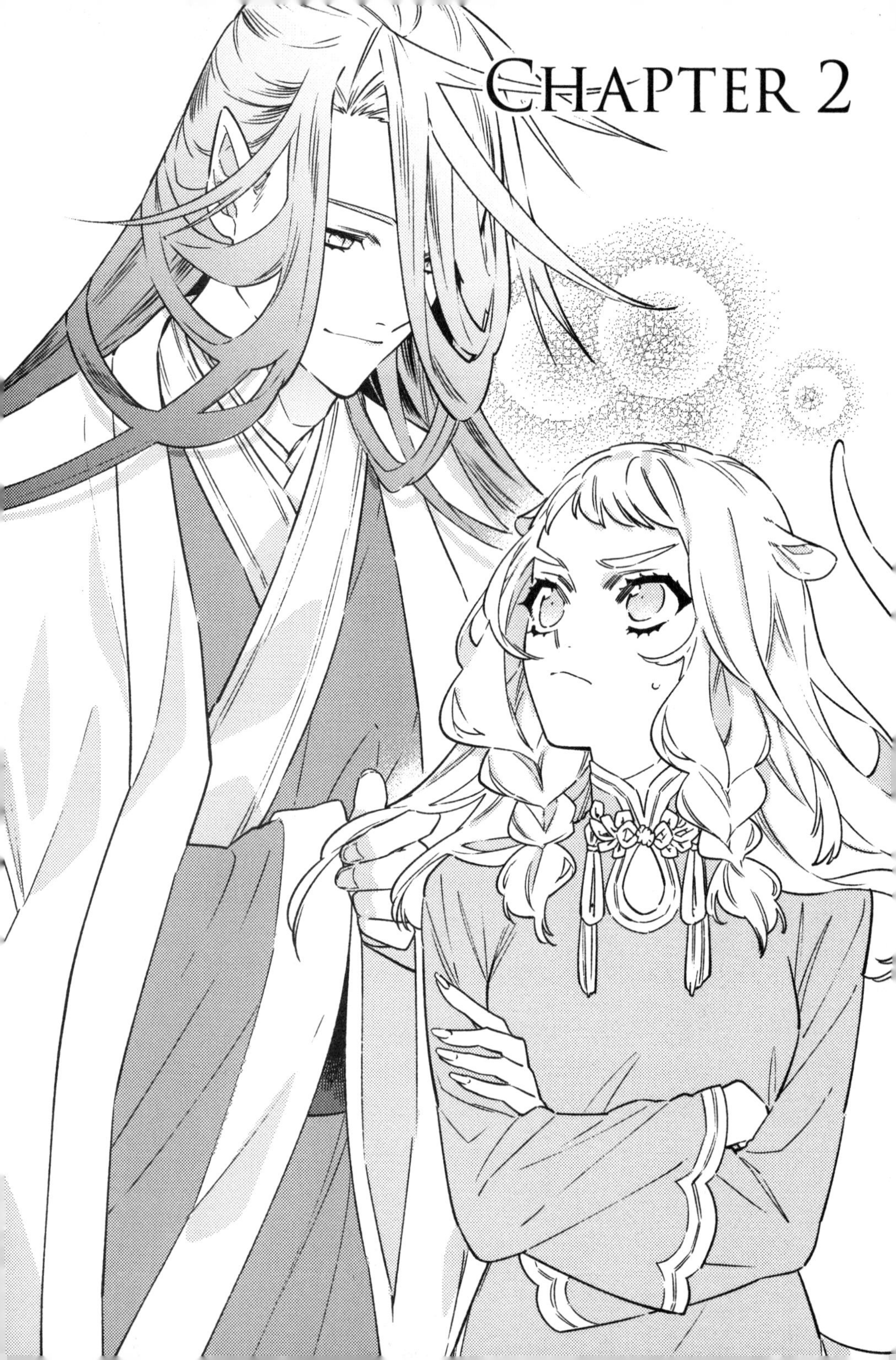

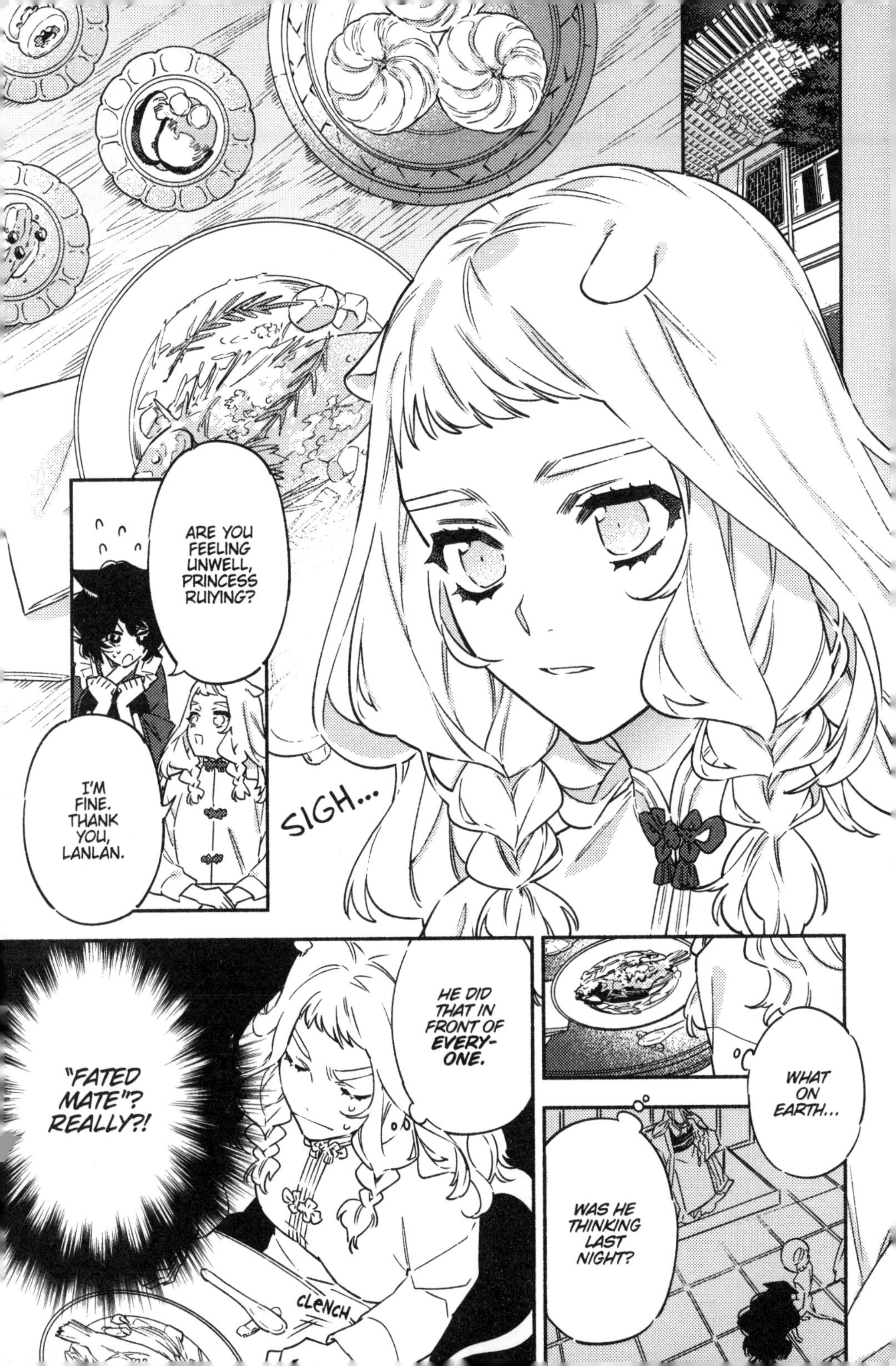
SIGH...
ARE YOU FEELING UNWELL, PRINCESS RUIYING?
I'M FINE. THANK YOU, LANLAN.
WHAT ON EARTH...
WAS HE THINKING LAST NIGHT?
HE DID THAT IN FRONT OF EVERY-ONE.
"FATED MATE"? REALLY?!
CLENCH

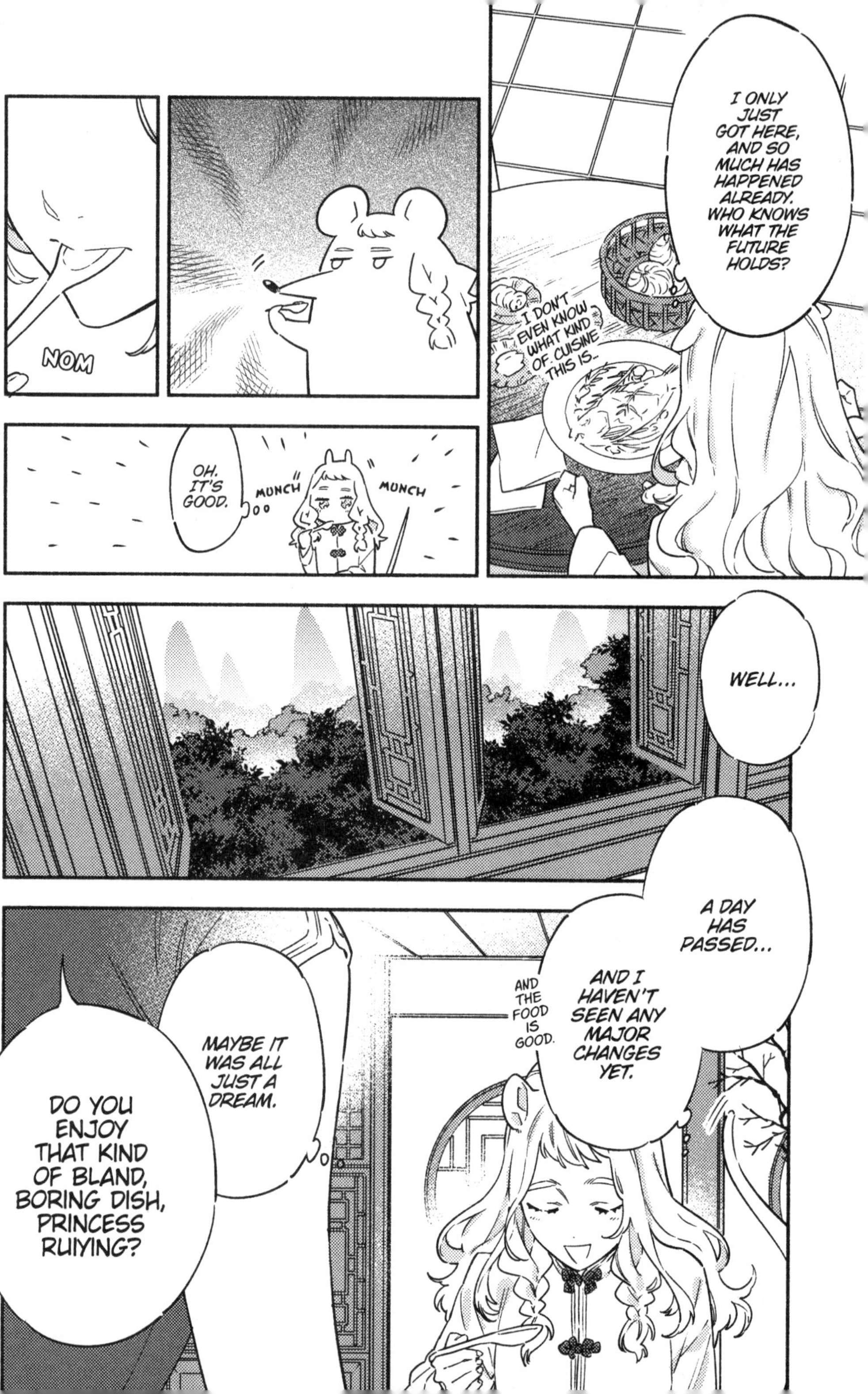
I ONLY JUST GOT HERE, AND SO MUCH HAS HAPPENED ALREADY. WHO KNOWS WHAT THE FUTURE HOLDS?
I DON'T EVEN KNOW WHAT KIND OF CUISINE THIS IS.
NOM
MUNCH
MUNCH
OH. IT'S GOOD.
WELL...
A DAY HAS PASSED...
AND I HAVEN'T SEEN ANY MAJOR CHANGES YET.
AND THE FOOD IS GOOD.
MAYBE IT WAS ALL JUST A DREAM.
DO YOU ENJOY THAT KIND OF BLAND, BORING DISH, PRINCESS RUIYING?

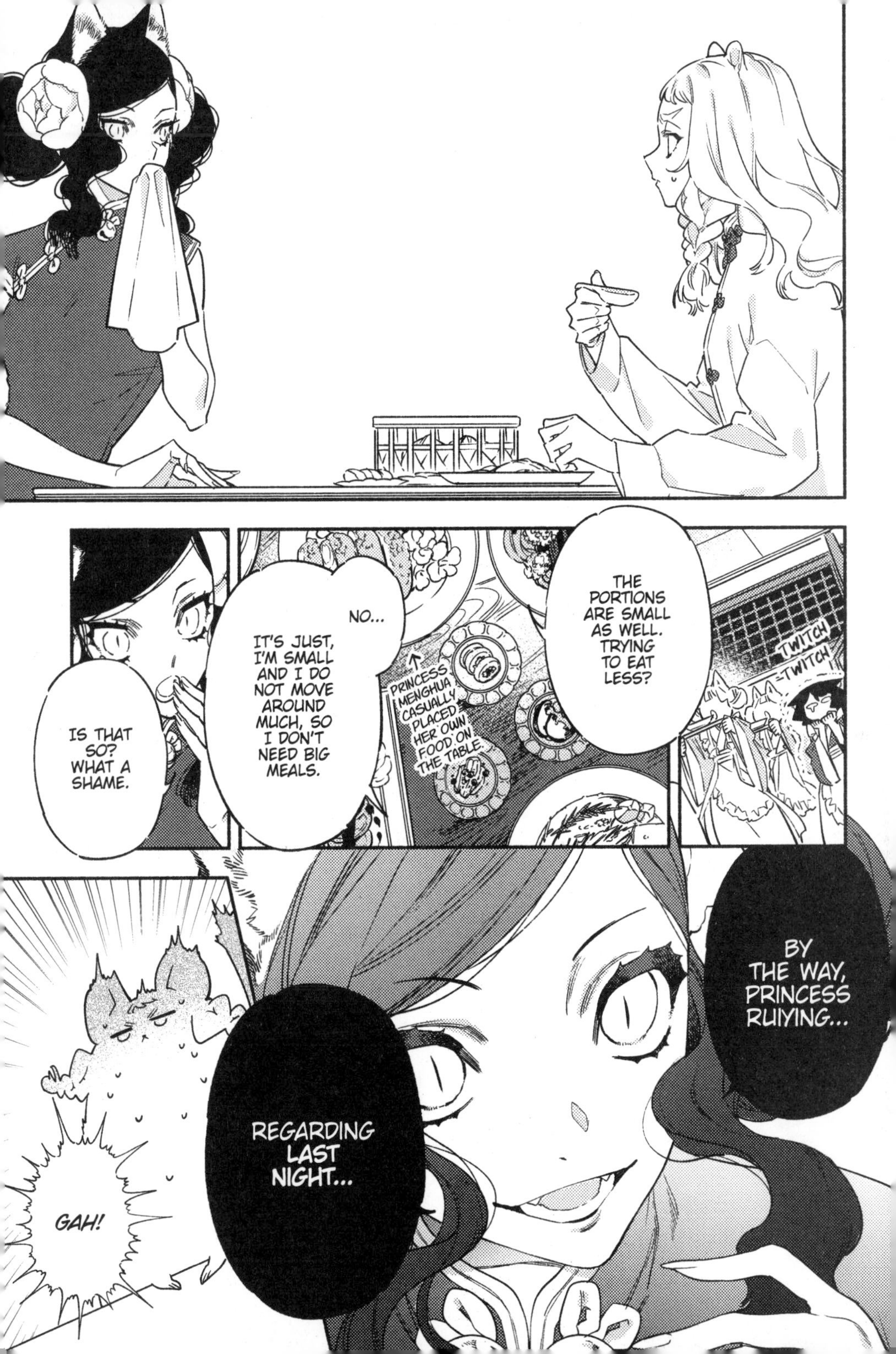
TWITCH
TWITCH
THE PORTIONS ARE SMALL AS WELL. TRYING TO EAT LESS?
PRINCESS MENGHUA CASUALLY PLACED HER OWN FOOD ON THE TABLE.
NO...
IT'S JUST, I'M SMALL AND I DO NOT MOVE AROUND MUCH, SO I DON'T NEED BIG MEALS.
IS THAT SO? WHAT A SHAME.
BY THE WAY, PRINCESS RUIYING...
REGARDING LAST NIGHT...
GAH!

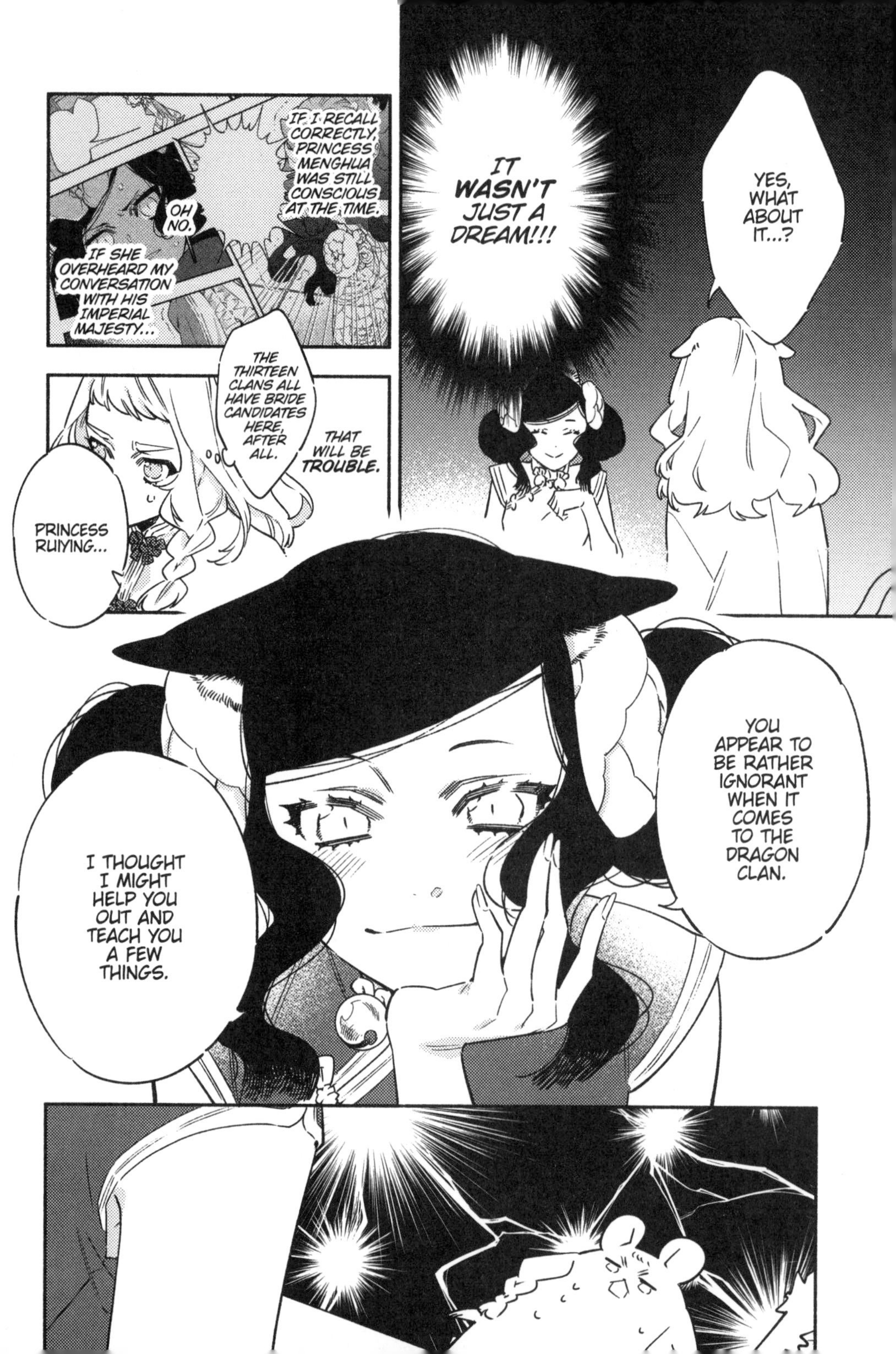
YES, WHAT ABOUT IT...?
IT WASN'T JUST A DREAM!!!
IF I RECALL CORRECTLY, PRINCESS MENGHUA WAS STILL CONSCIOUS AT THE TIME.
OH NO.
IF SHE OVERHEARD MY CONVERSATION WITH HIS IMPERIAL MAJESTY...
THE THIRTEEN CLANS ALL HAVE BRIDE CANDIDATES HERE, AFTER ALL.
THAT WILL BE TROUBLE.
PRINCESS RUIYING...
YOU APPEAR TO BE RATHER IGNORANT WHEN IT COMES TO THE DRAGON CLAN.
I THOUGHT I MIGHT HELP YOU OUT AND TEACH YOU A FEW THINGS.

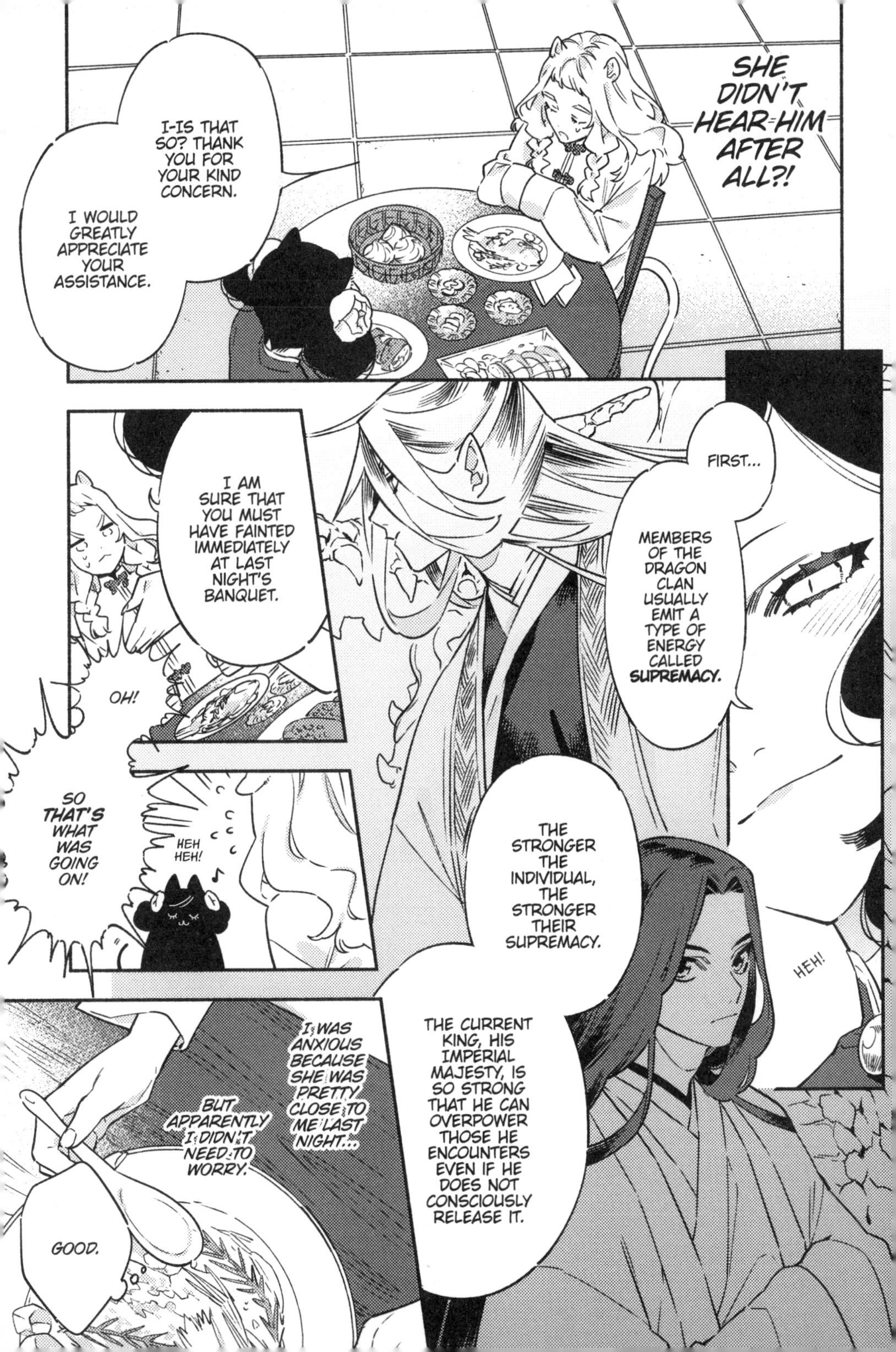
SHE DIDN'T HEAR HIM AFTER ALL?!
I-IS THAT SO? THANK YOU FOR YOUR KIND CONCERN.
I WOULD GREATLY APPRECIATE YOUR ASSISTANCE.
FIRST...
MEMBERS OF THE DRAGON CLAN USUALLY EMIT A TYPE OF ENERGY CALLED **SUPREMACY.**
THE STRONGER THE INDIVIDUAL, THE STRONGER THEIR SUPREMACY.
HEH!
THE CURRENT KING, HIS IMPERIAL MAJESTY, IS SO STRONG THAT HE CAN OVERPOWER THOSE HE ENCOUNTERS EVEN IF HE DOES NOT CONSCIOUSLY RELEASE IT.
I AM SURE THAT YOU MUST HAVE FAINTED IMMEDIATELY AT LAST NIGHT'S BANQUET.
OH!
SO ***THAT'S*** WHAT WAS GOING ON!
HEH HEH!
I WAS ANXIOUS BECAUSE SHE WAS PRETTY CLOSE TO ME LAST NIGHT...
BUT APPARENTLY I DIDN'T NEED TO WORRY.
GOOD.

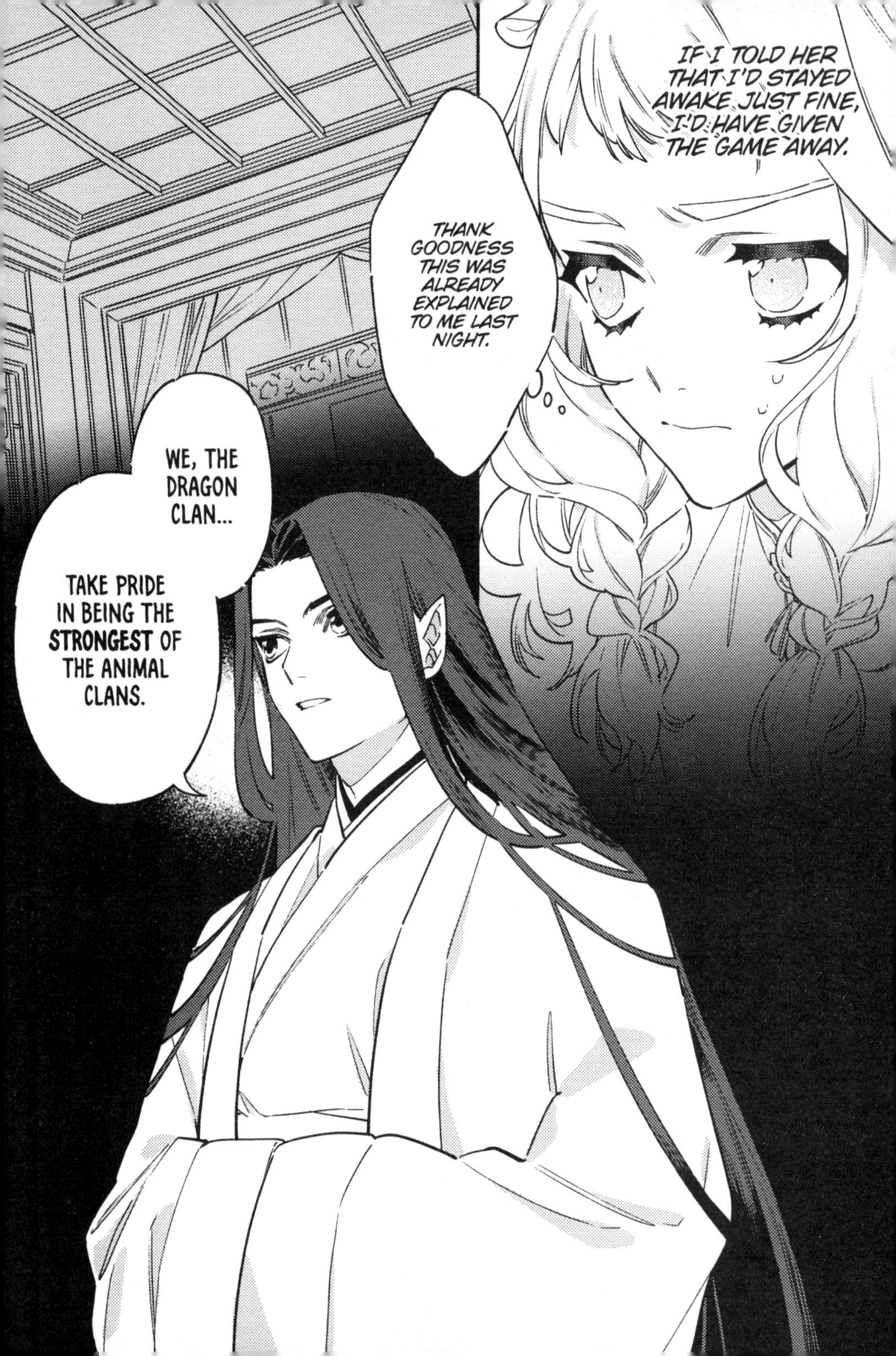
IF I TOLD HER THAT I'D STAYED AWAKE JUST FINE, I'D HAVE GIVEN THE GAME AWAY.
THANK GOODNESS THIS WAS ALREADY EXPLAINED TO ME LAST NIGHT.
WE, THE DRAGON CLAN...
TAKE PRIDE IN BEING THE STRONGEST OF THE ANIMAL CLANS.

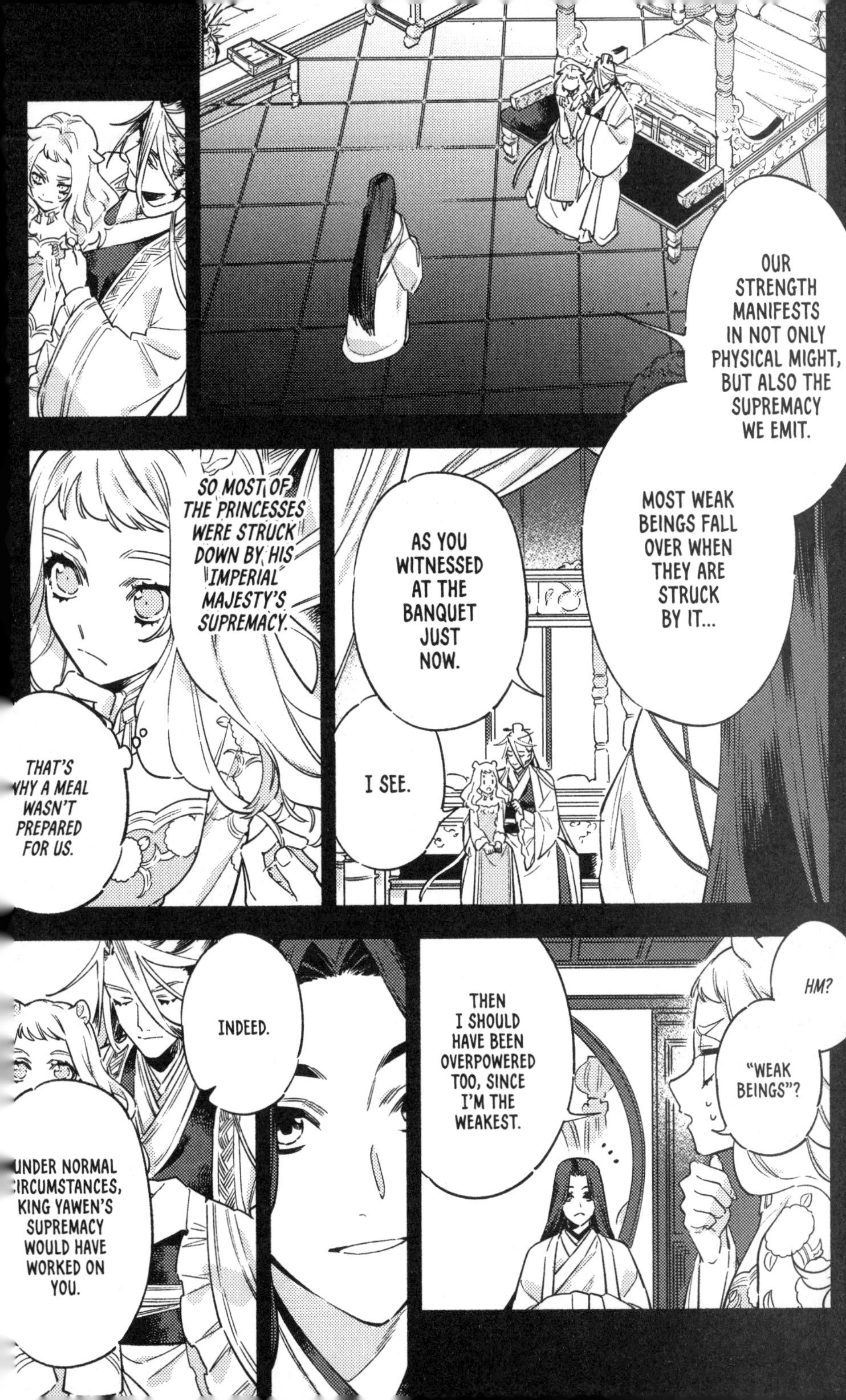
OUR STRENGTH MANIFESTS IN NOT ONLY PHYSICAL MIGHT, BUT ALSO THE SUPREMACY WE EMIT.
MOST WEAK BEINGS FALL OVER WHEN THEY ARE STRUCK BY IT...
AS YOU WITNESSED AT THE BANQUET JUST NOW.
I SEE.
SO MOST OF THE PRINCESSES WERE STRUCK DOWN BY HIS IMPERIAL MAJESTY'S SUPREMACY.
THAT'S WHY A MEAL WASN'T PREPARED FOR US.
HM?
"WEAK BEINGS"?
THEN I SHOULD HAVE BEEN OVERPOWERED TOO, SINCE I'M THE WEAKEST.
INDEED.
UNDER NORMAL CIRCUMSTANCES, KING YAWEN'S SUPREMACY WOULD HAVE WORKED ON YOU.

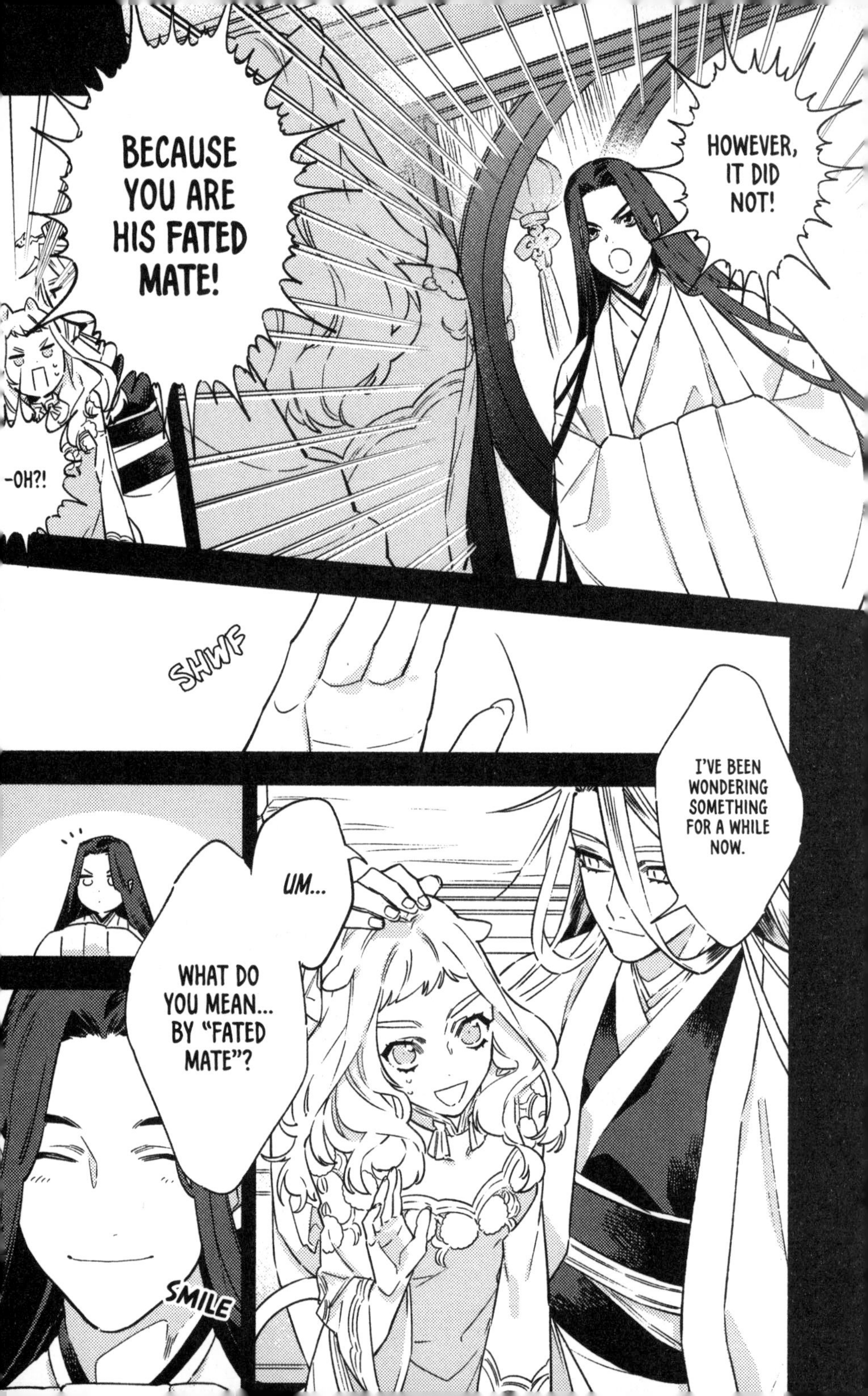
HOWEVER, IT DID NOT!
BECAUSE YOU ARE HIS FATED MATE!
-OH?!
SHWF
I'VE BEEN WONDERING SOMETHING FOR A WHILE NOW.
UM...
WHAT DO YOU MEAN... BY "FATED MATE"?
SMILE

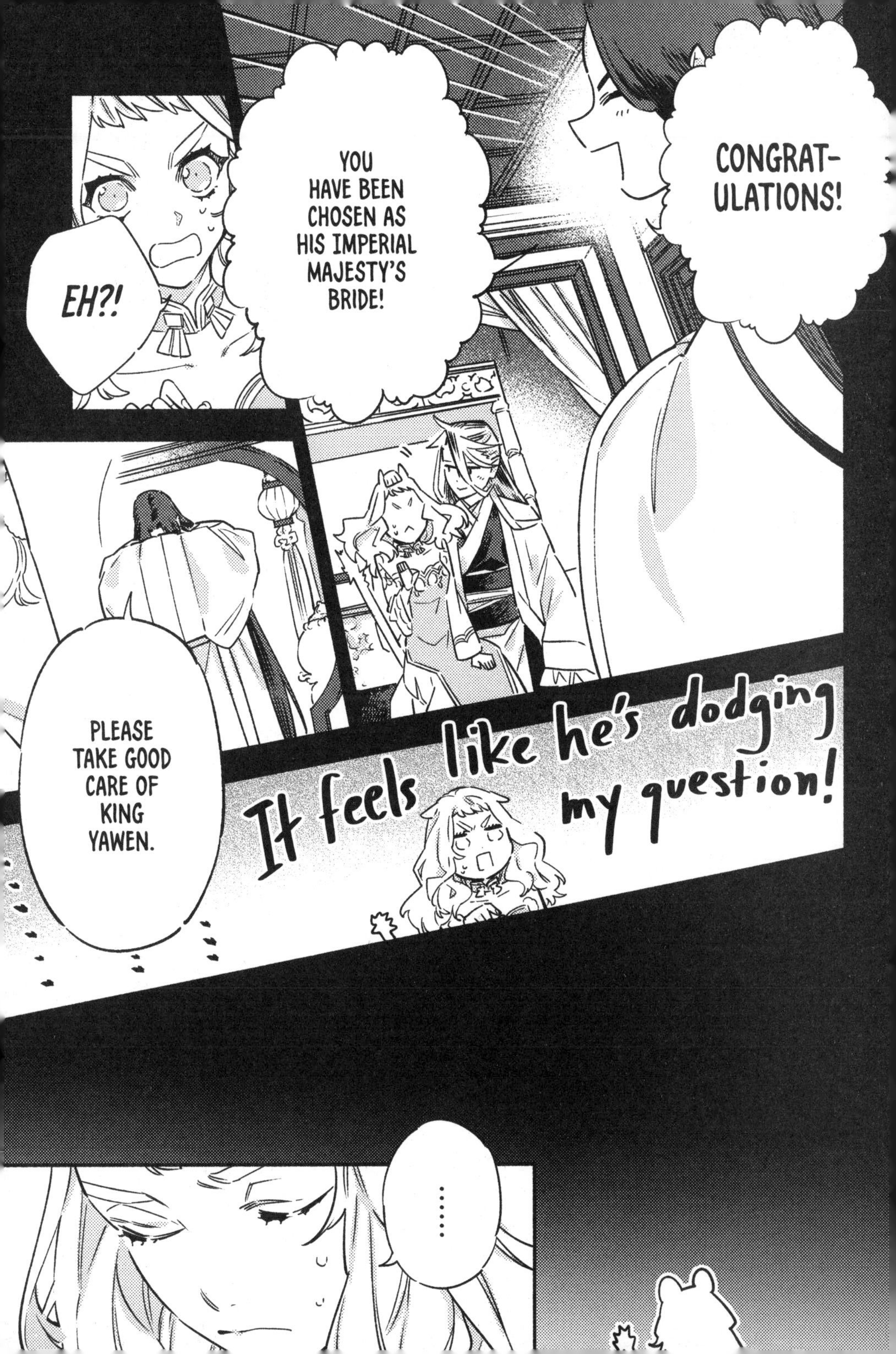
CONGRAT-ULATIONS!
YOU HAVE BEEN CHOSEN AS HIS IMPERIAL MAJESTY'S BRIDE!
EH?!
PLEASE TAKE GOOD CARE OF KING YAWEN.
It feels like he's dodging my question!
......

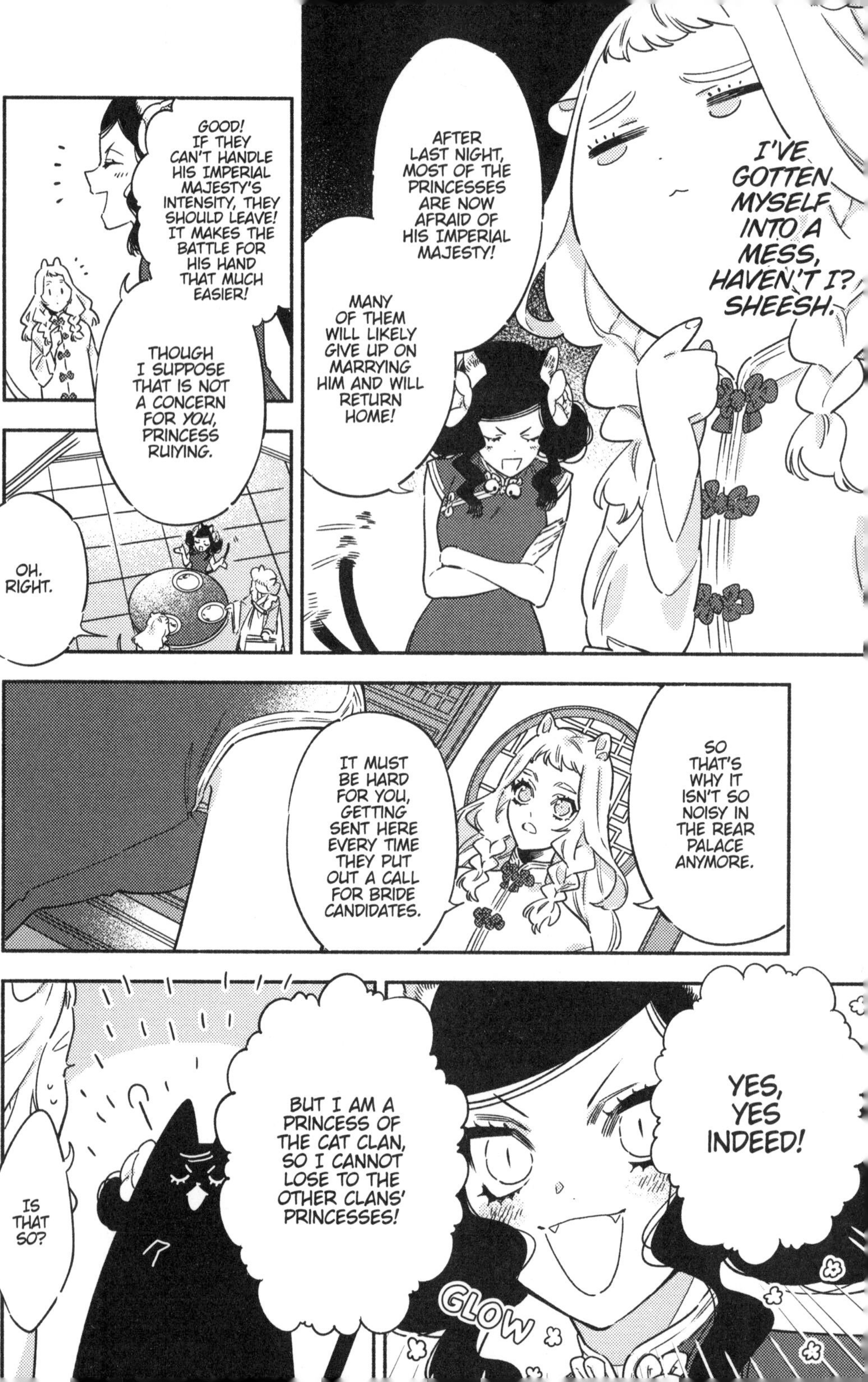
I'VE GOTTEN MYSELF INTO A MESS, HAVEN'T I? SHEESH.
AFTER LAST NIGHT, MOST OF THE PRINCESSES ARE NOW AFRAID OF HIS IMPERIAL MAJESTY!
MANY OF THEM WILL LIKELY GIVE UP ON MARRYING HIM AND WILL RETURN HOME!
GOOD! IF THEY CAN'T HANDLE HIS IMPERIAL MAJESTY'S INTENSITY, THEY SHOULD LEAVE! IT MAKES THE BATTLE FOR HIS HAND THAT MUCH EASIER!
THOUGH I SUPPOSE THAT IS NOT A CONCERN FOR *YOU*, PRINCESS RUIYING.
OH. RIGHT.
SO THAT'S WHY IT ISN'T SO NOISY IN THE REAR PALACE ANYMORE.
IT MUST BE HARD FOR YOU, GETTING SENT HERE EVERY TIME THEY PUT OUT A CALL FOR BRIDE CANDIDATES.
YES, YES INDEED!
GLOW
BUT I AM A PRINCESS OF THE CAT CLAN, SO I CANNOT LOSE TO THE OTHER CLANS' PRINCESSES!
IS THAT SO?

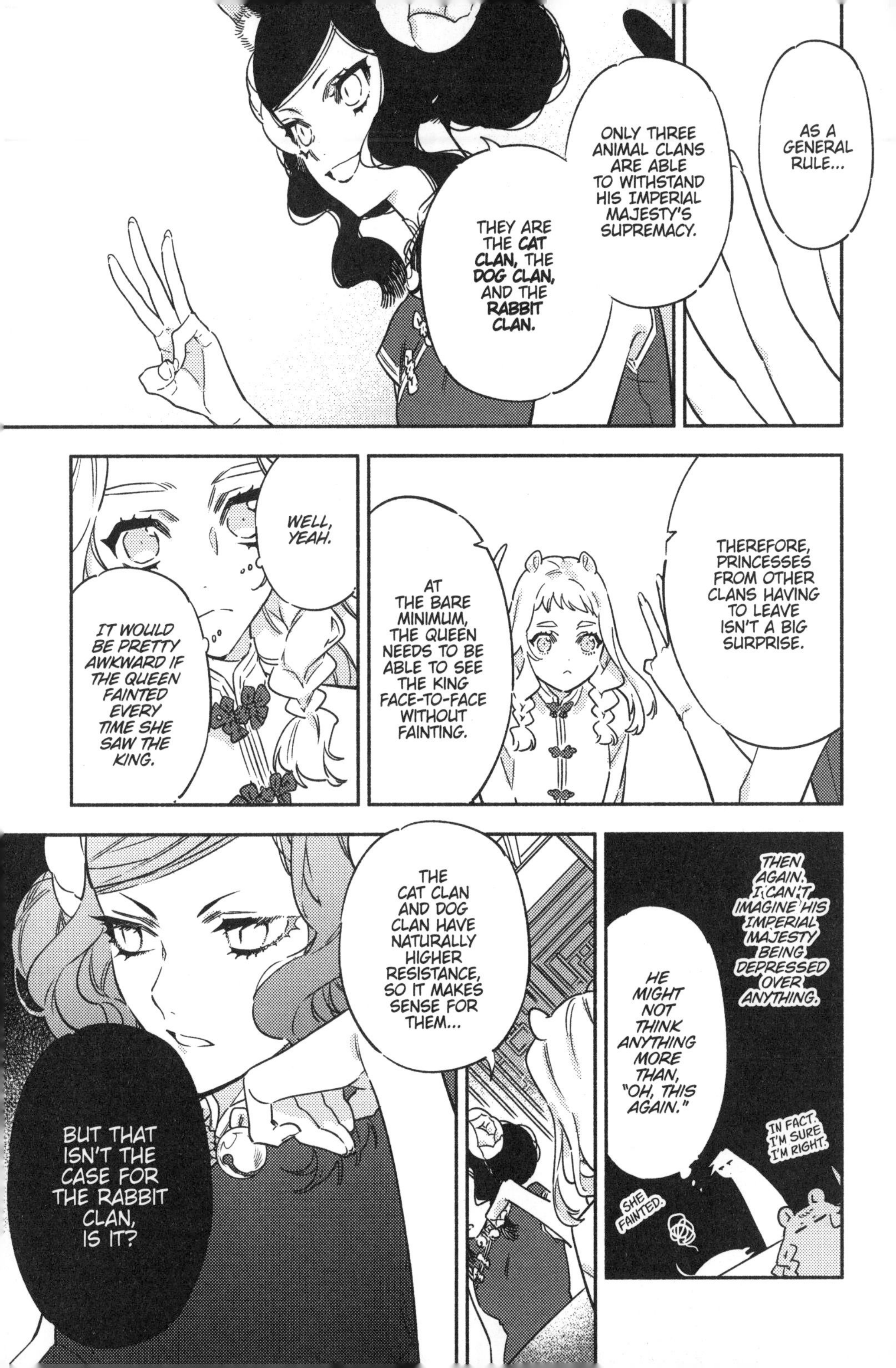
AS A GENERAL RULE...
ONLY THREE ANIMAL CLANS ARE ABLE TO WITHSTAND HIS IMPERIAL MAJESTY'S SUPREMACY.
THEY ARE THE CAT CLAN, THE DOG CLAN, AND THE RABBIT CLAN.
THEREFORE, PRINCESSES FROM OTHER CLANS HAVING TO LEAVE ISN'T A BIG SURPRISE.
AT THE BARE MINIMUM, THE QUEEN NEEDS TO BE ABLE TO SEE THE KING FACE-TO-FACE WITHOUT FAINTING.
WELL, YEAH.
IT WOULD BE PRETTY AWKWARD IF THE QUEEN FAINTED EVERY TIME SHE SAW THE KING.
THEN AGAIN, I CAN'T IMAGINE HIS IMPERIAL MAJESTY BEING DEPRESSED OVER ANYTHING.
HE MIGHT NOT THINK ANYTHING MORE THAN, "OH, THIS AGAIN."
IN FACT, I'M SURE I'M RIGHT.
SHE FAINTED.
THE CAT CLAN AND DOG CLAN HAVE NATURALLY HIGHER RESISTANCE, SO IT MAKES SENSE FOR THEM...
BUT THAT ISN'T THE CASE FOR THE RABBIT CLAN, IS IT?

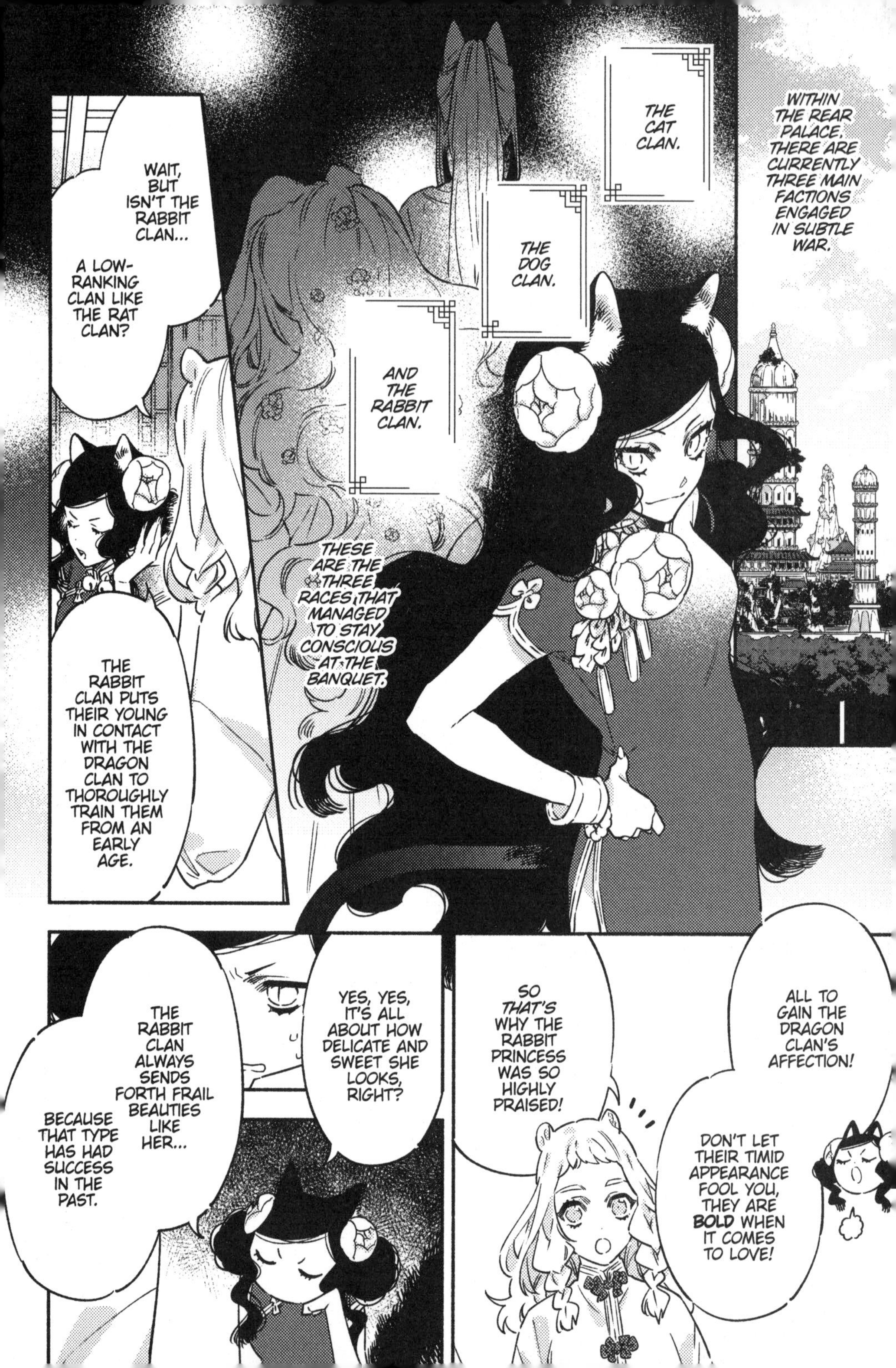
WITHIN THE REAR PALACE, THERE ARE CURRENTLY THREE MAIN FACTIONS ENGAGED IN SUBTLE WAR.
THE CAT CLAN.
THE DOG CLAN.
AND THE RABBIT CLAN.
THESE ARE THE THREE RACES THAT MANAGED TO STAY CONSCIOUS AT THE BANQUET.
WAIT, BUT ISN'T THE RABBIT CLAN...
A LOW-RANKING CLAN LIKE THE RAT CLAN?
THE RABBIT CLAN PUTS THEIR YOUNG IN CONTACT WITH THE DRAGON CLAN TO THOROUGHLY TRAIN THEM FROM AN EARLY AGE.
ALL TO GAIN THE DRAGON CLAN'S AFFECTION!
DON'T LET THEIR TIMID APPEARANCE FOOL YOU, THEY ARE **BOLD** WHEN IT COMES TO LOVE!
SO *THAT'S* WHY THE RABBIT PRINCESS WAS SO HIGHLY PRAISED!
YES, YES, IT'S ALL ABOUT HOW DELICATE AND SWEET SHE LOOKS, RIGHT?
THE RABBIT CLAN ALWAYS SENDS FORTH FRAIL BEAUTIES LIKE HER...
BECAUSE THAT TYPE HAS HAD SUCCESS IN THE PAST.

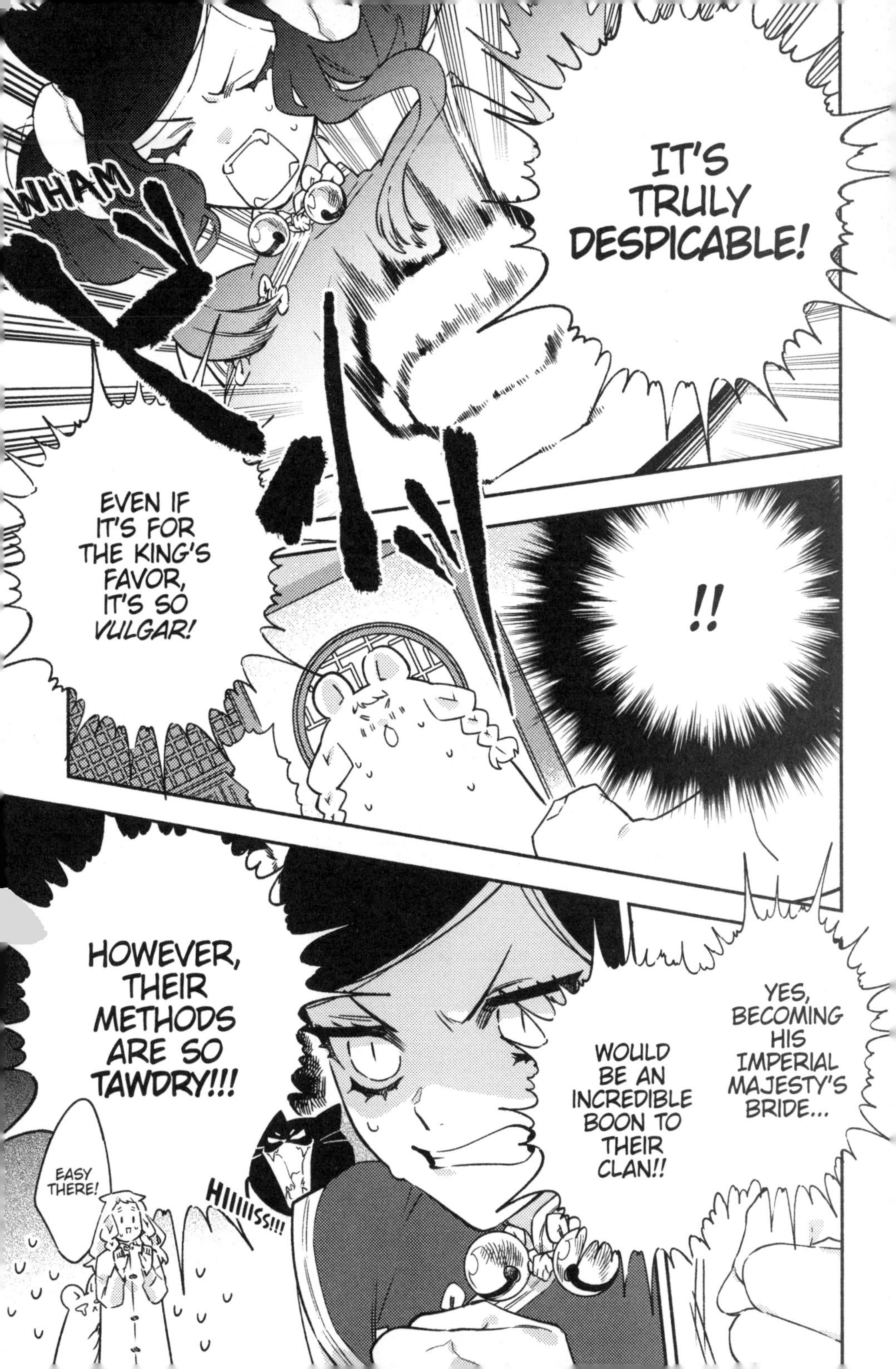
IT'S TRULY DESPICABLE!
WHAM
EVEN IF IT'S FOR THE KING'S FAVOR, IT'S SO *VULGAR!*
!!
YES, BECOMING HIS IMPERIAL MAJESTY'S BRIDE...
WOULD BE AN INCREDIBLE BOON TO THEIR CLAN!!
HOWEVER, THEIR METHODS ARE SO TAWDRY!!!
HIIIIISS!!!
EASY THERE!

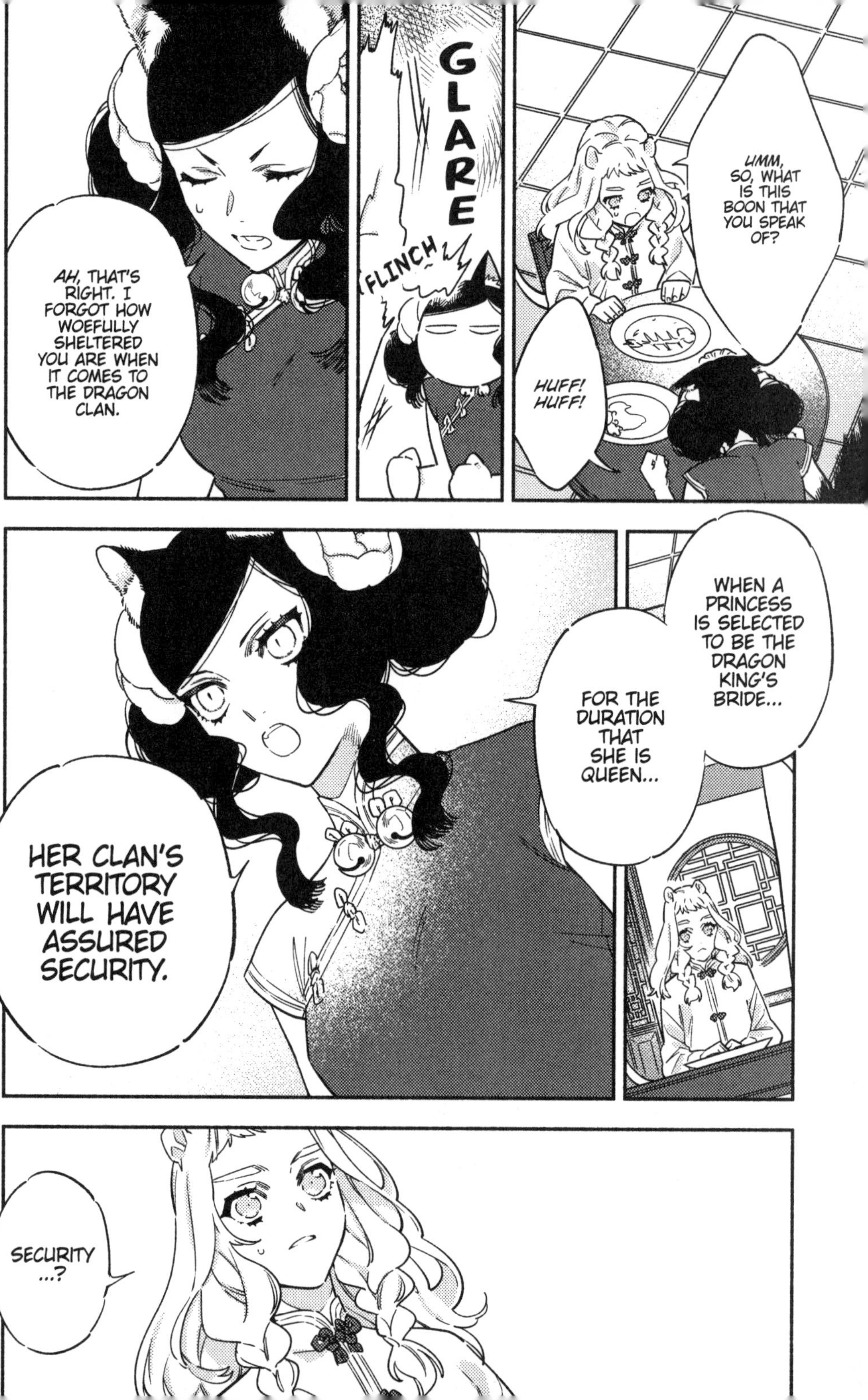
UMM, SO, WHAT IS THIS BOON THAT YOU SPEAK OF?
HUFF! HUFF!
GLARE
FLINCH
AH, THAT'S RIGHT. I FORGOT HOW WOEFULLY SHELTERED YOU ARE WHEN IT COMES TO THE DRAGON CLAN.
WHEN A PRINCESS IS SELECTED TO BE THE DRAGON KING'S BRIDE...
FOR THE DURATION THAT SHE IS QUEEN...
HER CLAN'S TERRITORY WILL HAVE ASSURED SECURITY.
SECURITY ...?

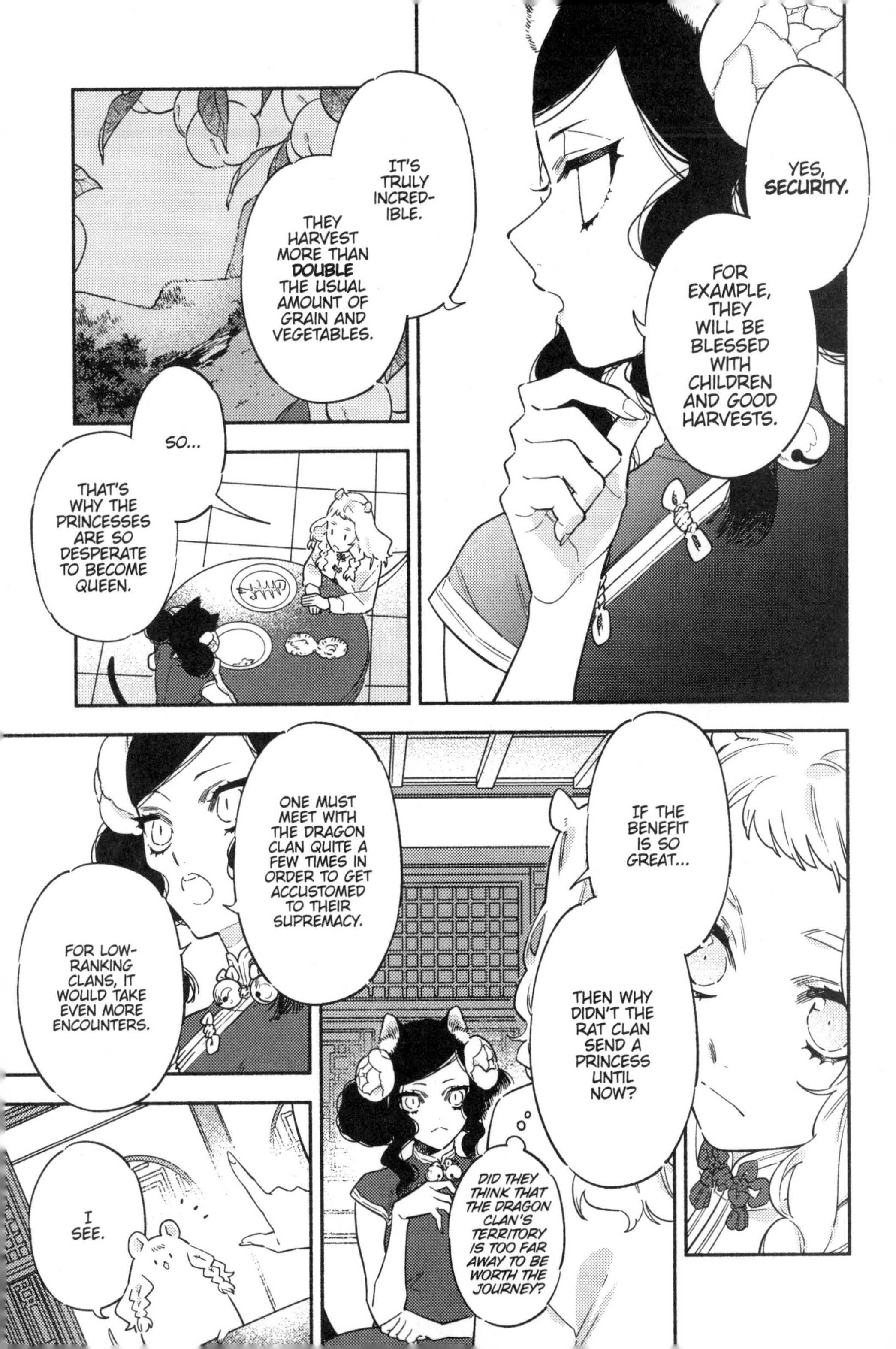

YES, SECURITY.
FOR EXAMPLE, THEY WILL BE BLESSED WITH CHILDREN AND GOOD HARVESTS.
IT'S TRULY INCREDIBLE.
THEY HARVEST MORE THAN DOUBLE THE USUAL AMOUNT OF GRAIN AND VEGETABLES.
SO...
THAT'S WHY THE PRINCESSES ARE SO DESPERATE TO BECOME QUEEN.
IF THE BENEFIT IS SO GREAT...
THEN WHY DIDN'T THE RAT CLAN SEND A PRINCESS UNTIL NOW?
DID THEY THINK THAT THE DRAGON CLAN'S TERRITORY IS TOO FAR AWAY TO BE WORTH THE JOURNEY?
ONE MUST MEET WITH THE DRAGON CLAN QUITE A FEW TIMES IN ORDER TO GET ACCUSTOMED TO THEIR SUPREMACY.
FOR LOW-RANKING CLANS, IT WOULD TAKE EVEN MORE ENCOUNTERS.
I SEE.

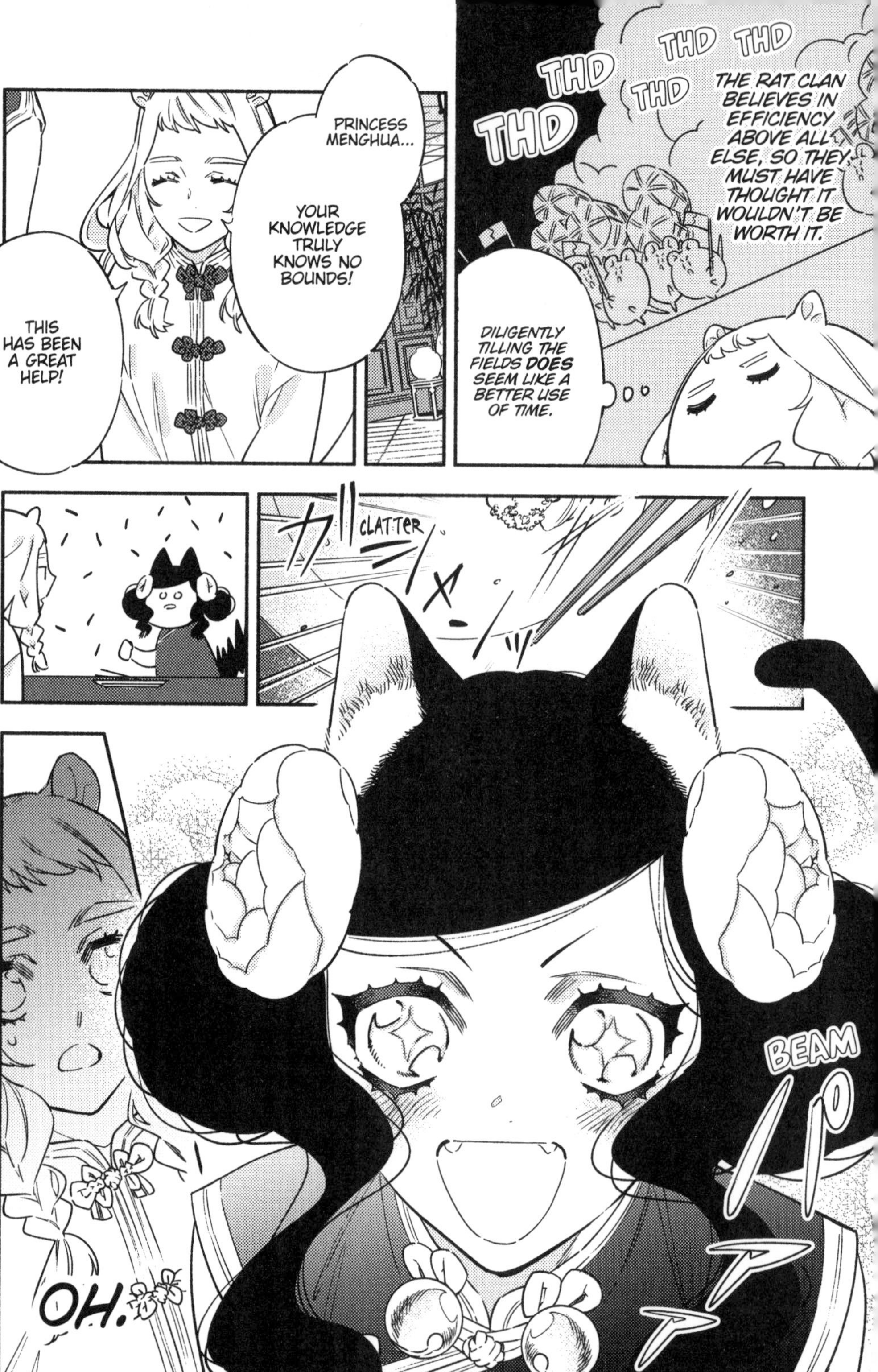
THD THD THD THD THD
THE RAT CLAN BELIEVES IN EFFICIENCY ABOVE ALL ELSE, SO THEY MUST HAVE THOUGHT IT WOULDN'T BE WORTH IT.
DILIGENTLY TILLING THE FIELDS **DOES** SEEM LIKE A BETTER USE OF TIME.
PRINCESS MENGHUA...
YOUR KNOWLEDGE TRULY KNOWS NO BOUNDS!
THIS HAS BEEN A GREAT HELP!
CLATTER
BEAM
OH.

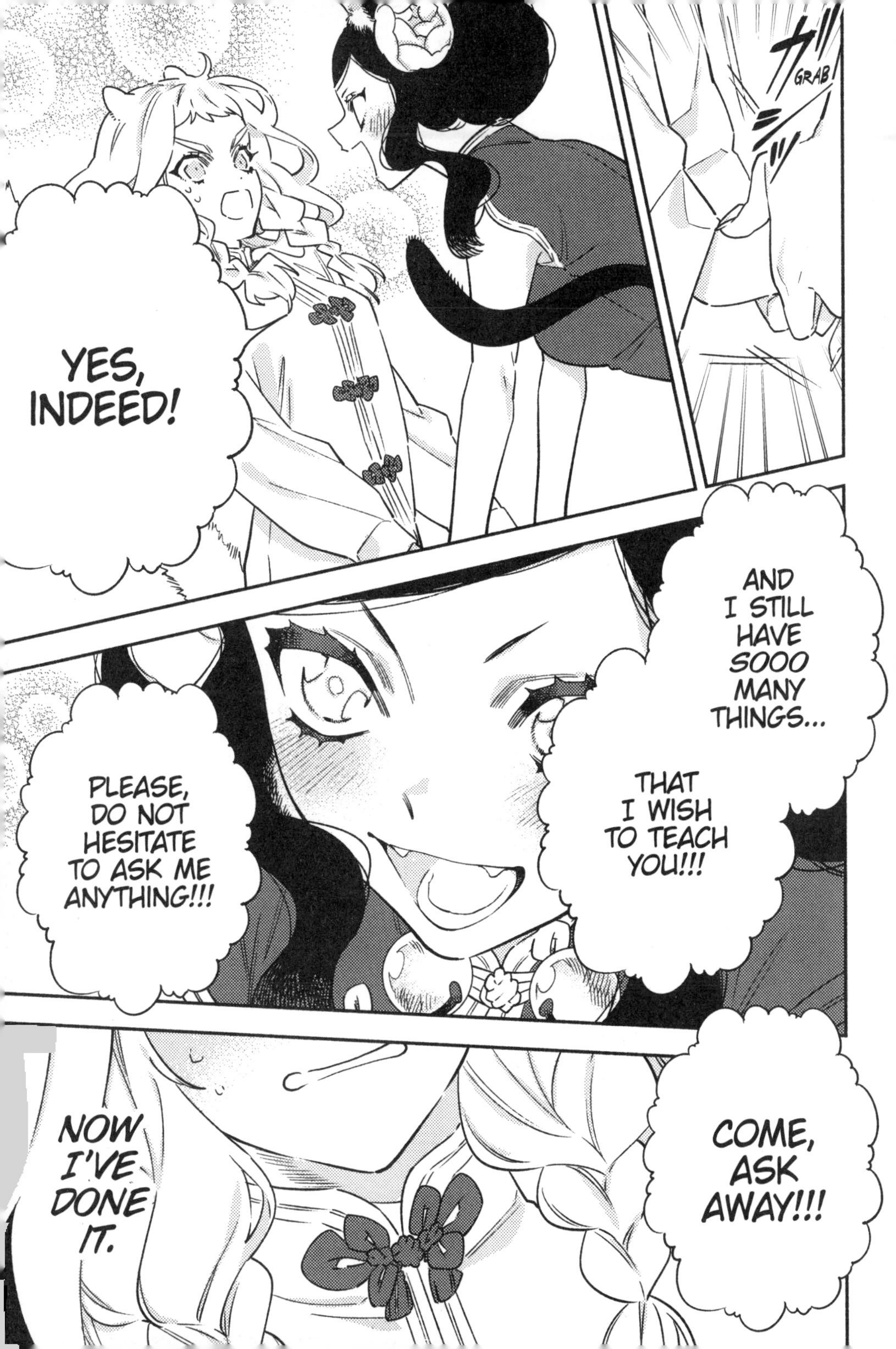
GRAB
YES, INDEED!
AND I STILL HAVE SOOO MANY THINGS...
THAT I WISH TO TEACH YOU!!!
PLEASE, DO NOT HESITATE TO ASK ME ANYTHING!!!
COME, ASK AWAY!!!
NOW I'VE DONE IT.

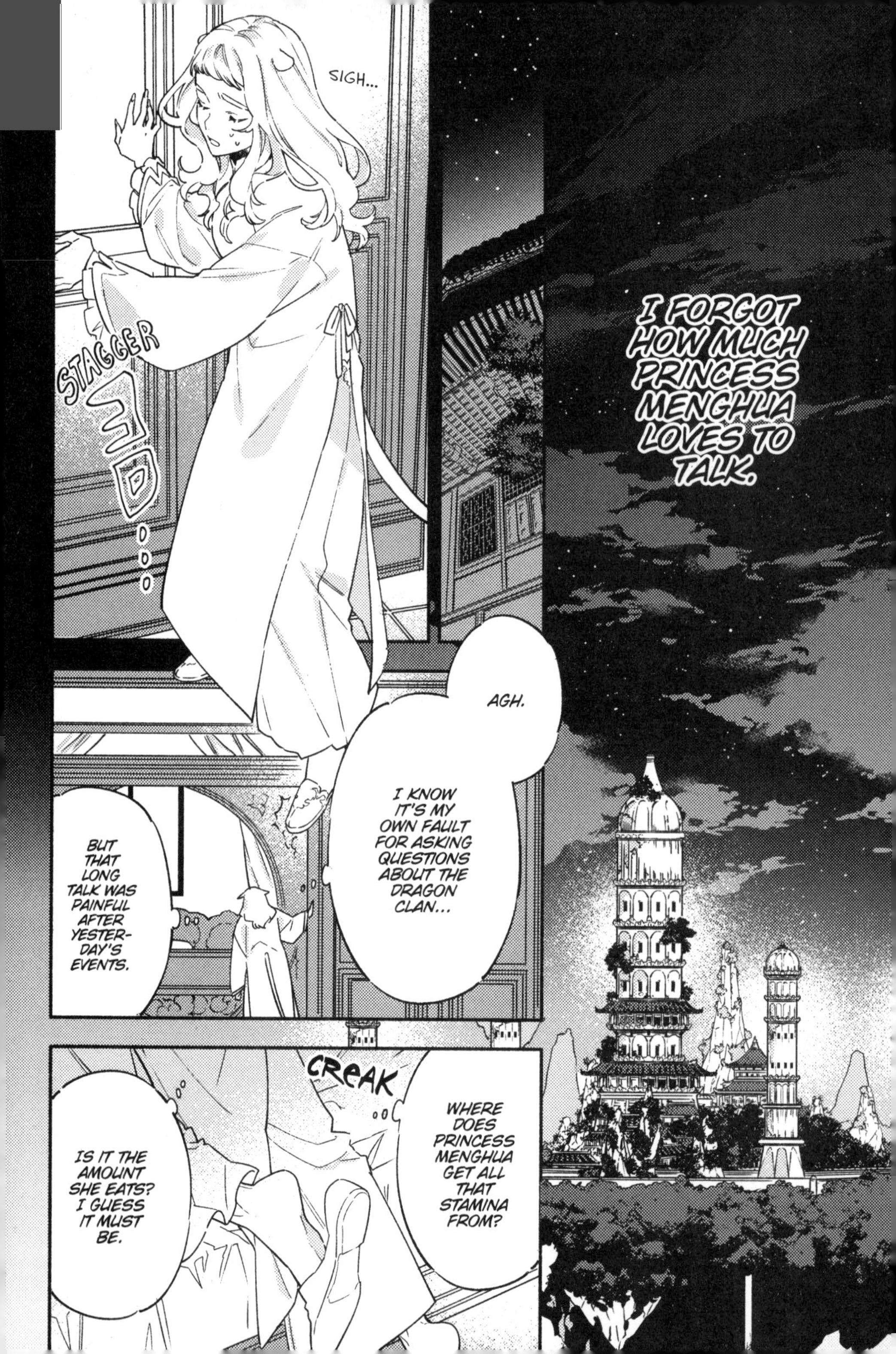

I FORGOT HOW MUCH PRINCESS MENGHUA LOVES TO TALK.
SIGH...
STAGGER
AGH.
I KNOW IT'S MY OWN FAULT FOR ASKING QUESTIONS ABOUT THE DRAGON CLAN...
BUT THAT LONG TALK WAS PAINFUL AFTER YESTER-DAY'S EVENTS.
CREAK
WHERE DOES PRINCESS MENGHUA GET ALL THAT STAMINA FROM?
IS IT THE AMOUNT SHE EATS? I GUESS IT MUST BE.

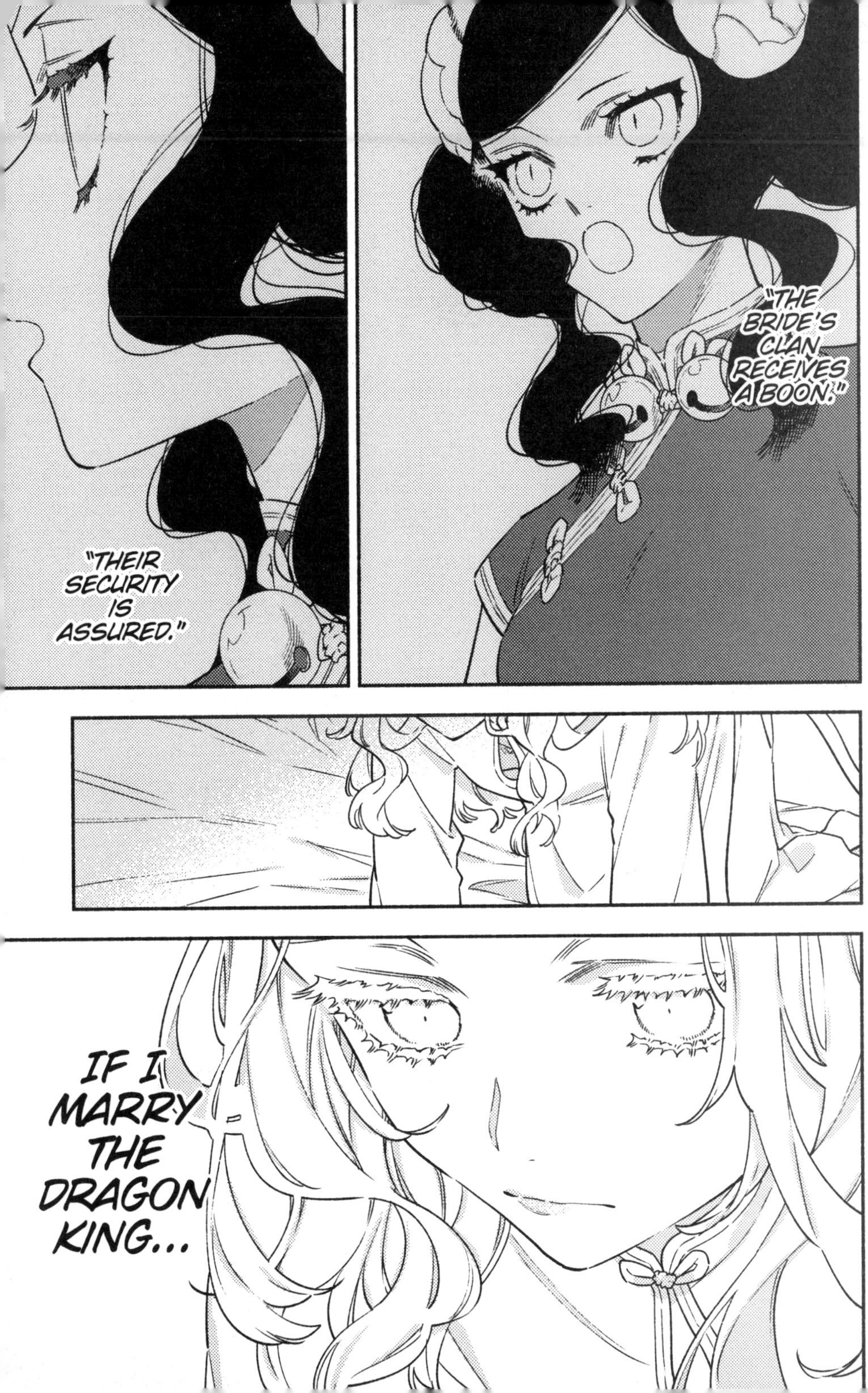
"THE BRIDE'S CLAN RECEIVES A BOON."
"THEIR SECURITY IS ASSURED."
IF I MARRY THE DRAGON KING...

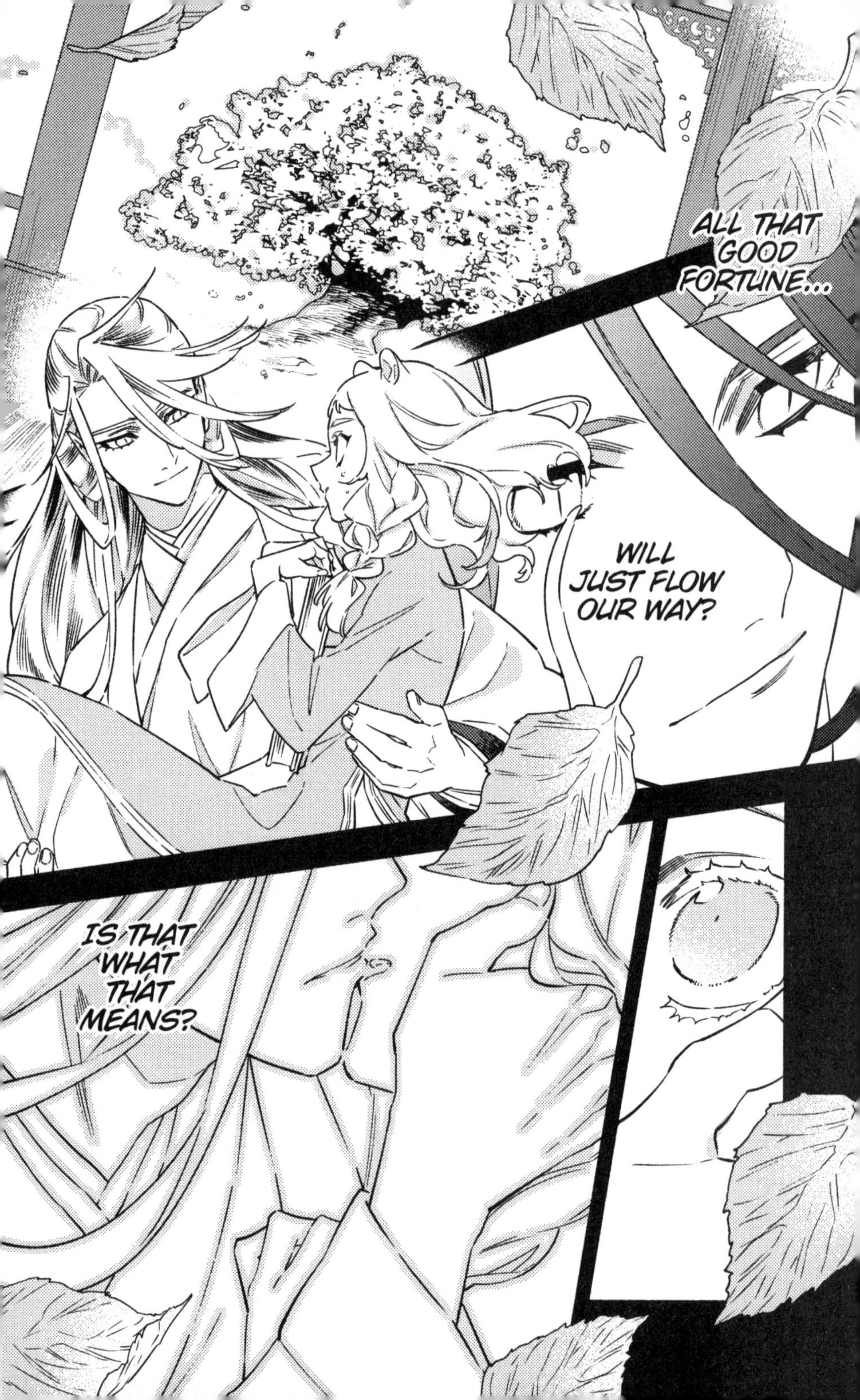
ALL THAT GOOD FORTUNE...
WILL JUST FLOW OUR WAY?
IS THAT WHAT THAT MEANS?

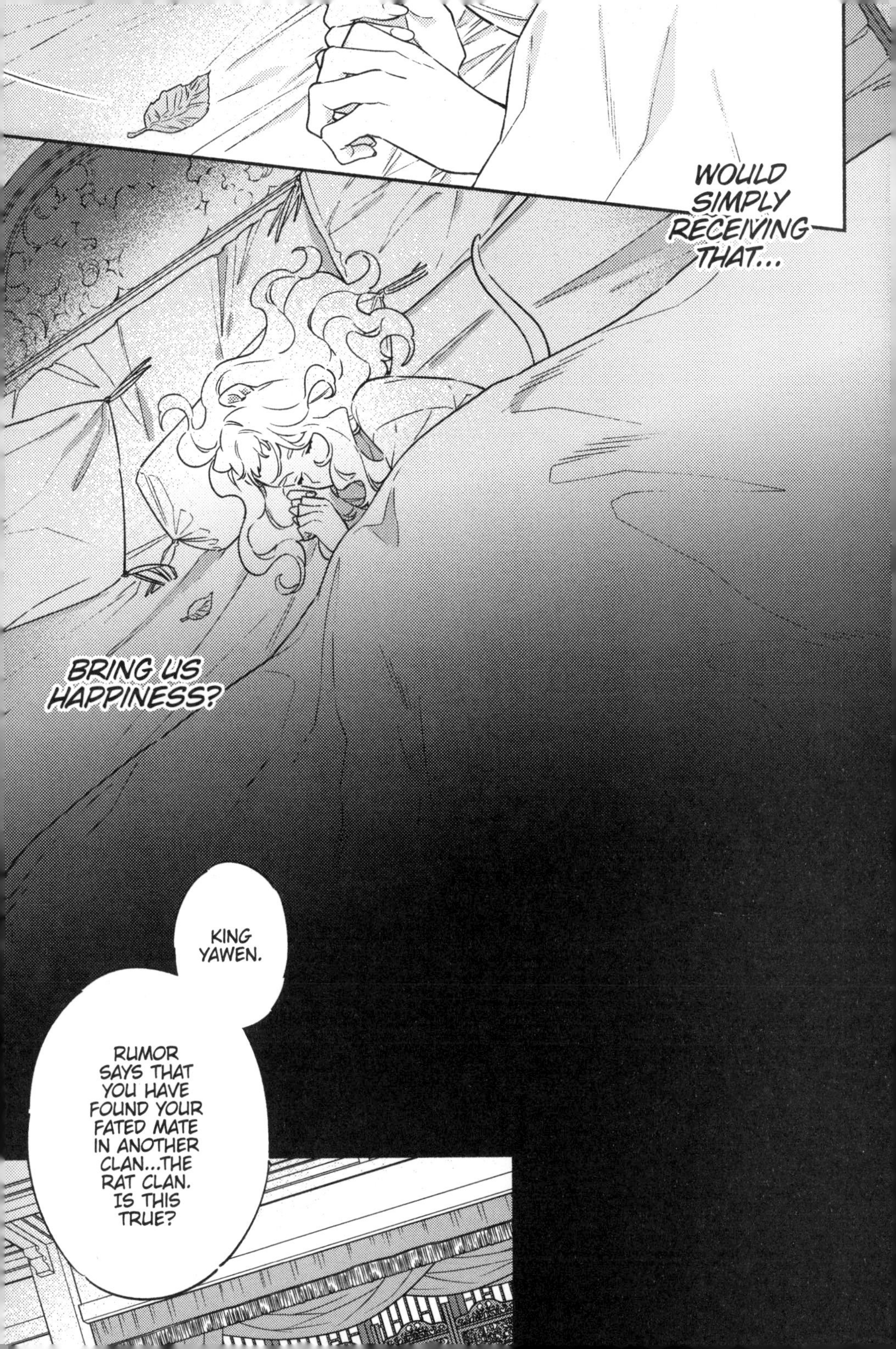
WOULD SIMPLY RECEIVING THAT...
BRING US HAPPINESS?
KING YAWEN.
RUMOR SAYS THAT YOU HAVE FOUND YOUR FATED MATE IN ANOTHER CLAN...THE RAT CLAN. IS THIS TRUE?

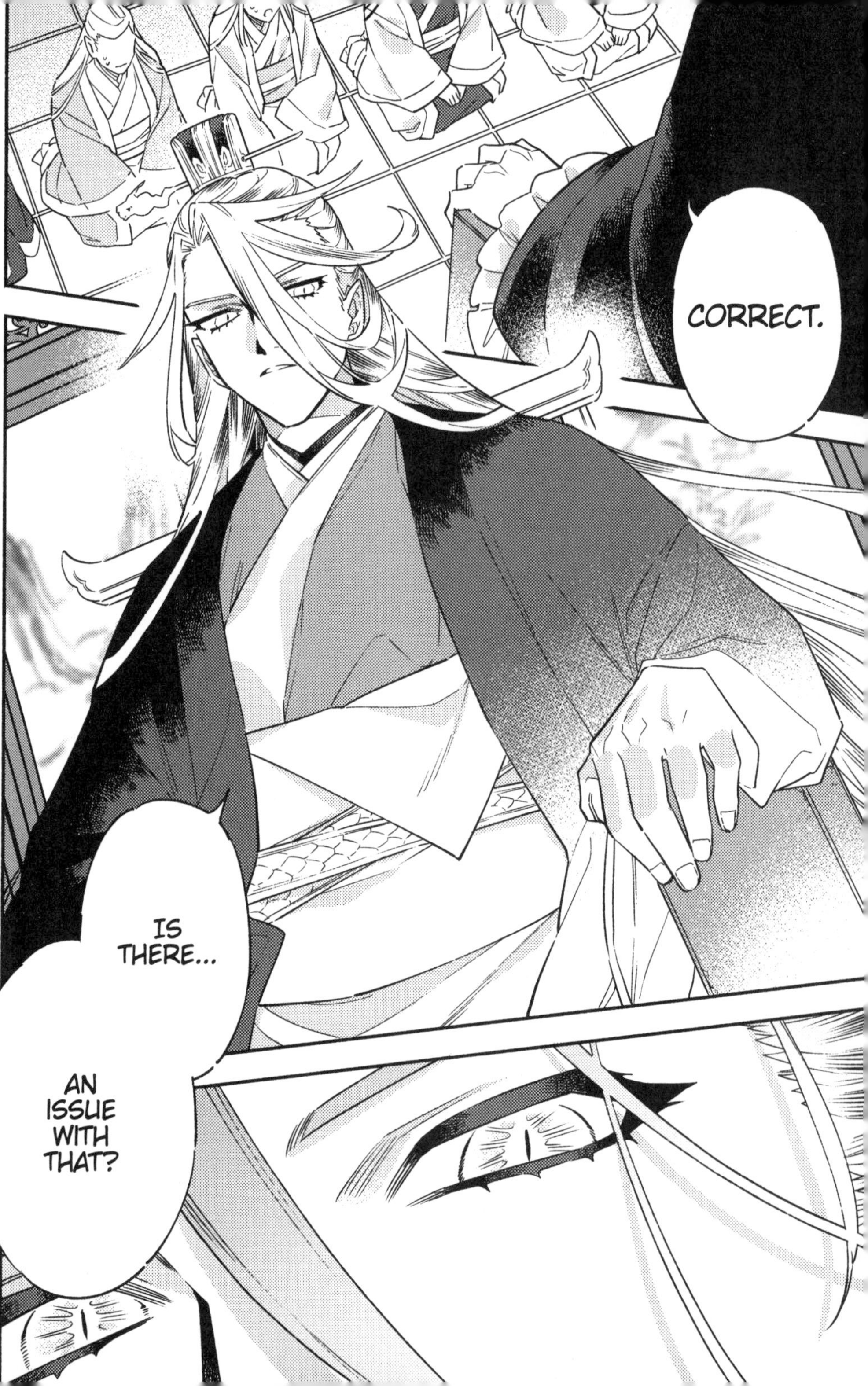
CORRECT.
IS THERE...
AN ISSUE WITH THAT?

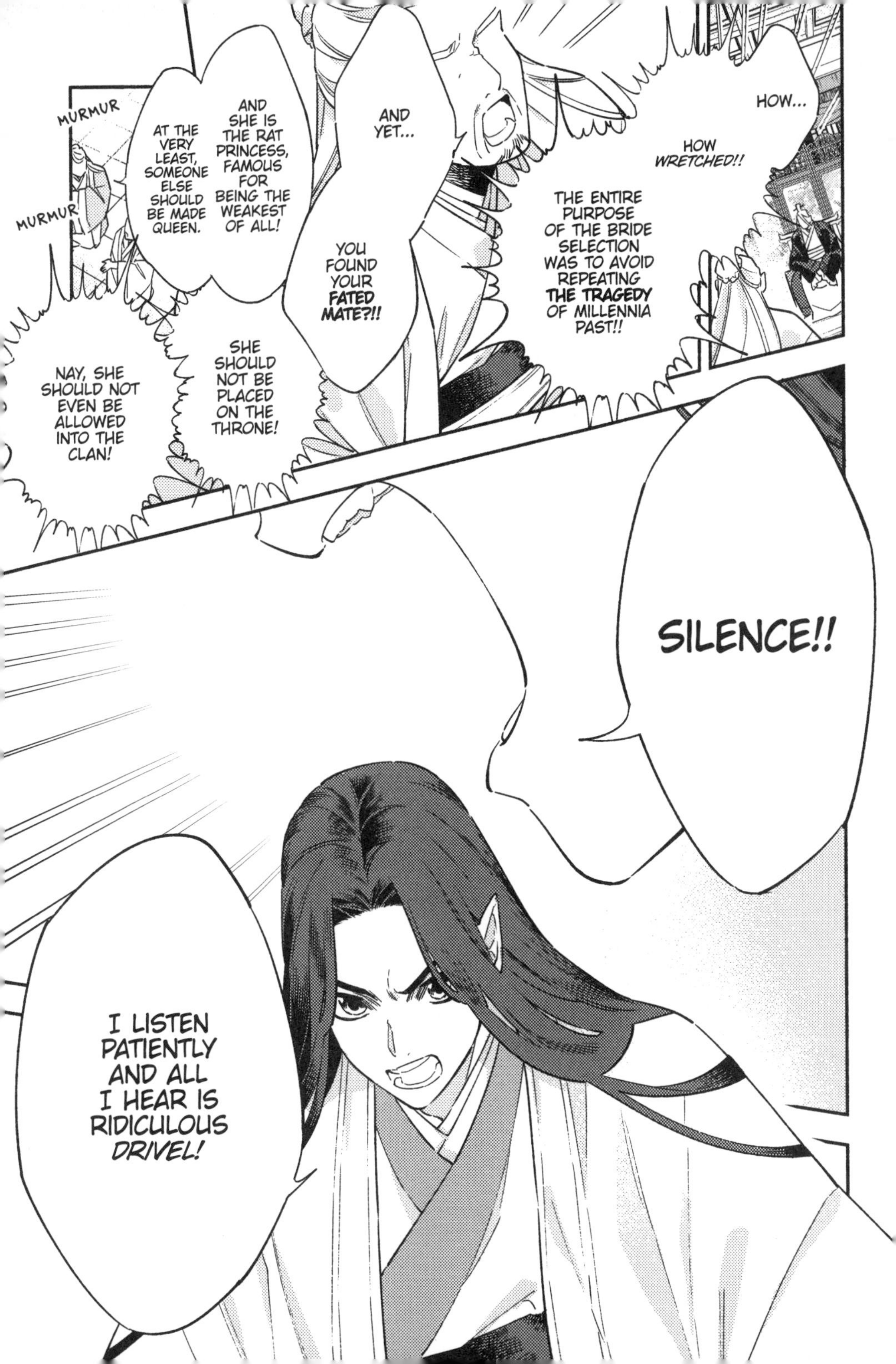
HOW...
HOW WRETCHED!!
THE ENTIRE PURPOSE OF THE BRIDE SELECTION WAS TO AVOID REPEATING **THE TRAGEDY** OF MILLENNIA PAST!!
AND YET...
YOU FOUND YOUR **FATED MATE?!!**
AND SHE IS THE RAT PRINCESS, FAMOUS FOR BEING THE WEAKEST OF ALL!
AT THE VERY LEAST, SOMEONE ELSE SHOULD BE MADE QUEEN.
MURMUR
MURMUR
SHE SHOULD NOT BE PLACED ON THE THRONE!
NAY, SHE SHOULD NOT EVEN BE ALLOWED INTO THE CLAN!
SILENCE!!
I LISTEN PATIENTLY AND ALL I HEAR IS RIDICULOUS *DRIVEL!*

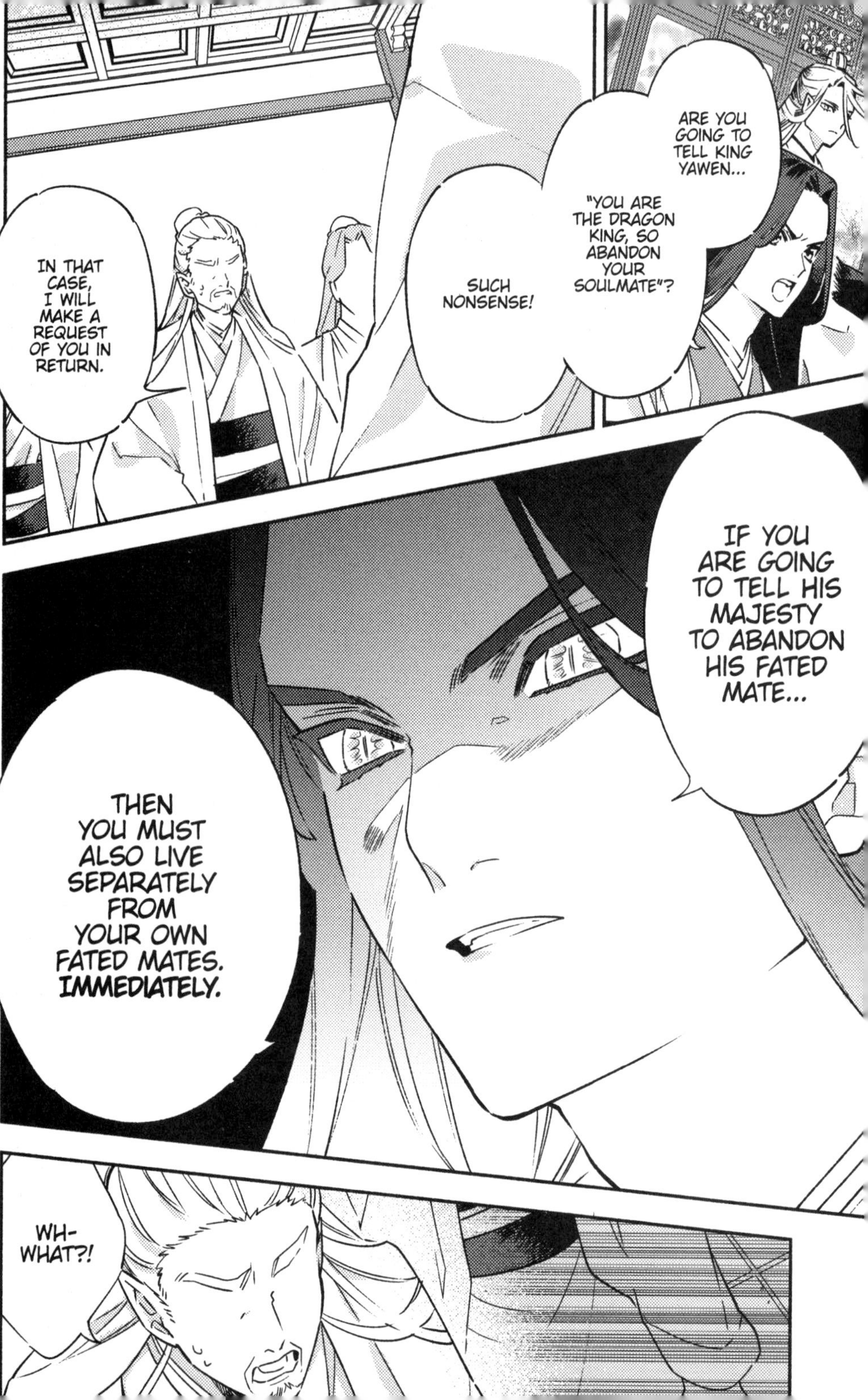
ARE YOU GOING TO TELL KING YAWEN...
"YOU ARE THE DRAGON KING, SO ABANDON YOUR SOULMATE"?
SUCH NONSENSE!
IN THAT CASE, I WILL MAKE A REQUEST OF YOU IN RETURN.
IF YOU ARE GOING TO TELL HIS MAJESTY TO ABANDON HIS FATED MATE...
THEN YOU MUST ALSO LIVE SEPARATELY FROM YOUR OWN FATED MATES. **IMMEDIATELY.**
WH-WHAT?!

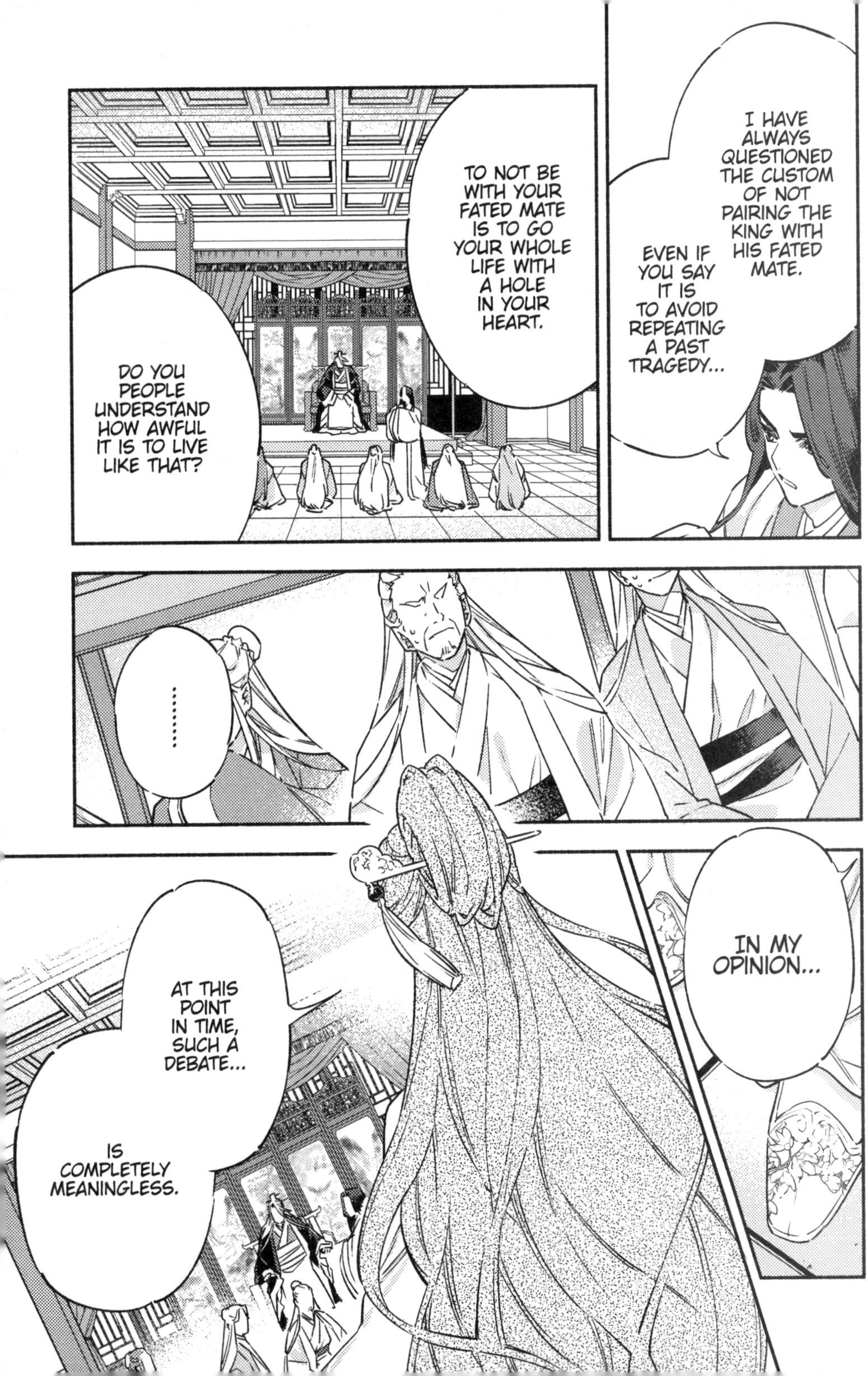
I HAVE ALWAYS QUESTIONED THE CUSTOM OF NOT PAIRING THE KING WITH HIS FATED MATE.
EVEN IF YOU SAY IT IS TO AVOID REPEATING A PAST TRAGEDY...
TO NOT BE WITH YOUR FATED MATE IS TO GO YOUR WHOLE LIFE WITH A HOLE IN YOUR HEART.
DO YOU PEOPLE UNDERSTAND HOW AWFUL IT IS TO LIVE LIKE THAT?
......
IN MY OPINION...
AT THIS POINT IN TIME, SUCH A DEBATE...
IS COMPLETELY MEANINGLESS.

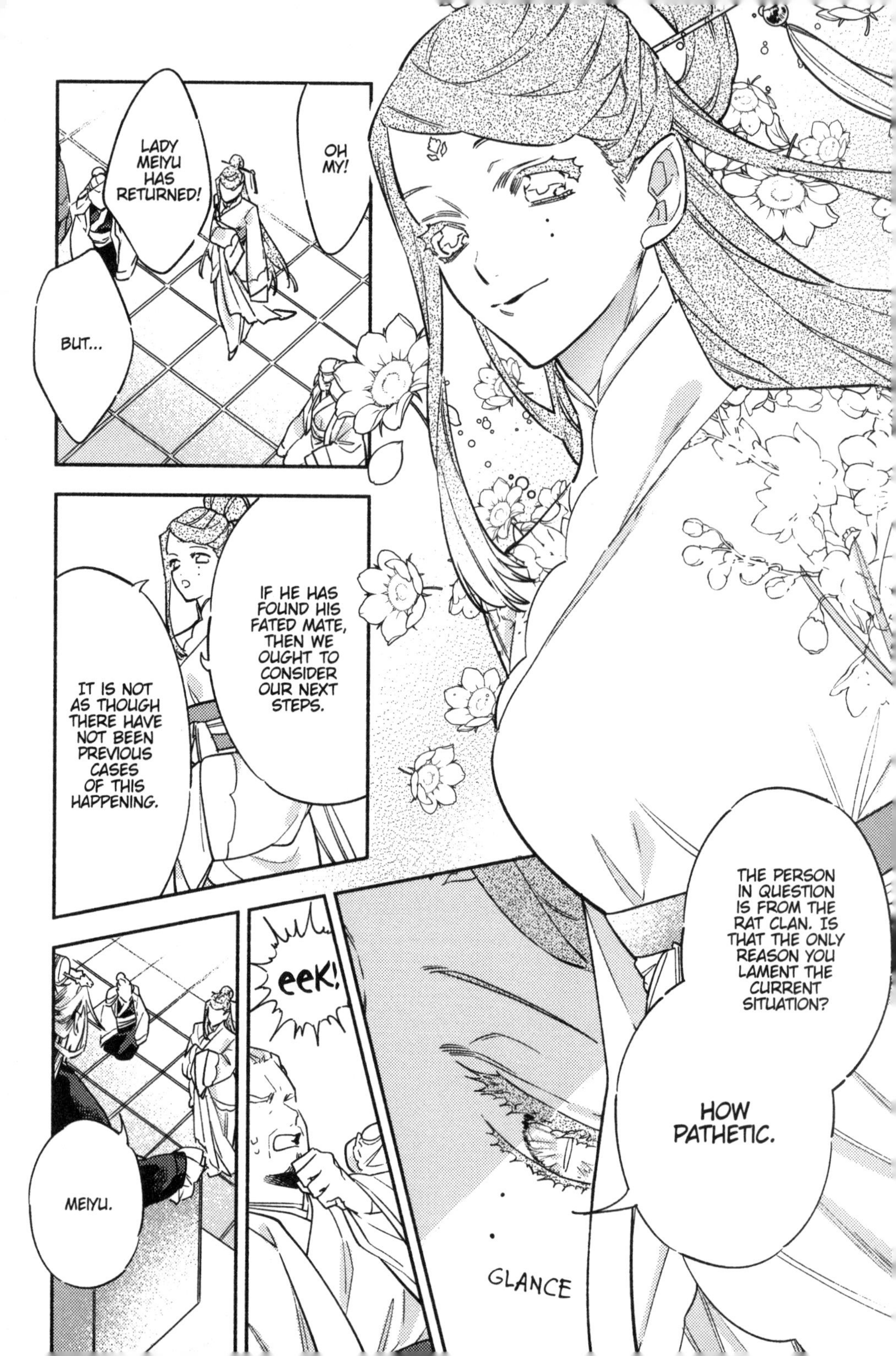

OH MY!
LADY MEIYU HAS RETURNED!
BUT...
IF HE HAS FOUND HIS FATED MATE, THEN WE OUGHT TO CONSIDER OUR NEXT STEPS.
IT IS NOT AS THOUGH THERE HAVE NOT BEEN PREVIOUS CASES OF THIS HAPPENING.
THE PERSON IN QUESTION IS FROM THE RAT CLAN. IS THAT THE ONLY REASON YOU LAMENT THE CURRENT SITUATION?
HOW PATHETIC.
GLANCE
eek!
MEIYU.

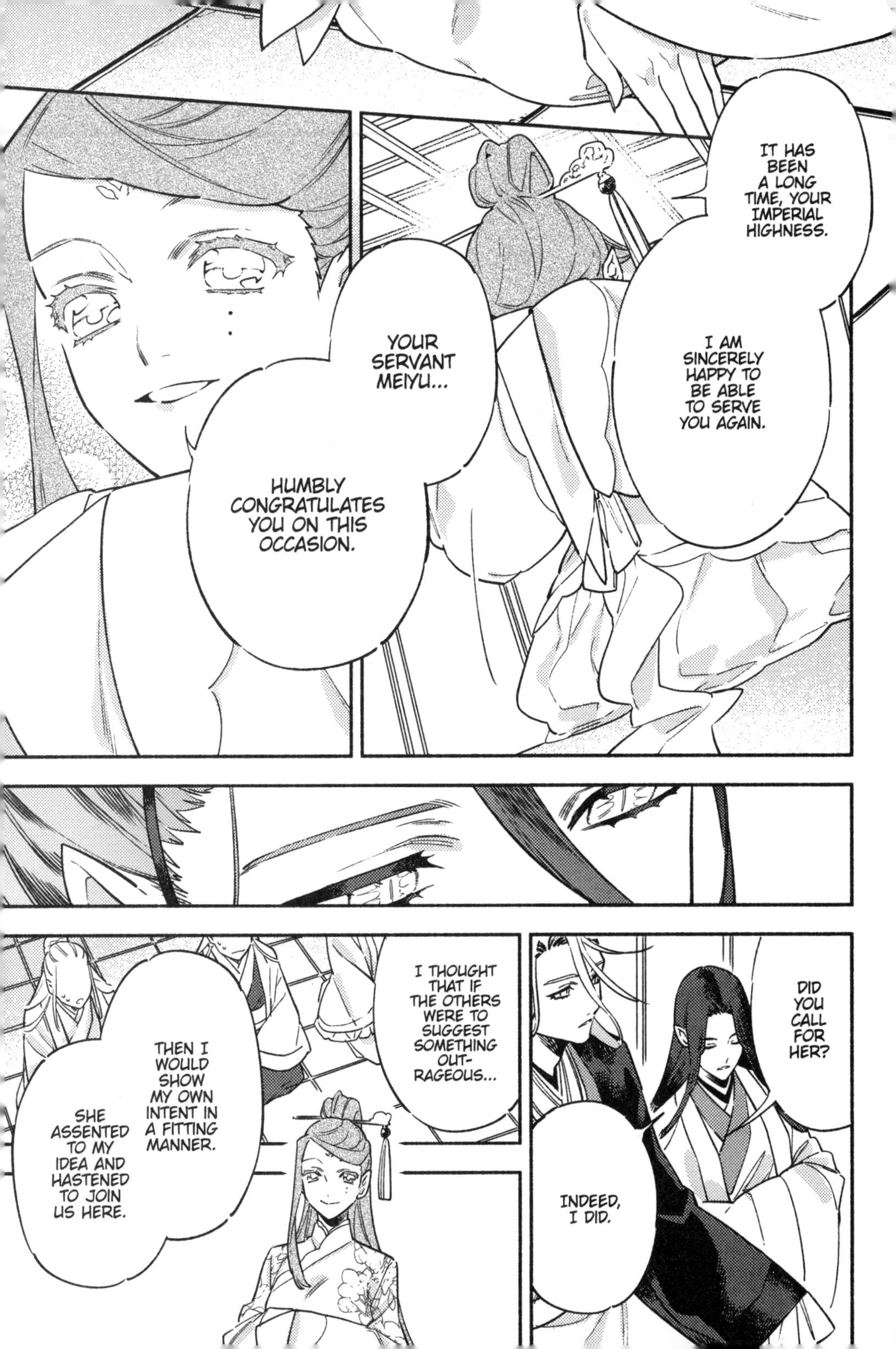
IT HAS BEEN A LONG TIME, YOUR IMPERIAL HIGHNESS.
I AM SINCERELY HAPPY TO BE ABLE TO SERVE YOU AGAIN.
YOUR SERVANT MEIYU...
HUMBLY CONGRATULATES YOU ON THIS OCCASION.
DID YOU CALL FOR HER?
INDEED, I DID.
I THOUGHT THAT IF THE OTHERS WERE TO SUGGEST SOMETHING OUT-RAGEOUS...
THEN I WOULD SHOW MY OWN INTENT IN A FITTING MANNER.
SHE ASSENTED TO MY IDEA AND HASTENED TO JOIN US HERE.

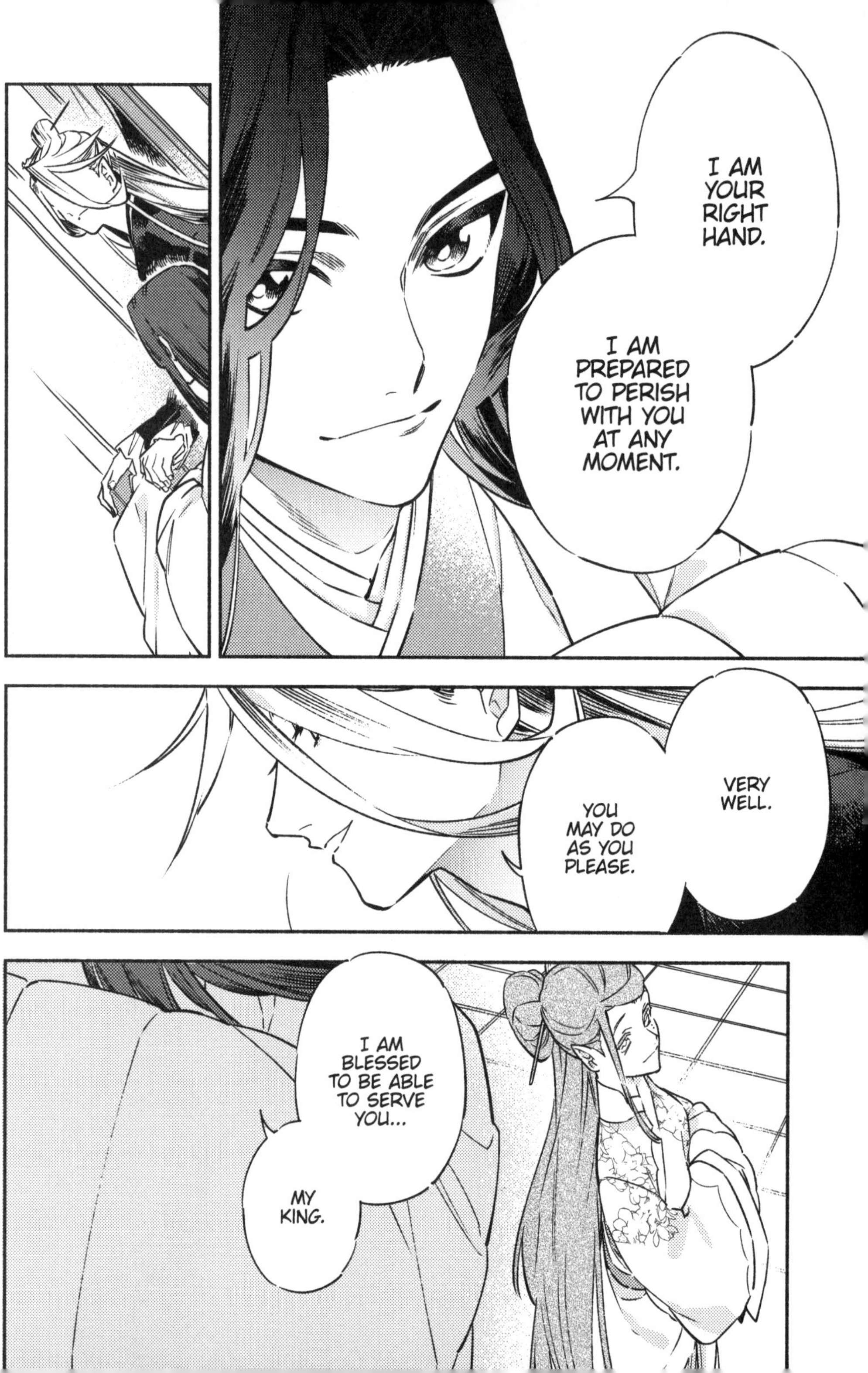
I AM YOUR RIGHT HAND.
I AM PREPARED TO PERISH WITH YOU AT ANY MOMENT.
VERY WELL.
YOU MAY DO AS YOU PLEASE.
I AM BLESSED TO BE ABLE TO SERVE YOU...
MY KING.

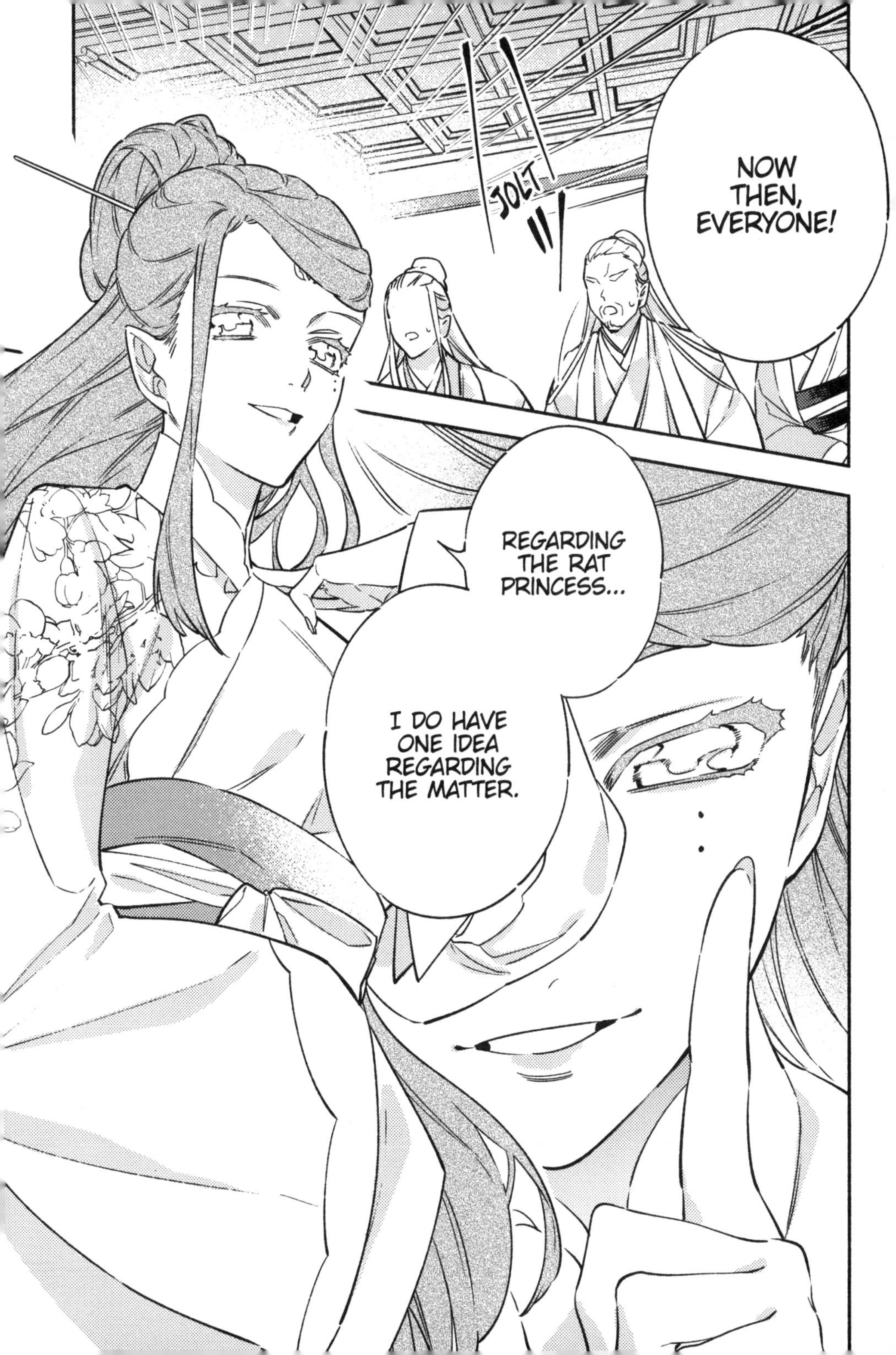
NOW THEN, EVERYONE!
JOLT
REGARDING THE RAT PRINCESS...
I DO HAVE ONE IDEA REGARDING THE MATTER.

THE DRAGON KING'S IMPERIAL WRATH

FALLING IN LOVE
WITH THE BOOKISH PRINCESS
OF THE RAT CLAN

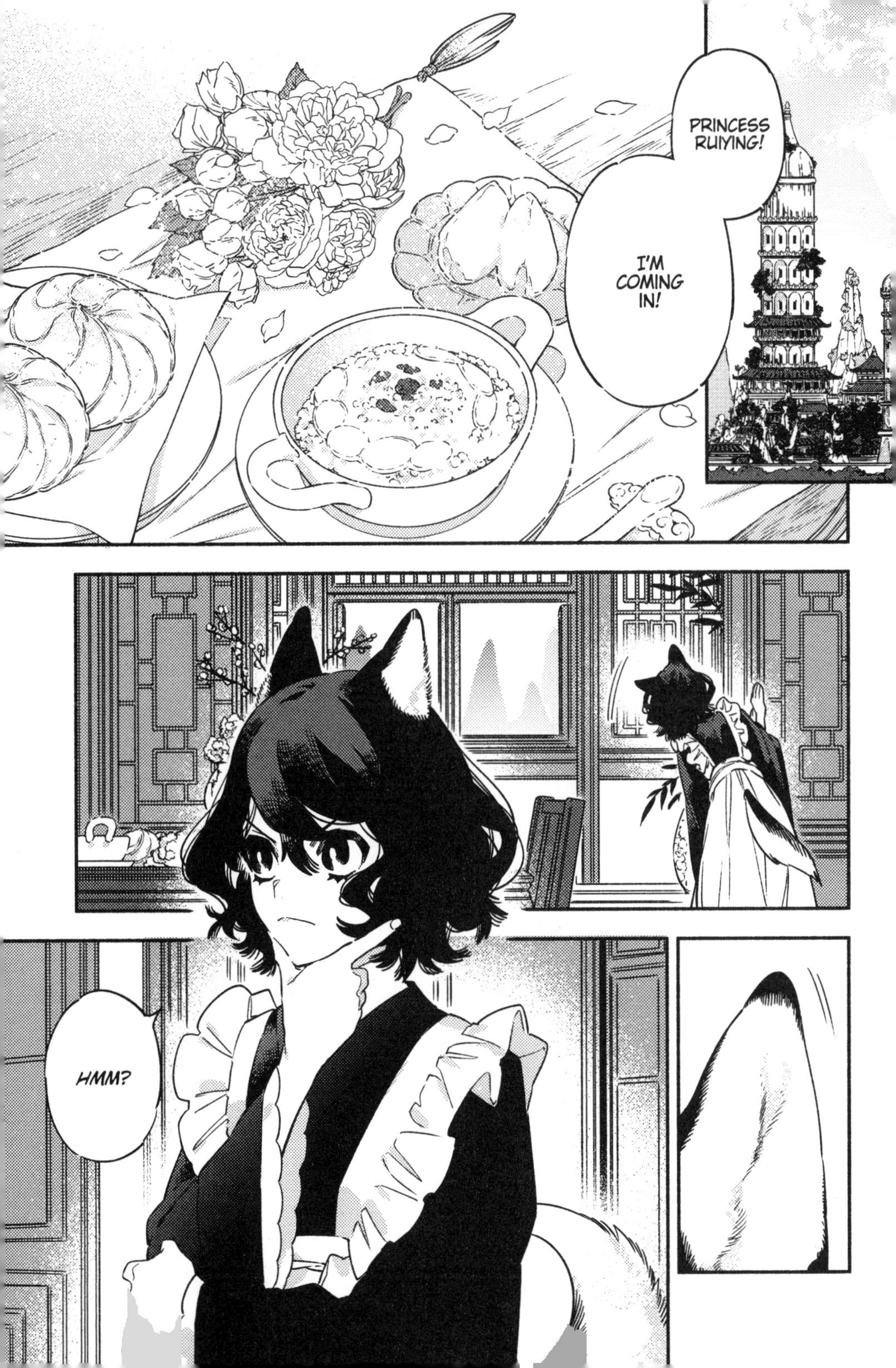
PRINCESS RUIYING!
I'M COMING IN!
HMM?

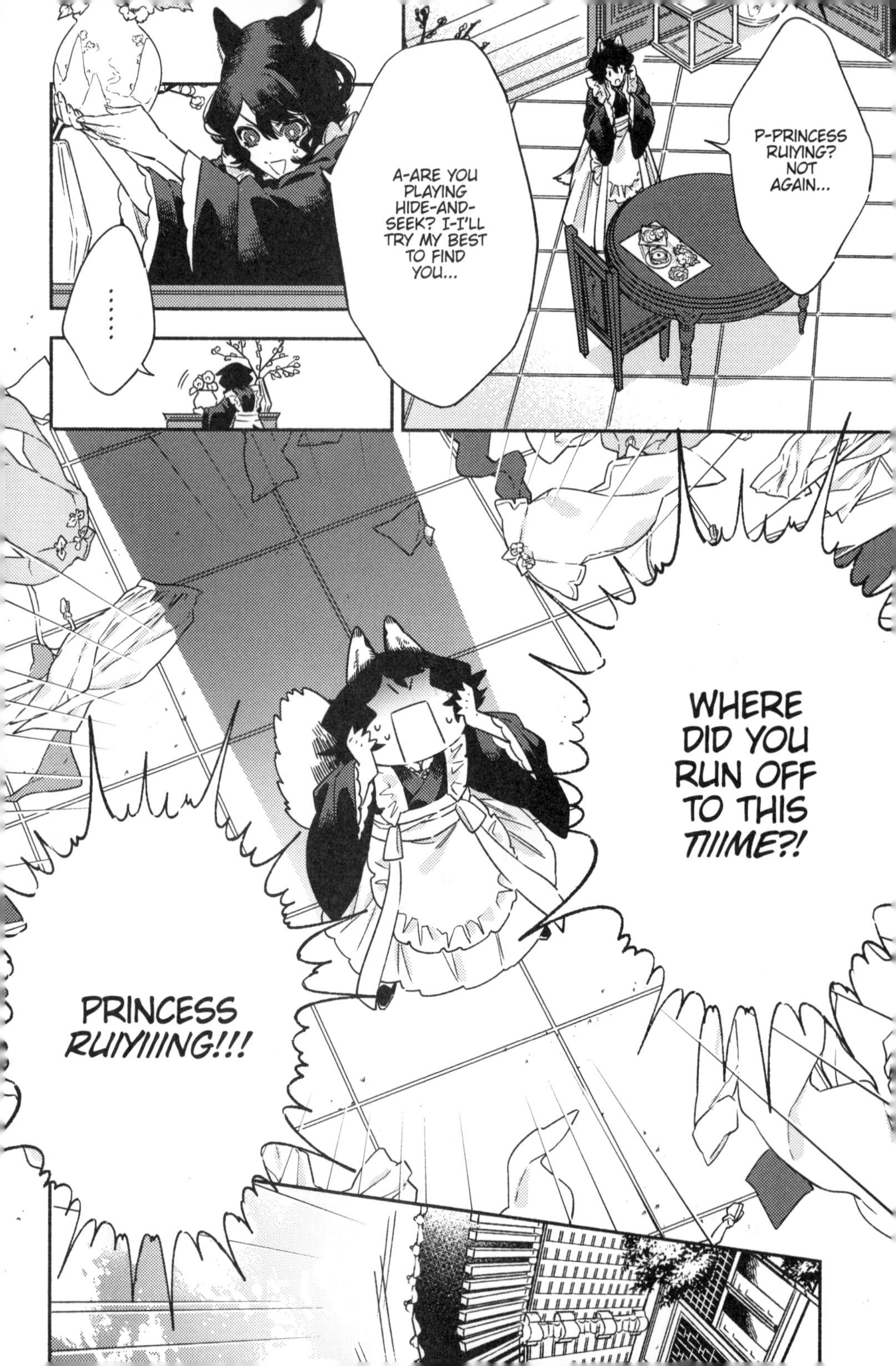
P-PRINCESS RUIYING? NOT AGAIN...
A-ARE YOU PLAYING HIDE-AND-SEEK? I-I'LL TRY MY BEST TO FIND YOU...
......
WHERE DID YOU RUN OFF TO THIS TIIIME?!
PRINCESS RUIYIIING!!!

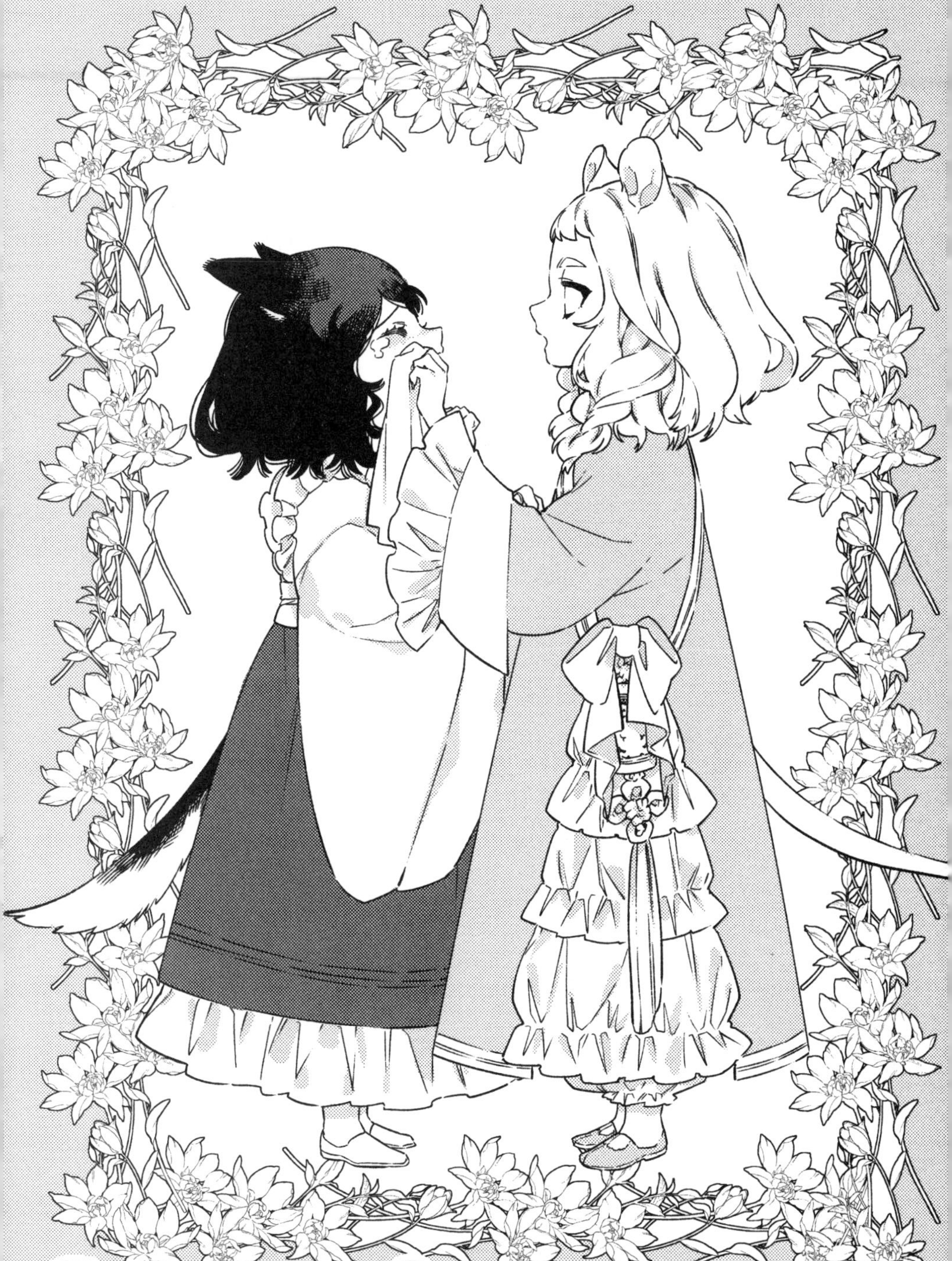

CHAPTER 3

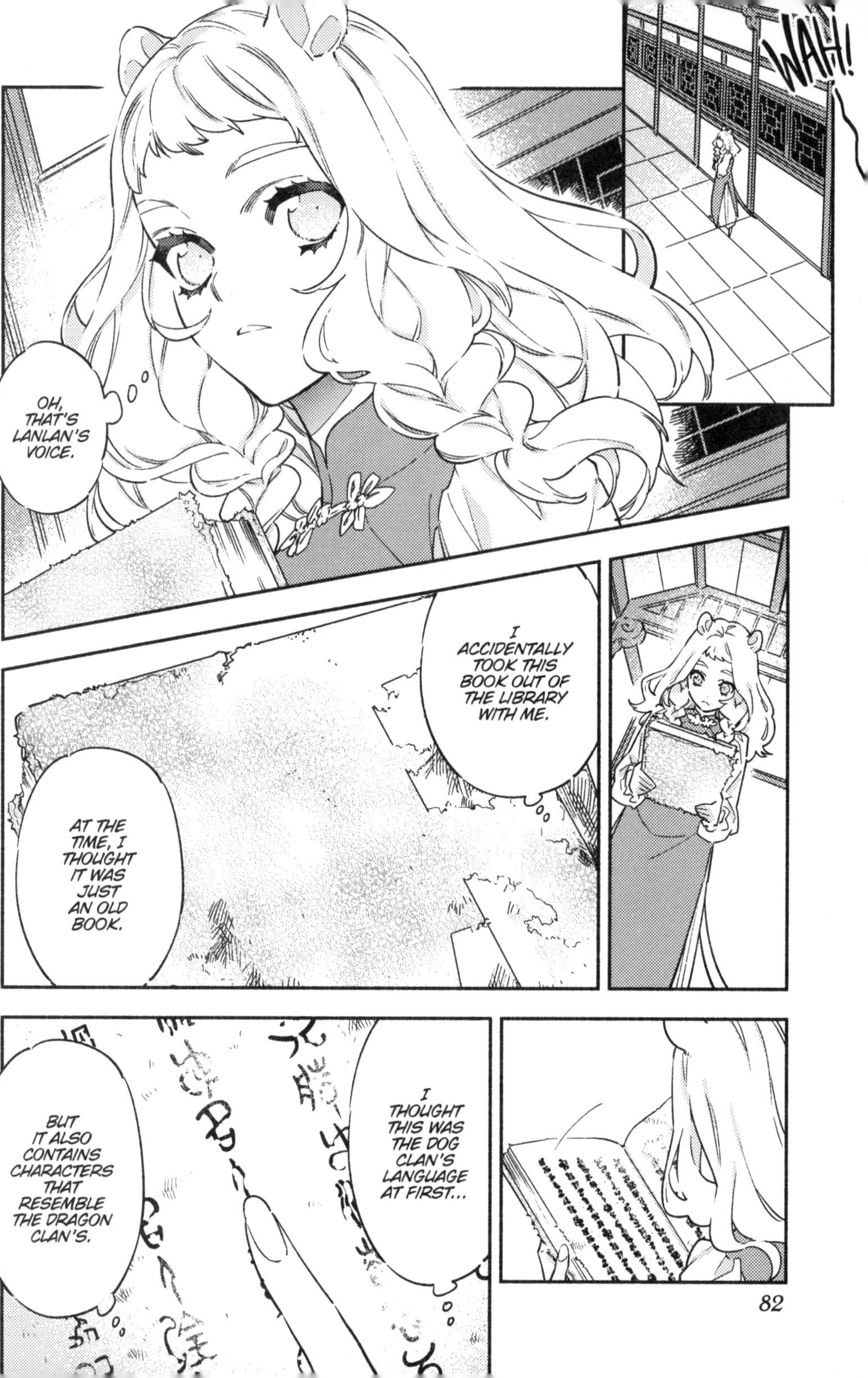
WAH!
OH, THAT'S LANLAN'S VOICE.
I ACCIDENTALLY TOOK THIS BOOK OUT OF THE LIBRARY WITH ME.
AT THE TIME, I THOUGHT IT WAS JUST AN OLD BOOK.
I THOUGHT THIS WAS THE DOG CLAN'S LANGUAGE AT FIRST...
BUT IT ALSO CONTAINS CHARACTERS THAT RESEMBLE THE DRAGON CLAN'S.

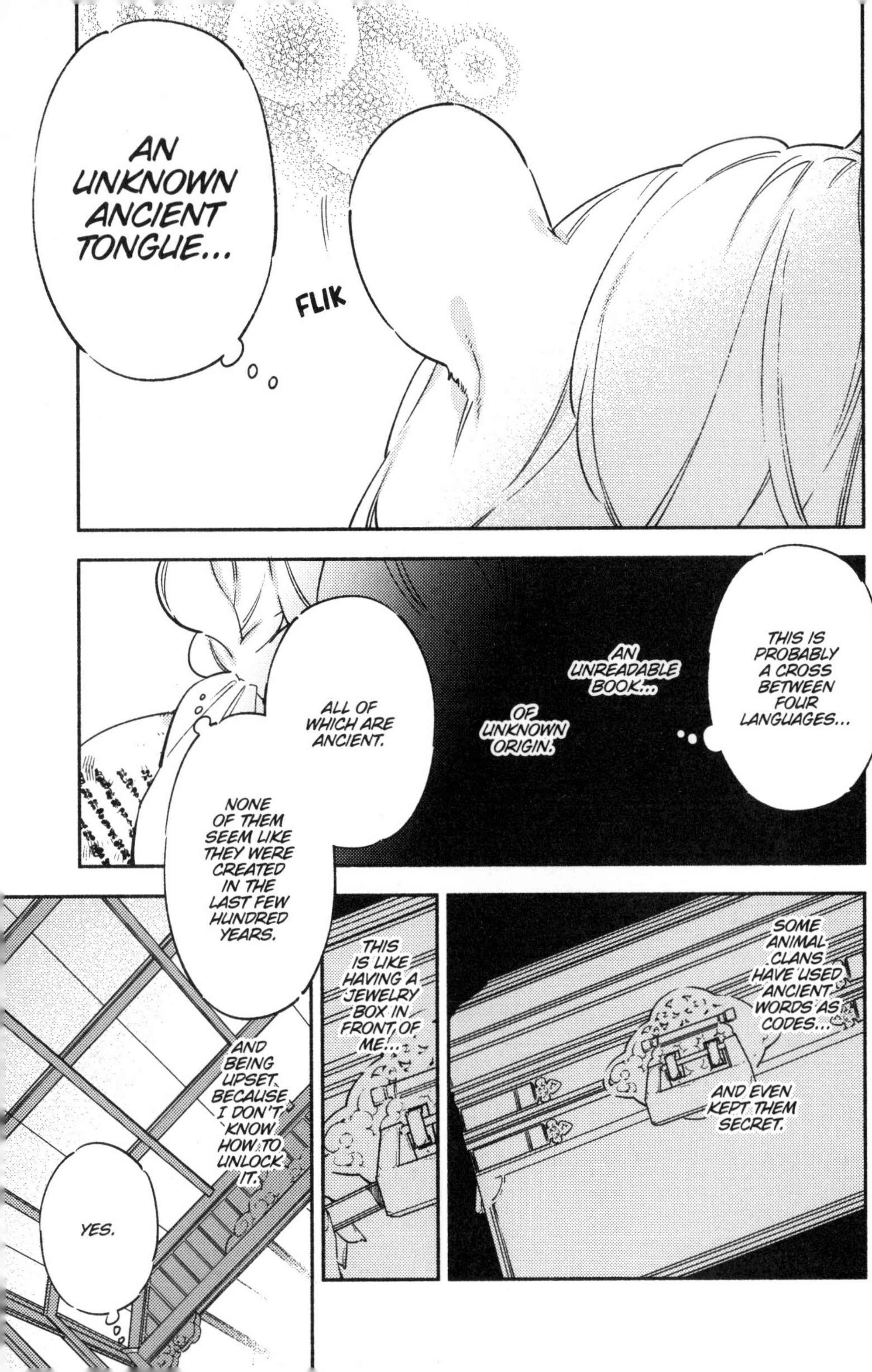
AN UNKNOWN ANCIENT TONGUE...
FLIK
THIS IS PROBABLY A CROSS BETWEEN FOUR LANGUAGES...
AN UNREADABLE BOOK...
OF UNKNOWN ORIGIN.
ALL OF WHICH ARE ANCIENT.
NONE OF THEM SEEM LIKE THEY WERE CREATED IN THE LAST FEW HUNDRED YEARS.
SOME ANIMAL CLANS HAVE USED ANCIENT WORDS AS CODES...
AND EVEN KEPT THEM SECRET.
THIS IS LIKE HAVING A JEWELRY BOX IN FRONT OF ME...
AND BEING UPSET BECAUSE I DON'T KNOW HOW TO UNLOCK IT.
YES.

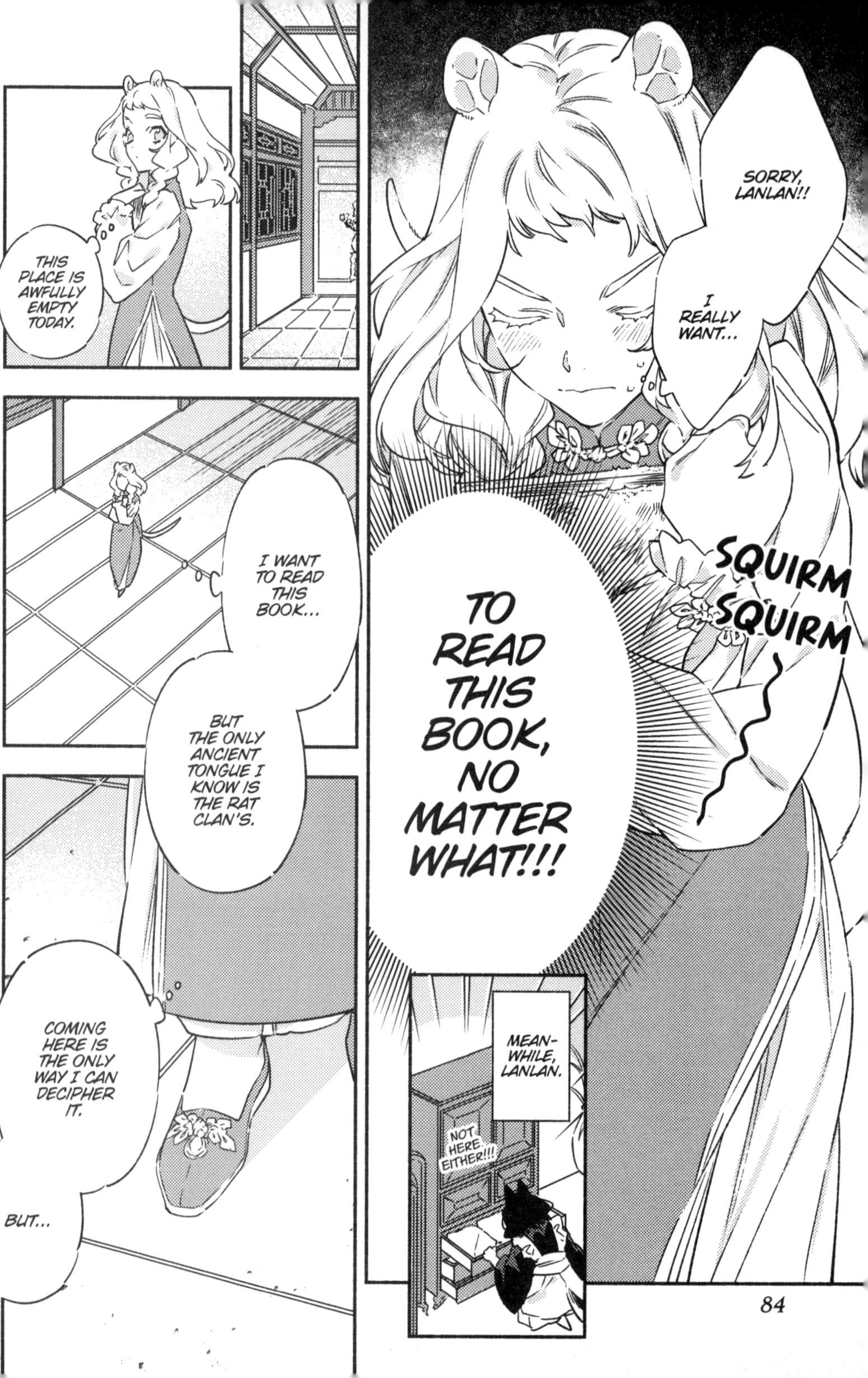
THIS PLACE IS AWFULLY EMPTY TODAY.
I WANT TO READ THIS BOOK...
BUT THE ONLY ANCIENT TONGUE I KNOW IS THE RAT CLAN'S.
COMING HERE IS THE ONLY WAY I CAN DECIPHER IT.
BUT...
SORRY, LANLAN!!
I REALLY WANT...
TO READ THIS BOOK, NO MATTER WHAT!!!
SQUIRM SQUIRM
MEAN-WHILE, LANLAN.
NOT HERE EITHER!!!

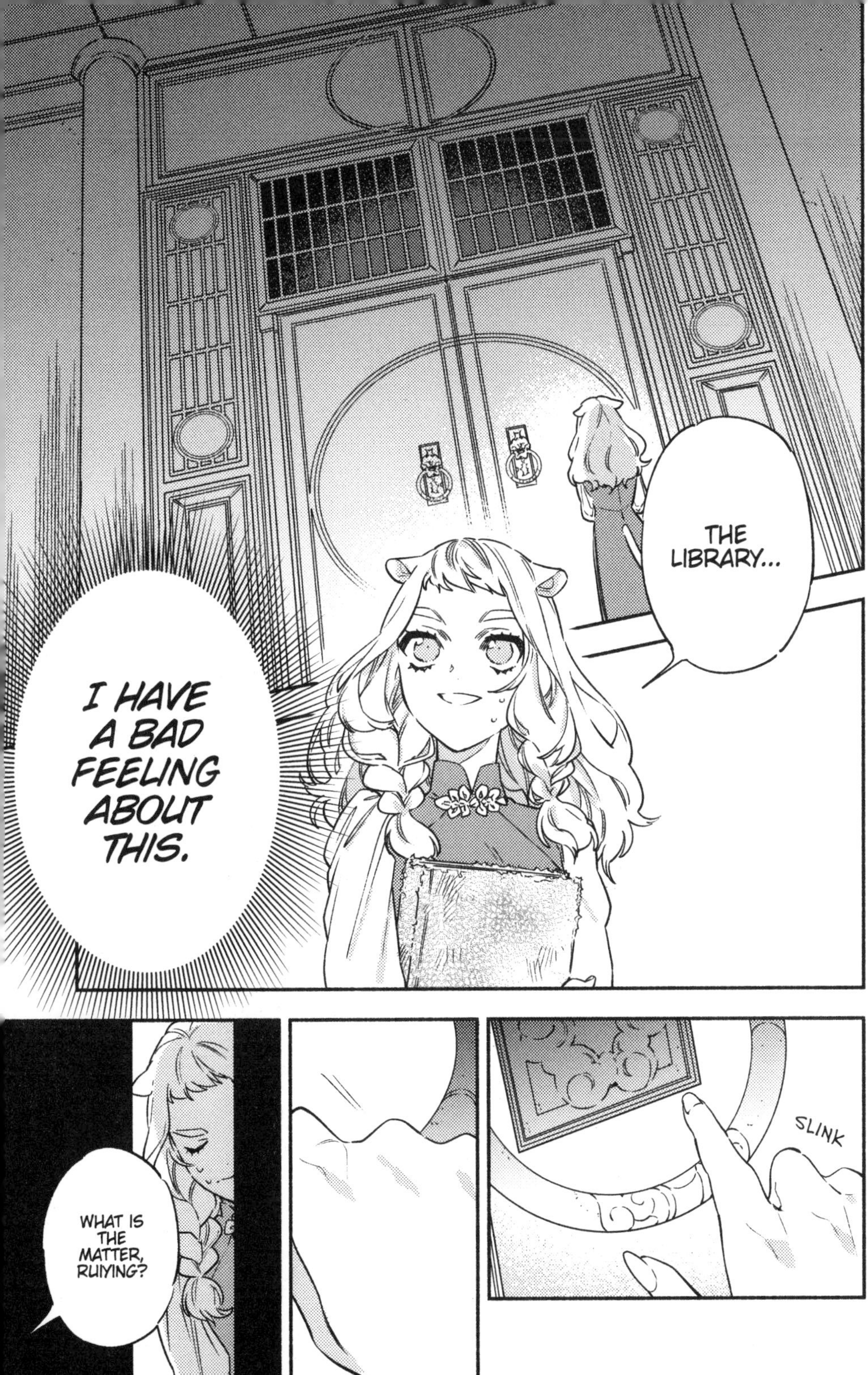
THE LIBRARY...
I HAVE A BAD FEELING ABOUT THIS.
SLINK
WHAT IS THE MATTER, RUIYING?

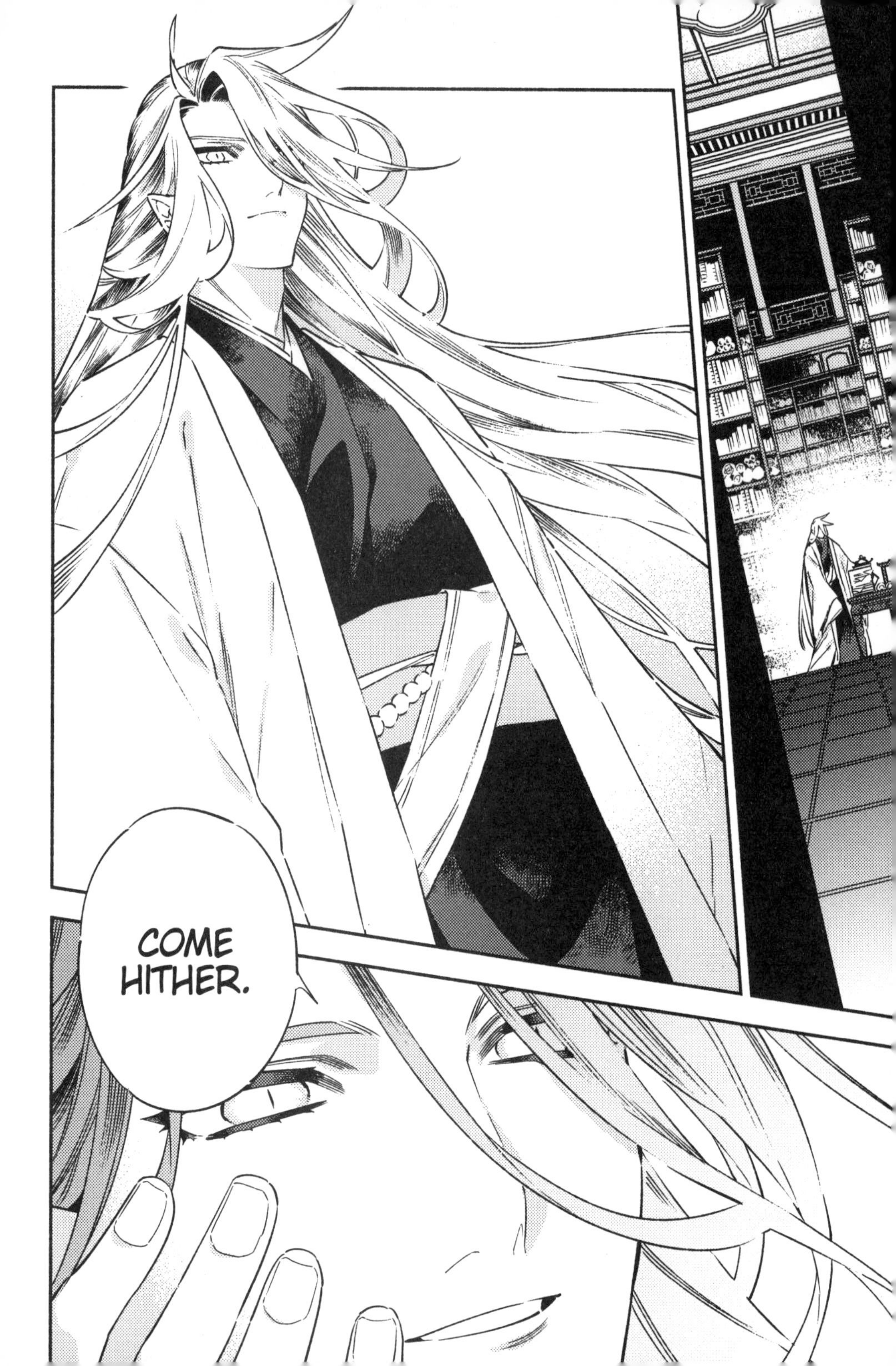
COME HITHER.

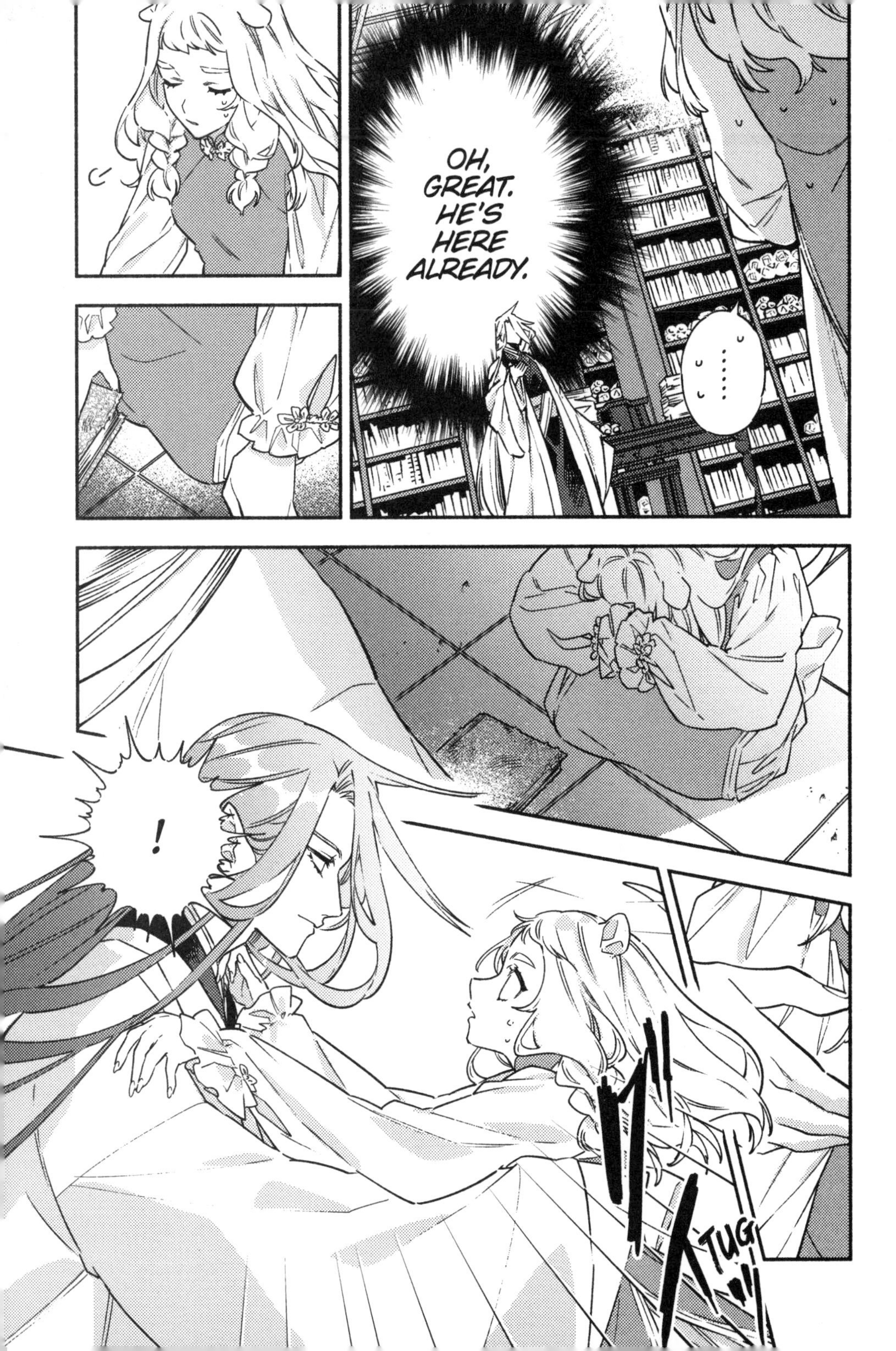
OH, GREAT. HE'S HERE ALREADY.
......
!
TUG

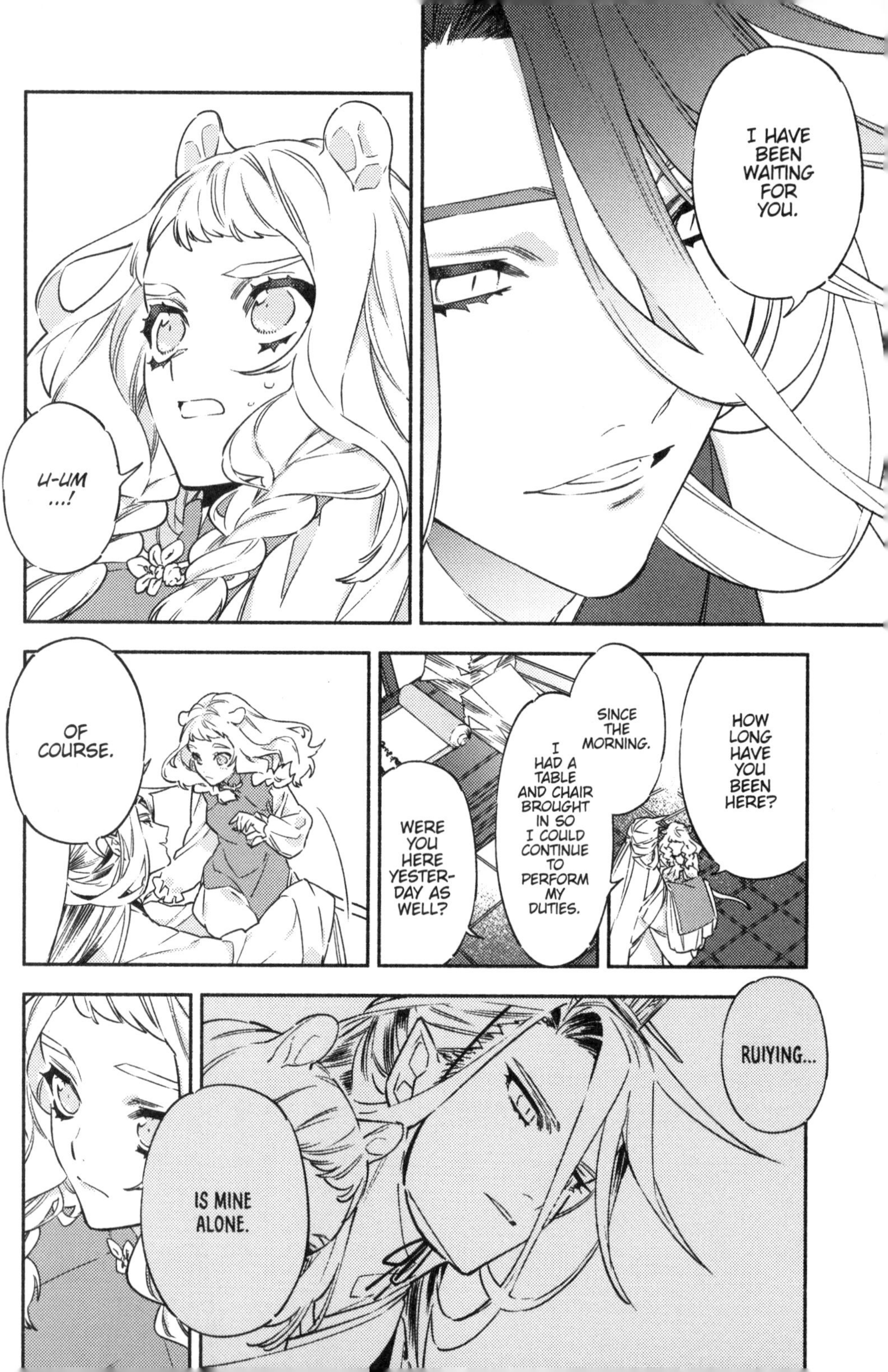
I HAVE BEEN WAITING FOR YOU.
U-UM ...!
HOW LONG HAVE YOU BEEN HERE?
SINCE THE MORNING.
I HAD A TABLE AND CHAIR BROUGHT IN SO I COULD CONTINUE TO PERFORM MY DUTIES.
WERE YOU HERE YESTER-DAY AS WELL?
OF COURSE.
RUIYING...
IS MINE ALONE.

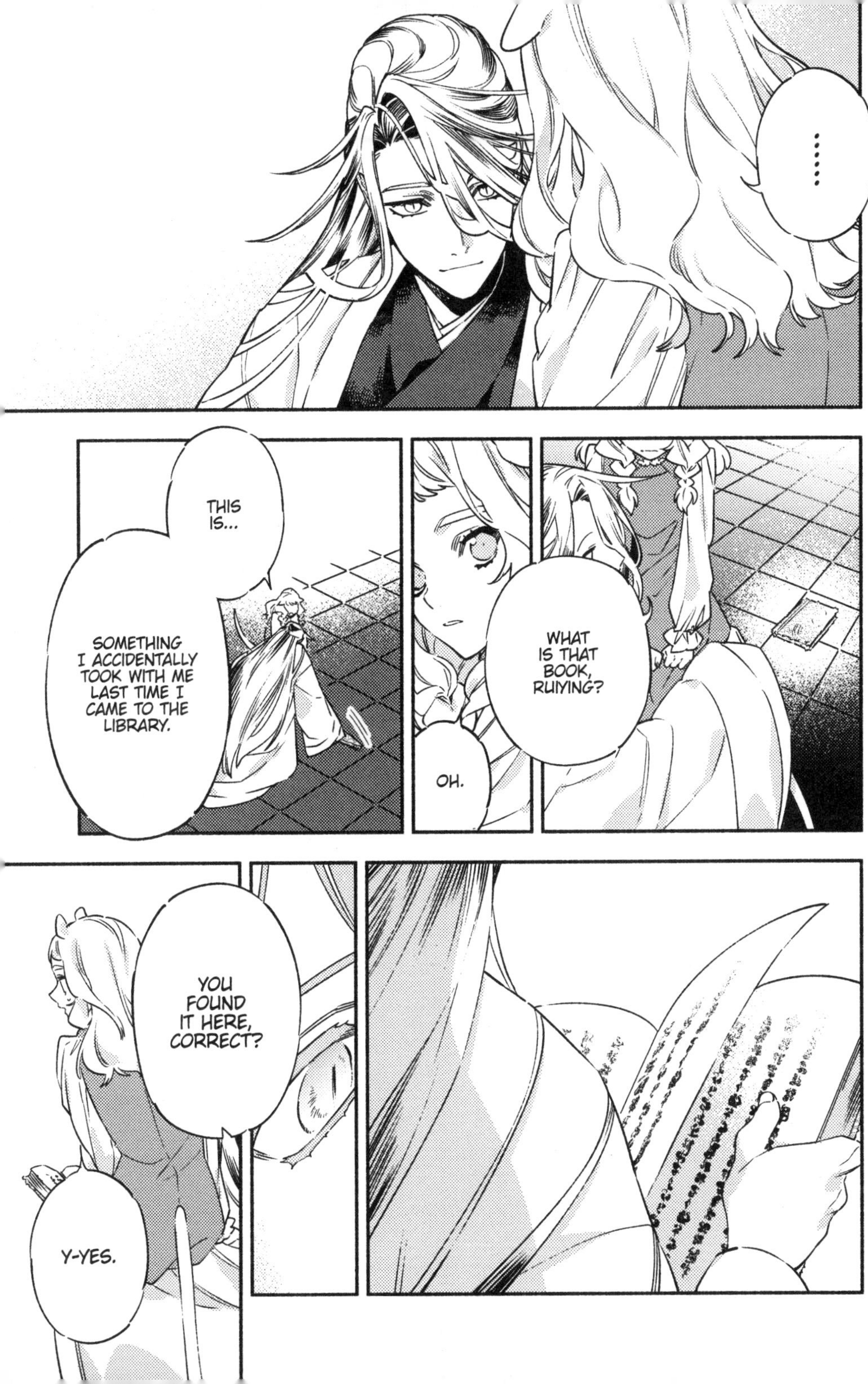
......
WHAT IS THAT BOOK, RUIYING?
OH.
THIS IS...
SOMETHING I ACCIDENTALLY TOOK WITH ME LAST TIME I CAME TO THE LIBRARY.
YOU FOUND IT HERE, CORRECT?
Y-YES.

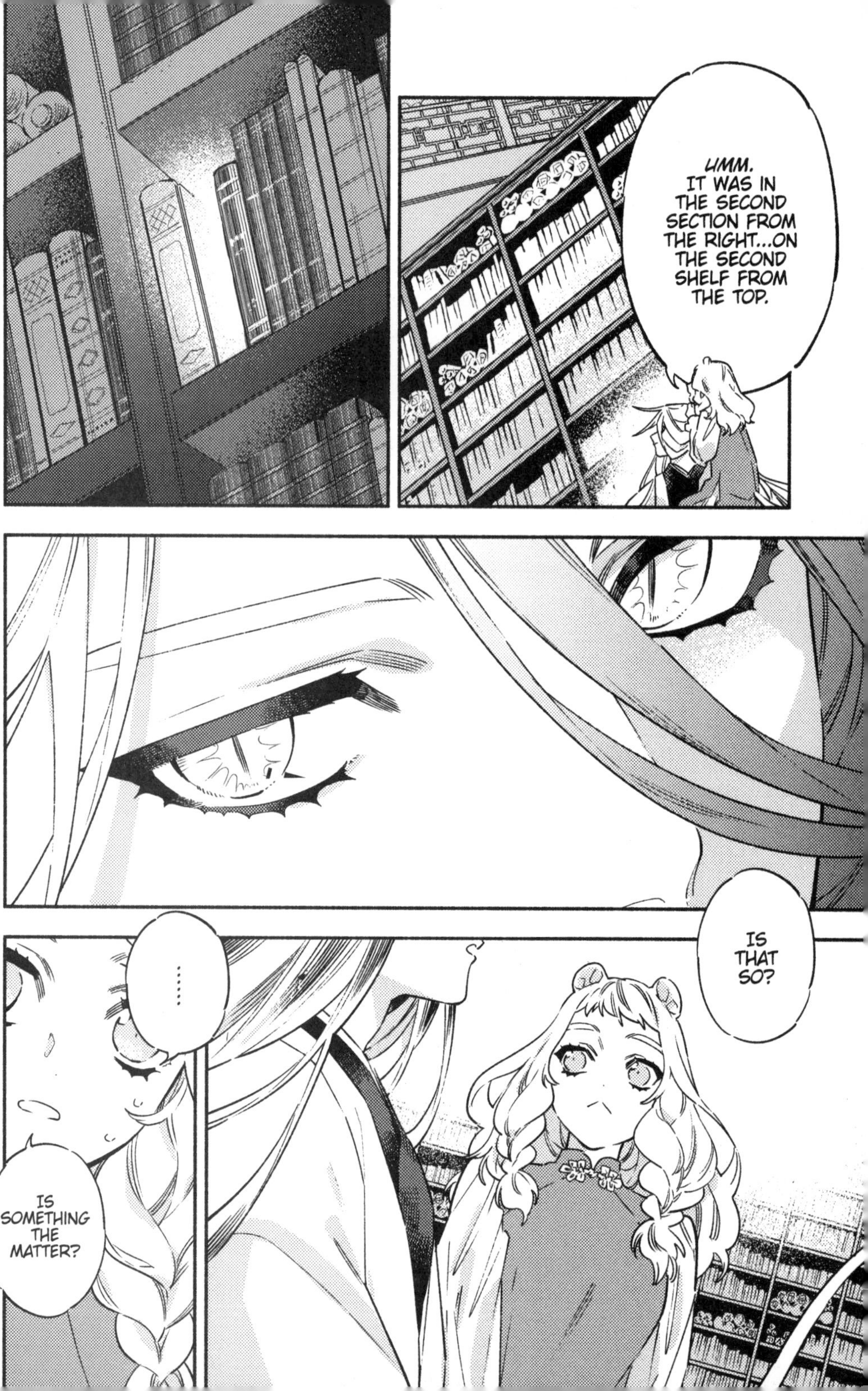
UMM. IT WAS IN THE SECOND SECTION FROM THE RIGHT...ON THE SECOND SHELF FROM THE TOP.
IS THAT SO?
......
IS SOMETHING THE MATTER?

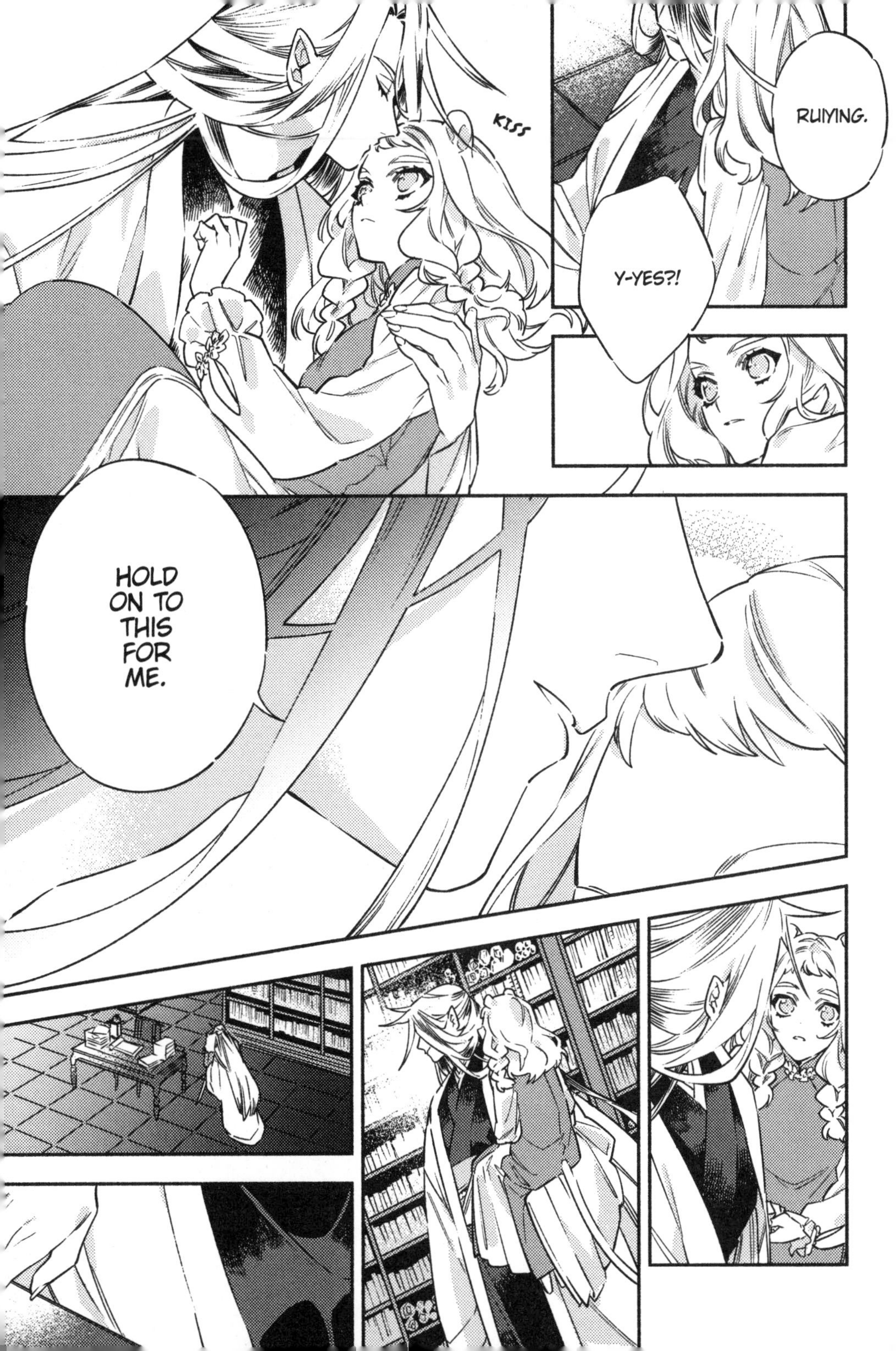
RUIYING.
Y-YES?!
KISS
HOLD ON TO THIS FOR ME.

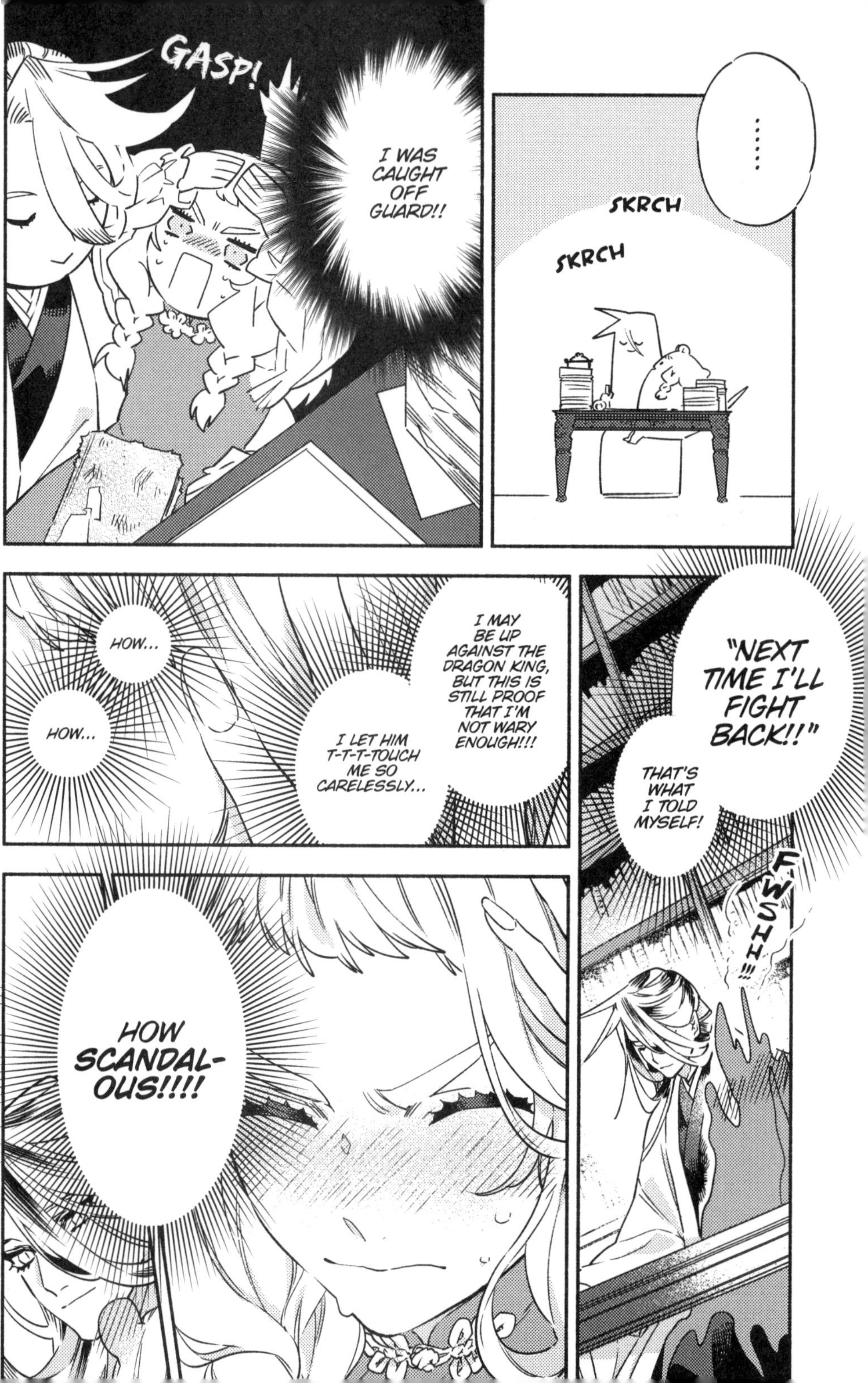

……
SKRCH
SKRCH
GASP!
I WAS CAUGHT OFF GUARD!!
"NEXT TIME I'LL FIGHT BACK!!"
THAT'S WHAT I TOLD MYSELF!
FWSHH!!!
I MAY BE UP AGAINST THE DRAGON KING, BUT THIS IS STILL PROOF THAT I'M NOT WARY ENOUGH!!!
I LET HIM T-T-T-TOUCH ME SO CARELESSLY...
HOW...
HOW...
HOW SCANDAL-OUS!!!!

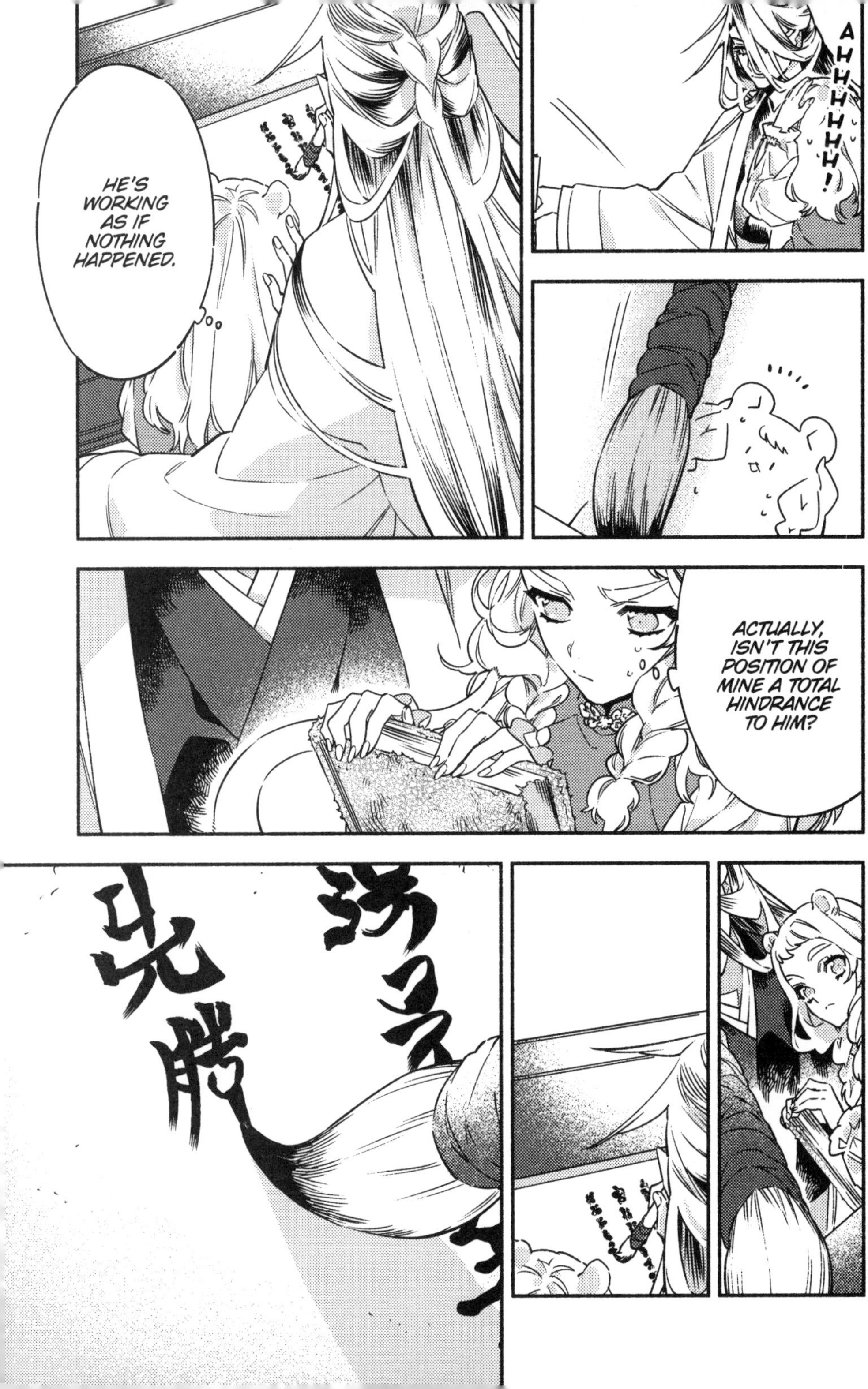
AHHHHHH!
HE'S WORKING AS IF NOTHING HAPPENED.
ACTUALLY, ISN'T THIS POSITION OF MINE A TOTAL HINDRANCE TO HIM?

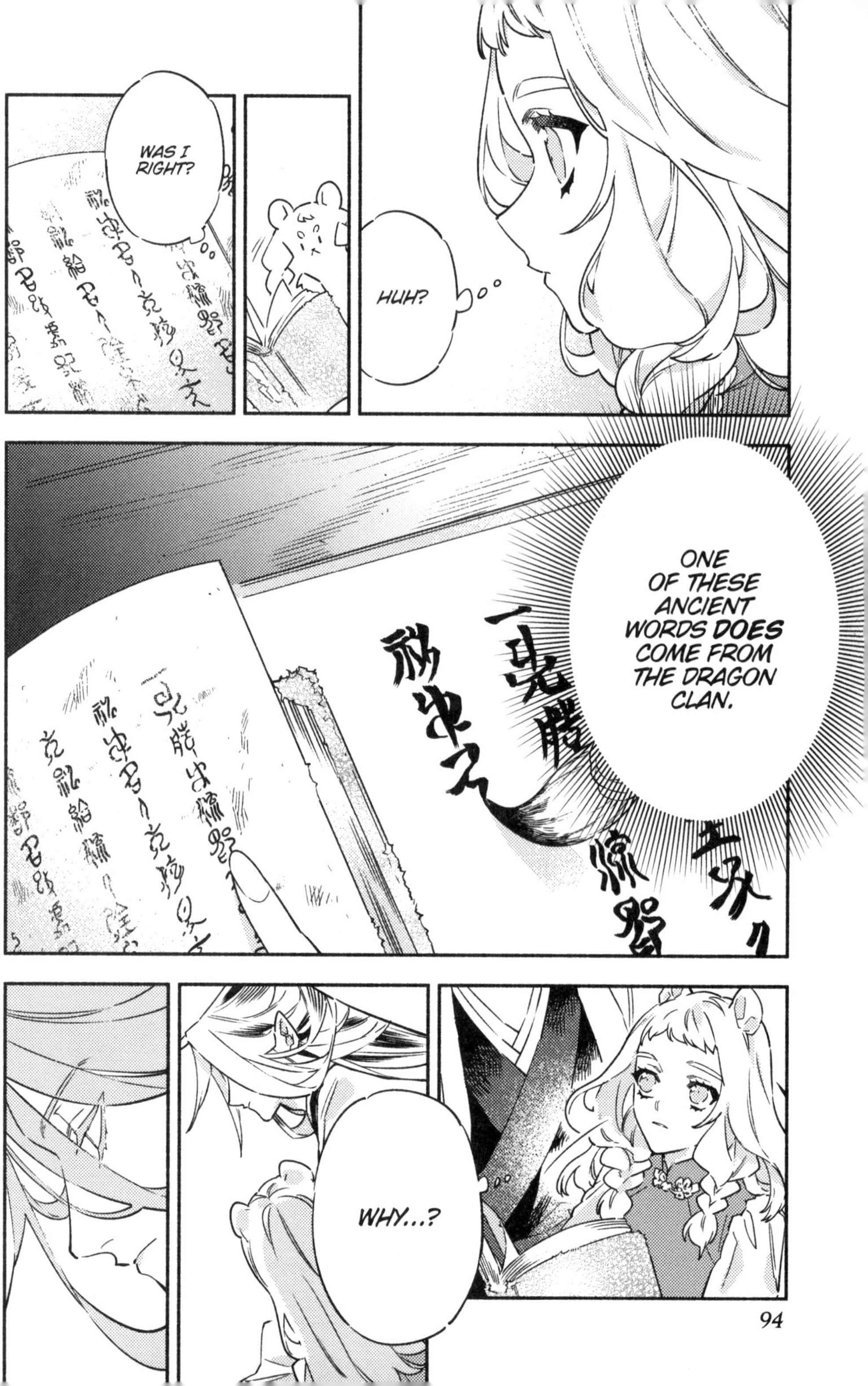
HUH?
WAS I RIGHT?
ONE OF THESE ANCIENT WORDS DOES COME FROM THE DRAGON CLAN.
WHY...?

......

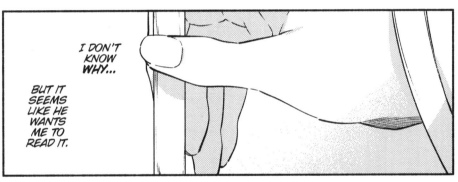

I DON'T KNOW WHY...

BUT IT SEEMS LIKE HE WANTS ME TO READ IT.

WHAT A WEIRD PERSON.

BA-THUMP

BA-THUMP

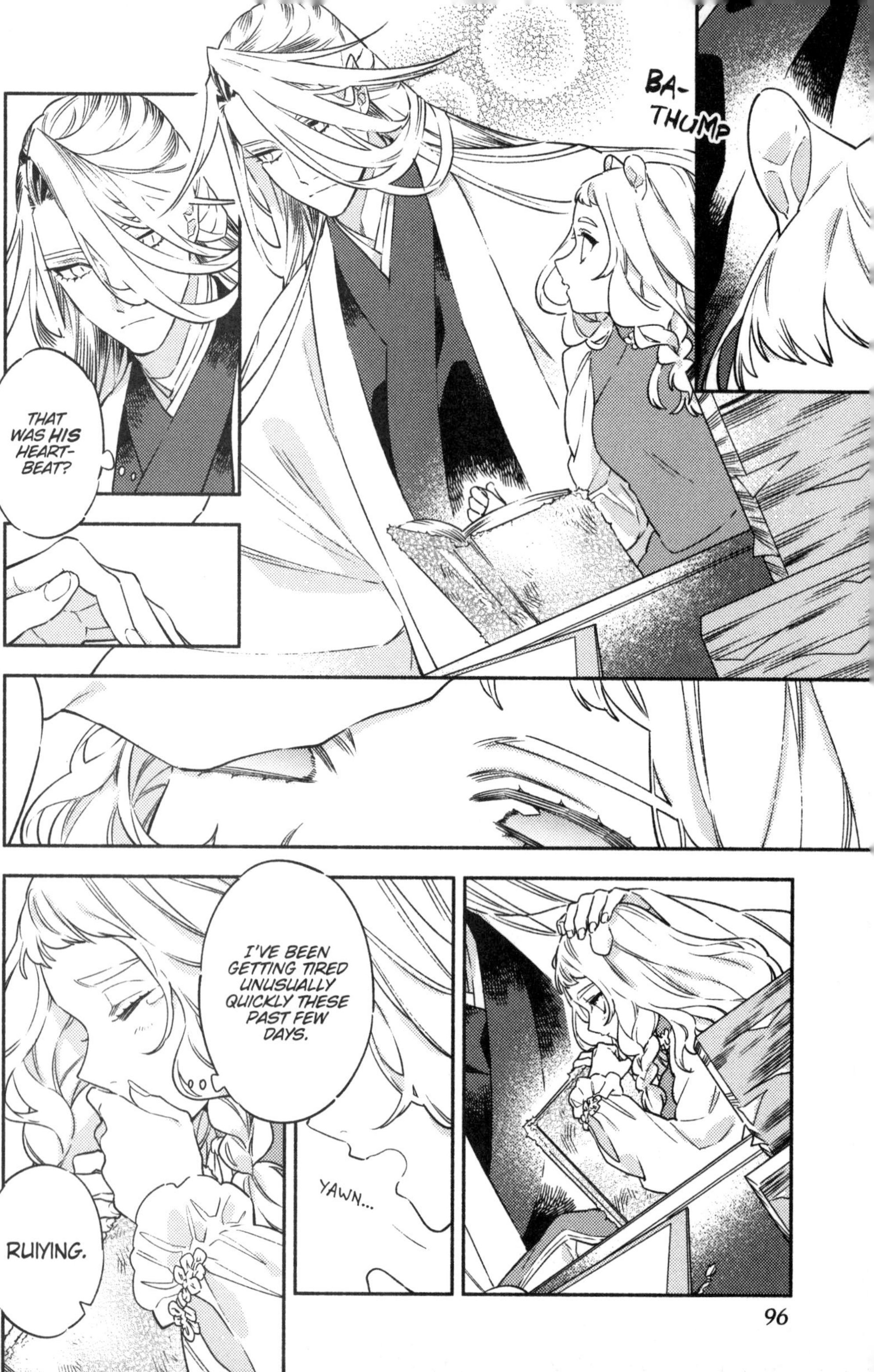
BA-THUMP
THAT WAS HIS HEART-BEAT?
I'VE BEEN GETTING TIRED UNUSUALLY QUICKLY THESE PAST FEW DAYS.
YAWN...
RUIYING.

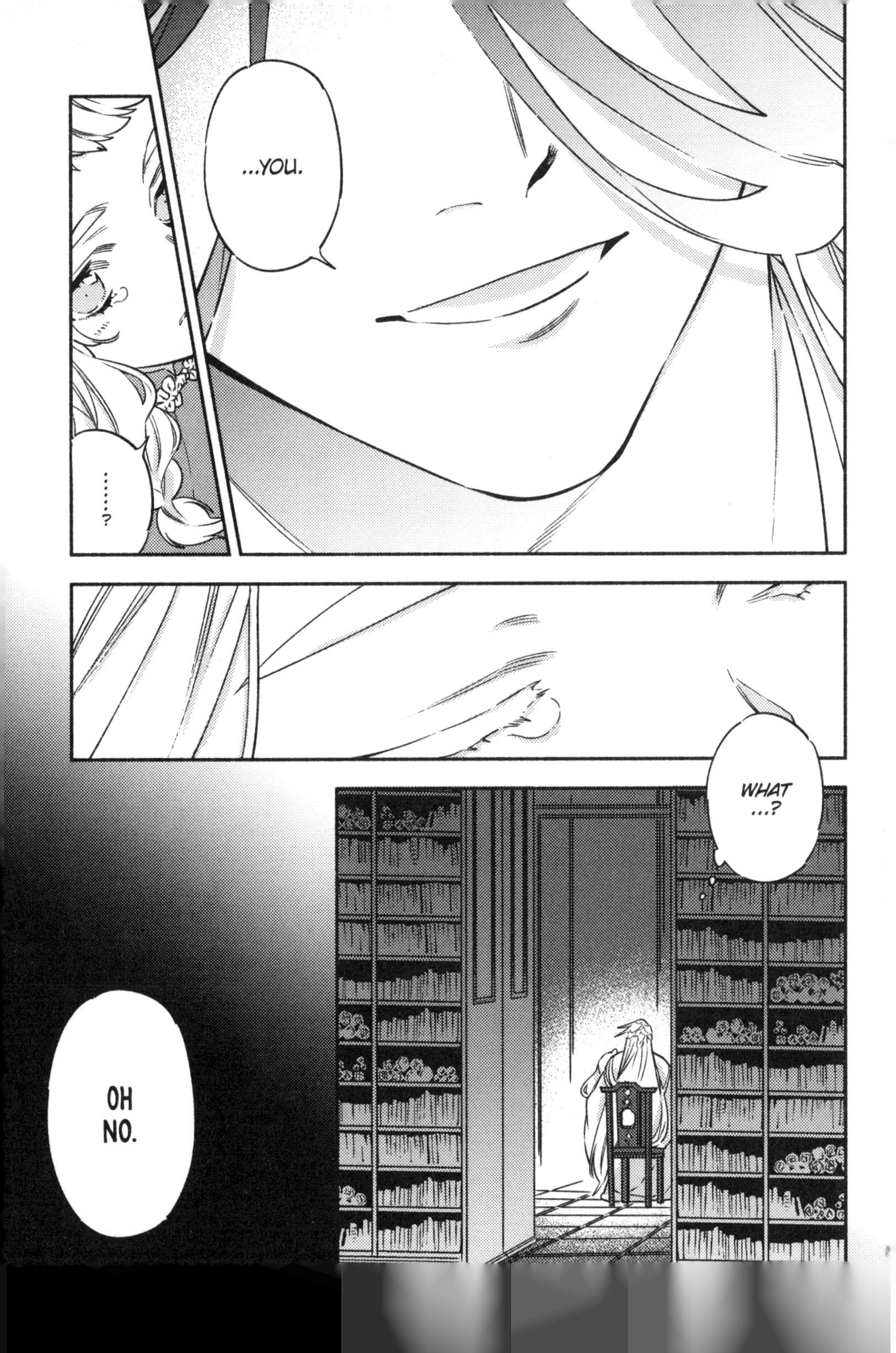
...YOU.
......?
WHAT ...?
OH NO.

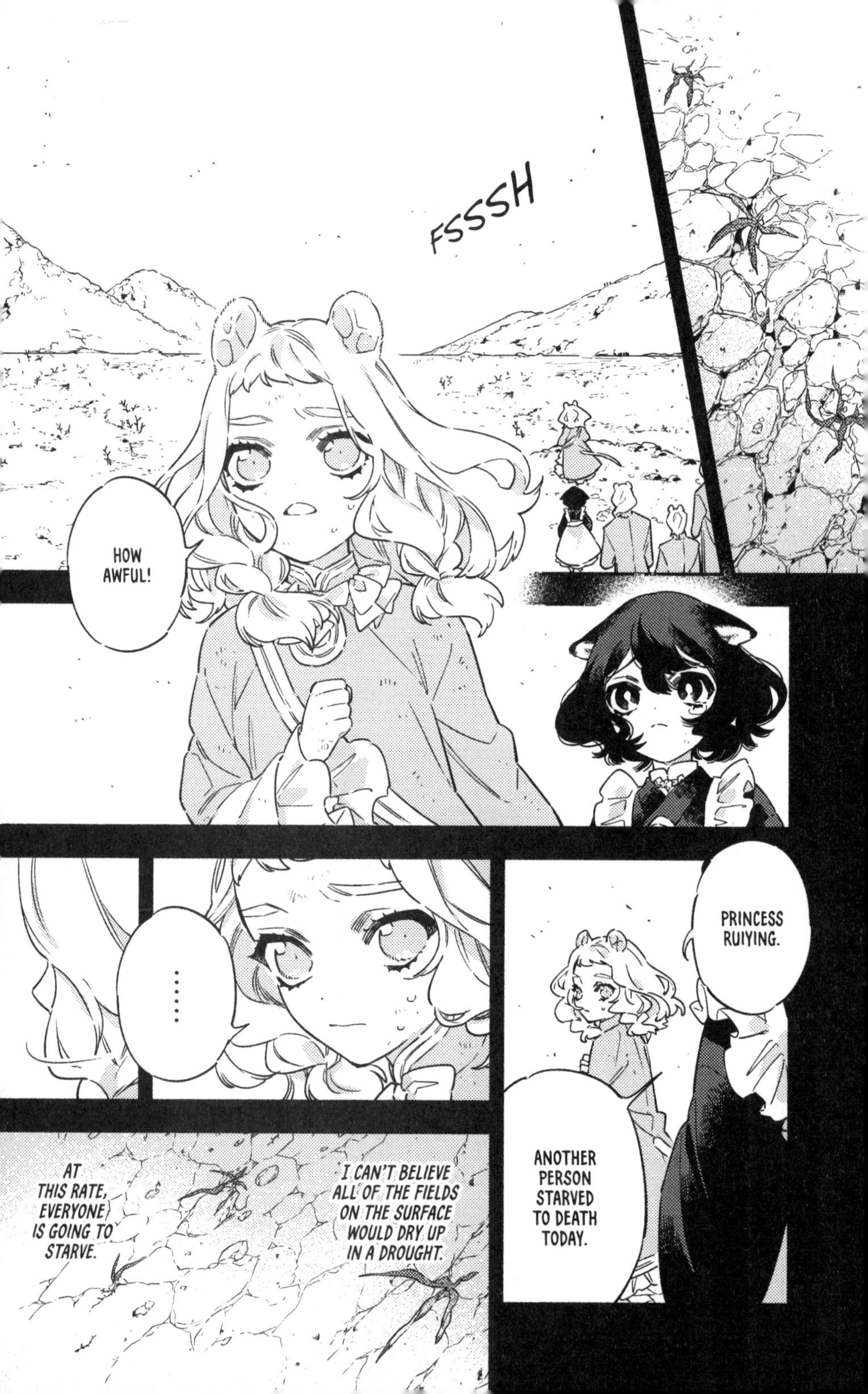
FSSSH
HOW AWFUL!
PRINCESS RUIYING.
ANOTHER PERSON STARVED TO DEATH TODAY.
......
I CAN'T BELIEVE ALL OF THE FIELDS ON THE SURFACE WOULD DRY UP IN A DROUGHT.
AT THIS RATE, EVERYONE IS GOING TO STARVE.

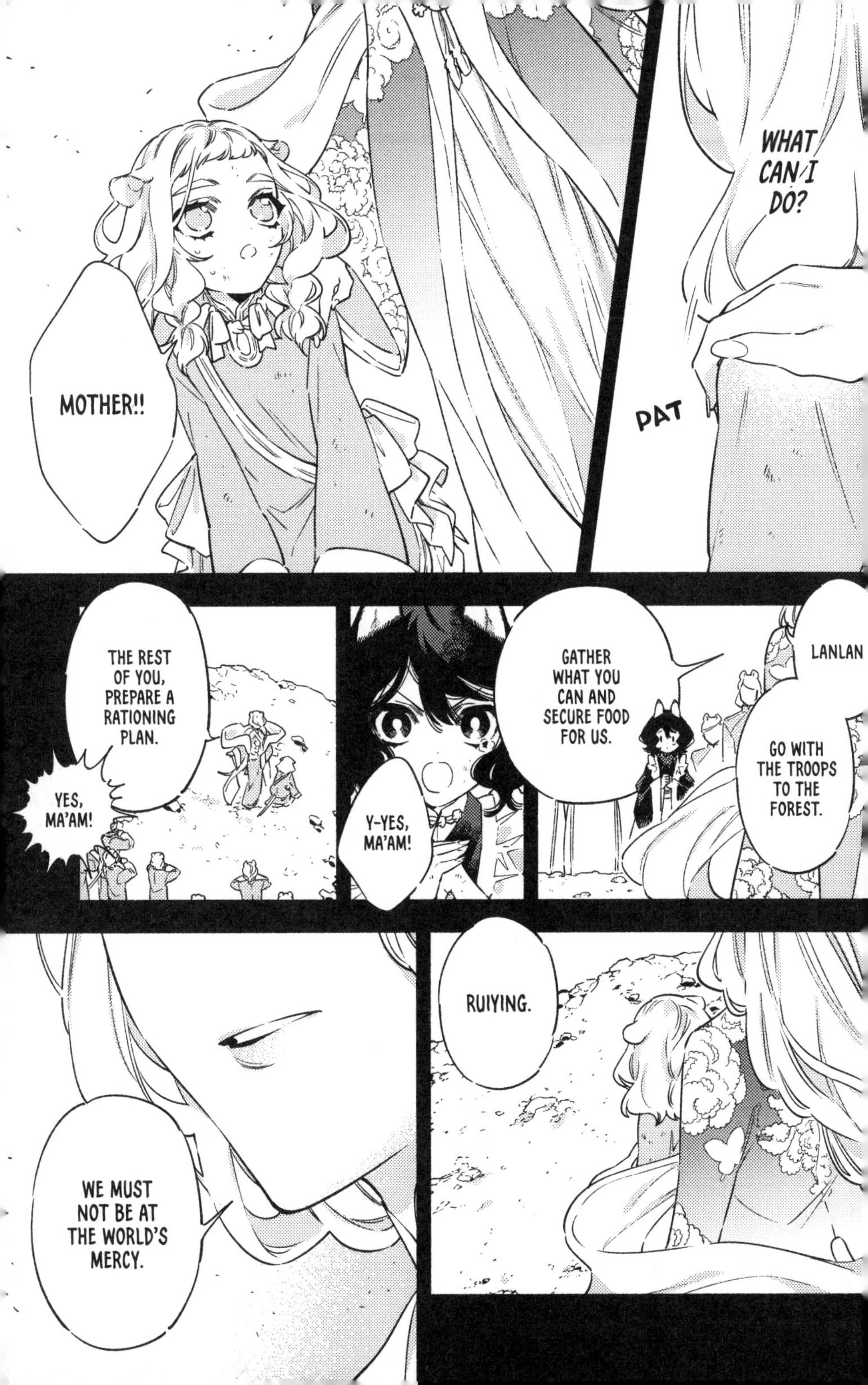
WHAT CAN I DO?
PAT
MOTHER!!
LANLAN
GO WITH THE TROOPS TO THE FOREST.
GATHER WHAT YOU CAN AND SECURE FOOD FOR US.
Y-YES, MA'AM!
THE REST OF YOU, PREPARE A RATIONING PLAN.
YES, MA'AM!
RUIYING.
WE MUST NOT BE AT THE WORLD'S MERCY.

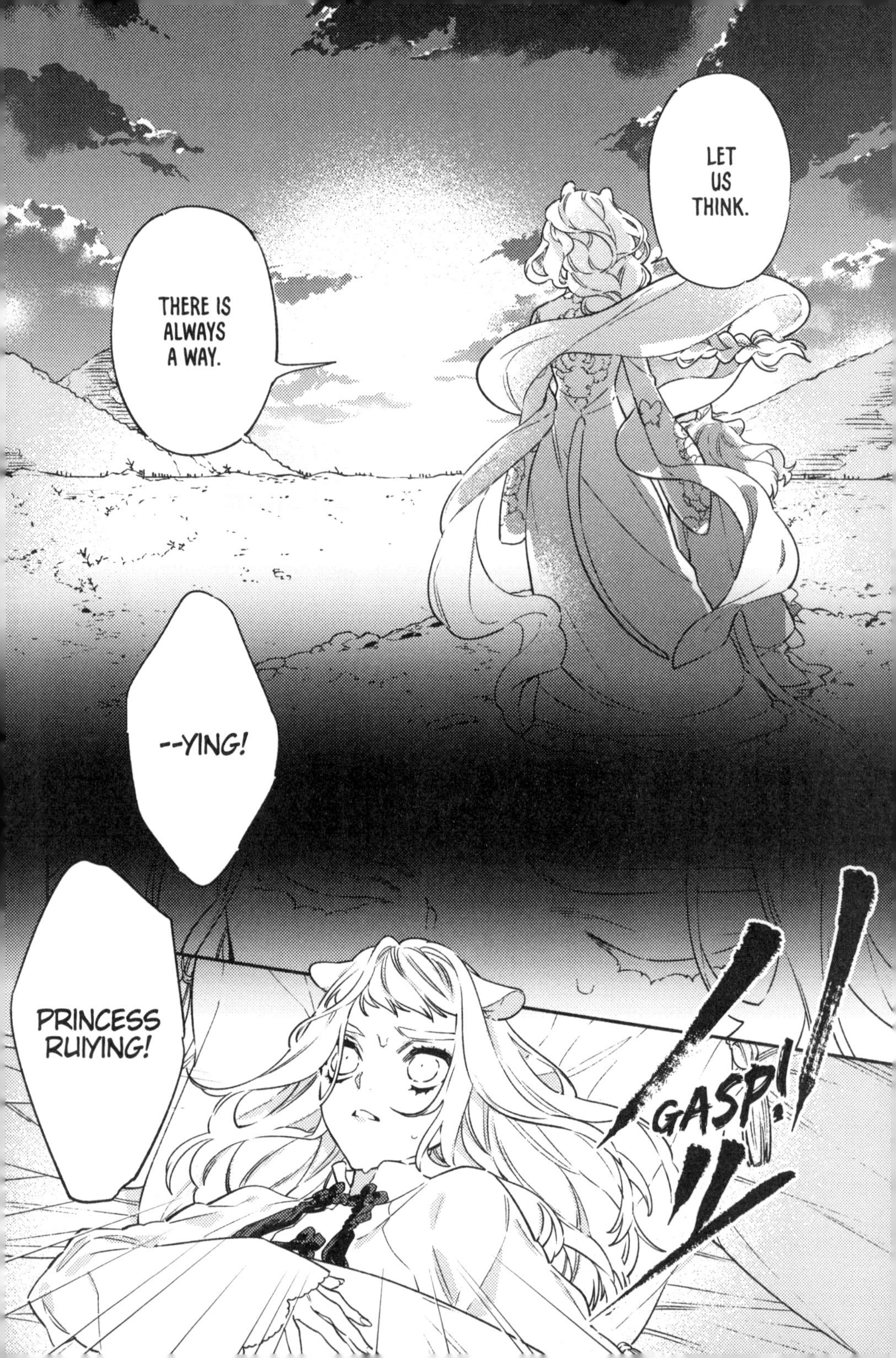
LET US THINK.
THERE IS ALWAYS A WAY.
--YING!
PRINCESS RUIYING!
GASP!

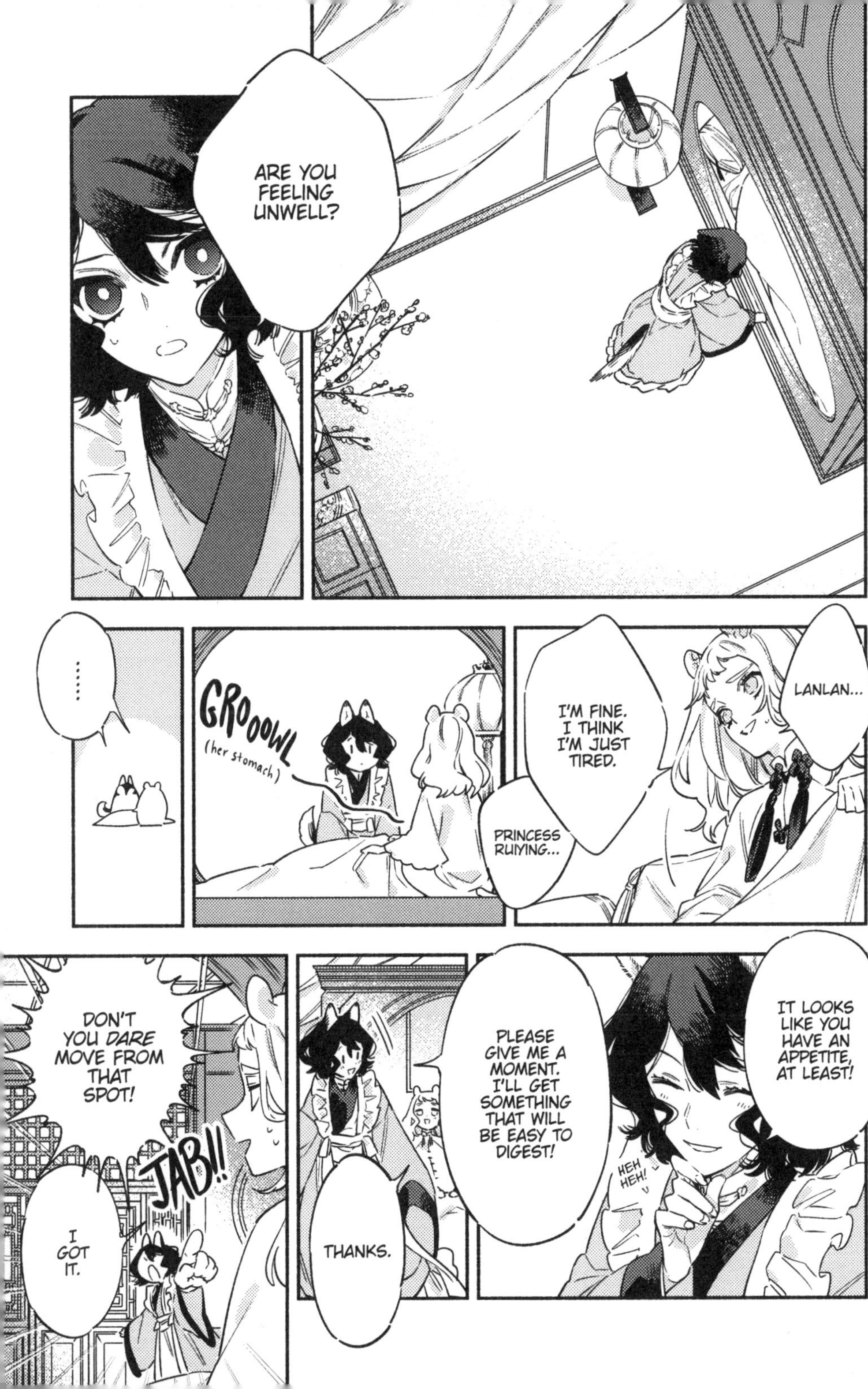
ARE YOU FEELING UNWELL?
LANLAN...
I'M FINE. I THINK I'M JUST TIRED.
PRINCESS RUIYING...
GROOOWL
(her stomach)
......
IT LOOKS LIKE YOU HAVE AN APPETITE, AT LEAST!
HEH HEH!
PLEASE GIVE ME A MOMENT. I'LL GET SOMETHING THAT WILL BE EASY TO DIGEST!
THANKS.
DON'T YOU *DARE* MOVE FROM THAT SPOT!
JAB!!
I GOT IT.

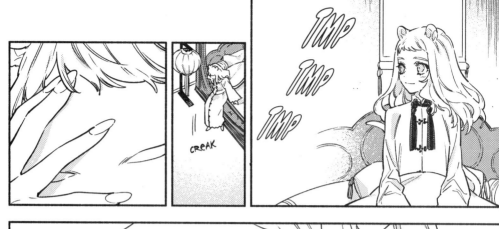

TMP
TMP
TMP

CREAK

SIGH...

WHY DO I FEEL SO FATIGUED?

YESTERDAY...

PAD

PAD

PAD

I WENT TO THE LIBRARY AND SAW HIS IMPERIAL MAJESTY...

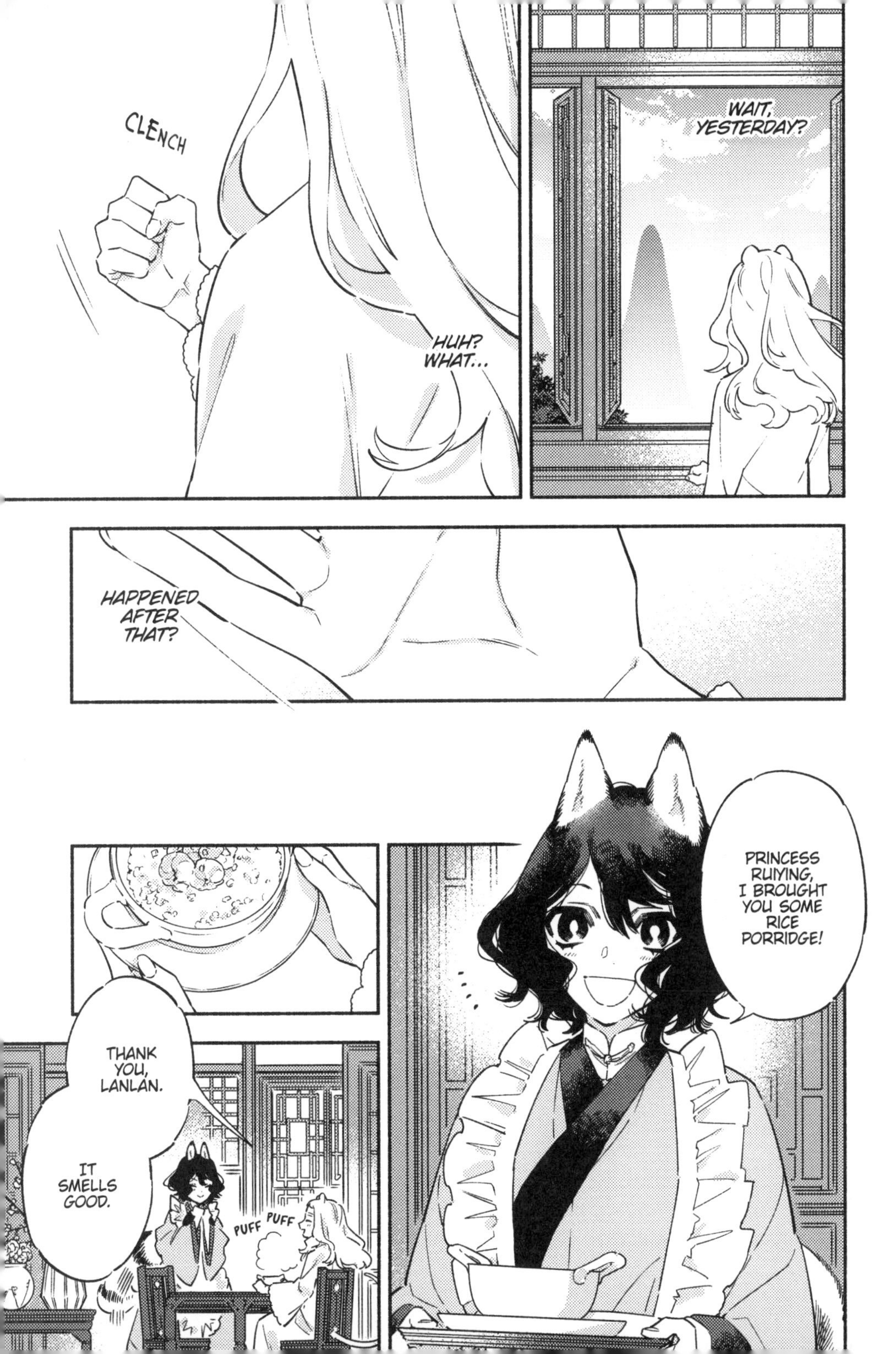
WAIT, YESTERDAY?
CLENCH
HUH? WHAT...
HAPPENED AFTER THAT?
PRINCESS RUIYING, I BROUGHT YOU SOME RICE PORRIDGE!
THANK YOU, LANLAN.
IT SMELLS GOOD.
PUFF PUFF

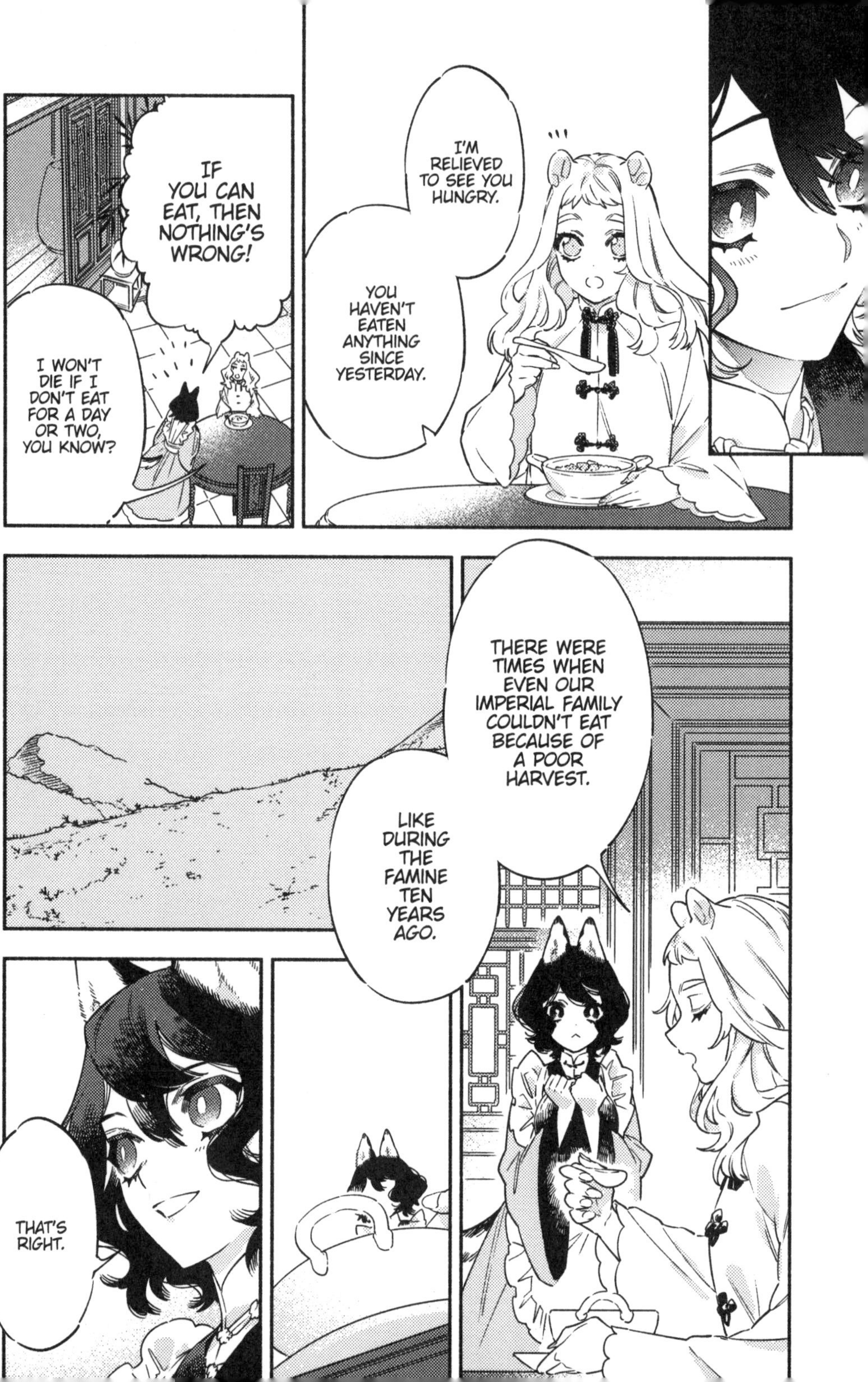
I'M RELIEVED TO SEE YOU HUNGRY.
YOU HAVEN'T EATEN ANYTHING SINCE YESTERDAY.
IF YOU CAN EAT, THEN NOTHING'S WRONG!
I WON'T DIE IF I DON'T EAT FOR A DAY OR TWO, YOU KNOW?
THERE WERE TIMES WHEN EVEN OUR IMPERIAL FAMILY COULDN'T EAT BECAUSE OF A POOR HARVEST.
LIKE DURING THE FAMINE TEN YEARS AGO.
THAT'S RIGHT.

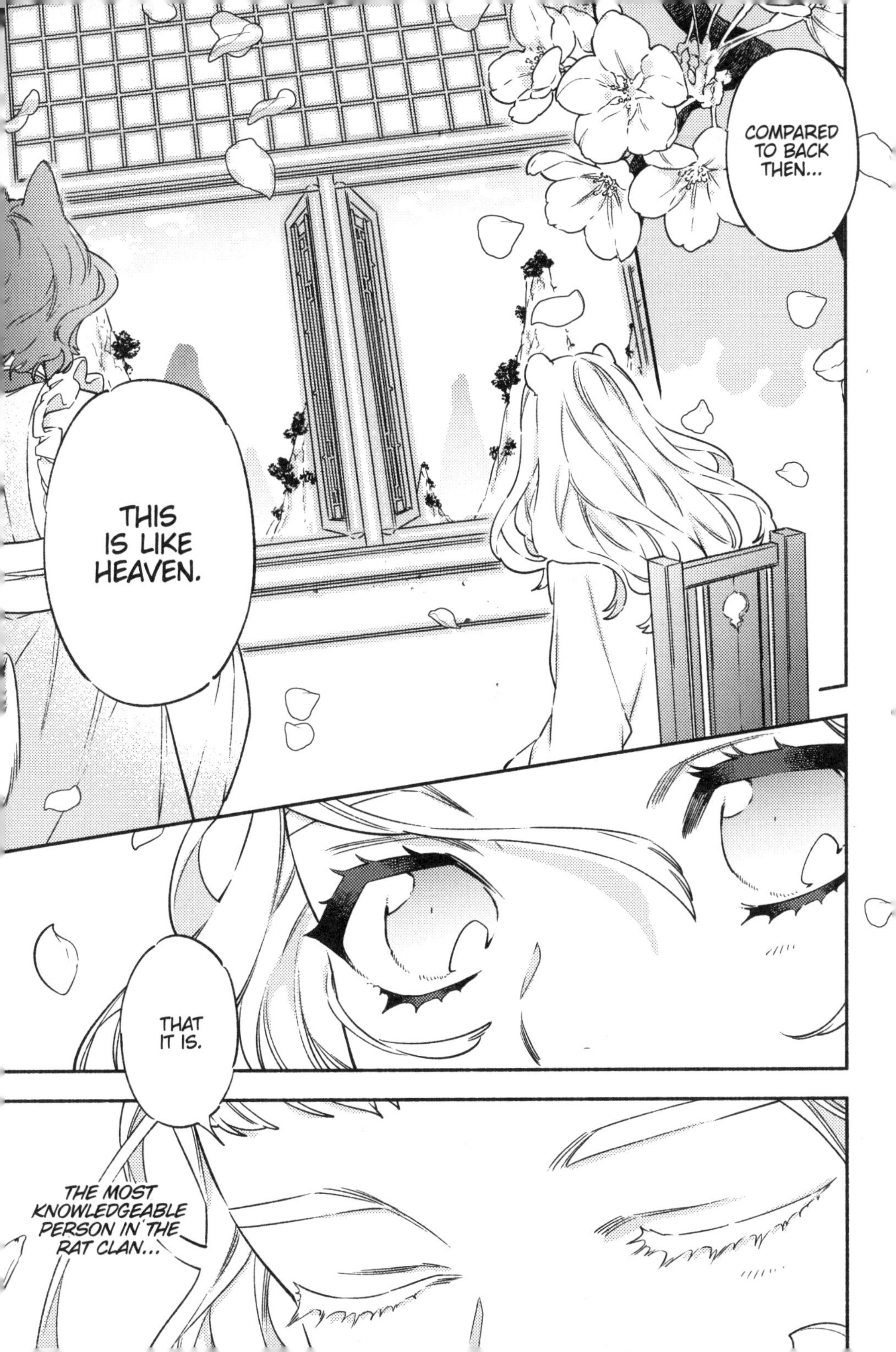
COMPARED TO BACK THEN...
THIS IS LIKE HEAVEN.
THAT IT IS.
THE MOST KNOWLEDGEABLE PERSON IN THE RAT CLAN...

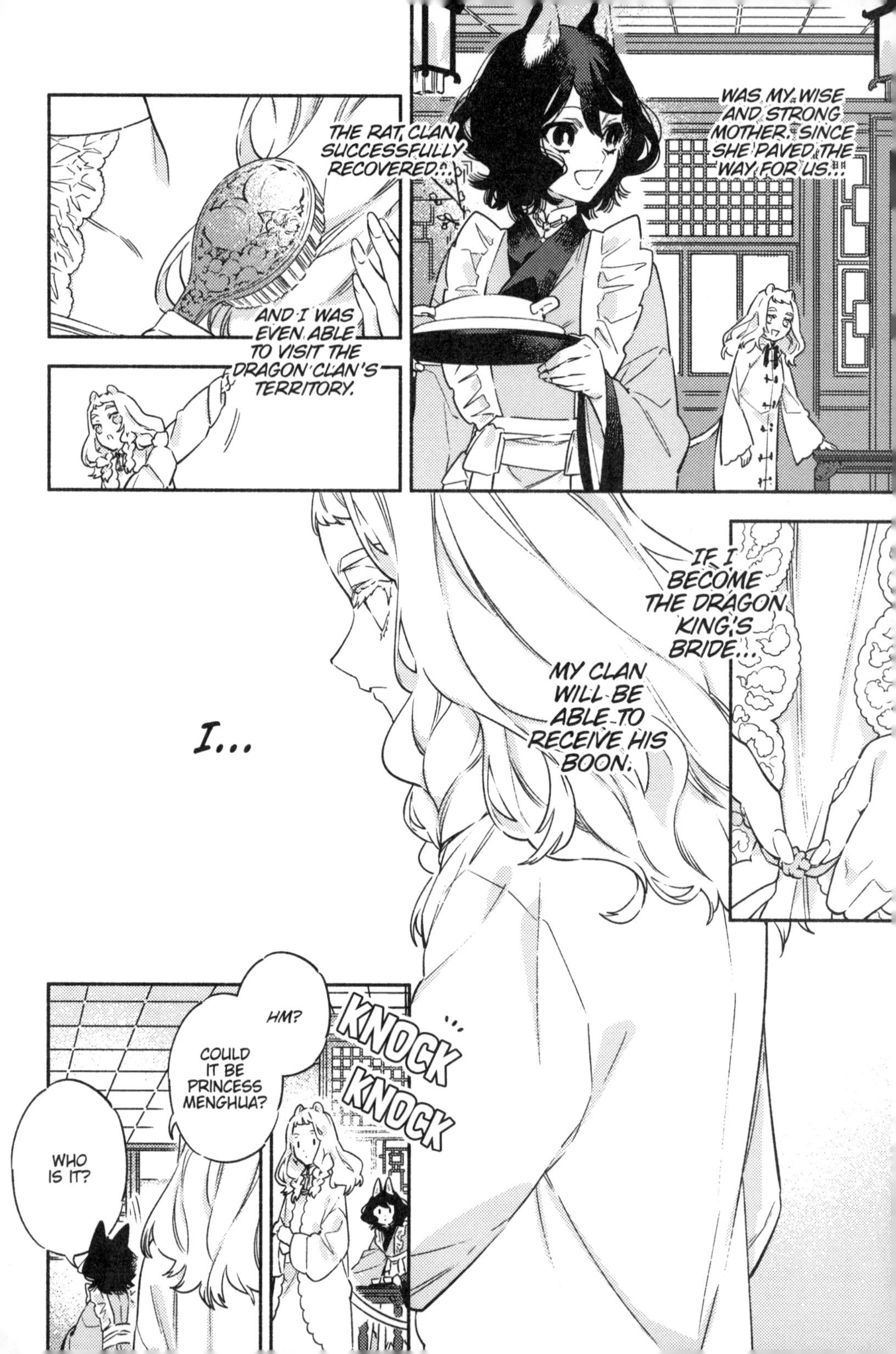
WAS MY WISE AND STRONG MOTHER. SINCE SHE PAVED THE WAY FOR US...
THE RAT CLAN SUCCESSFULLY RECOVERED...
AND I WAS EVEN ABLE TO VISIT THE DRAGON CLAN'S TERRITORY.
IF I BECOME THE DRAGON KING'S BRIDE...
MY CLAN WILL BE ABLE TO RECEIVE HIS BOON.
I...
KNOCK
KNOCK
...
HM?
COULD IT BE PRINCESS MENGHUA?
WHO IS IT?

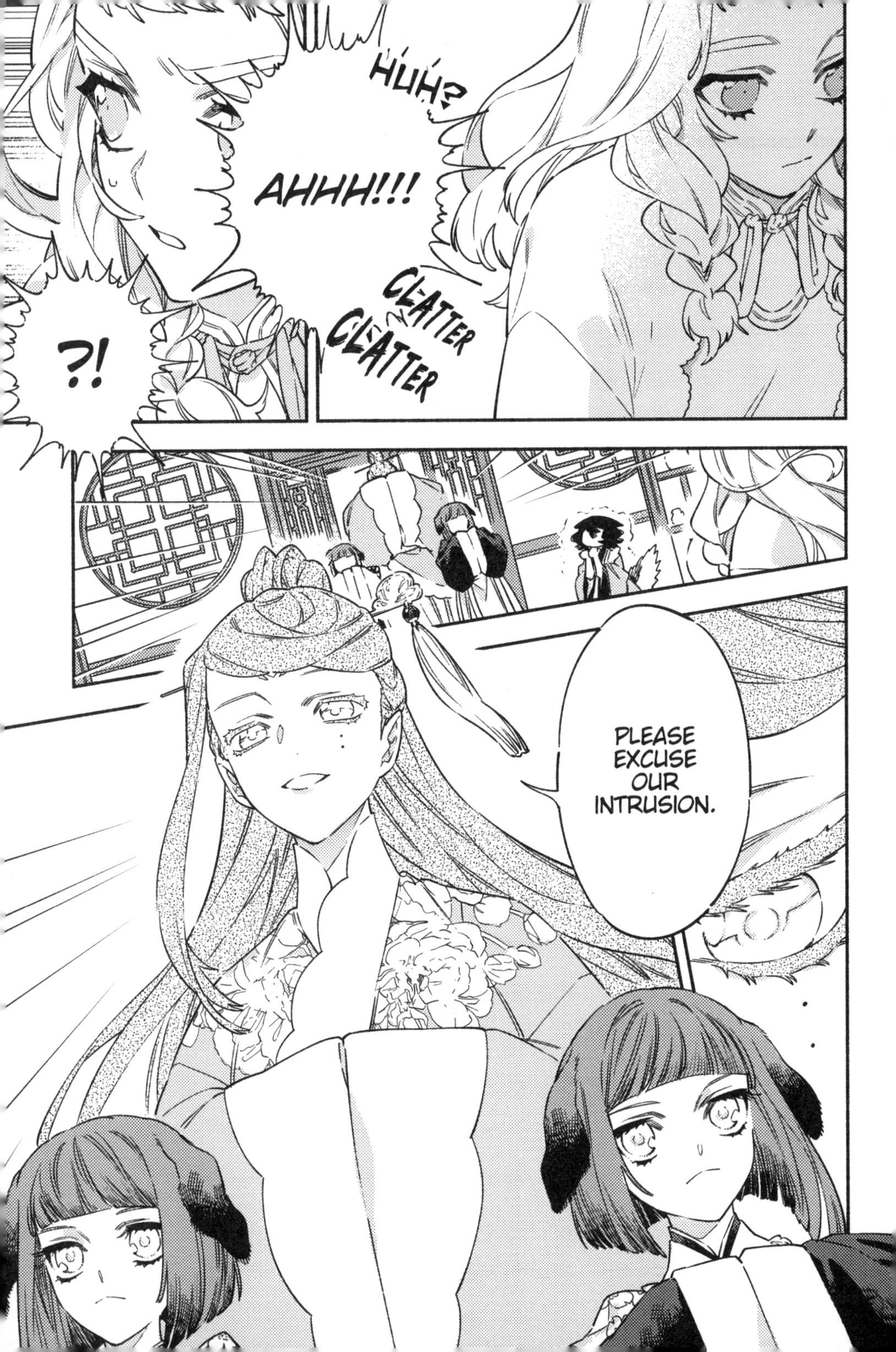
HUH?
AHHH!!!
CLATTER
CLATTER
?!
PLEASE EXCUSE OUR INTRUSION.

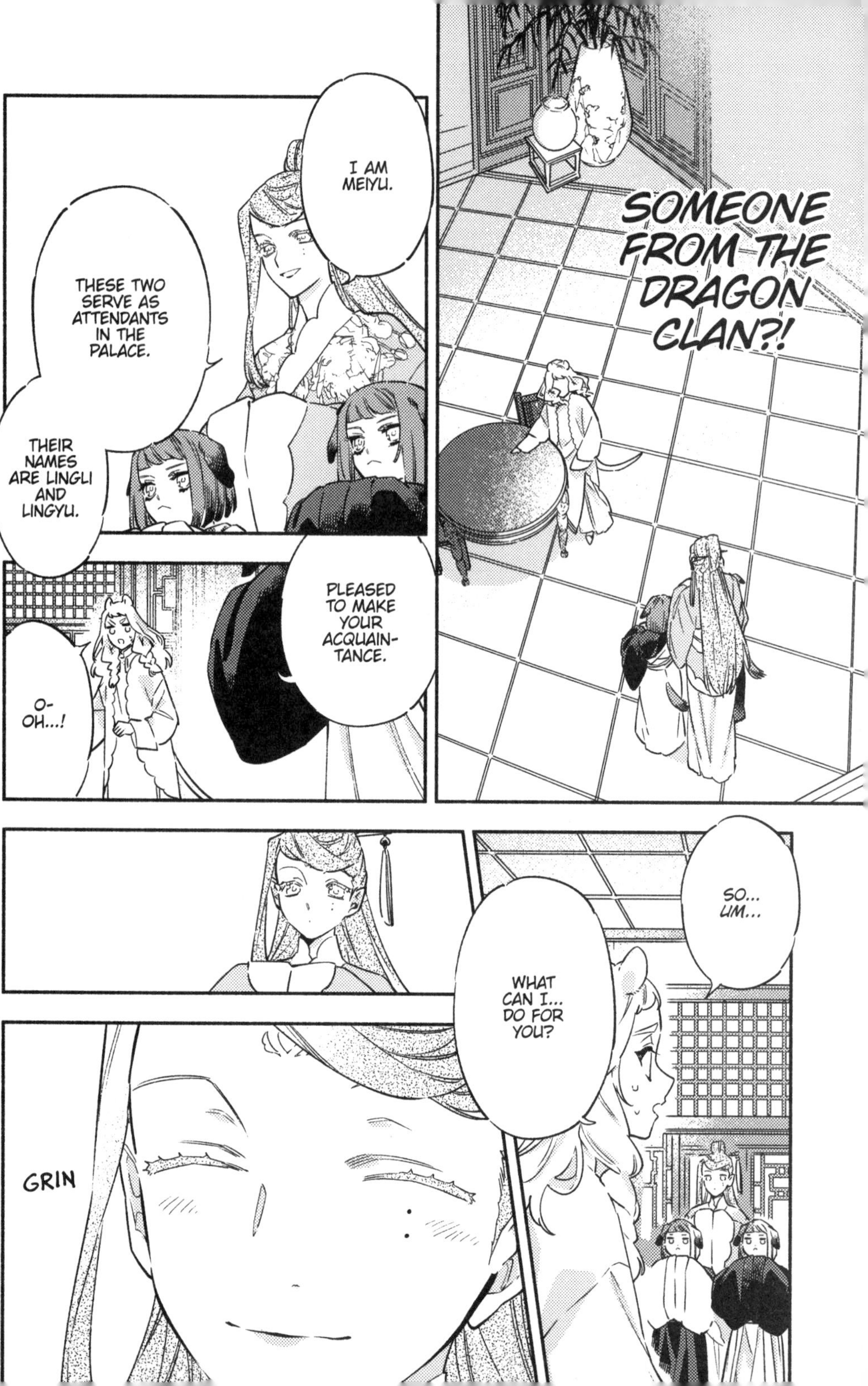
SOMEONE FROM THE DRAGON CLAN?!
I AM MEIYU.
THESE TWO SERVE AS ATTENDANTS IN THE PALACE.
THEIR NAMES ARE LINGLI AND LINGYU.
PLEASED TO MAKE YOUR ACQUAIN-TANCE.
O-OH...!
SO... UM...
WHAT CAN I... DO FOR YOU?
GRIN

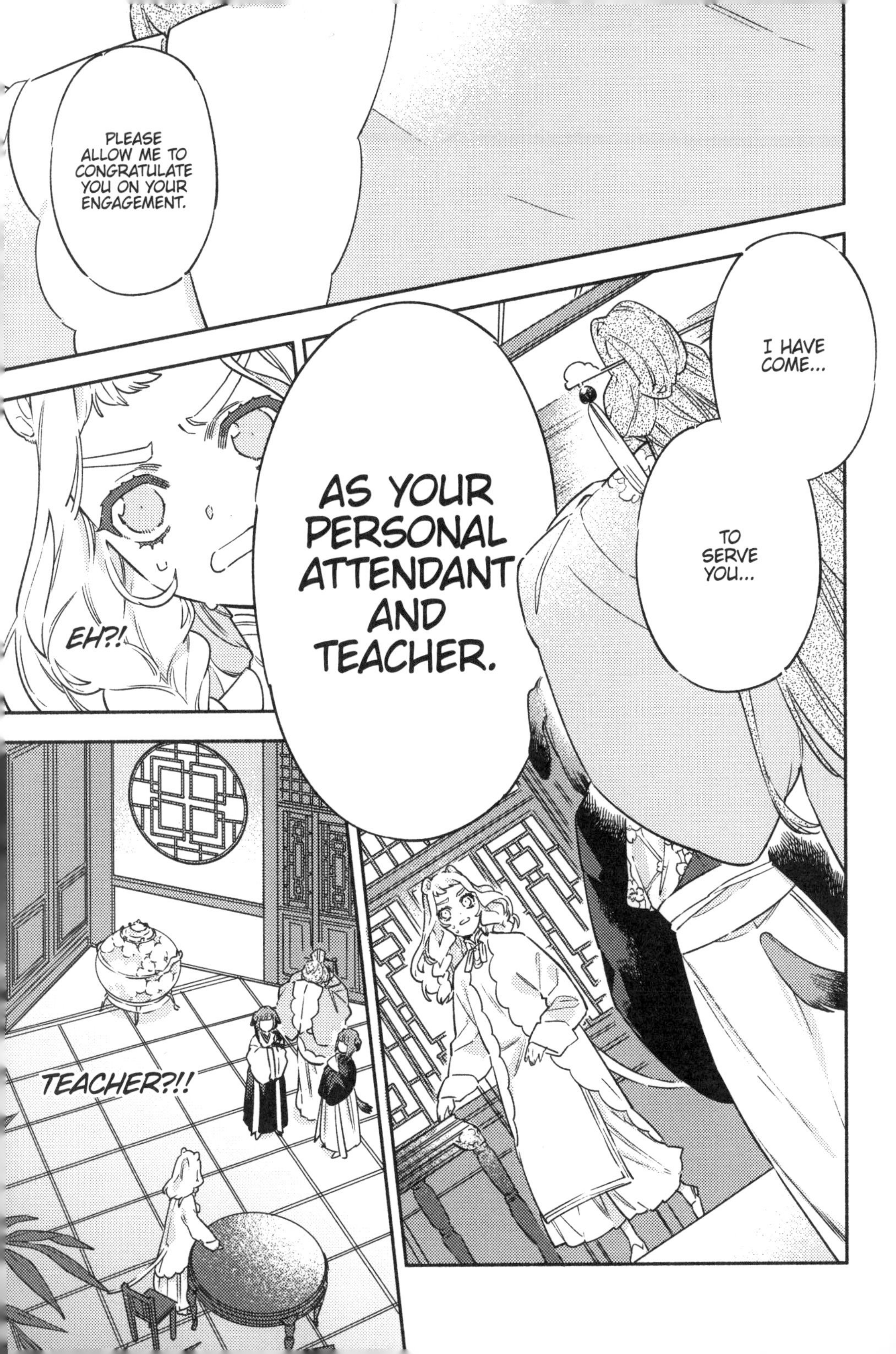
PLEASE ALLOW ME TO CONGRATULATE YOU ON YOUR ENGAGEMENT.
I HAVE COME...
TO SERVE YOU...
AS YOUR PERSONAL ATTENDANT AND TEACHER.
EH?!
TEACHER?!!

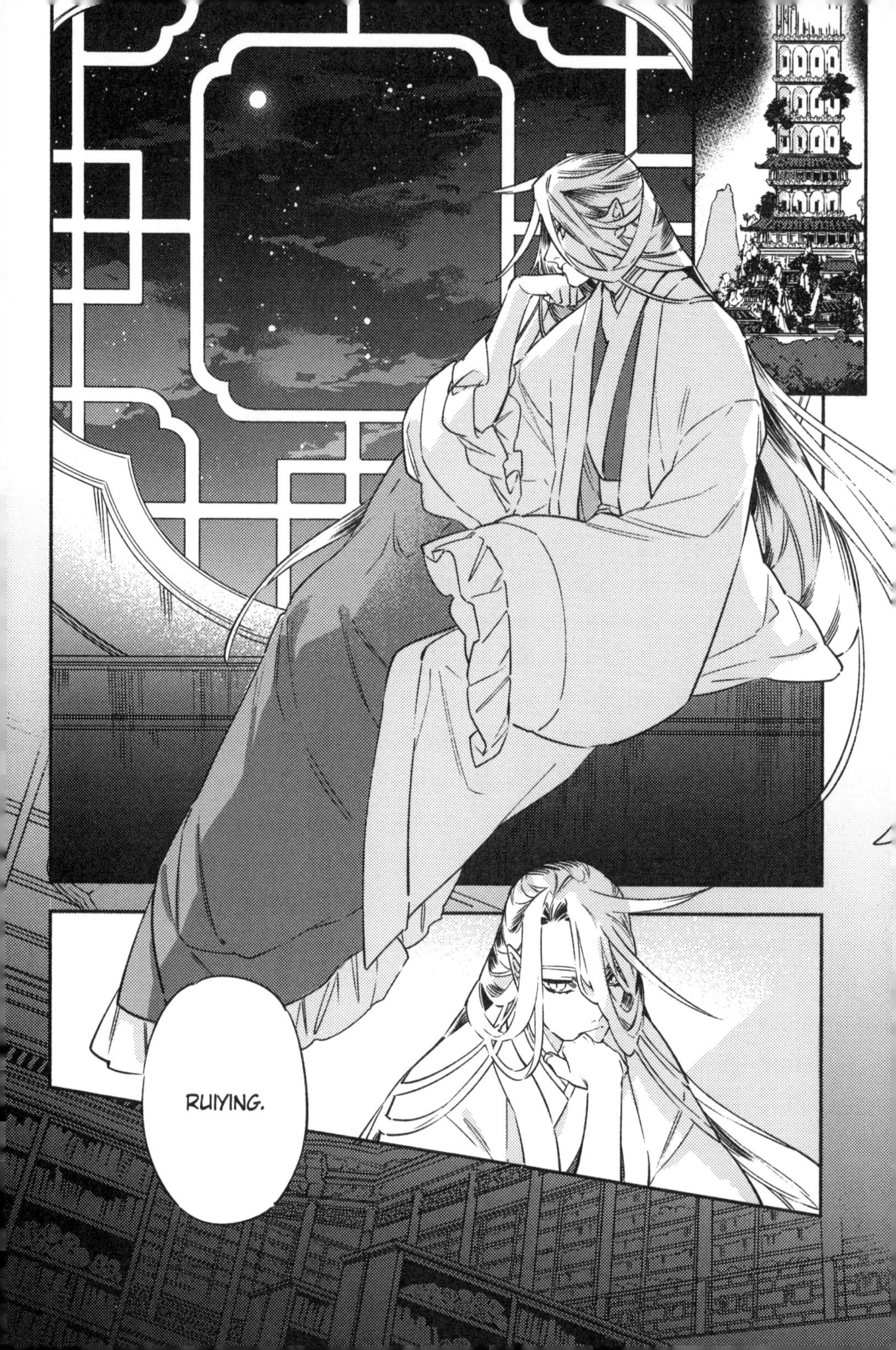
RUIYING.

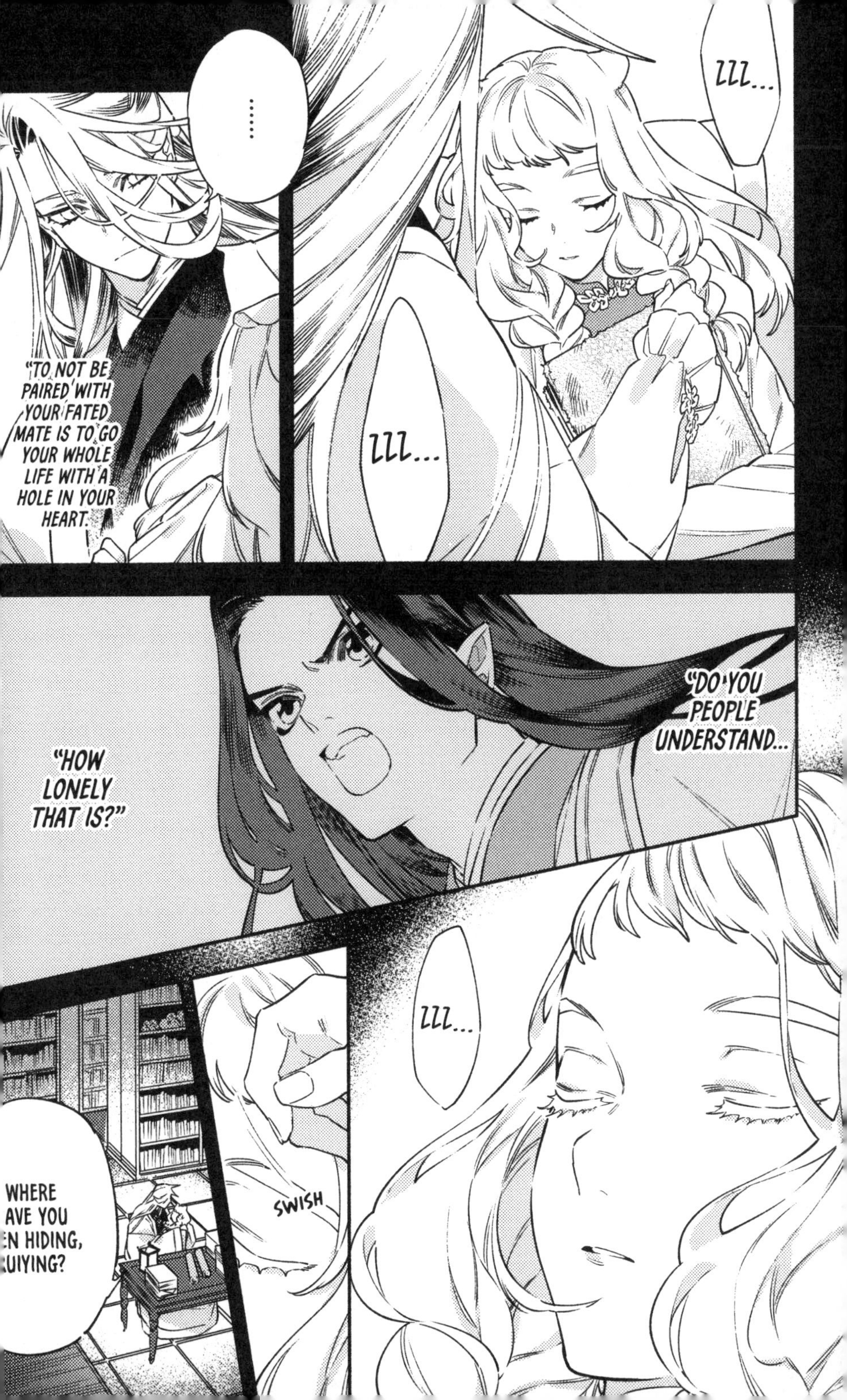
ZZZ...
ZZZ...
......
"TO NOT BE PAIRED WITH YOUR FATED MATE IS TO GO YOUR WHOLE LIFE WITH A HOLE IN YOUR HEART.
"DO YOU PEOPLE UNDERSTAND...
"HOW LONELY THAT IS?"
ZZZ...
SWISH
WHERE
AVE YOU
EN HIDING,
UIYING?

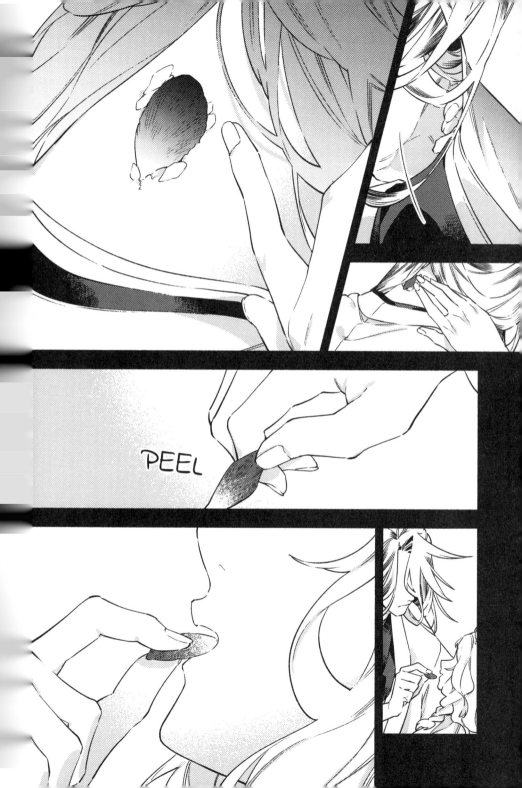

PEEL

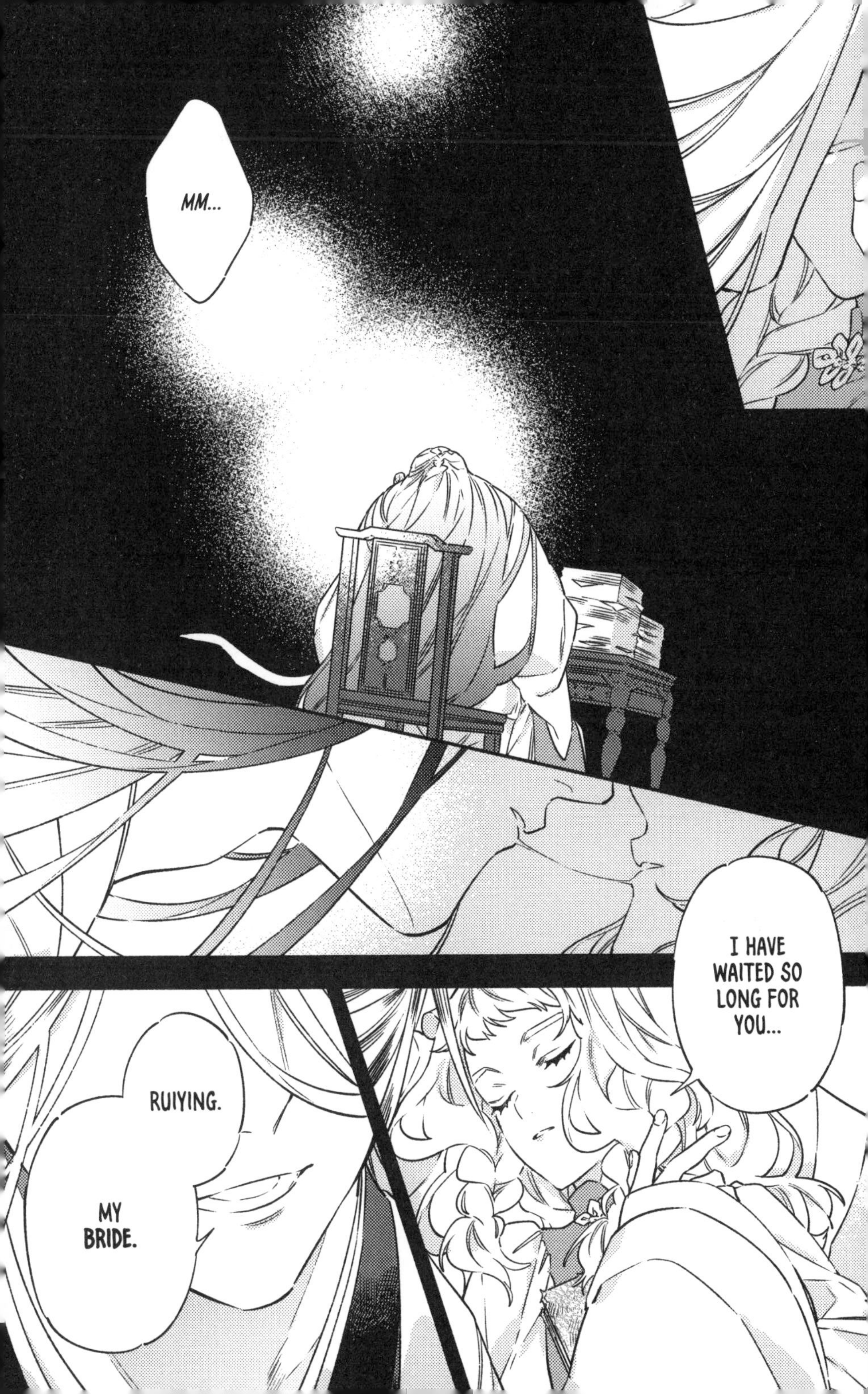
MM...
I HAVE WAITED SO LONG FOR YOU...
RUIYING.
MY BRIDE.

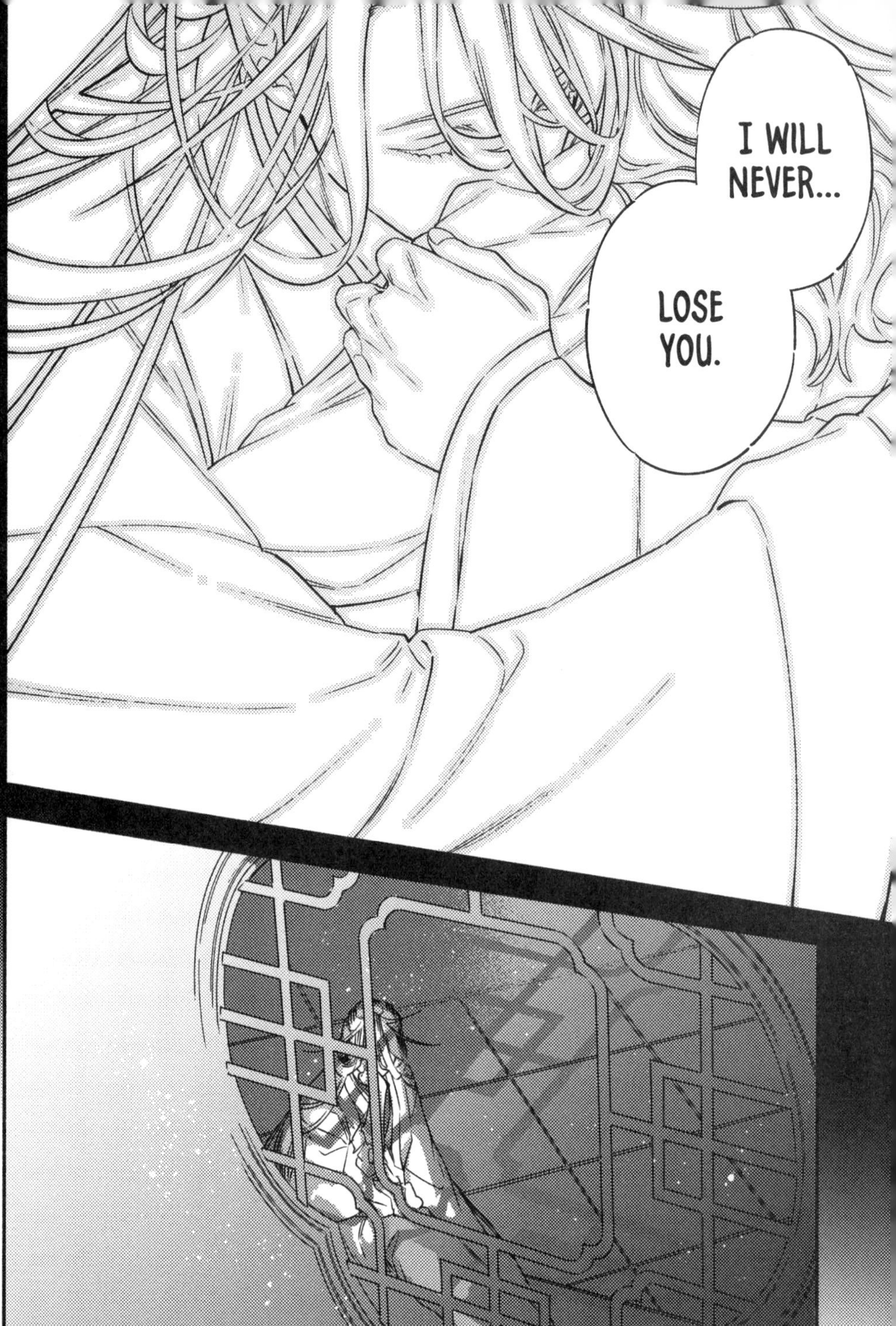
I WILL NEVER...
LOSE YOU.

THE DRAGON KING'S IMPERIAL WRATH

FALLING IN LOVE
WITH THE BOOKISH PRINCESS
OF THE RAT CLAN

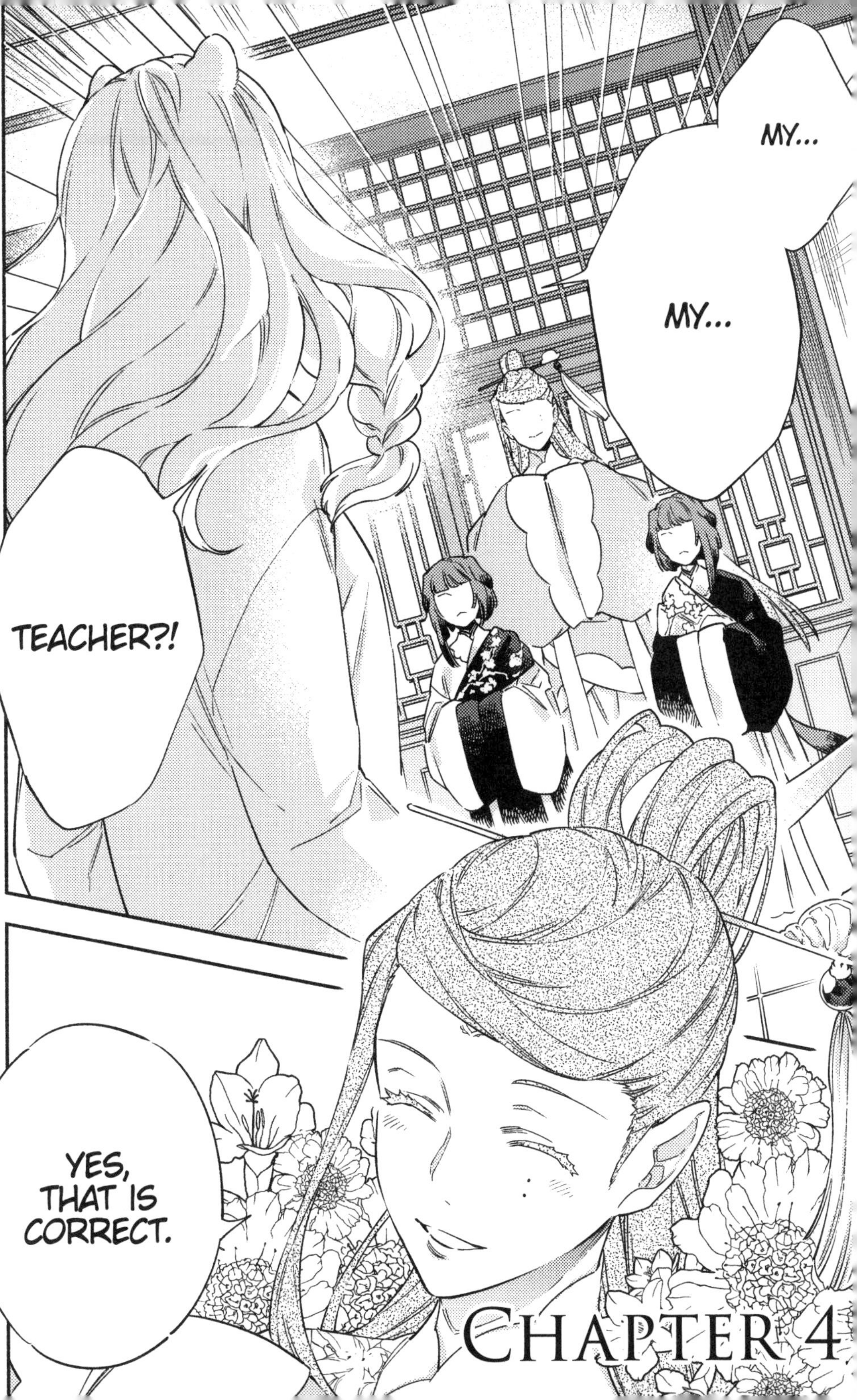
MY...
MY...
TEACHER?!
YES, THAT IS CORRECT.
CHAPTER 4

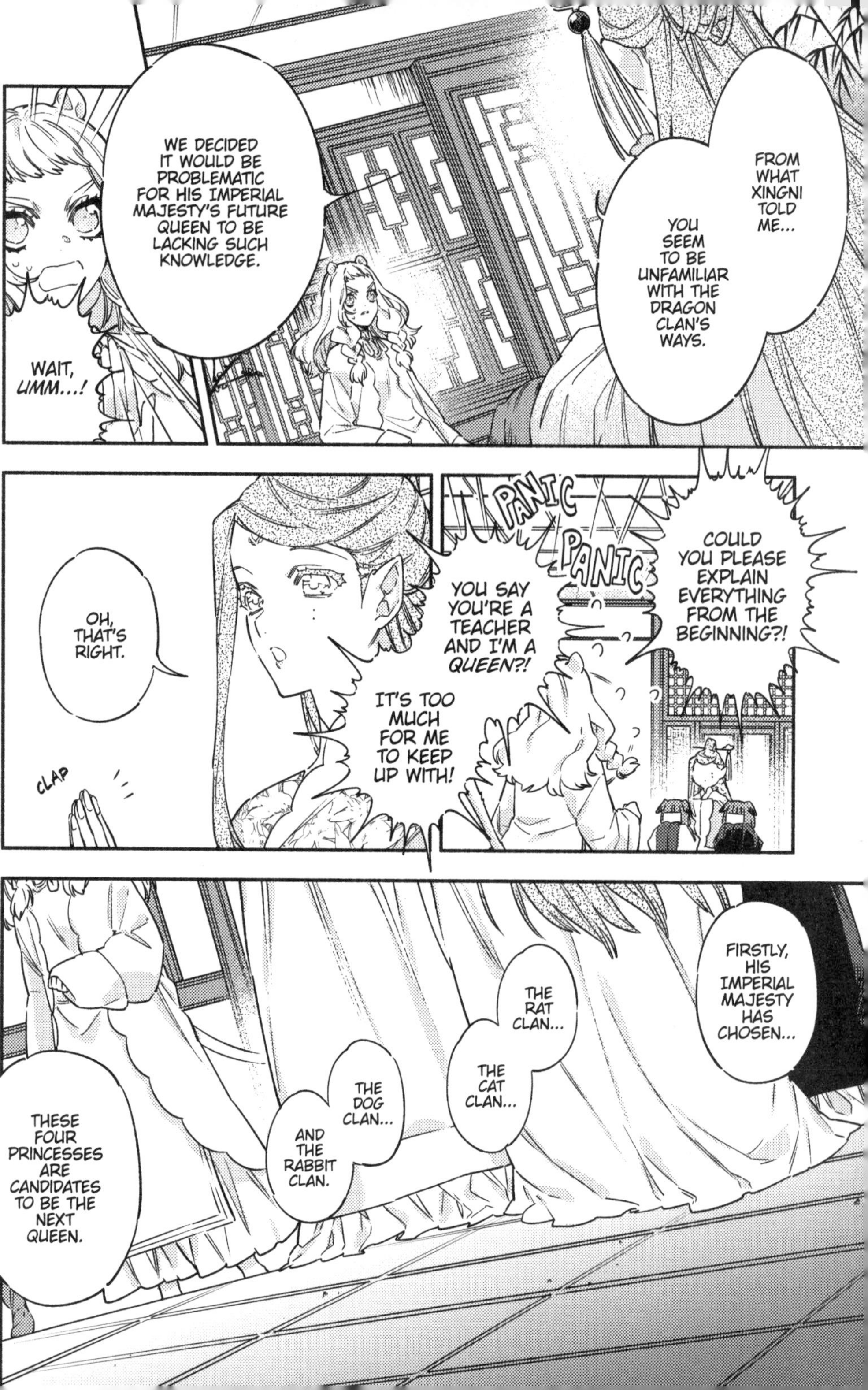
FROM WHAT XINGNI TOLD ME...
YOU SEEM TO BE UNFAMILIAR WITH THE DRAGON CLAN'S WAYS.
WE DECIDED IT WOULD BE PROBLEMATIC FOR HIS IMPERIAL MAJESTY'S FUTURE QUEEN TO BE LACKING SUCH KNOWLEDGE.
WAIT, UMM...!
PANIC
PANIC
COULD YOU PLEASE EXPLAIN EVERYTHING FROM THE BEGINNING?!
YOU SAY YOU'RE A TEACHER AND I'M A QUEEN?!
IT'S TOO MUCH FOR ME TO KEEP UP WITH!
OH, THAT'S RIGHT.
CLAP
FIRSTLY, HIS IMPERIAL MAJESTY HAS CHOSEN...
THE RAT CLAN...
THE CAT CLAN...
THE DOG CLAN...
AND THE RABBIT CLAN.
THESE FOUR PRINCESSES ARE CANDIDATES TO BE THE NEXT QUEEN.

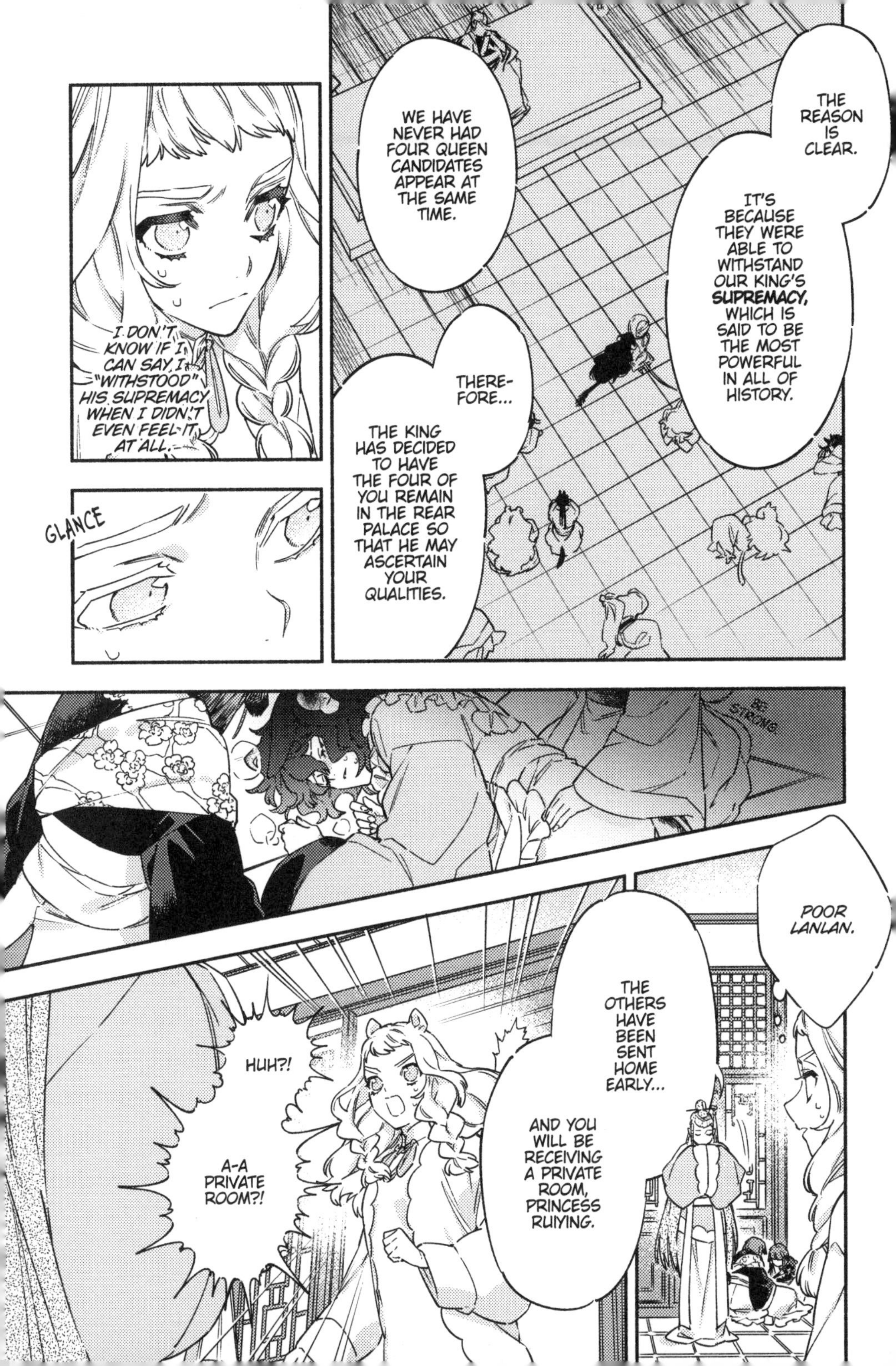
THE REASON IS CLEAR.
IT'S BECAUSE THEY WERE ABLE TO WITHSTAND OUR KING'S **SUPREMACY,** WHICH IS SAID TO BE THE MOST POWERFUL IN ALL OF HISTORY.
WE HAVE NEVER HAD FOUR QUEEN CANDIDATES APPEAR AT THE SAME TIME.
THERE-FORE...
THE KING HAS DECIDED TO HAVE THE FOUR OF YOU REMAIN IN THE REAR PALACE SO THAT HE MAY ASCERTAIN YOUR QUALITIES.
I DON'T KNOW IF I CAN SAY I "WITHSTOOD" HIS SUPREMACY WHEN I DIDN'T EVEN FEEL IT AT ALL.
GLANCE
BE STRONG.
POOR LANLAN.
THE OTHERS HAVE BEEN SENT HOME EARLY...
AND YOU WILL BE RECEIVING A PRIVATE ROOM, PRINCESS RUIYING.
HUH?!
A-A PRIVATE ROOM?!

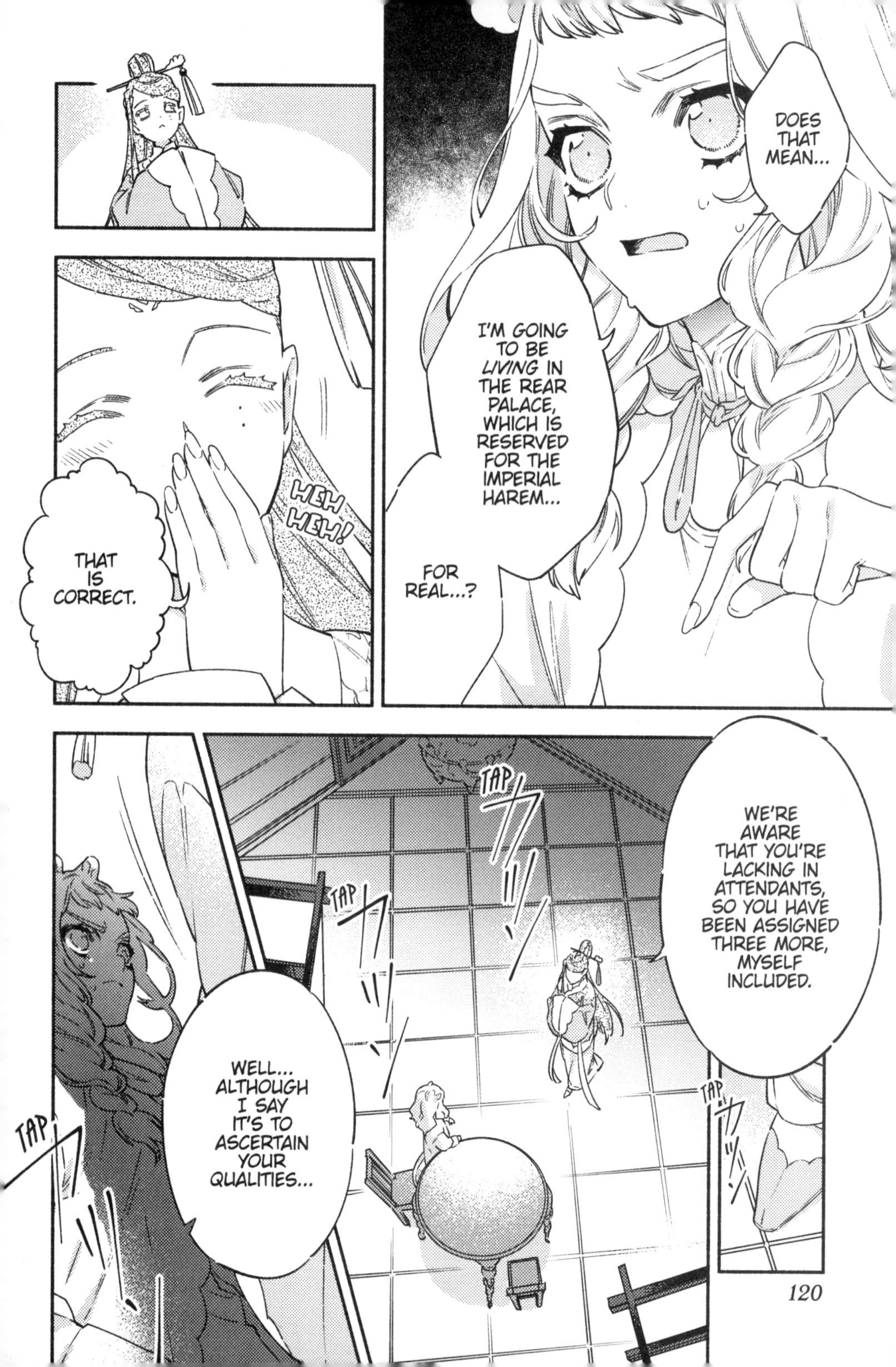
DOES THAT MEAN...
I'M GOING TO BE *LIVING* IN THE REAR PALACE, WHICH IS RESERVED FOR THE IMPERIAL HAREM...
FOR REAL...?
HEH HEH!
THAT IS CORRECT.
WE'RE AWARE THAT YOU'RE LACKING IN ATTENDANTS, SO YOU HAVE BEEN ASSIGNED THREE MORE, MYSELF INCLUDED.
TAP
TAP
TAP
WELL... ALTHOUGH I SAY IT'S TO ASCERTAIN YOUR QUALITIES...
TAP

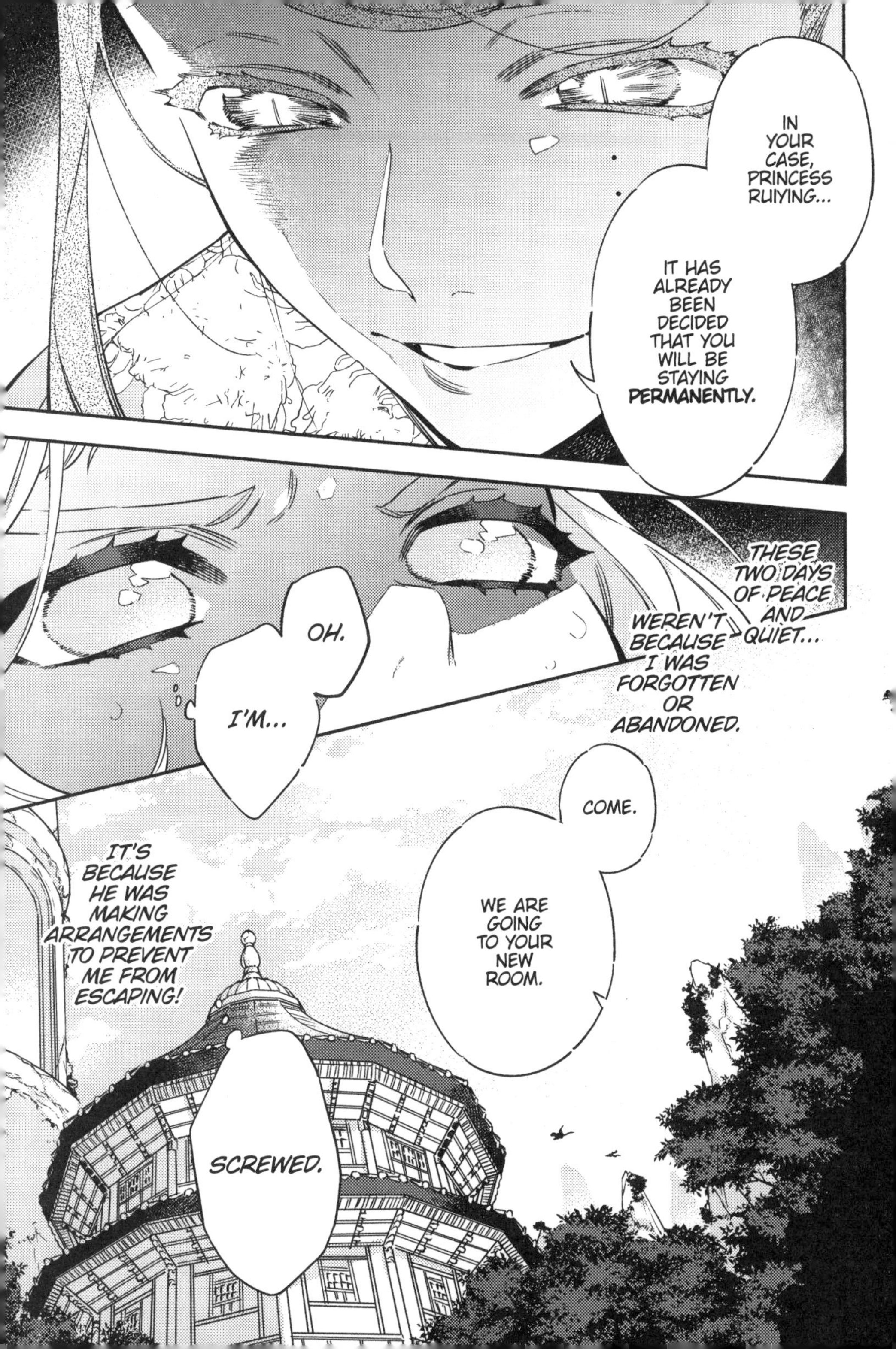
IN YOUR CASE, PRINCESS RUIYING...
IT HAS ALREADY BEEN DECIDED THAT YOU WILL BE STAYING **PERMANENTLY.**
THESE TWO DAYS OF PEACE AND QUIET...
WEREN'T BECAUSE I WAS FORGOTTEN OR ABANDONED.
OH.
I'M...
COME.
WE ARE GOING TO YOUR NEW ROOM.
IT'S BECAUSE HE WAS MAKING ARRANGEMENTS TO PREVENT ME FROM ESCAPING!
SCREWED.

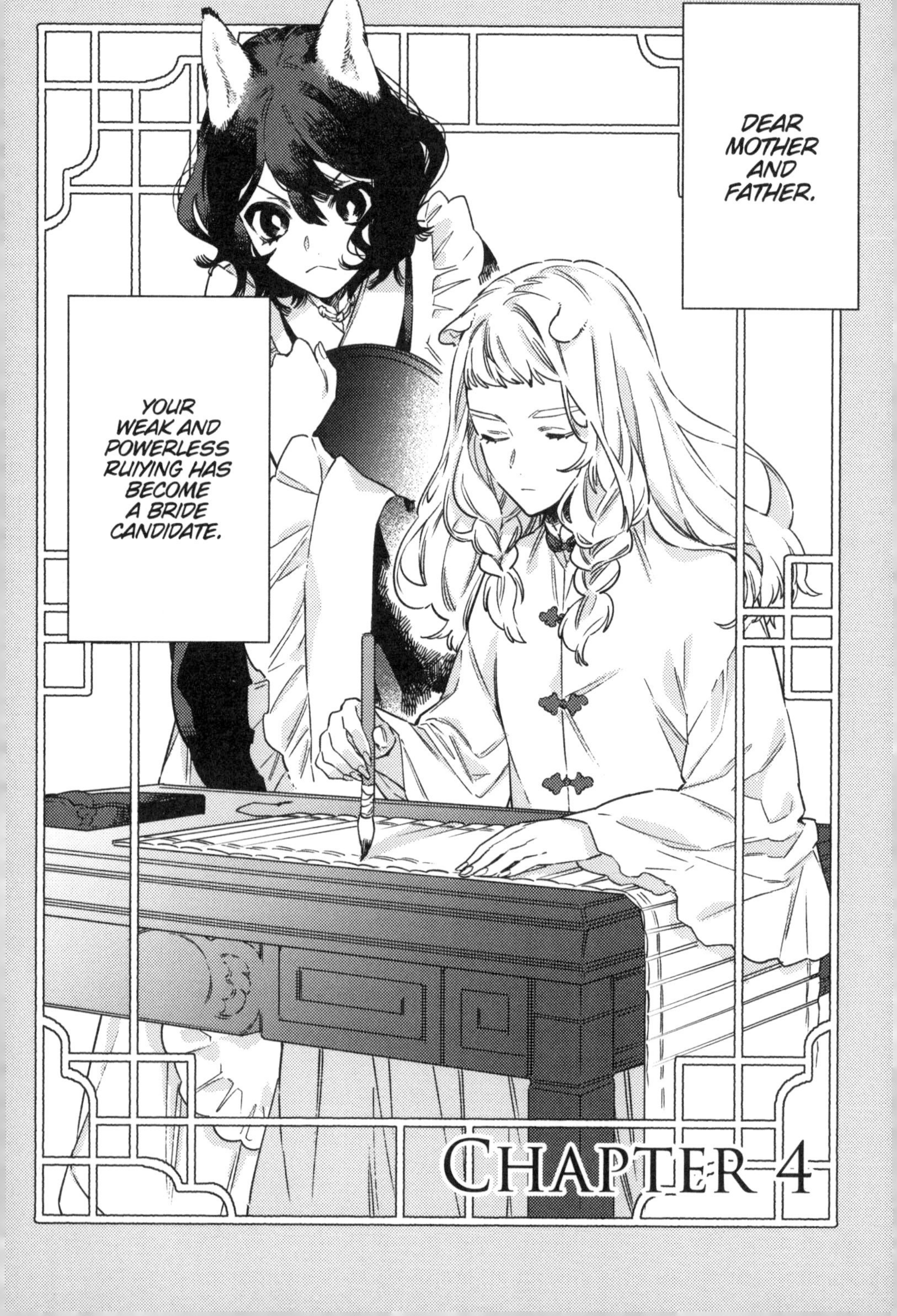
DEAR MOTHER AND FATHER.
YOUR WEAK AND POWERLESS RUIYING HAS BECOME A BRIDE CANDIDATE.
CHAPTER 4

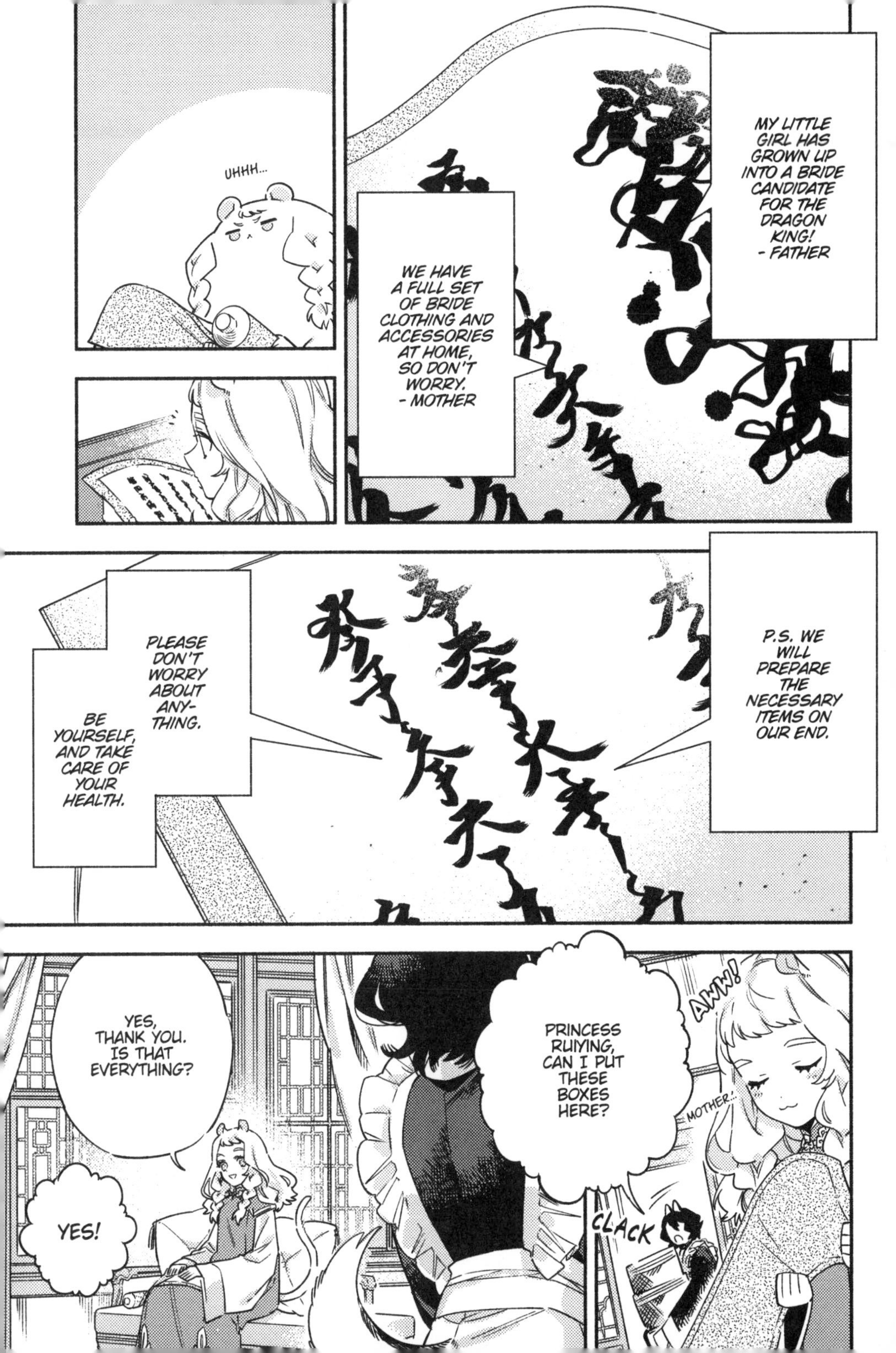
MY LITTLE GIRL HAS GROWN UP INTO A BRIDE CANDIDATE FOR THE DRAGON KING! - FATHER
WE HAVE A FULL SET OF BRIDE CLOTHING AND ACCESSORIES AT HOME, SO DON'T WORRY. - MOTHER
UHHH...
P.S. WE WILL PREPARE THE NECESSARY ITEMS ON OUR END.
PLEASE DON'T WORRY ABOUT ANY-THING.
BE YOURSELF, AND TAKE CARE OF YOUR HEALTH.
AWW!
MOTHER...
CLACK
PRINCESS RUIYING, CAN I PUT THESE BOXES HERE?
YES, THANK YOU. IS THAT EVERYTHING?
YES!

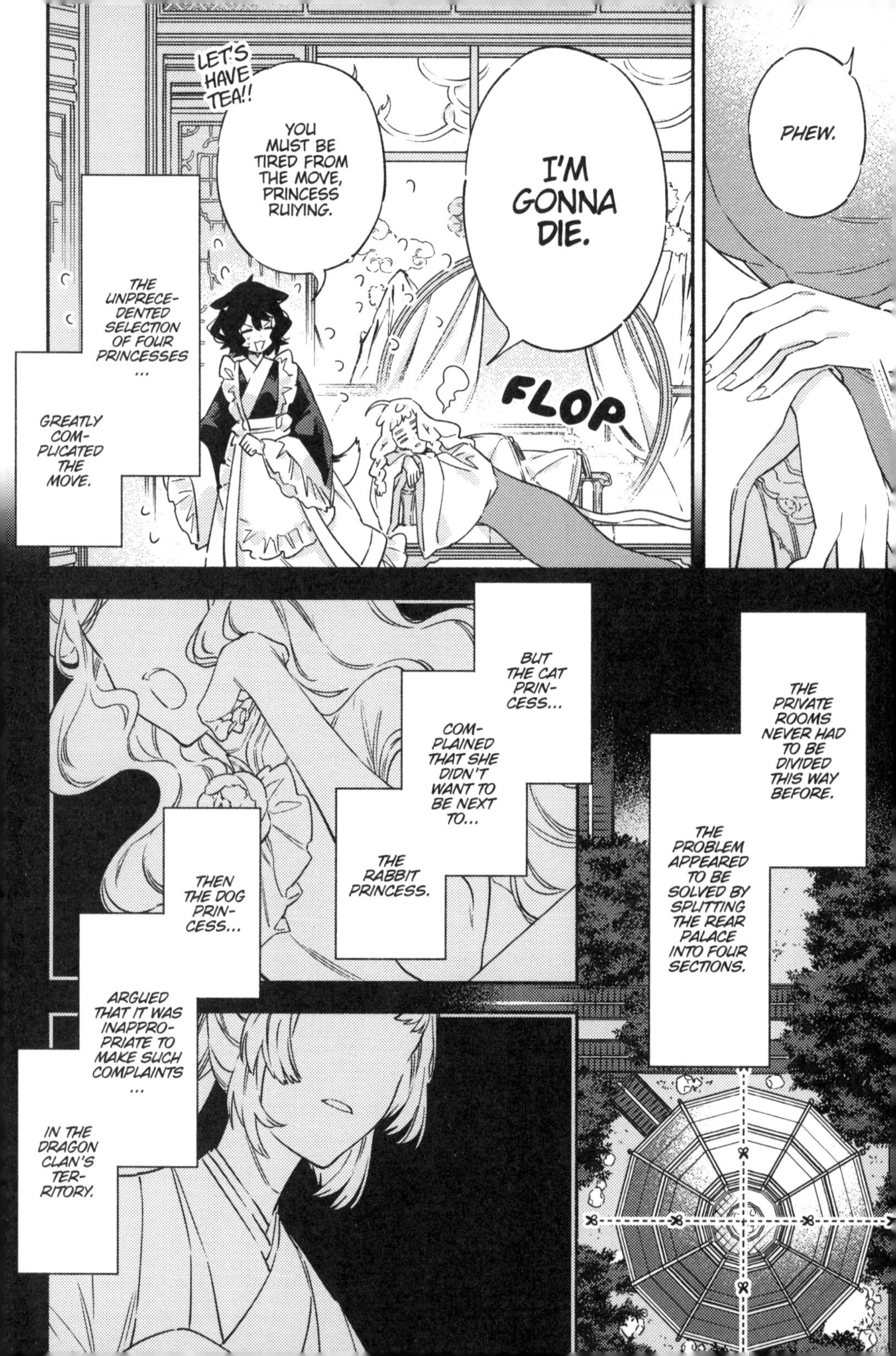
PHEW.
I'M GONNA DIE.
YOU MUST BE TIRED FROM THE MOVE, PRINCESS RUIYING.
LET'S HAVE TEA!!
FLOP
THE UNPRECEDENTED SELECTION OF FOUR PRINCESSES...
GREATLY COMPLICATED THE MOVE.
THE PRIVATE ROOMS NEVER HAD TO BE DIVIDED THIS WAY BEFORE.
THE PROBLEM APPEARED TO BE SOLVED BY SPLITTING THE REAR PALACE INTO FOUR SECTIONS.
BUT THE CAT PRINCESS...
COMPLAINED THAT SHE DIDN'T WANT TO BE NEXT TO...
THE RABBIT PRINCESS.
THEN THE DOG PRINCESS...
ARGUED THAT IT WAS INAPPROPRIATE TO MAKE SUCH COMPLAINTS...
IN THE DRAGON CLAN'S TERRITORY.

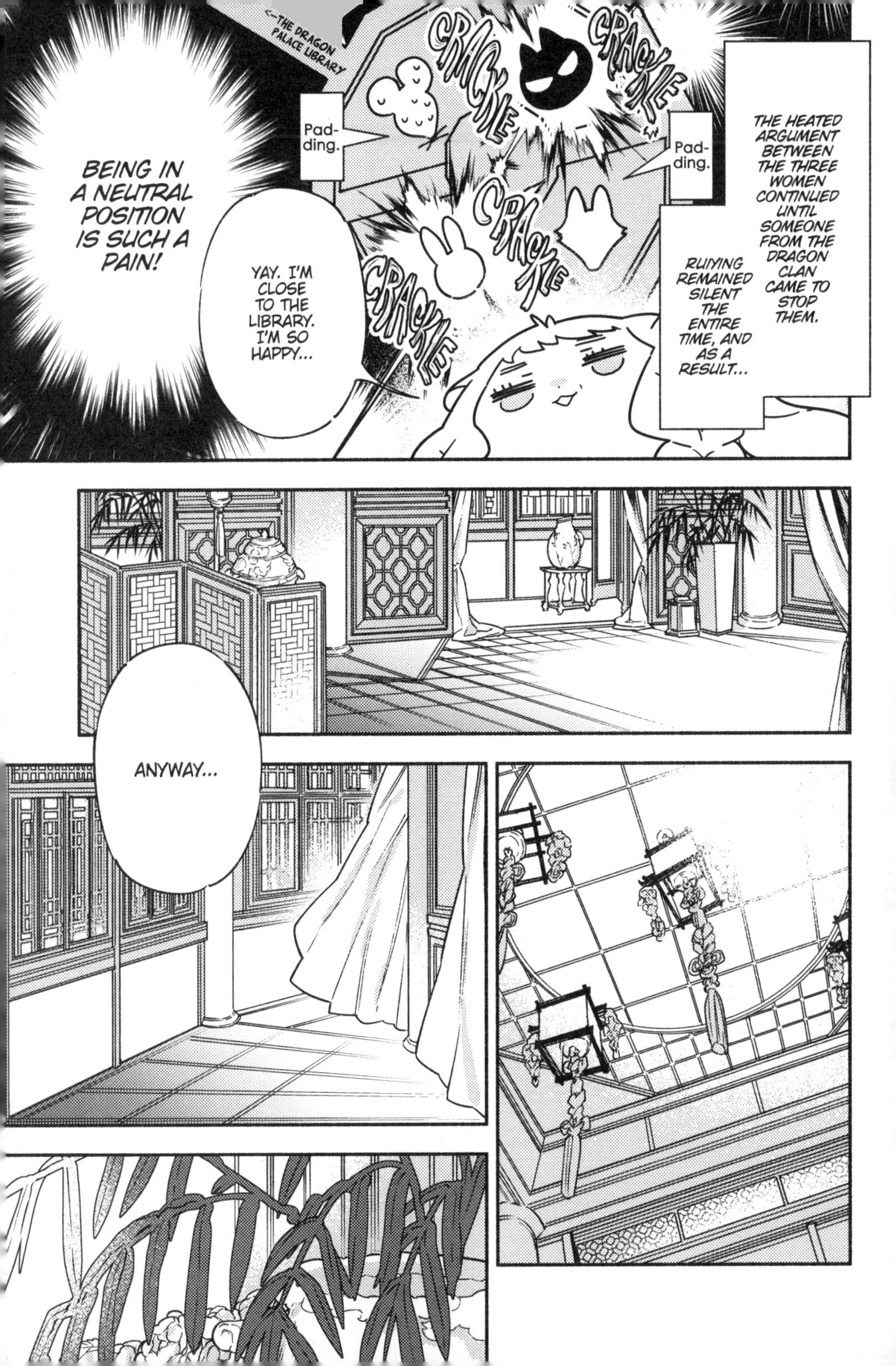

THE HEATED ARGUMENT BETWEEN THE THREE WOMEN CONTINUED UNTIL SOMEONE FROM THE DRAGON CLAN CAME TO STOP THEM.
RUIYING REMAINED SILENT THE ENTIRE TIME, AND AS A RESULT...
Pad-ding.
CRACKLE
CRACKLE
CRACKLE
CRACKLE
CRACKLE
Pad-ding.
<--THE DRAGON PALACE LIBRARY
YAY. I'M CLOSE TO THE LIBRARY. I'M SO HAPPY...
BEING IN A NEUTRAL POSITION IS SUCH A PAIN!
ANYWAY...

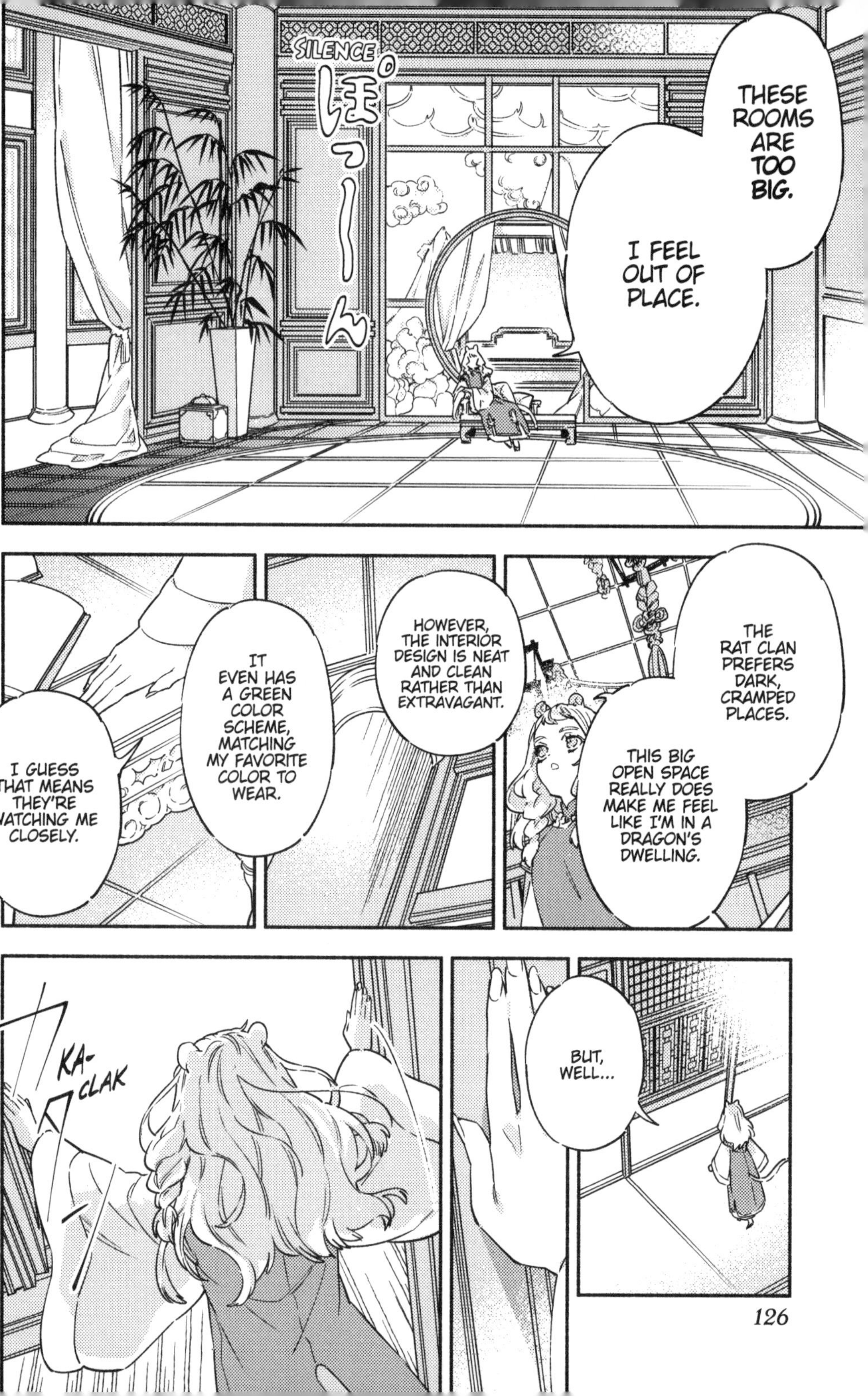
THESE ROOMS ARE TOO BIG.
I FEEL OUT OF PLACE.
SILENCE
ぽっーん
THE RAT CLAN PREFERS DARK, CRAMPED PLACES.
THIS BIG OPEN SPACE REALLY DOES MAKE ME FEEL LIKE I'M IN A DRAGON'S DWELLING.
HOWEVER, THE INTERIOR DESIGN IS NEAT AND CLEAN RATHER THAN EXTRAVAGANT.
IT EVEN HAS A GREEN COLOR SCHEME, MATCHING MY FAVORITE COLOR TO WEAR.
I GUESS THAT MEANS THEY'RE WATCHING ME CLOSELY.
BUT, WELL...
KA-CLAK

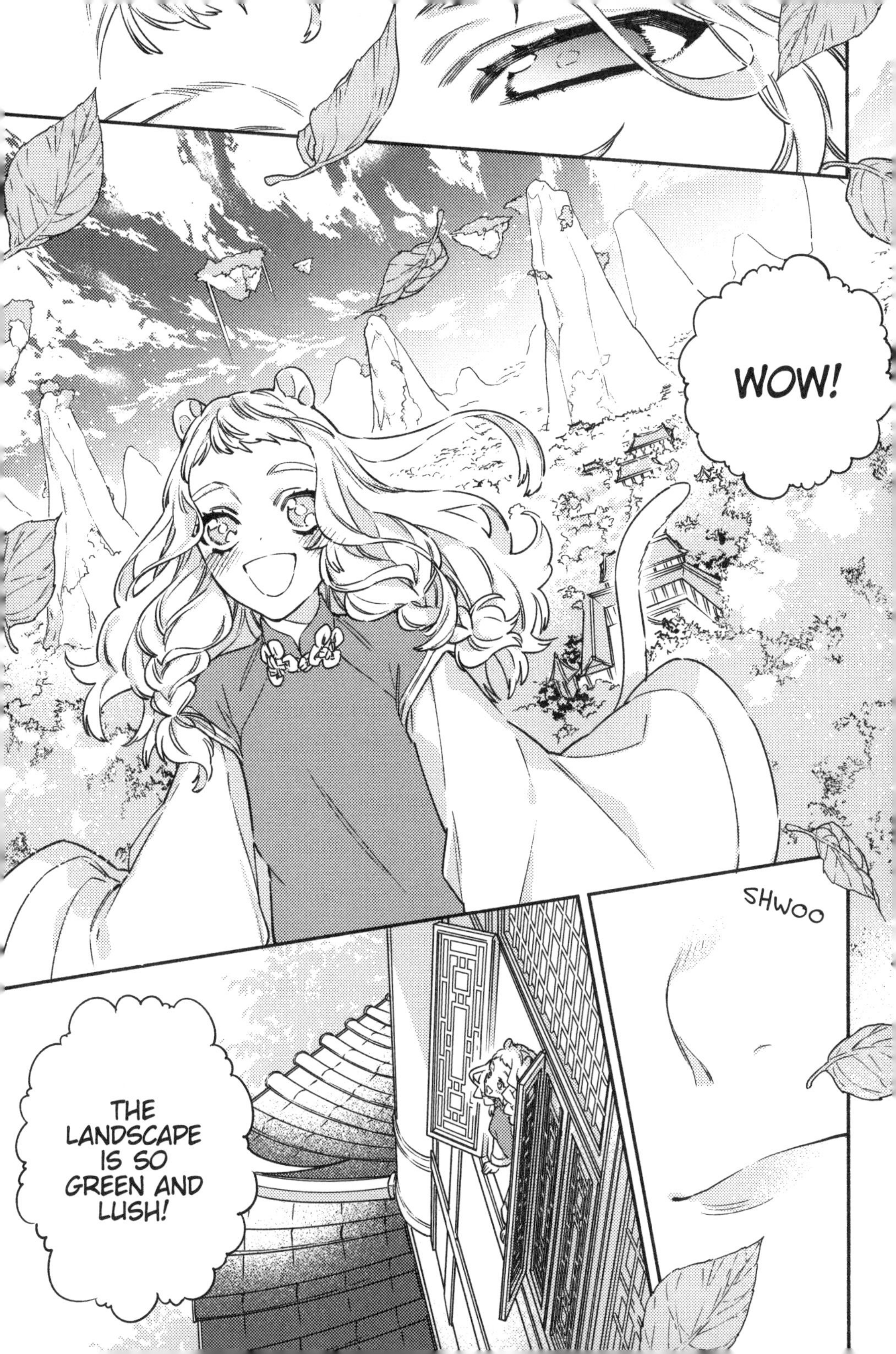
WOW!
SHWOO
THE LANDSCAPE IS SO GREEN AND LUSH!

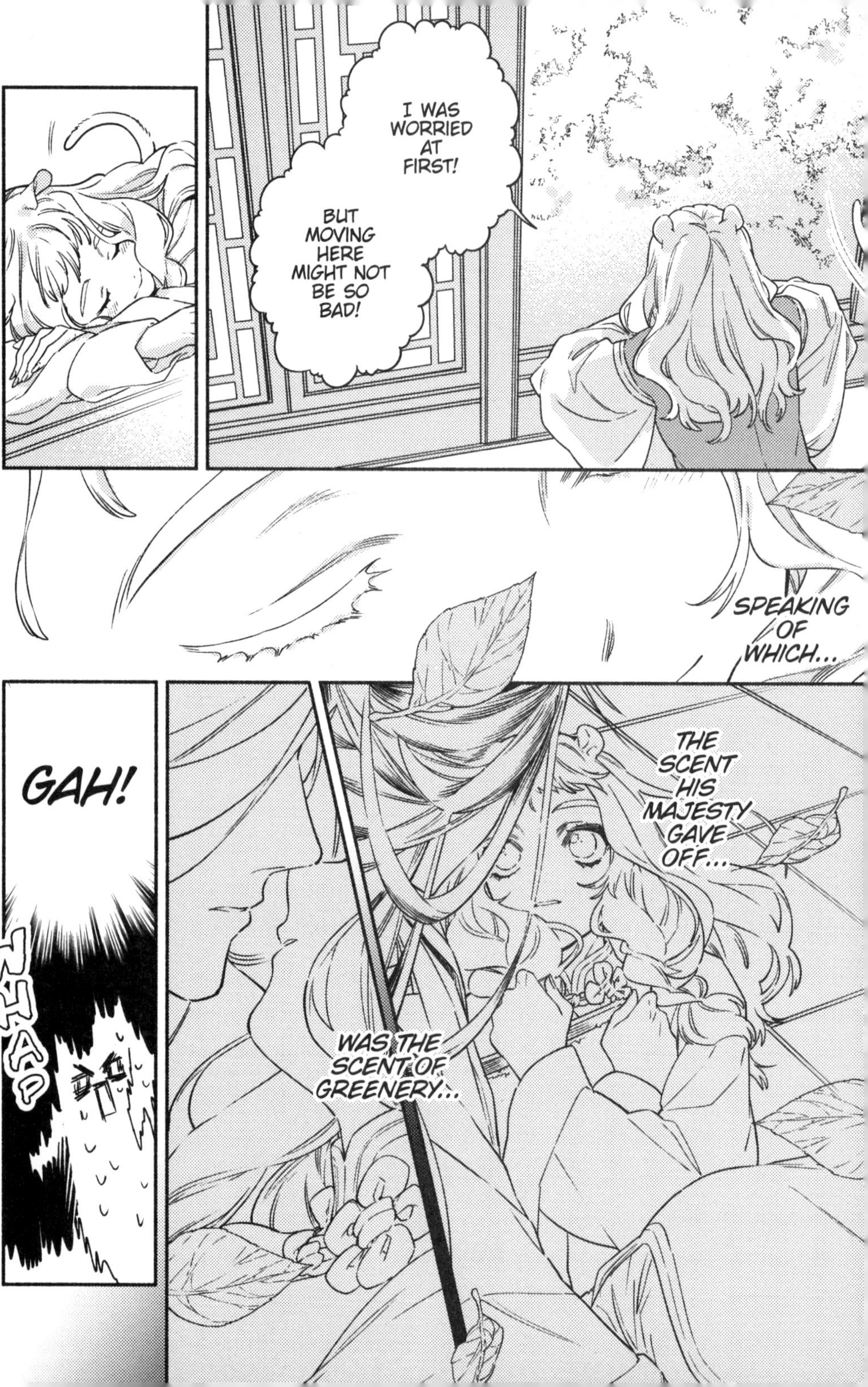
I WAS WORRIED AT FIRST!
BUT MOVING HERE MIGHT NOT BE SO BAD!
SPEAKING OF WHICH...
THE SCENT HIS MAJESTY GAVE OFF...
WAS THE SCENT OF GREENERY...
GAH!
WHAP

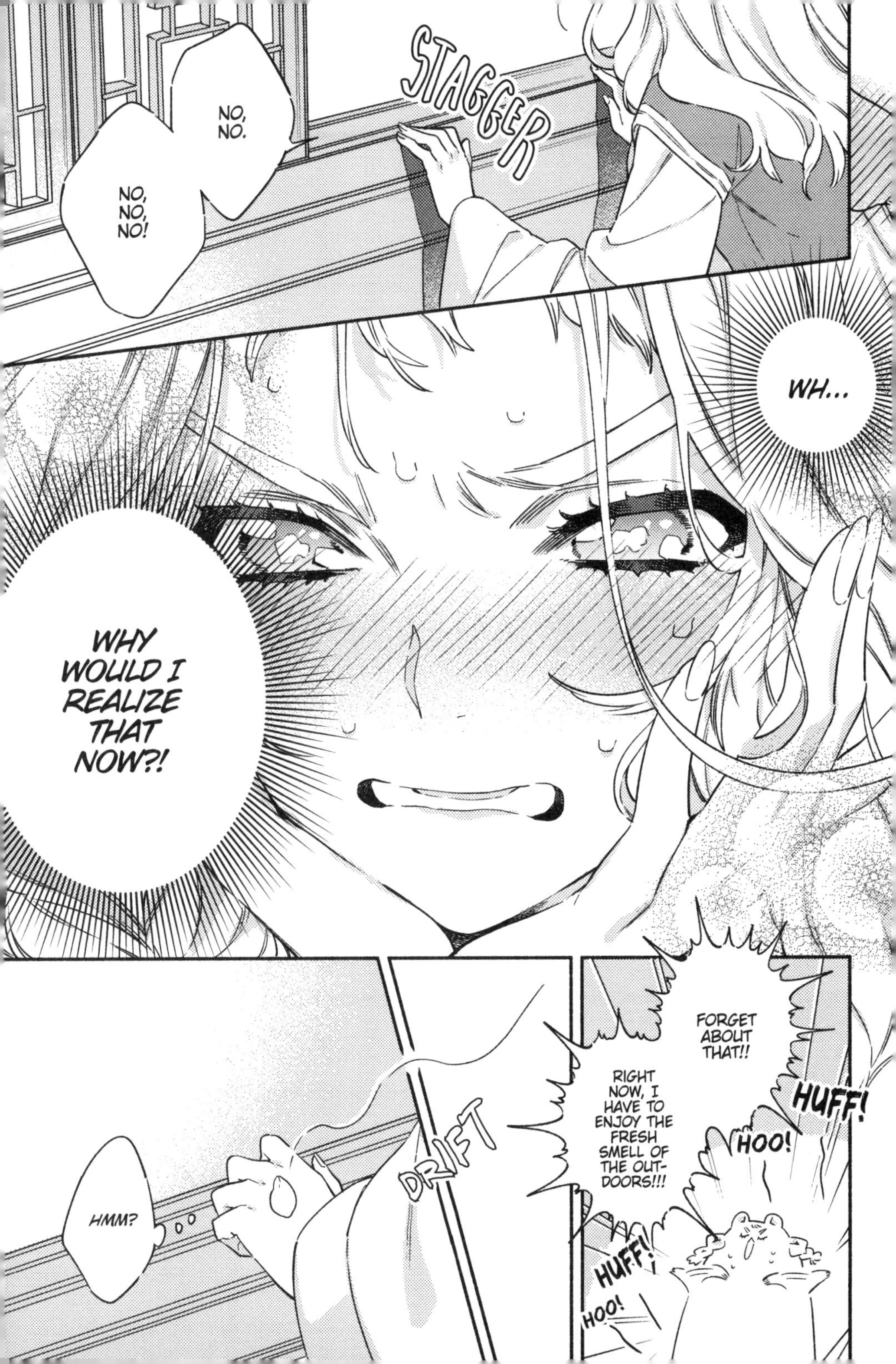
STAGGER
NO, NO.
NO, NO, NO!
WH...
WHY WOULD I REALIZE THAT NOW?!
FORGET ABOUT THAT!!
RIGHT NOW, I HAVE TO ENJOY THE FRESH SMELL OF THE OUT-DOORS!!!
HUFF!
HOO!
HUFF!
HOO!
DRIFT
HMM?

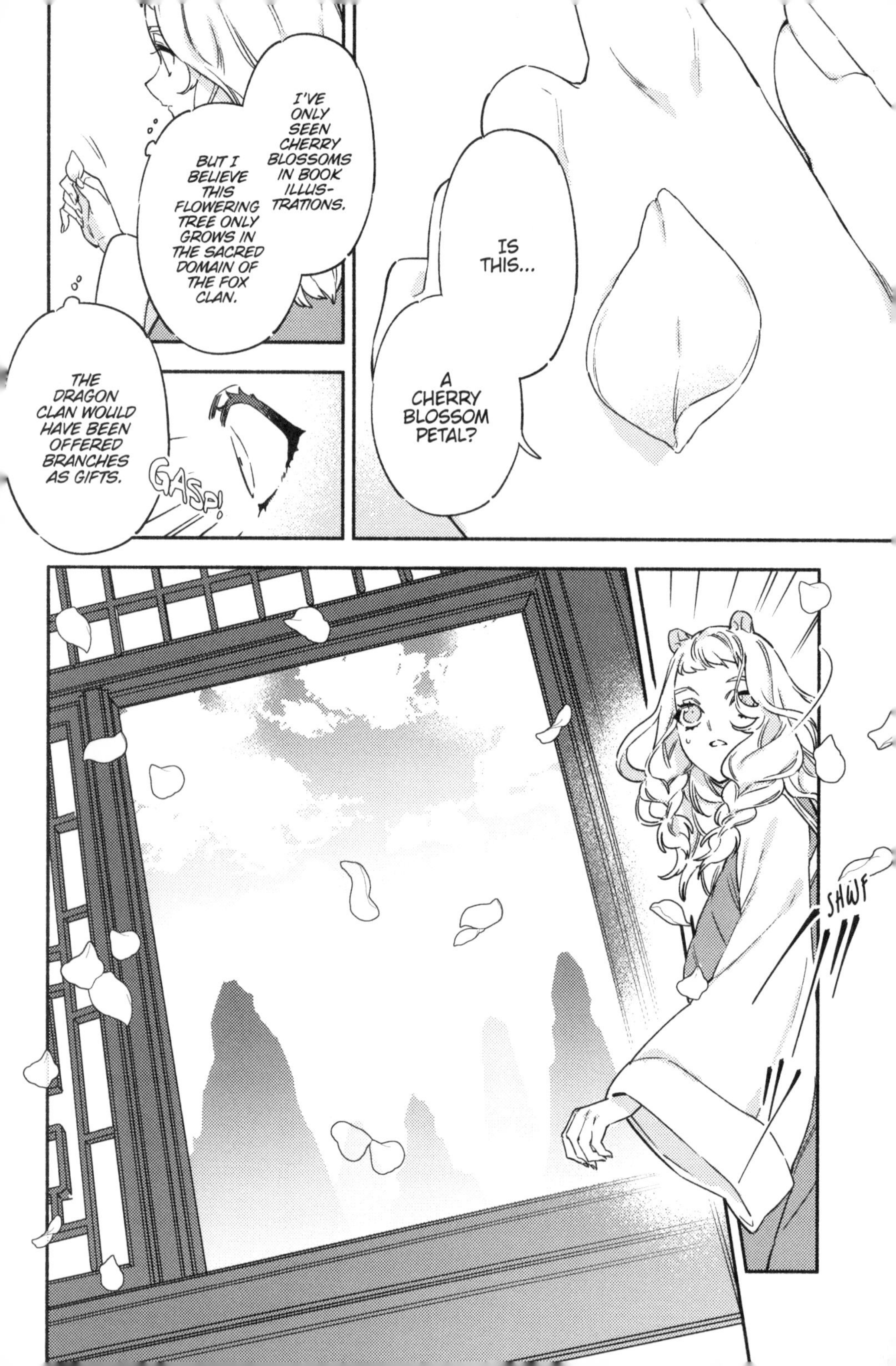
IS THIS...
A CHERRY BLOSSOM PETAL?
I'VE ONLY SEEN CHERRY BLOSSOMS IN BOOK ILLUS-TRATIONS.
BUT I BELIEVE THIS FLOWERING TREE ONLY GROWS IN THE SACRED DOMAIN OF THE FOX CLAN.
THE DRAGON CLAN WOULD HAVE BEEN OFFERED BRANCHES AS GIFTS.
GASP!
SHWF

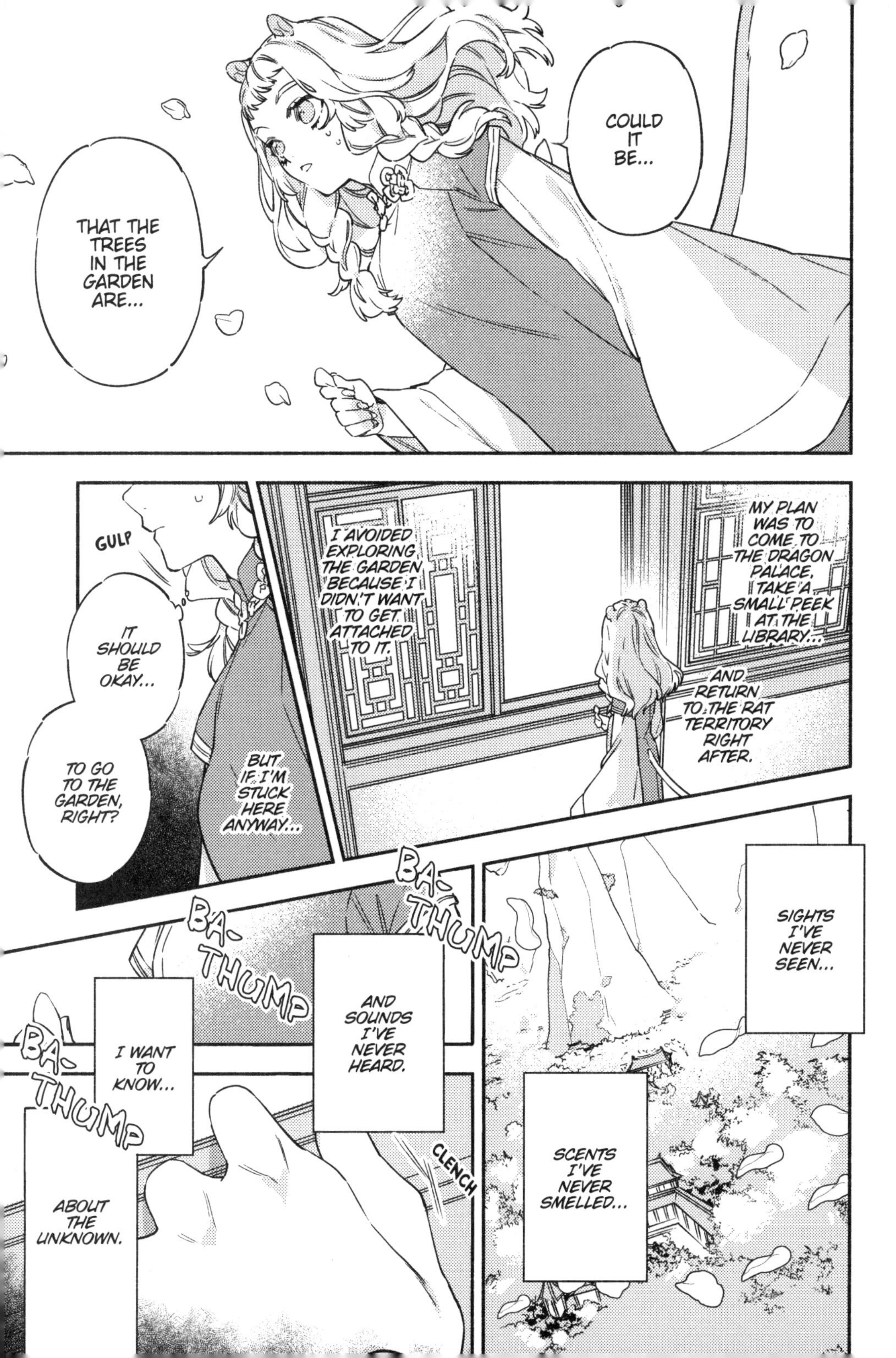
COULD IT BE...
THAT THE TREES IN THE GARDEN ARE...
MY PLAN WAS TO COME TO THE DRAGON PALACE, TAKE A SMALL PEEK AT THE LIBRARY...
AND RETURN TO THE RAT TERRITORY RIGHT AFTER.
I AVOIDED EXPLORING THE GARDEN BECAUSE I DIDN'T WANT TO GET ATTACHED TO IT.
GULP
BUT IF I'M STUCK HERE ANYWAY...
IT SHOULD BE OKAY...
TO GO TO THE GARDEN, RIGHT?
SIGHTS I'VE NEVER SEEN...
SCENTS I'VE NEVER SMELLED...
BA-THUMP
AND SOUNDS I'VE NEVER HEARD.
BA-THUMP
I WANT TO KNOW...
BA-THUMP
CLENCH
ABOUT THE UNKNOWN.

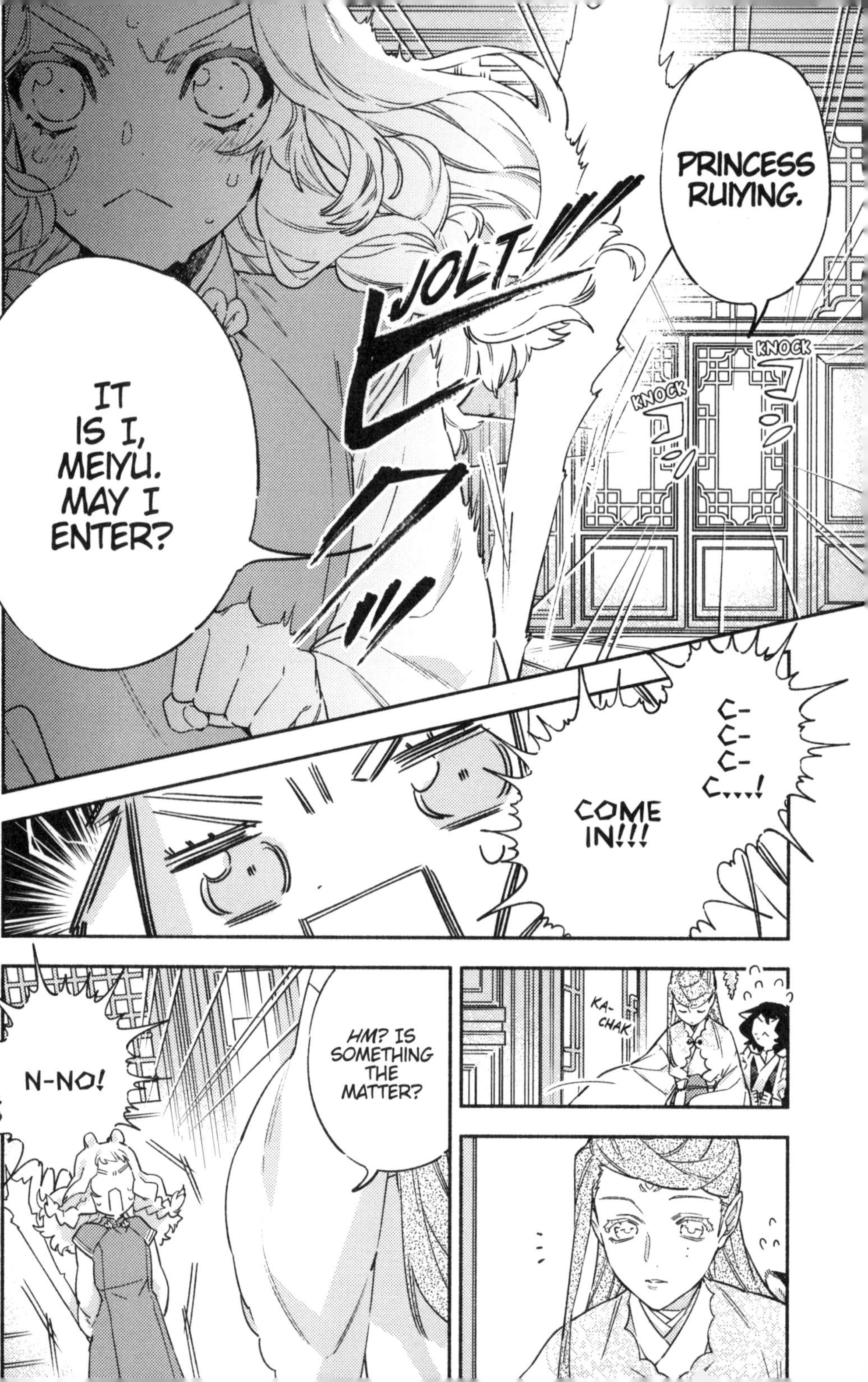
PRINCESS RUIYING.
KNOCK
KNOCK
JOLT
IT IS I, MEIYU. MAY I ENTER?
C-C-C-C...!
COME IN!!!
KA-CHAK
HM? IS SOMETHING THE MATTER?
N-NO!

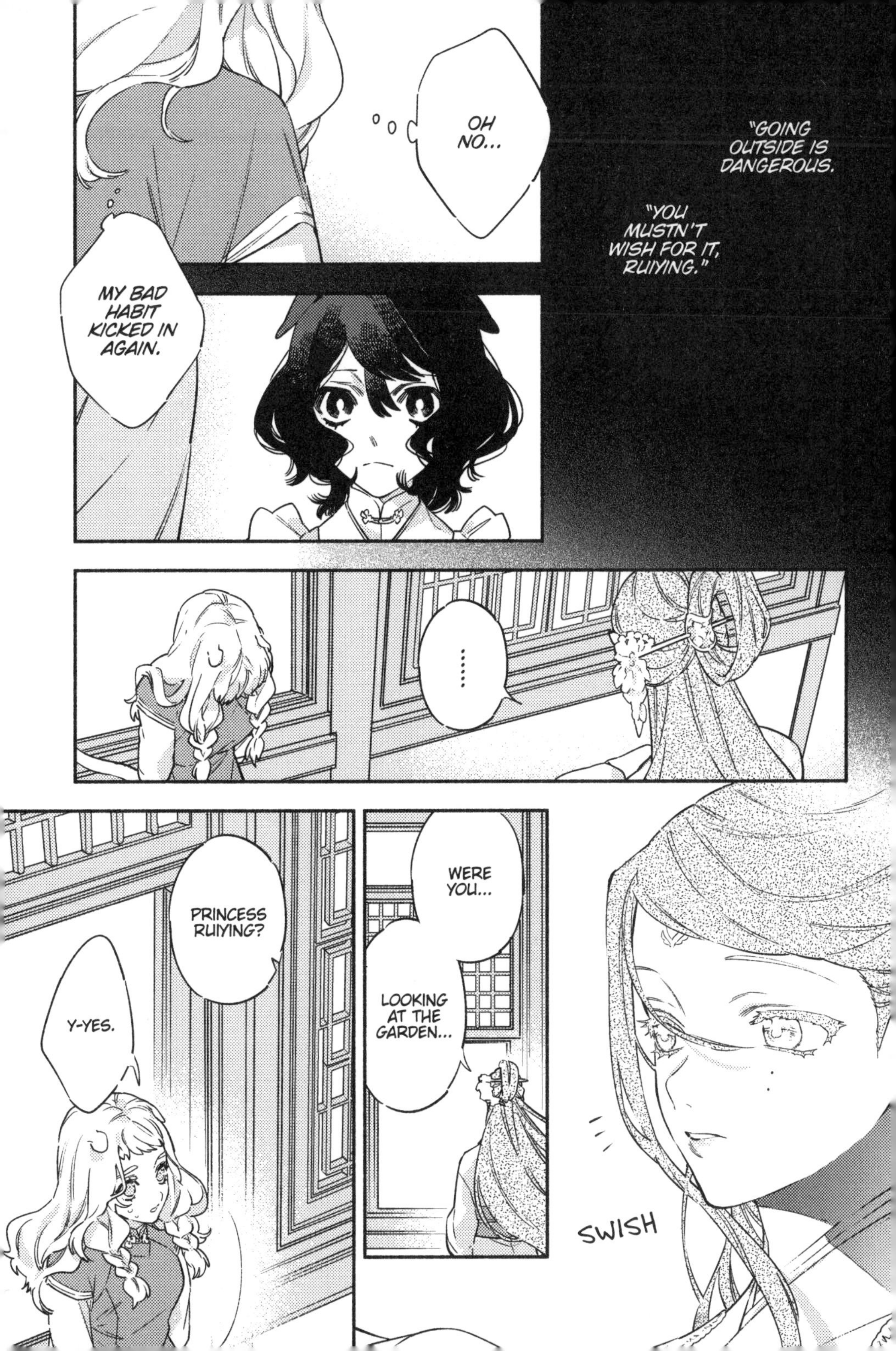

"GOING OUTSIDE IS DANGEROUS.
"YOU MUSTN'T WISH FOR IT, RUIYING."
OH NO...
MY BAD HABIT KICKED IN AGAIN.
......
SWISH
WERE YOU...
LOOKING AT THE GARDEN...
PRINCESS RUIYING?
Y-YES.

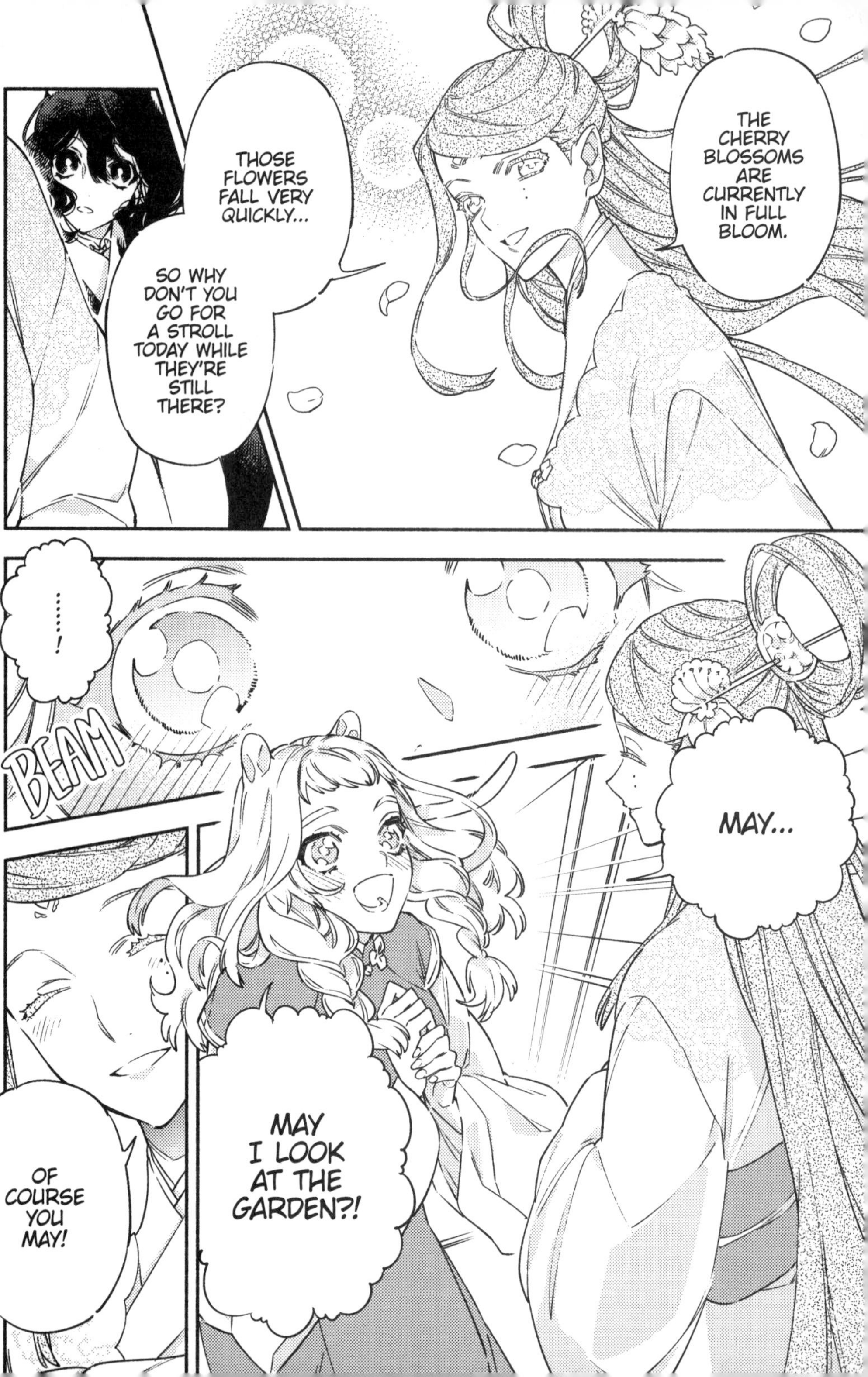
THE CHERRY BLOSSOMS ARE CURRENTLY IN FULL BLOOM.
THOSE FLOWERS FALL VERY QUICKLY...
SO WHY DON'T YOU GO FOR A STROLL TODAY WHILE THEY'RE STILL THERE?
MAY...
......!
BEAM
MAY I LOOK AT THE GARDEN?!
OF COURSE YOU MAY!

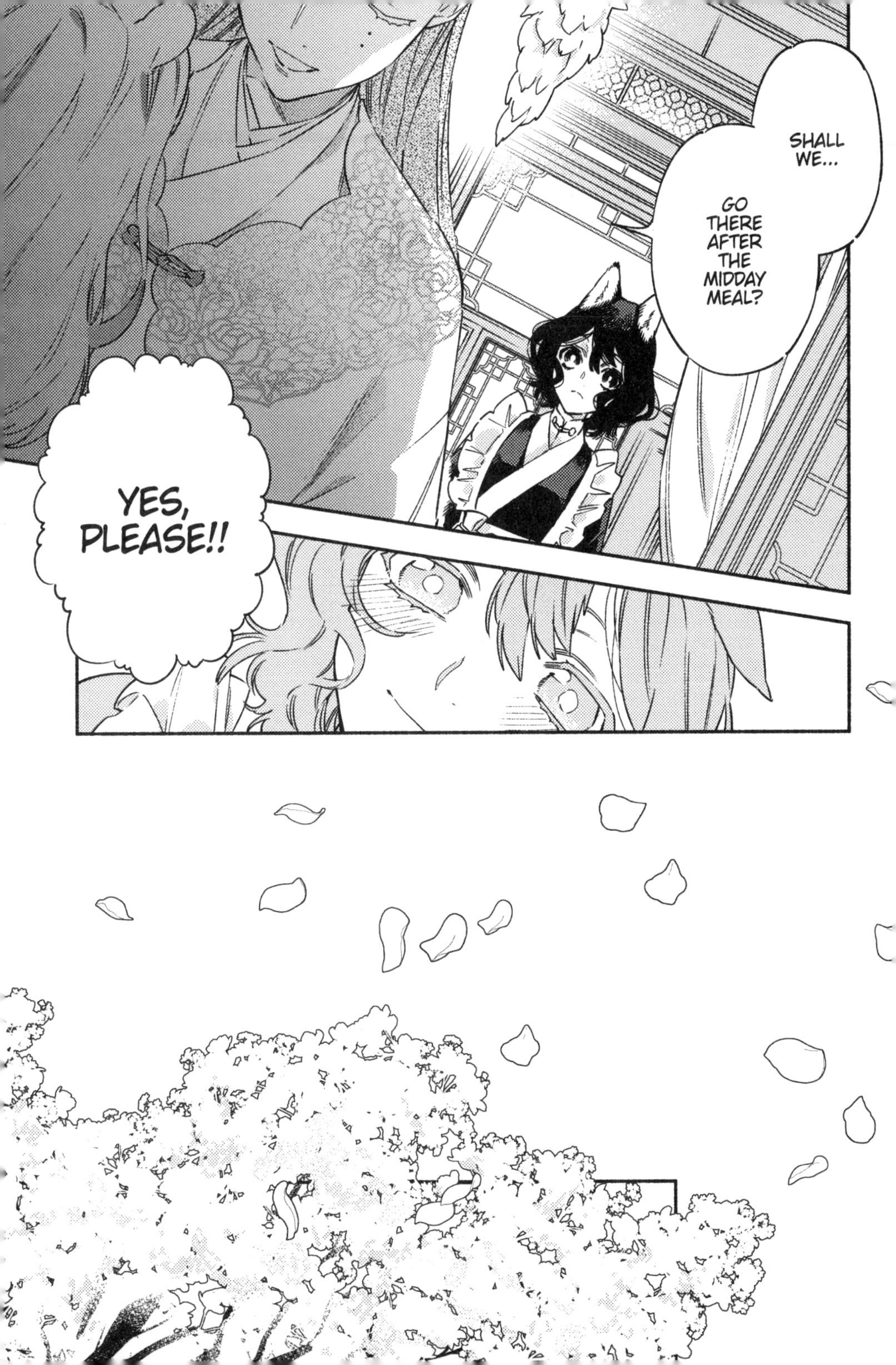
SHALL WE...
GO THERE AFTER THE MIDDAY MEAL?
YES, PLEASE!!

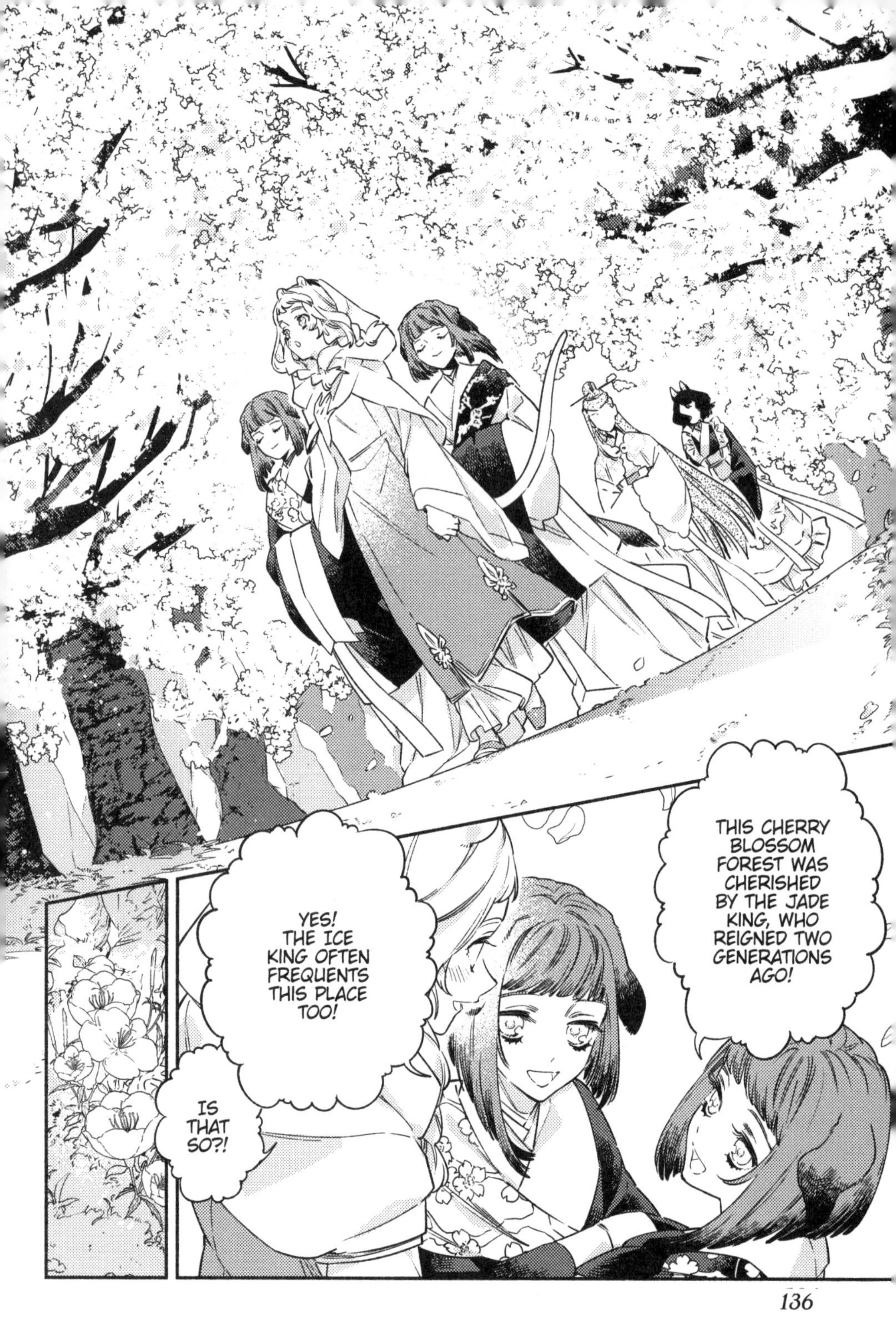
THIS CHERRY BLOSSOM FOREST WAS CHERISHED BY THE JADE KING, WHO REIGNED TWO GENERATIONS AGO!
YES! THE ICE KING OFTEN FREQUENTS THIS PLACE TOO!
IS THAT SO?!

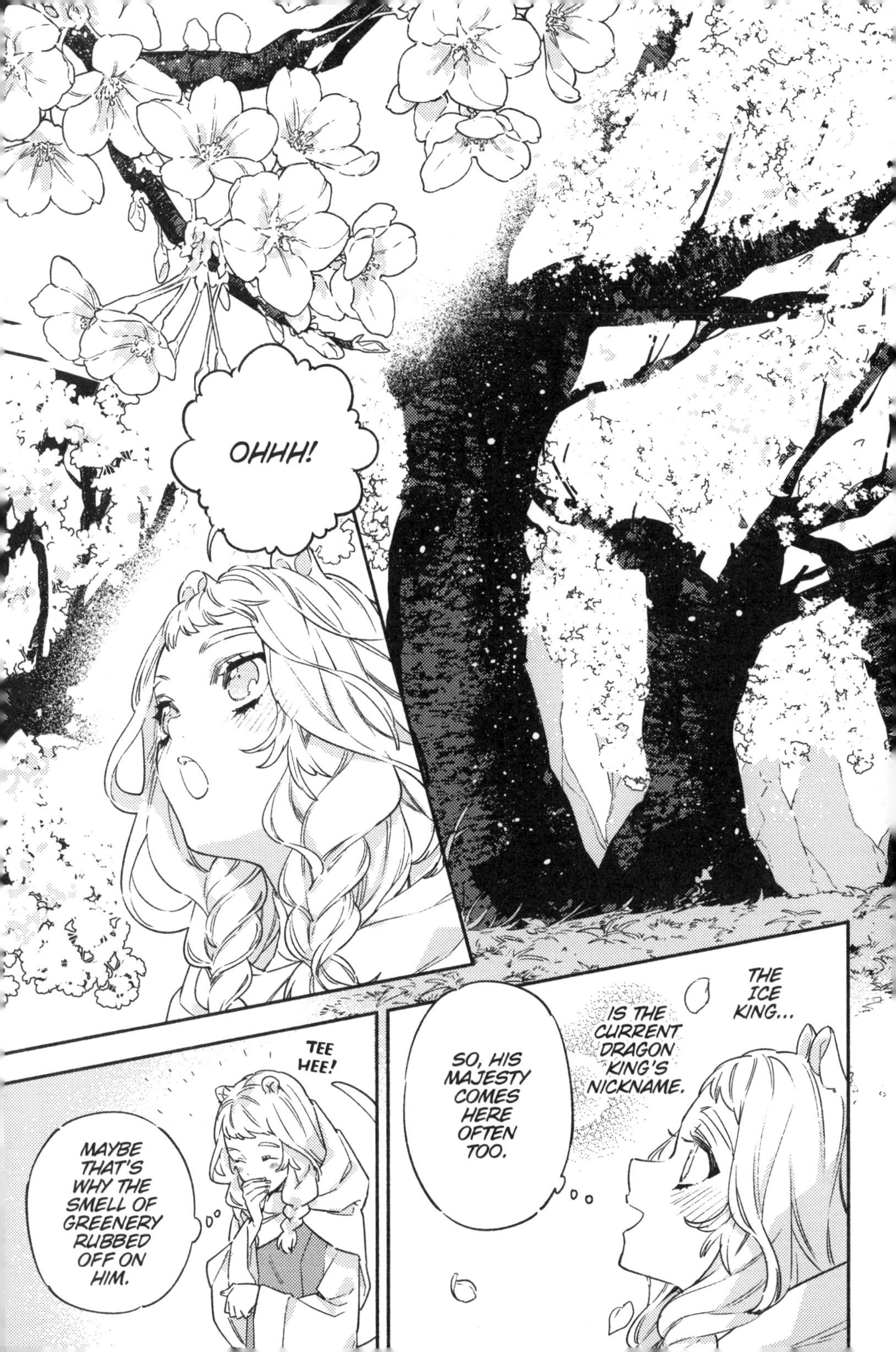
OHHH!
THE ICE KING...
IS THE CURRENT DRAGON KING'S NICKNAME.
SO, HIS MAJESTY COMES HERE OFTEN TOO.
TEE HEE!
MAYBE THAT'S WHY THE SMELL OF GREENERY RUBBED OFF ON HIM.

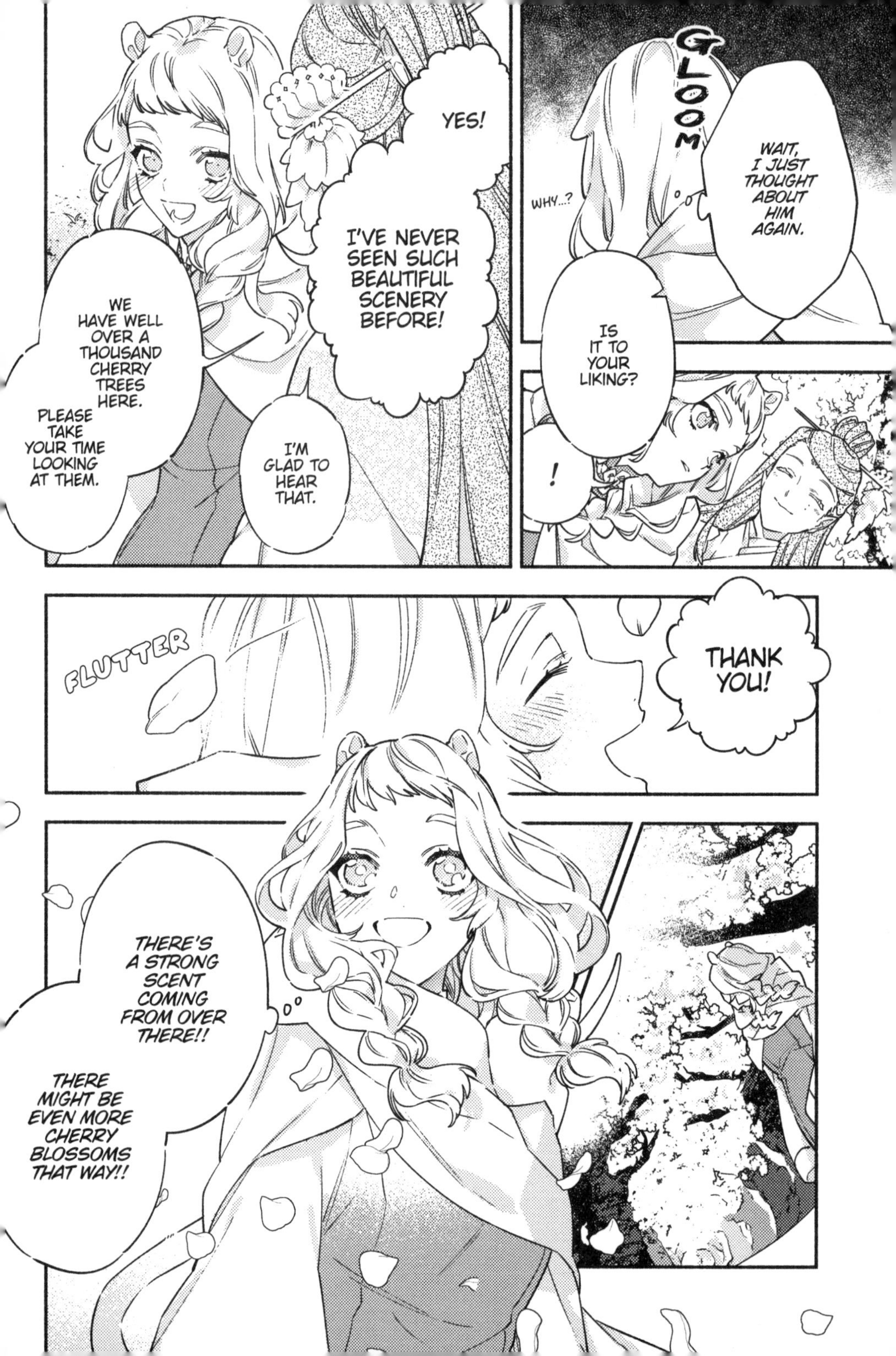
GLOOM
WAIT, I JUST THOUGHT ABOUT HIM AGAIN.
WHY...?
IS IT TO YOUR LIKING?
!
YES!
I'VE NEVER SEEN SUCH BEAUTIFUL SCENERY BEFORE!
I'M GLAD TO HEAR THAT.
WE HAVE WELL OVER A THOUSAND CHERRY TREES HERE.
PLEASE TAKE YOUR TIME LOOKING AT THEM.
THANK YOU!
FLUTTER
THERE'S A STRONG SCENT COMING FROM OVER THERE!!
THERE MIGHT BE EVEN MORE CHERRY BLOSSOMS THAT WAY!!

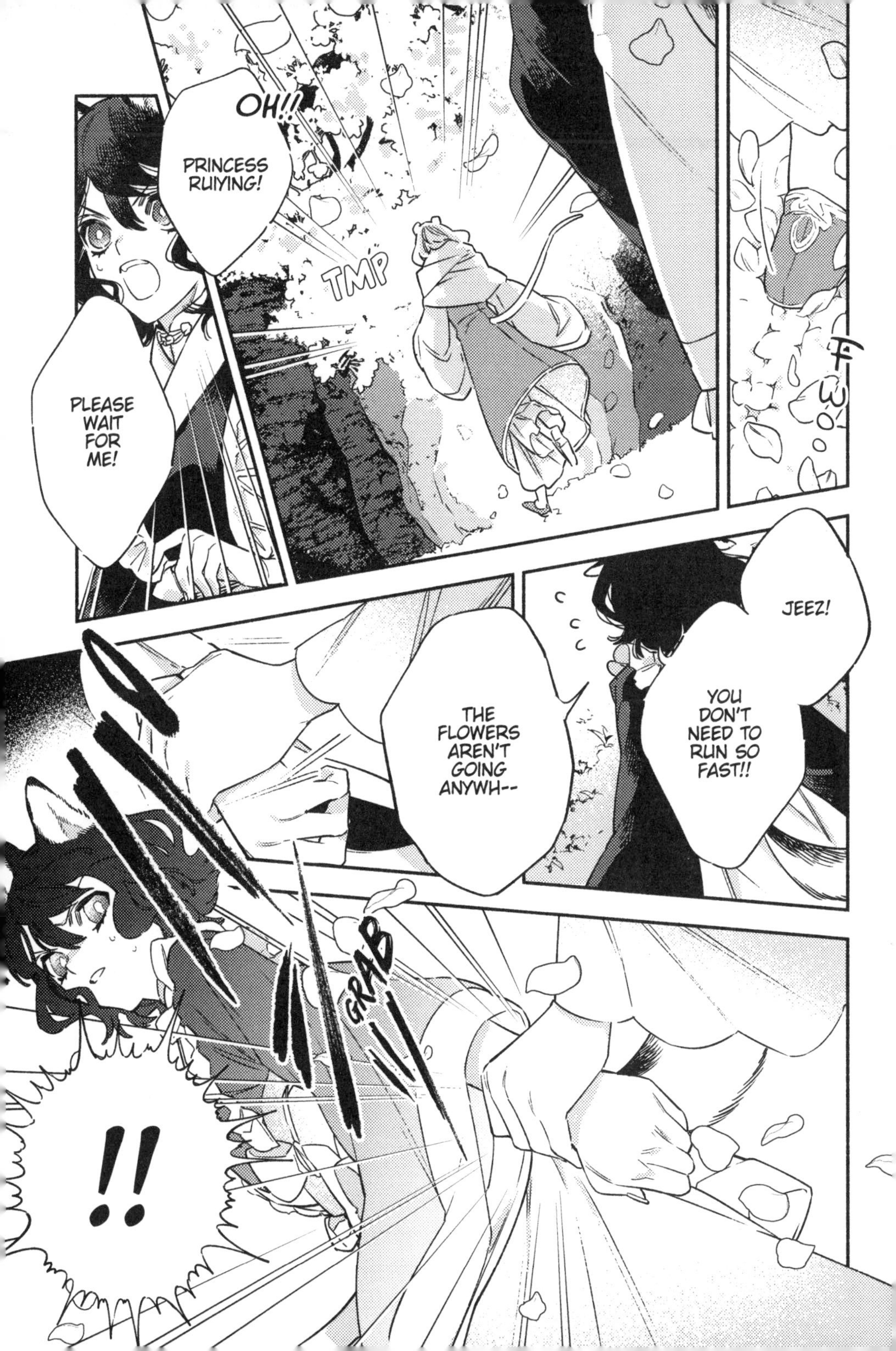
FWOO
OH!!
TMP
PRINCESS RUIYING!
PLEASE WAIT FOR ME!
JEEZ!
YOU DON'T NEED TO RUN SO FAST!!
THE FLOWERS AREN'T GOING ANYWH--
GRAB
!!

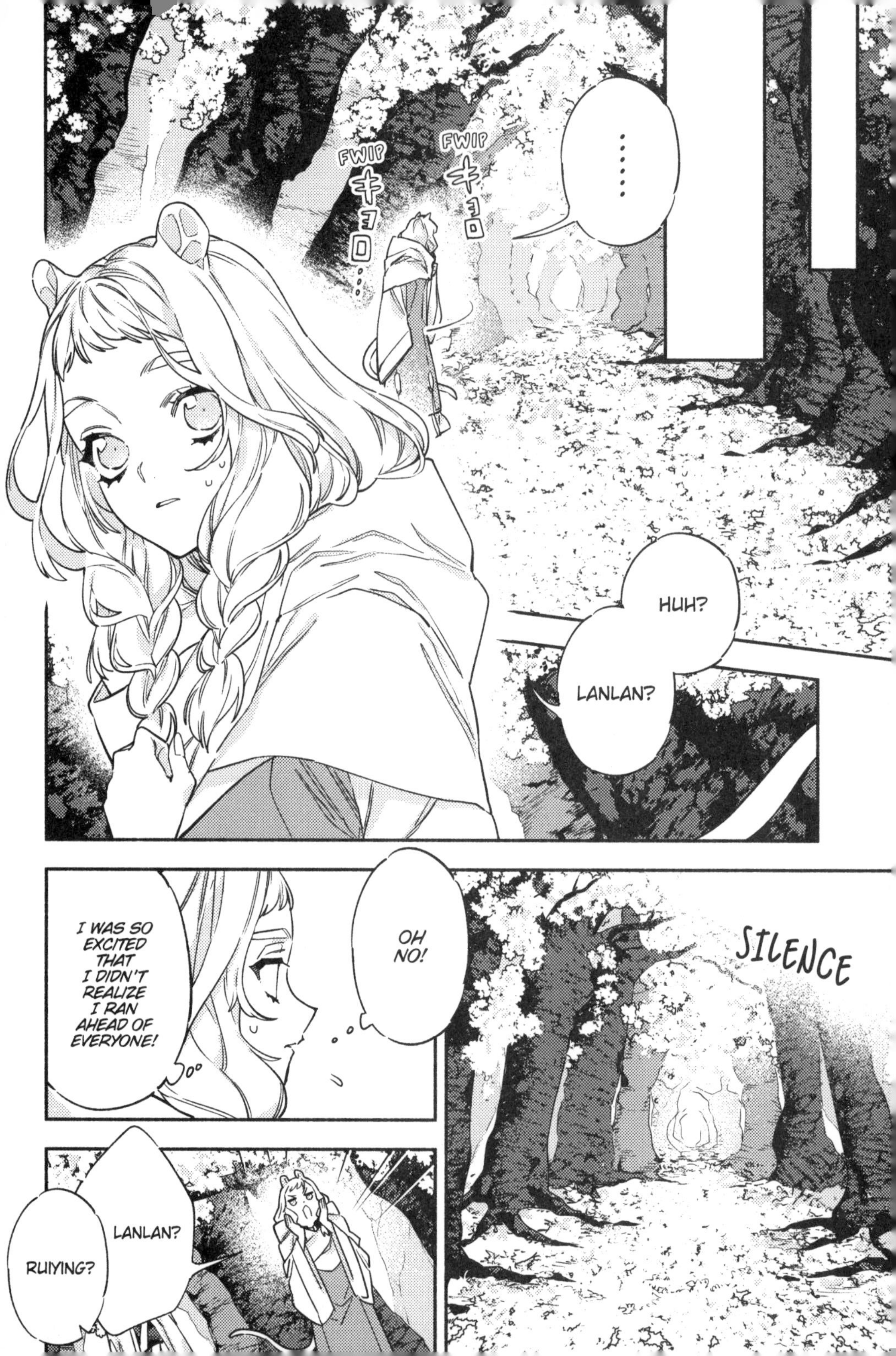
......
FWIP キョロ
FWIP キョロ...
HUH?
LANLAN?
SILENCE
OH NO!
I WAS SO EXCITED THAT I DIDN'T REALIZE I RAN AHEAD OF EVERYONE!
LANLAN?
RUIYING?

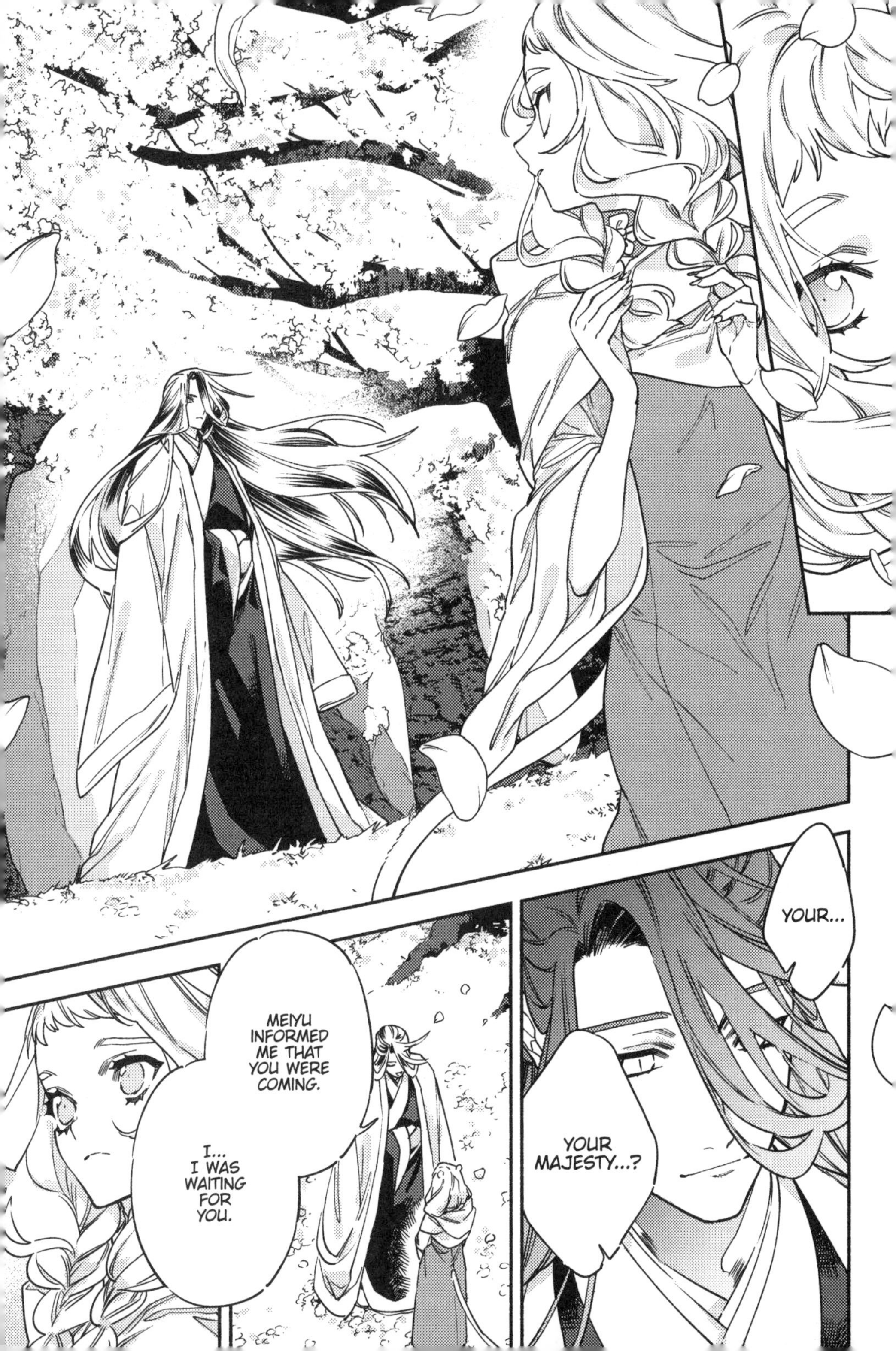
YOUR...
YOUR MAJESTY...?
MEIYU INFORMED ME THAT YOU WERE COMING.
I... I WAS WAITING FOR YOU.

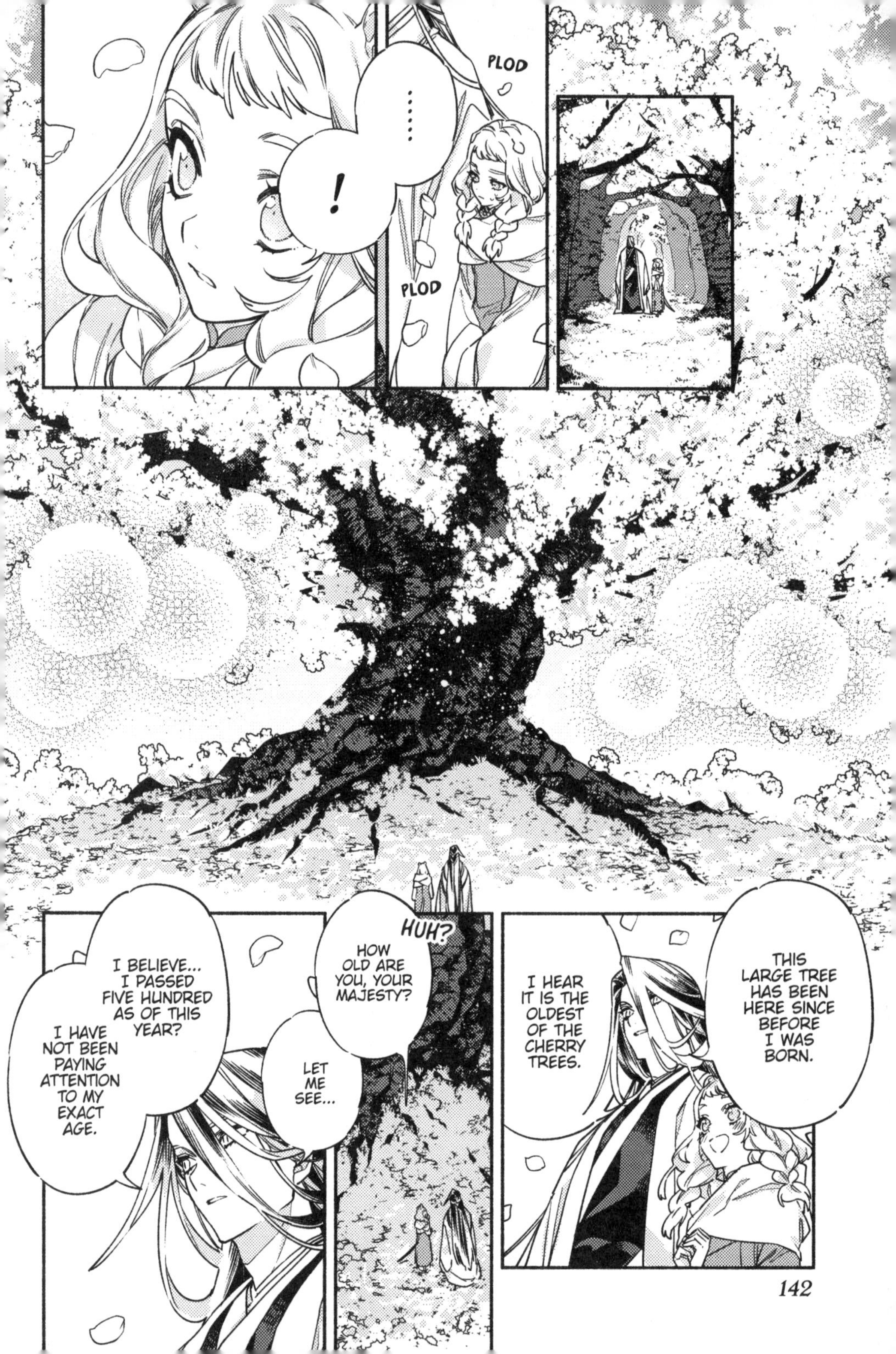
PLOD
PLOD
......
!
THIS LARGE TREE HAS BEEN HERE SINCE BEFORE I WAS BORN.
I HEAR IT IS THE OLDEST OF THE CHERRY TREES.
HUH?
HOW OLD ARE YOU, YOUR MAJESTY?
LET ME SEE...
I BELIEVE... I PASSED FIVE HUNDRED AS OF THIS YEAR?
I HAVE NOT BEEN PAYING ATTENTION TO MY EXACT AGE.

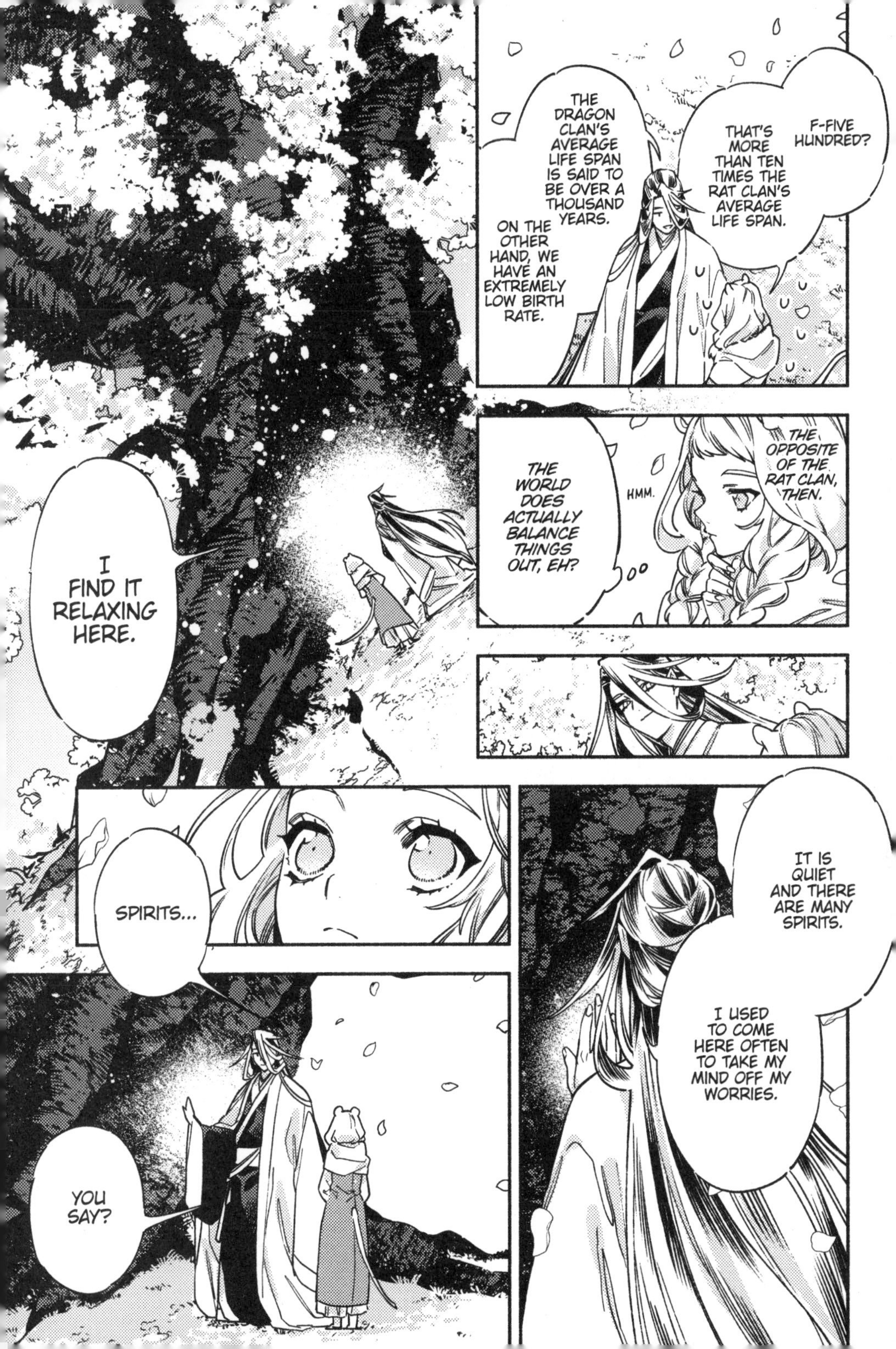
F-FIVE HUNDRED?
THAT'S MORE THAN TEN TIMES THE RAT CLAN'S AVERAGE LIFE SPAN.
THE DRAGON CLAN'S AVERAGE LIFE SPAN IS SAID TO BE OVER A THOUSAND YEARS.
ON THE OTHER HAND, WE HAVE AN EXTREMELY LOW BIRTH RATE.
THE OPPOSITE OF THE RAT CLAN, THEN.
HMM.
THE WORLD DOES ACTUALLY BALANCE THINGS OUT, EH?
I FIND IT RELAXING HERE.
IT IS QUIET AND THERE ARE MANY SPIRITS.
I USED TO COME HERE OFTEN TO TAKE MY MIND OFF MY WORRIES.
SPIRITS...
YOU SAY?

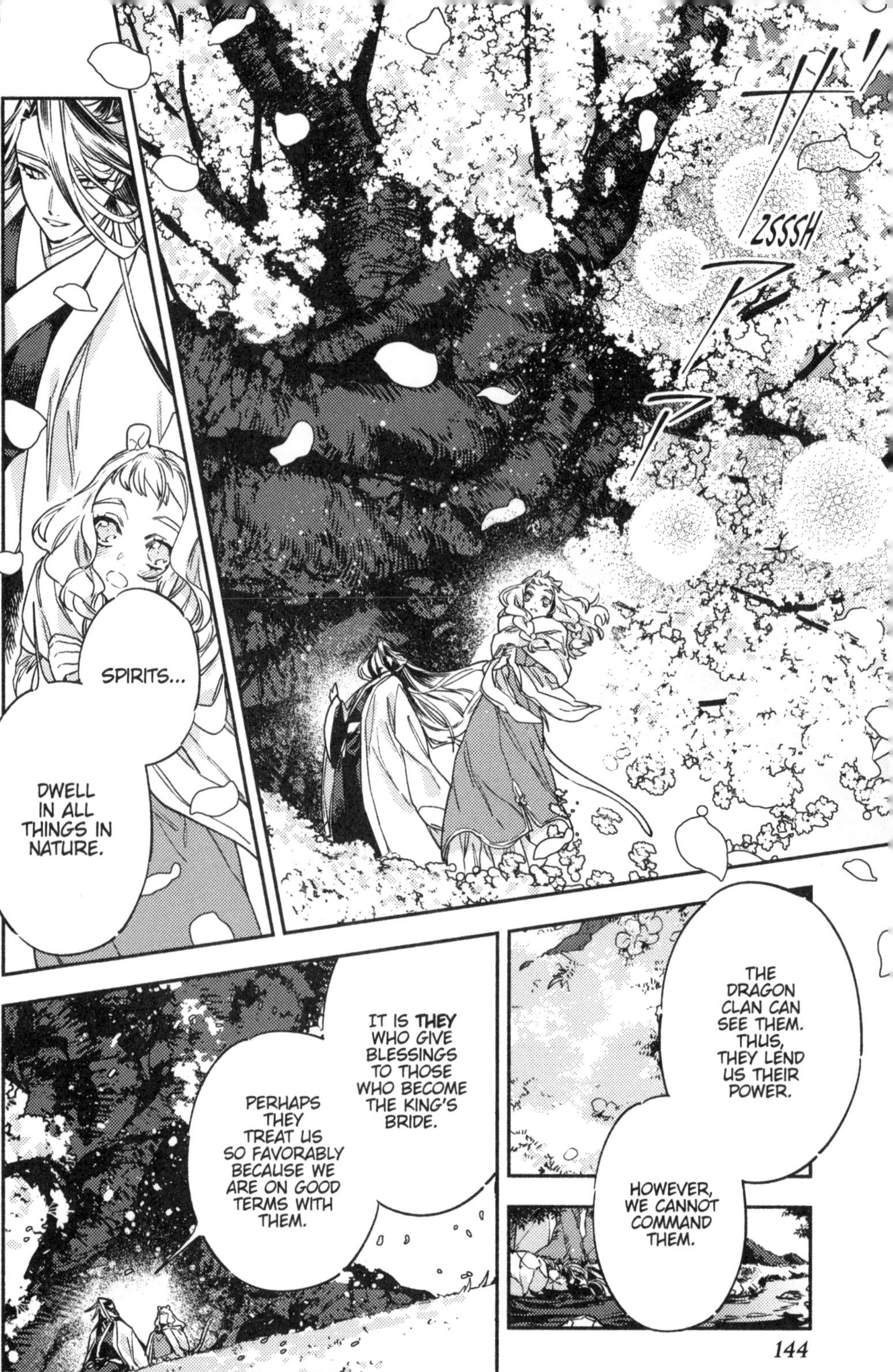
ZSSSH
SPIRITS...
DWELL IN ALL THINGS IN NATURE.
THE DRAGON CLAN CAN SEE THEM. THUS, THEY LEND US THEIR POWER.
HOWEVER, WE CANNOT COMMAND THEM.
IT IS **THEY** WHO GIVE BLESSINGS TO THOSE WHO BECOME THE KING'S BRIDE.
PERHAPS THEY TREAT US SO FAVORABLY BECAUSE WE ARE ON GOOD TERMS WITH THEM.

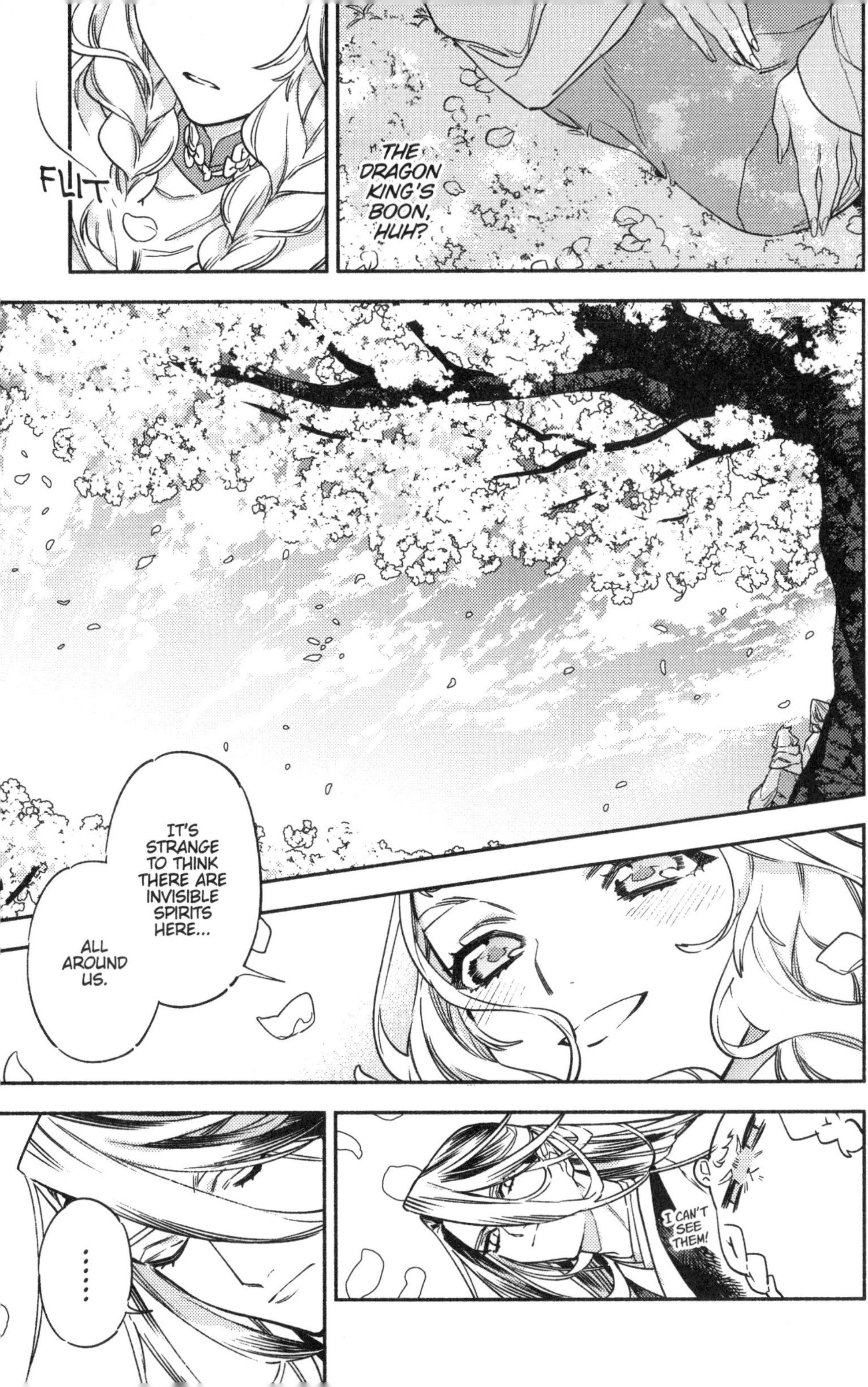
THE DRAGON KING'S BOON, HUH?
FLIT
IT'S STRANGE TO THINK THERE ARE INVISIBLE SPIRITS HERE...
ALL AROUND US.
I CAN'T SEE THEM!
......

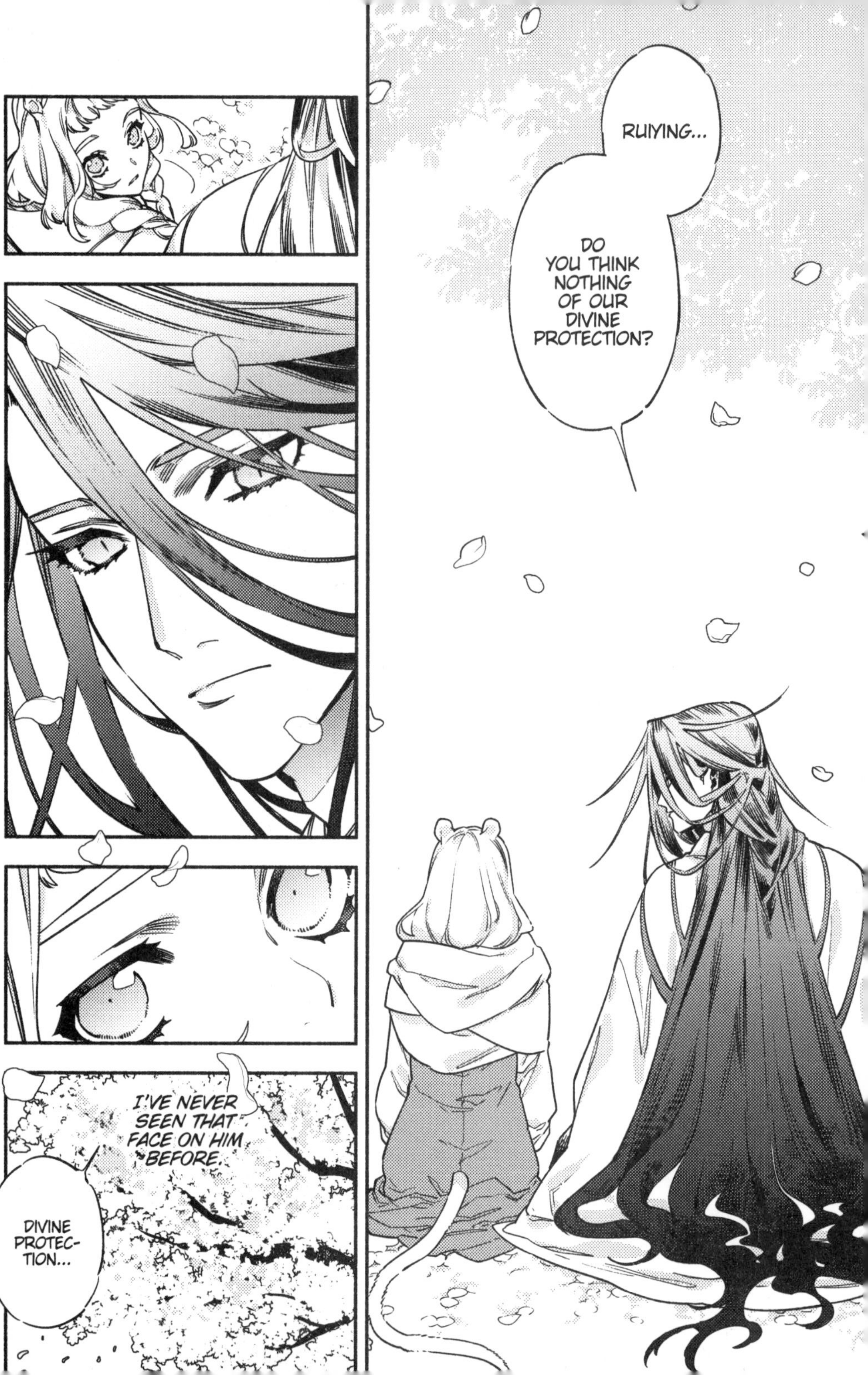
RUIYING...
DO YOU THINK NOTHING OF OUR DIVINE PROTECTION?
I'VE NEVER SEEN THAT FACE ON HIM BEFORE.
DIVINE PROTEC-TION...

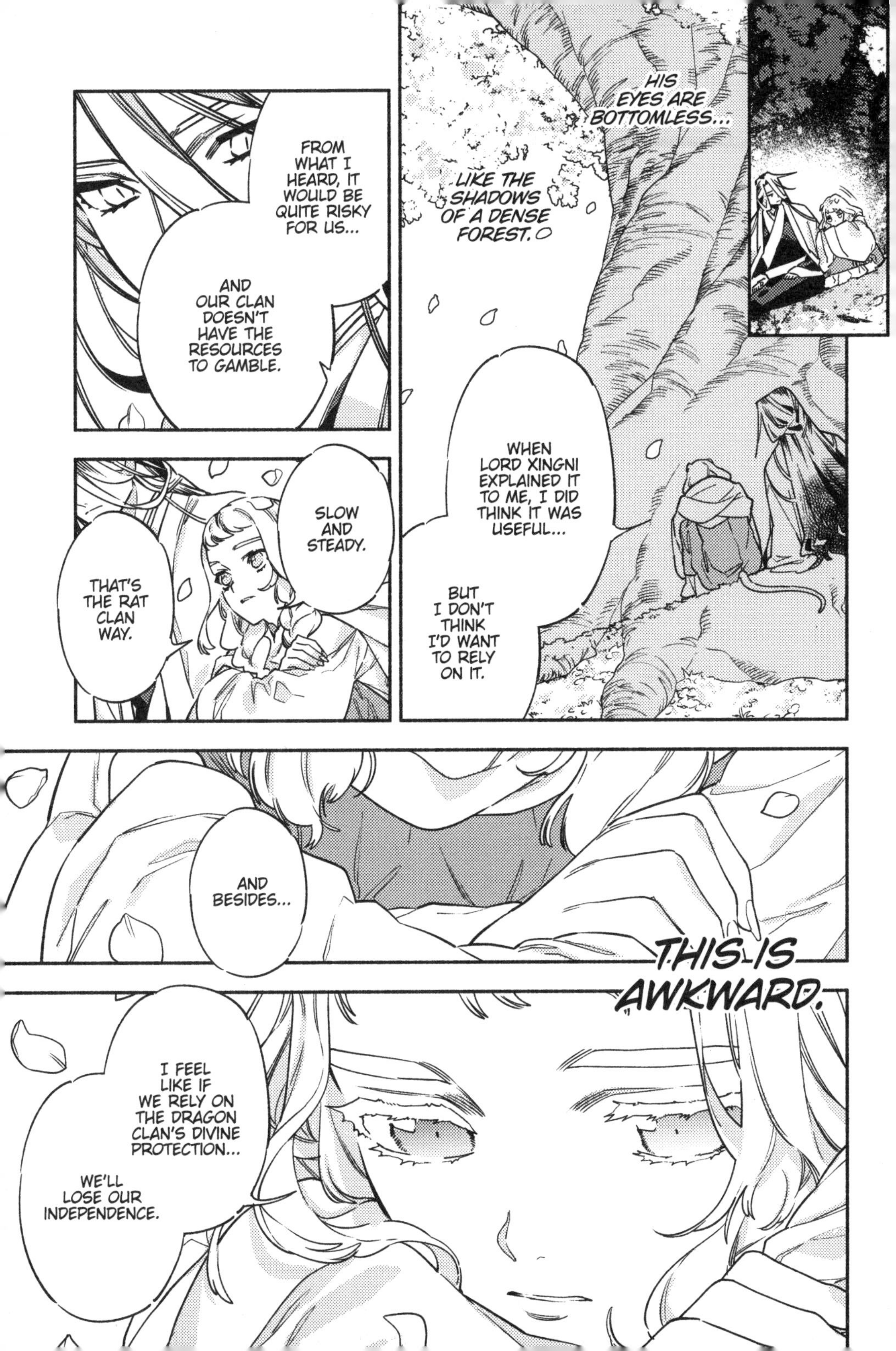
HIS EYES ARE BOTTOMLESS...
LIKE THE SHADOWS OF A DENSE FOREST.
WHEN LORD XINGNI EXPLAINED IT TO ME, I DID THINK IT WAS USEFUL...
BUT I DON'T THINK I'D WANT TO RELY ON IT.
FROM WHAT I HEARD, IT WOULD BE QUITE RISKY FOR US...
AND OUR CLAN DOESN'T HAVE THE RESOURCES TO GAMBLE.
SLOW AND STEADY.
THAT'S THE RAT CLAN WAY.
AND BESIDES...
THIS IS AWKWARD.
I FEEL LIKE IF WE RELY ON THE DRAGON CLAN'S DIVINE PROTECTION...
WE'LL LOSE OUR INDEPENDENCE.

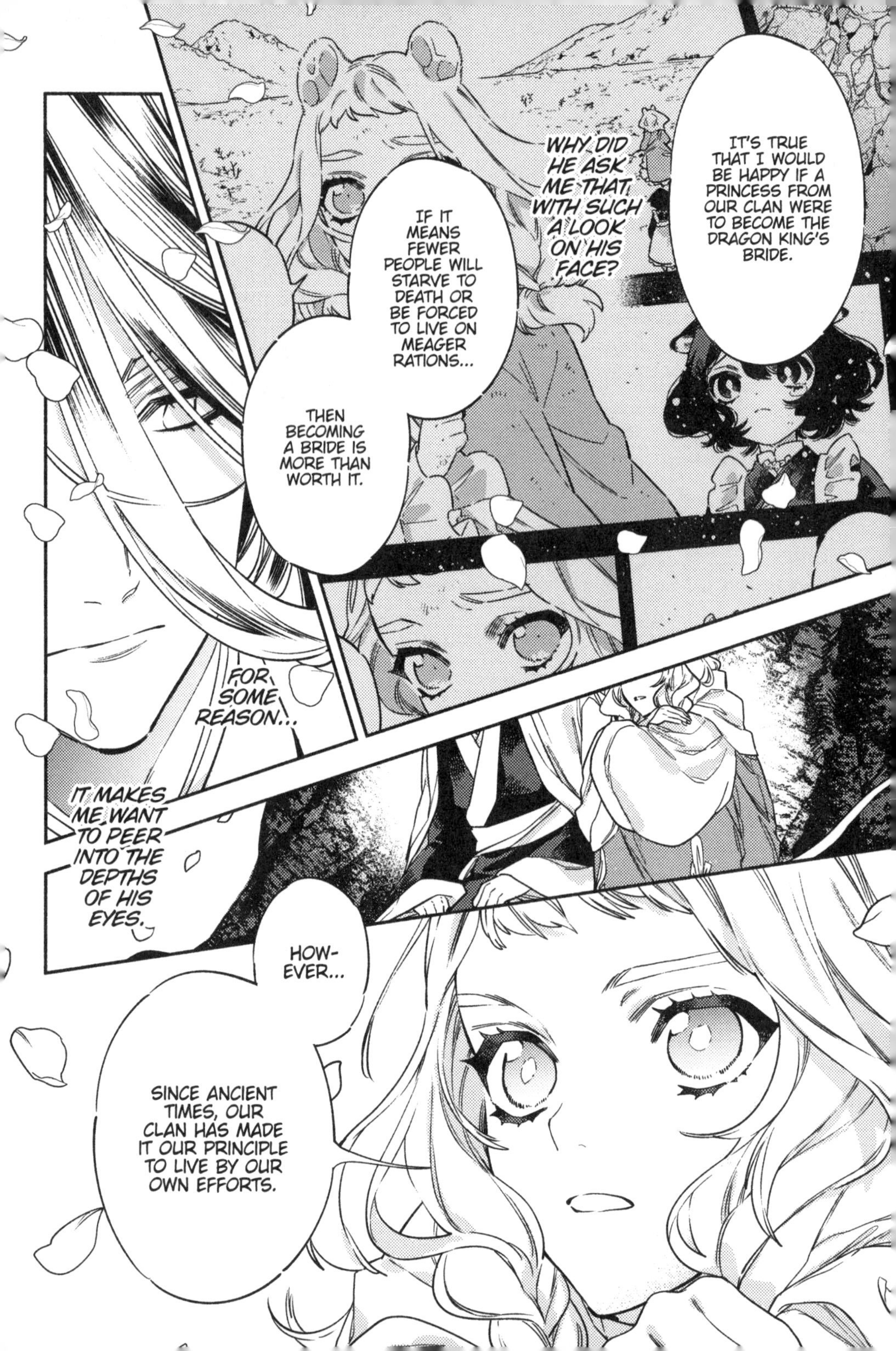
IT'S TRUE THAT I WOULD BE HAPPY IF A PRINCESS FROM OUR CLAN WERE TO BECOME THE DRAGON KING'S BRIDE.
WHY DID HE ASK ME THAT WITH SUCH A LOOK ON HIS FACE?
IF IT MEANS FEWER PEOPLE WILL STARVE TO DEATH OR BE FORCED TO LIVE ON MEAGER RATIONS...
THEN BECOMING A BRIDE IS MORE THAN WORTH IT.
FOR SOME REASON...
IT MAKES ME WANT TO PEER INTO THE DEPTHS OF HIS EYES.
HOW-EVER...
SINCE ANCIENT TIMES, OUR CLAN HAS MADE IT OUR PRINCIPLE TO LIVE BY OUR OWN EFFORTS.

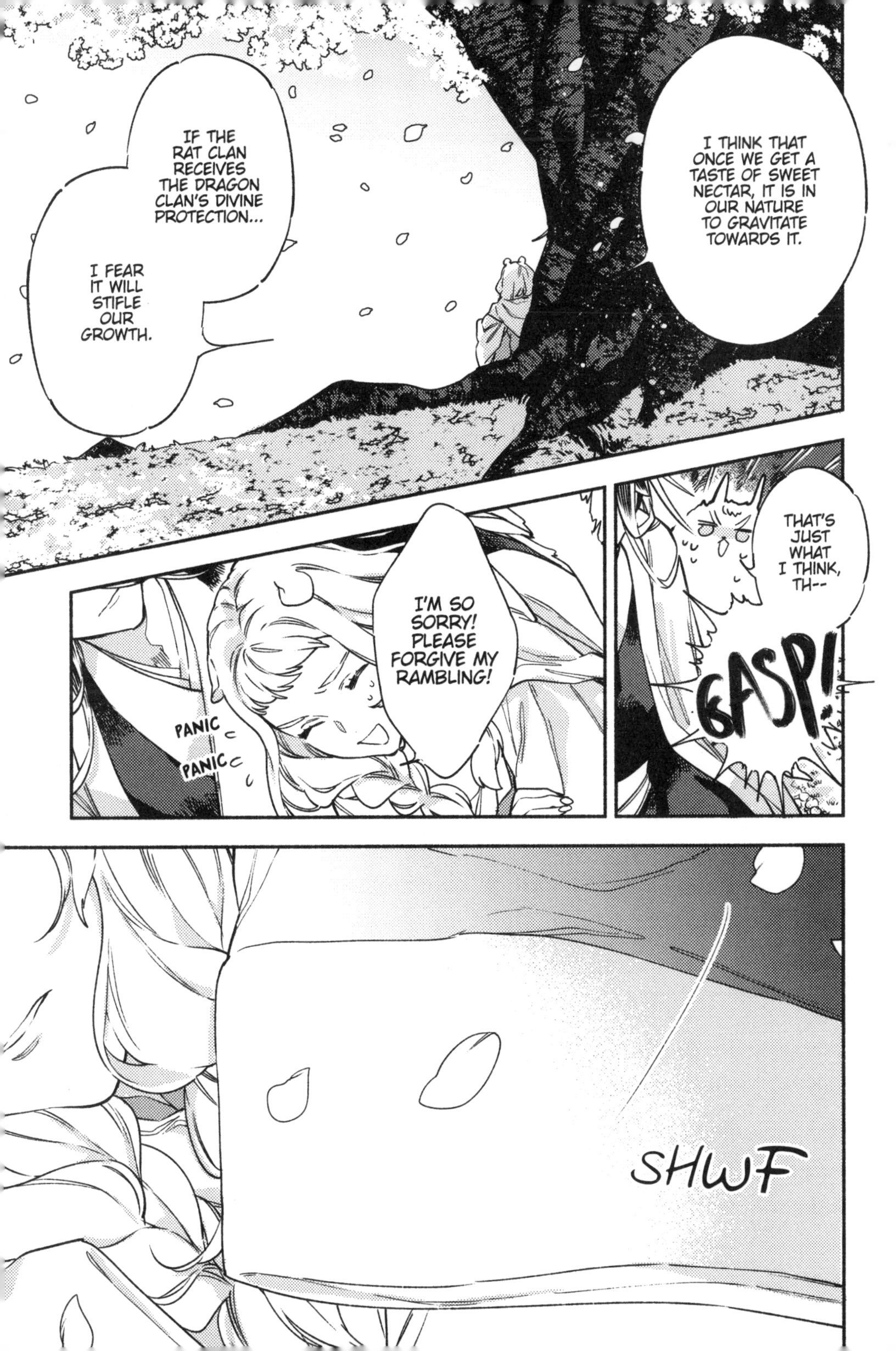
I THINK THAT ONCE WE GET A TASTE OF SWEET NECTAR, IT IS IN OUR NATURE TO GRAVITATE TOWARDS IT.
IF THE RAT CLAN RECEIVES THE DRAGON CLAN'S DIVINE PROTECTION...
I FEAR IT WILL STIFLE OUR GROWTH.
THAT'S JUST WHAT I THINK, TH--
GASP!
I'M SO SORRY! PLEASE FORGIVE MY RAMBLING!
PANIC
PANIC
SHWF

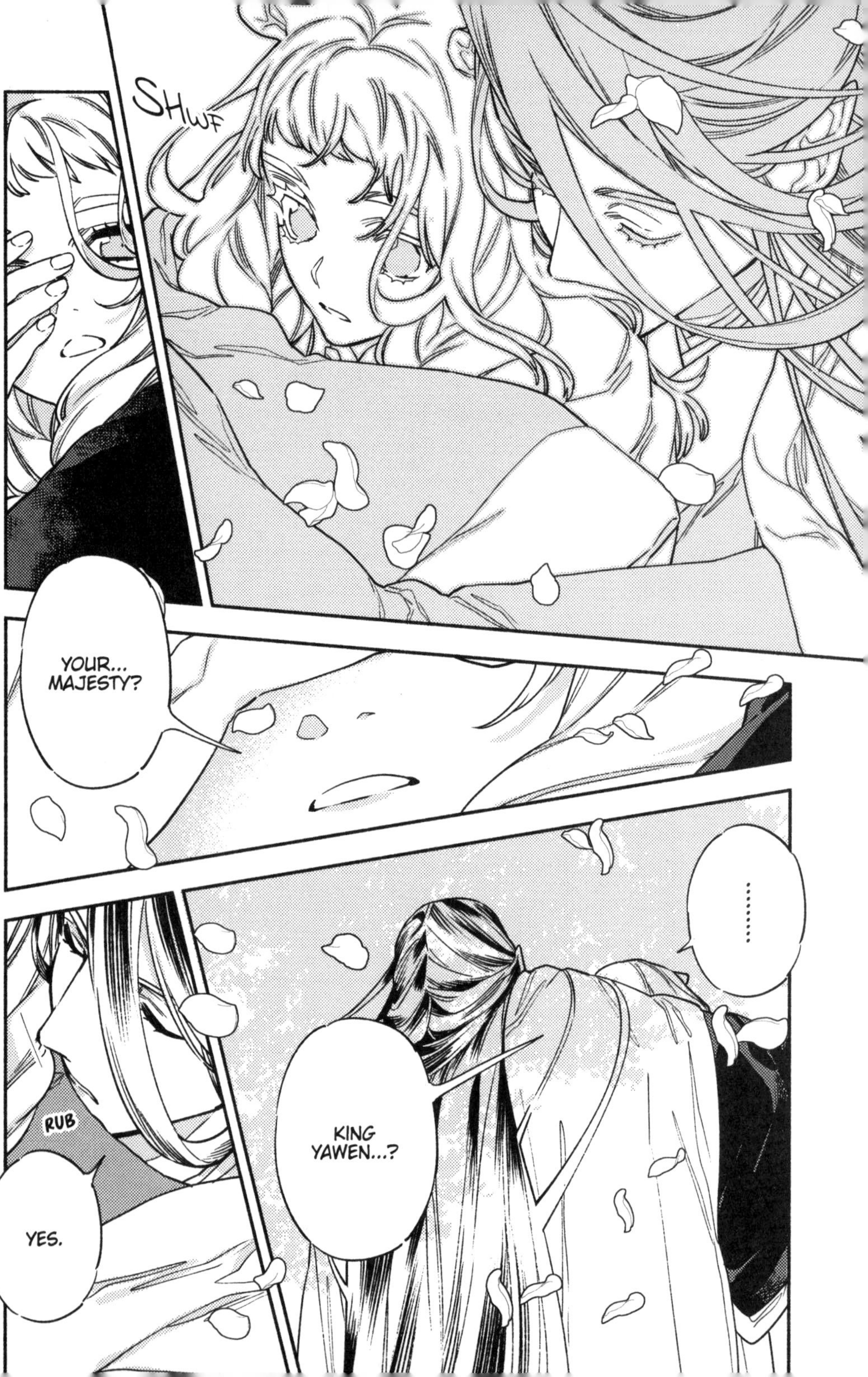
SHWF
YOUR... MAJESTY?
....
KING YAWEN...?
RUB
YES.

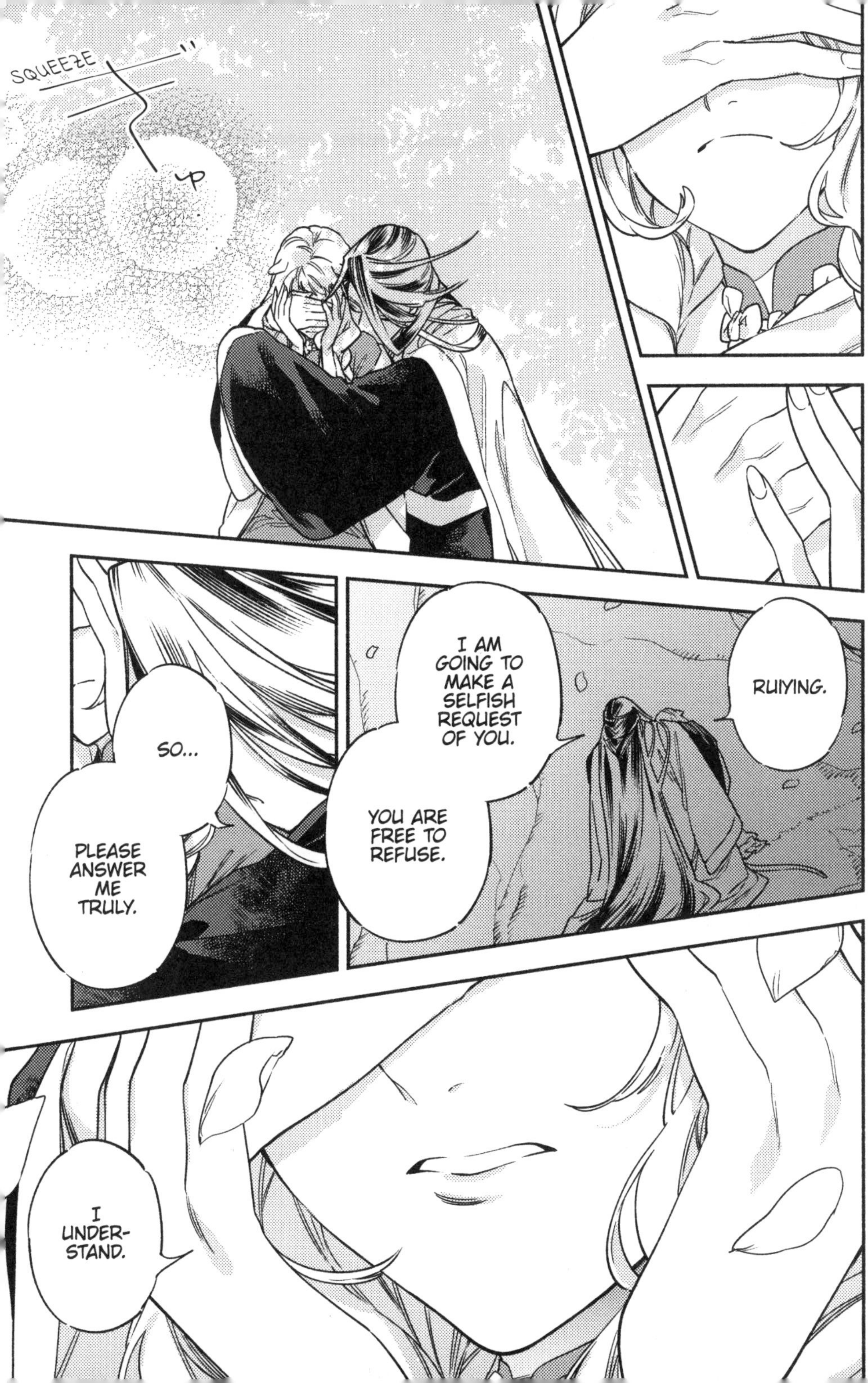
SQUEEZE
UP
RUIYING.
I AM GOING TO MAKE A SELFISH REQUEST OF YOU.
YOU ARE FREE TO REFUSE.
SO...
PLEASE ANSWER ME TRULY.
I UNDER-STAND.

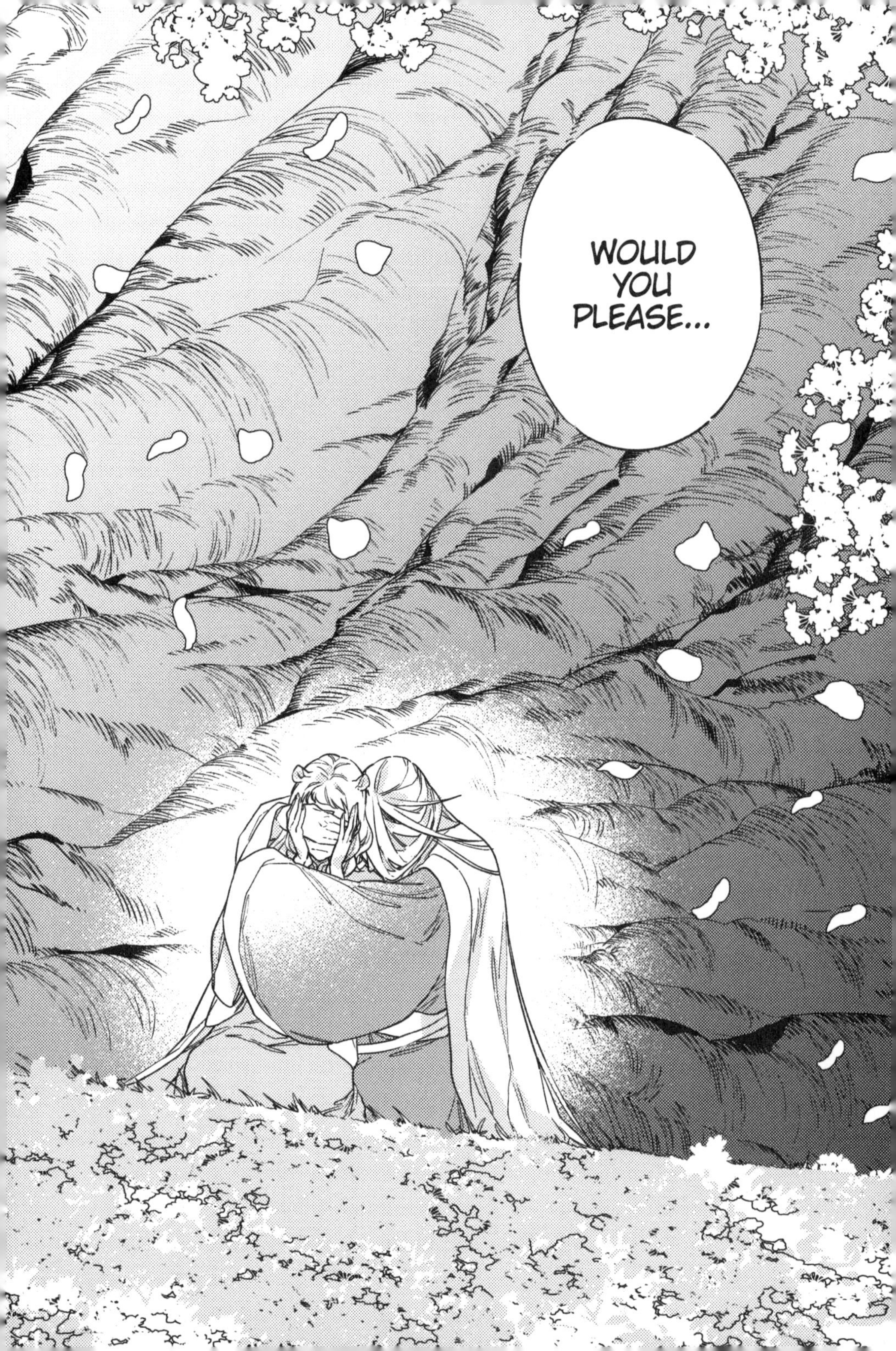
WOULD YOU PLEASE...

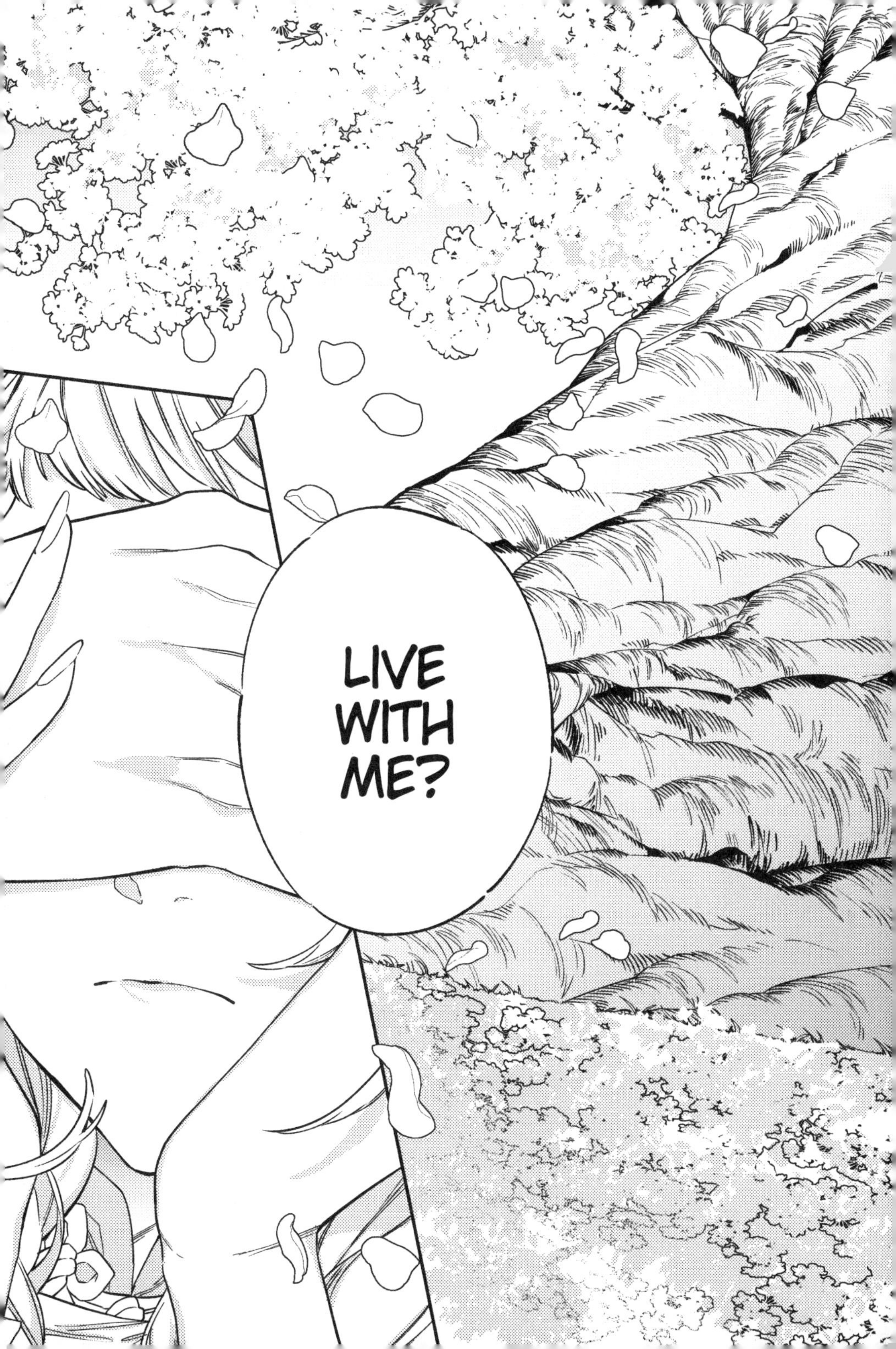
LIVE WITH ME?

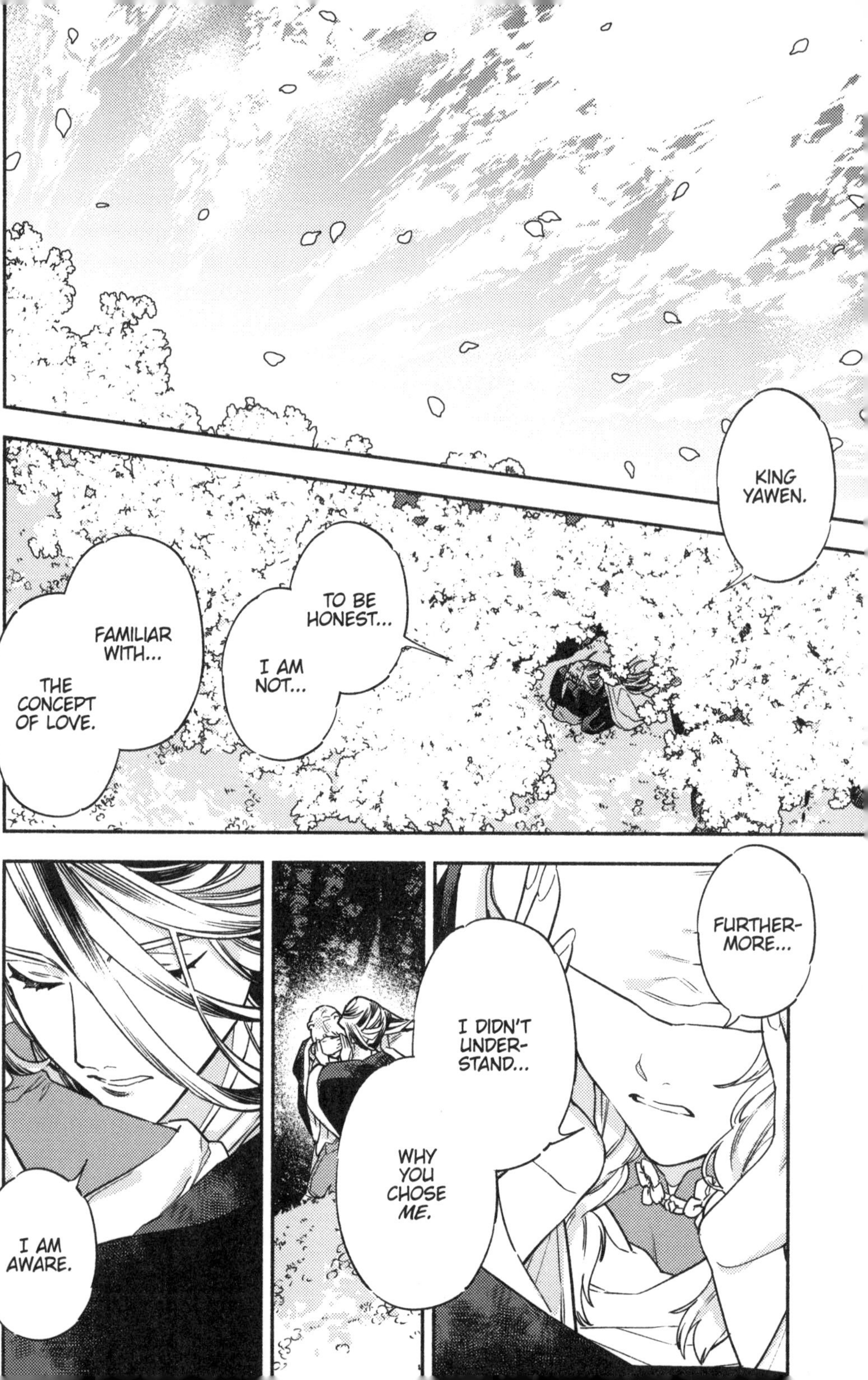
KING YAWEN.
TO BE HONEST...
I AM NOT...
FAMILIAR WITH...
THE CONCEPT OF LOVE.
FURTHER-MORE...
I DIDN'T UNDER-STAND...
WHY YOU CHOSE ME.
I AM AWARE.

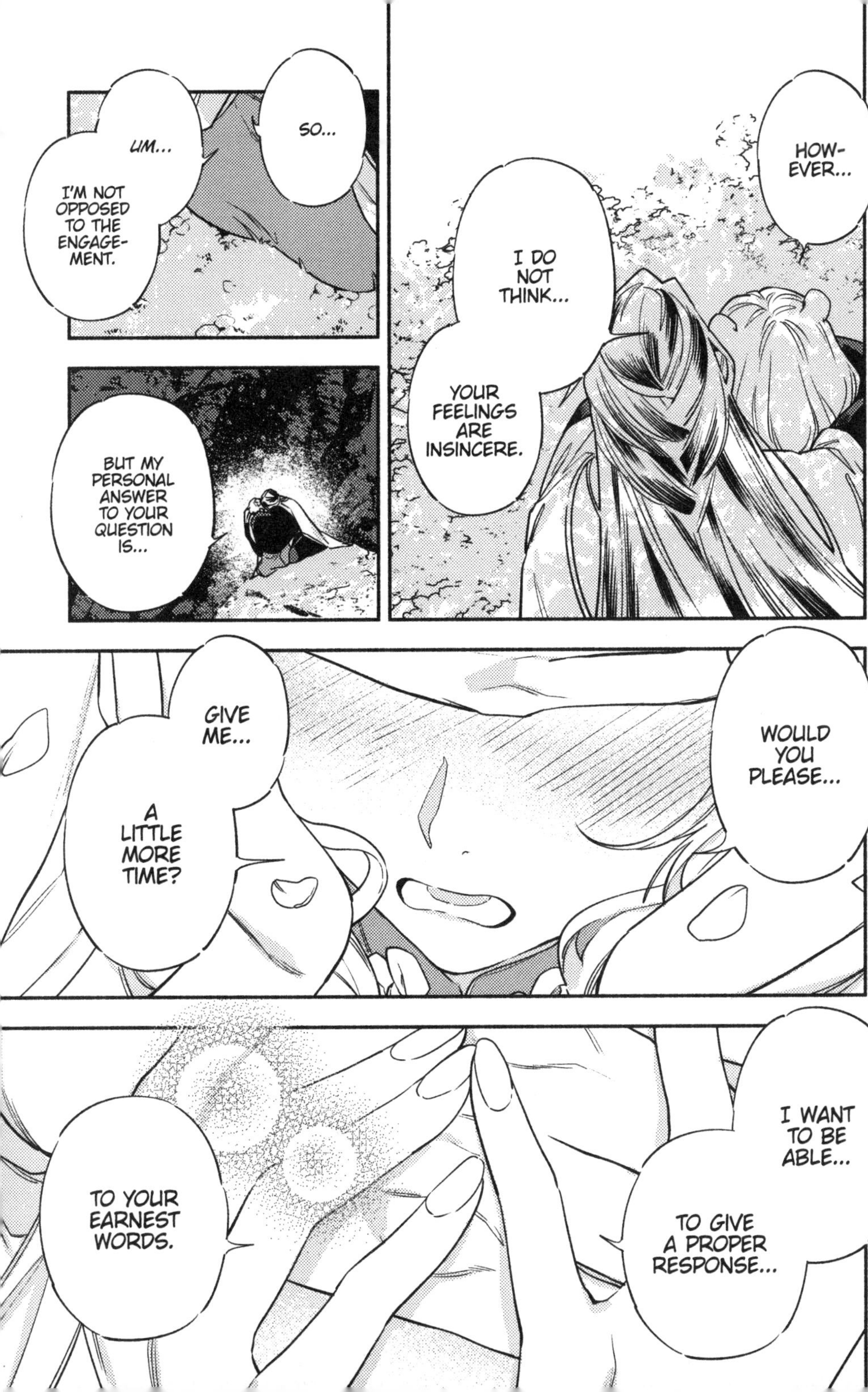
HOW-EVER...
I DO NOT THINK...
YOUR FEELINGS ARE INSINCERE.
SO...
UM...
I'M NOT OPPOSED TO THE ENGAGE-MENT.
BUT MY PERSONAL ANSWER TO YOUR QUESTION IS...
WOULD YOU PLEASE...
GIVE ME...
A LITTLE MORE TIME?
I WANT TO BE ABLE...
TO GIVE A PROPER RESPONSE...
TO YOUR EARNEST WORDS.

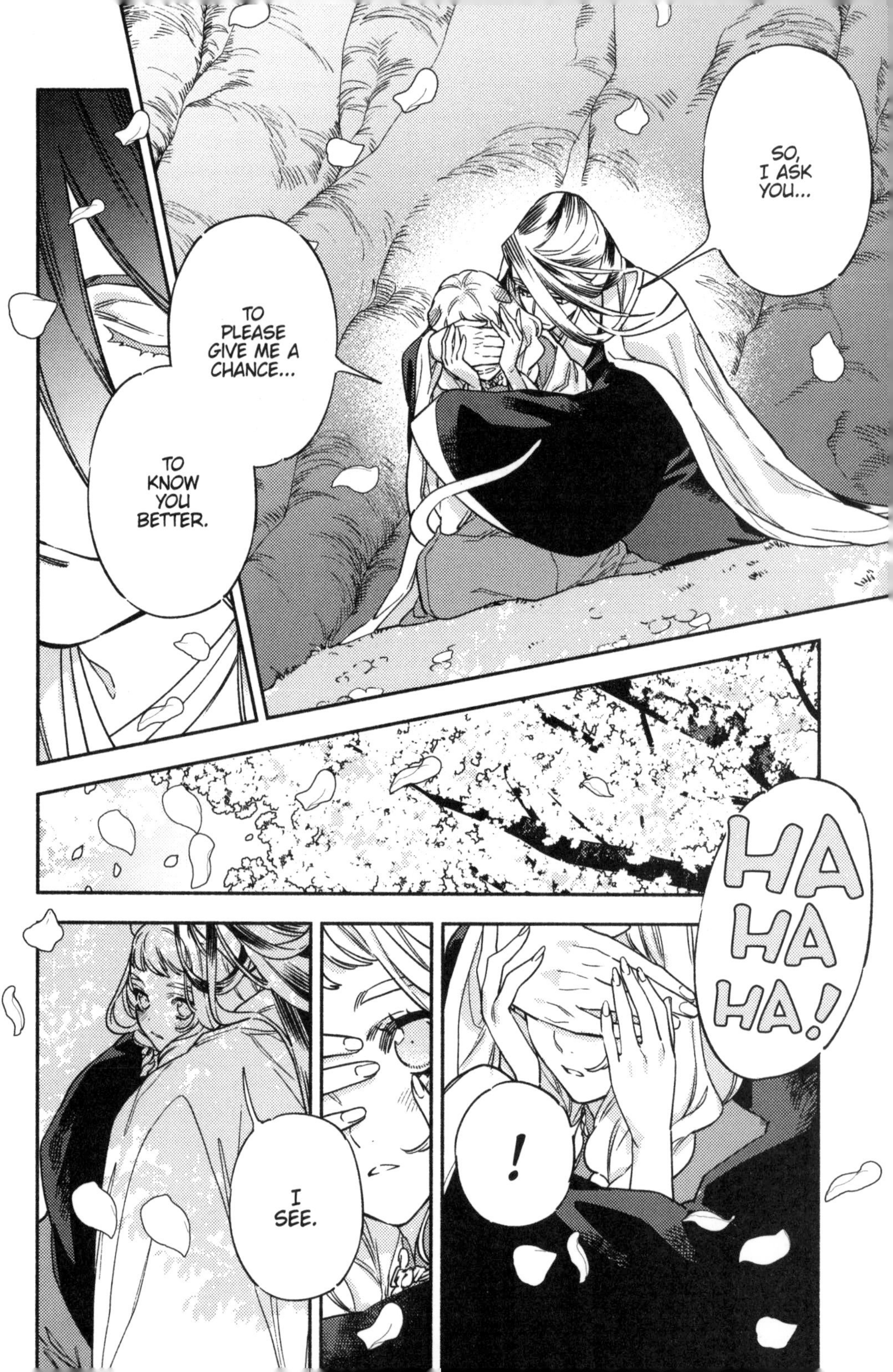
SO, I ASK YOU...
TO PLEASE GIVE ME A CHANCE...
TO KNOW YOU BETTER.
HA HA HA!
!
I SEE.

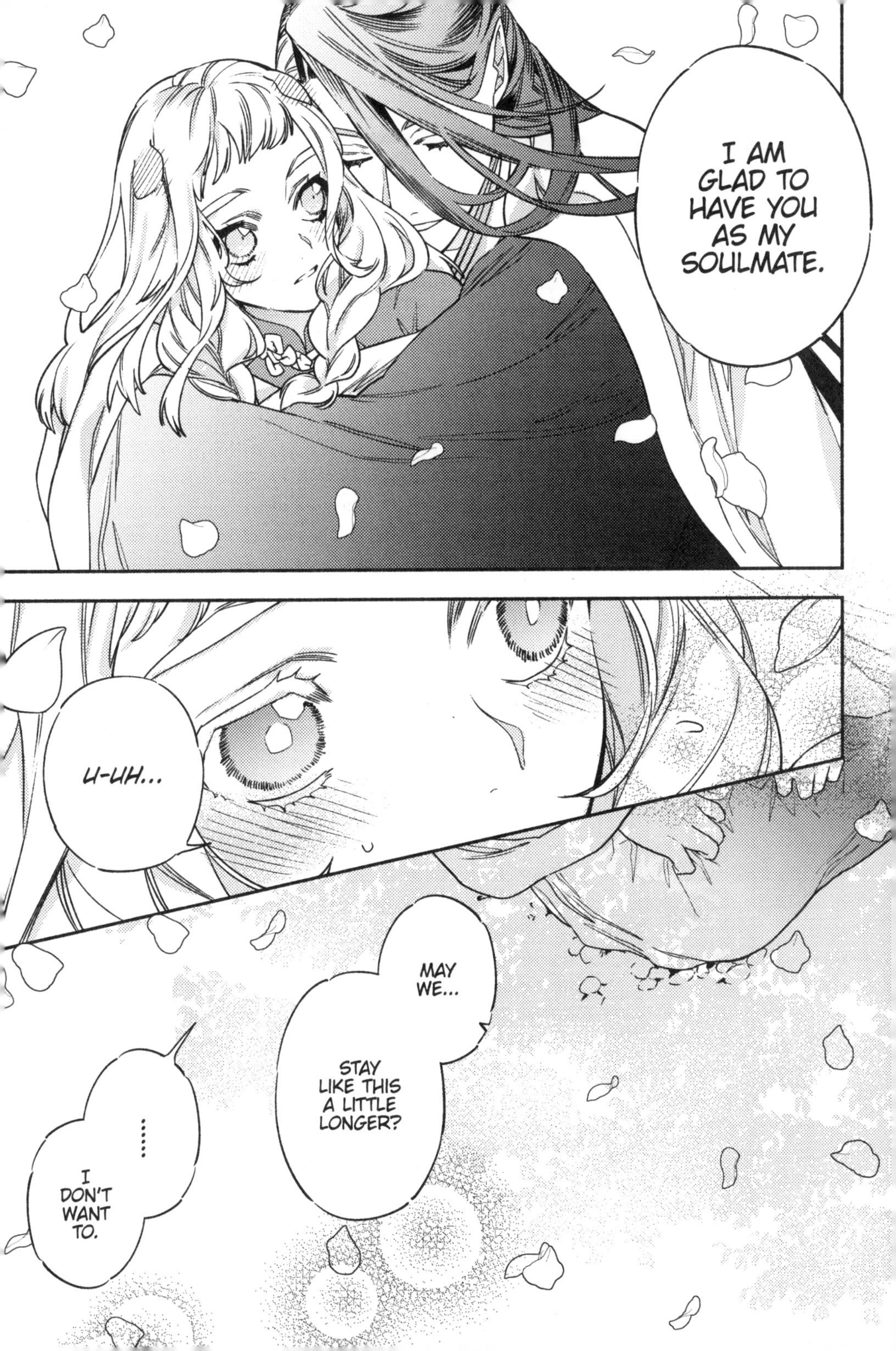
I AM GLAD TO HAVE YOU AS MY SOULMATE.
U-UH...
MAY WE...
STAY LIKE THIS A LITTLE LONGER?
......
I DON'T WANT TO.

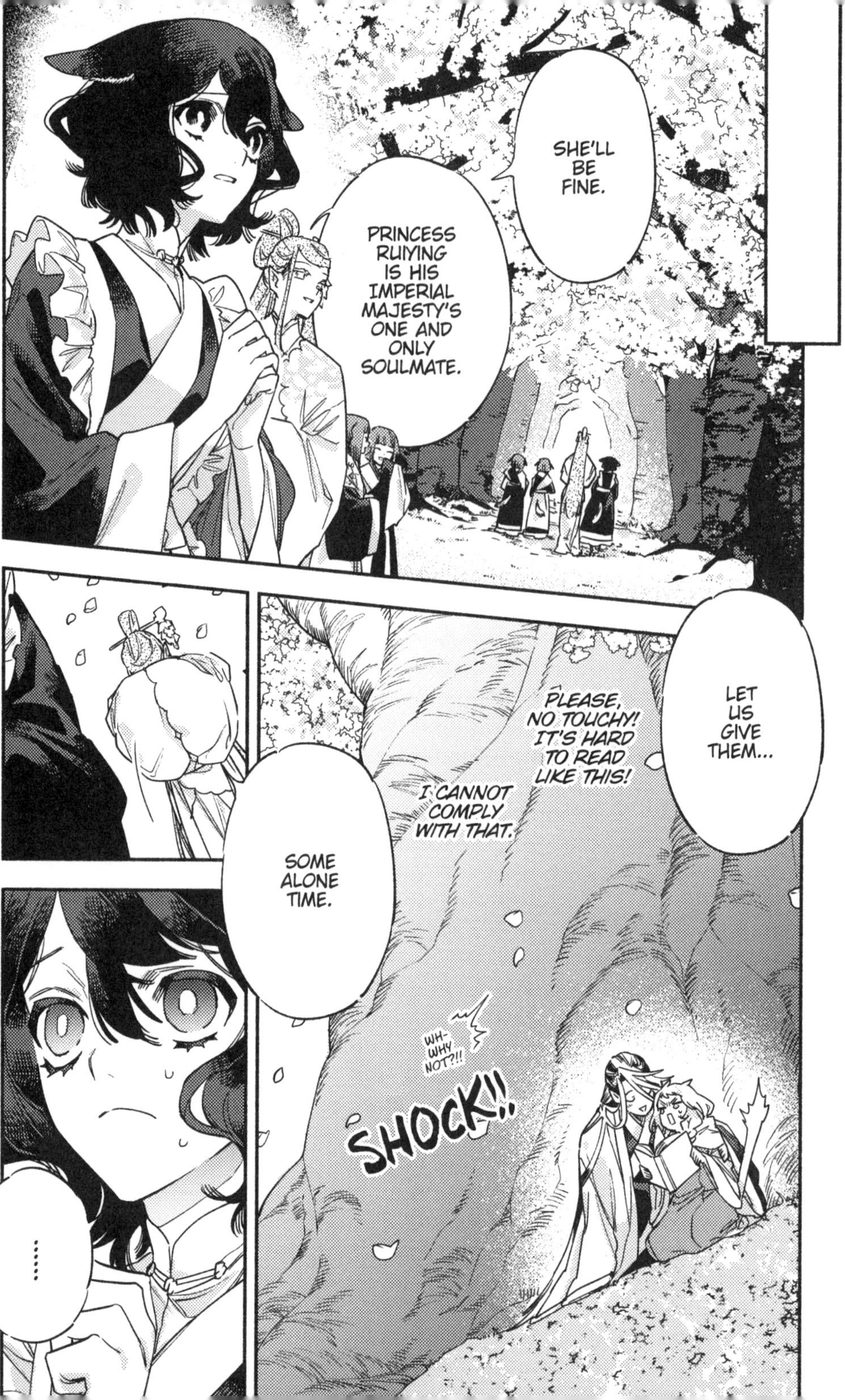
SHE'LL BE FINE.
PRINCESS RUIYING IS HIS IMPERIAL MAJESTY'S ONE AND ONLY SOULMATE.
LET US GIVE THEM...
SOME ALONE TIME.
PLEASE, NO TOUCHY! IT'S HARD TO READ LIKE THIS!
I CANNOT COMPLY WITH THAT.
WH- WHY NOT?!!
SHOCK!!
......

THE DRAGON KING'S IMPERIAL WRATH

FALLING IN LOVE
WITH THE BOOKISH PRINCESS
OF THE RAT CLAN

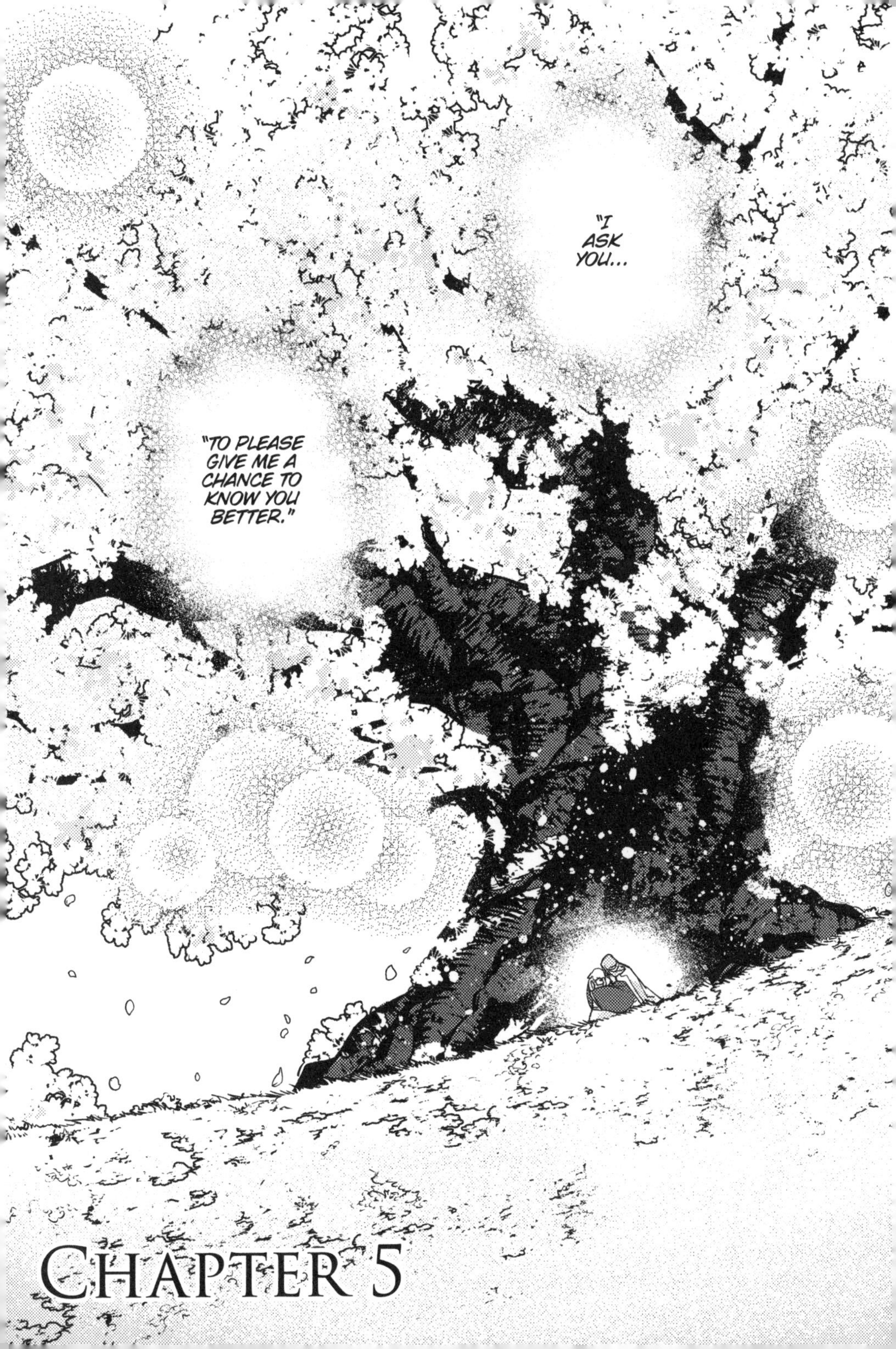
"I ASK YOU...
"TO PLEASE GIVE ME A CHANCE TO KNOW YOU BETTER."
CHAPTER 5

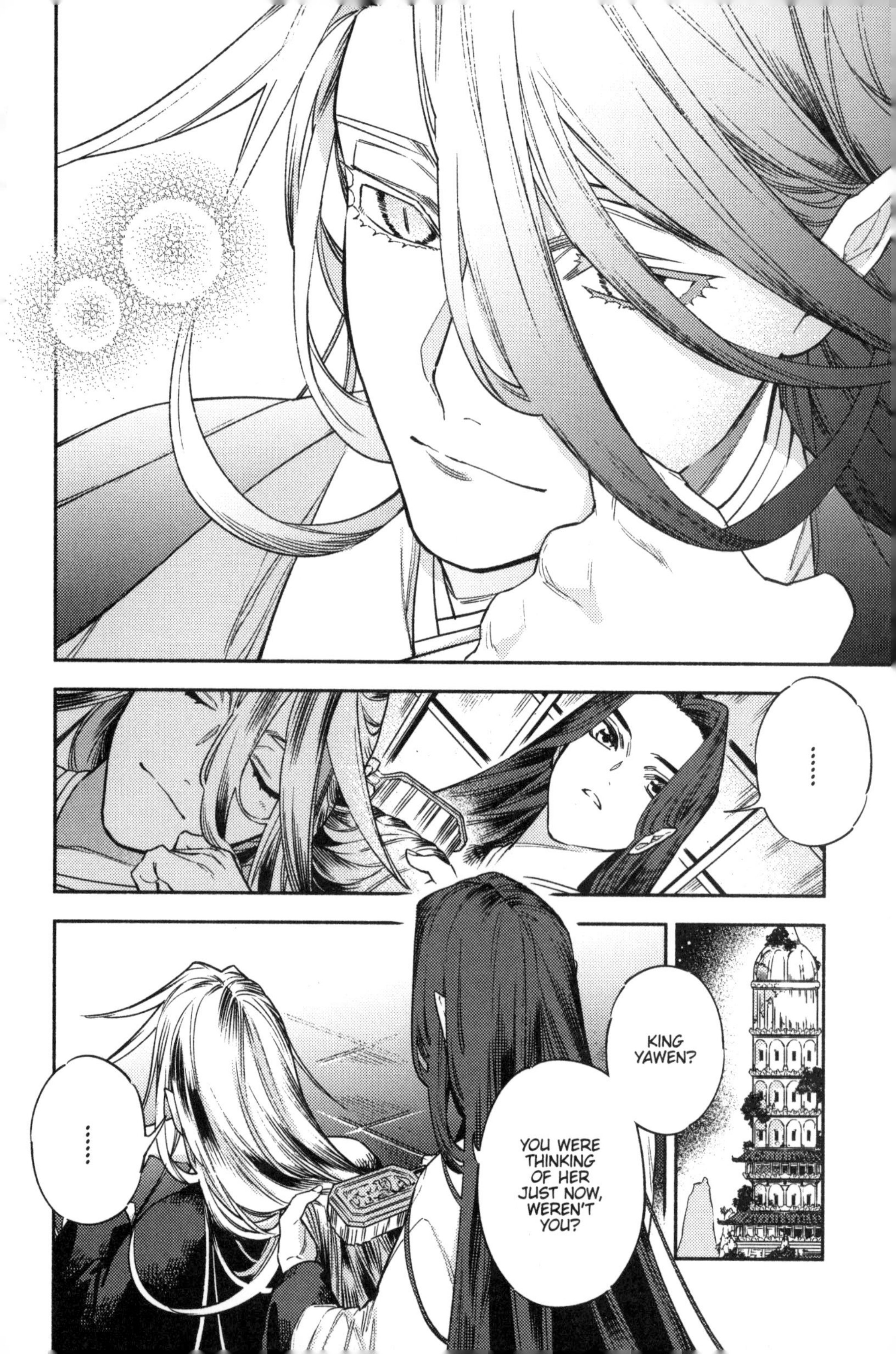
......
KING YAWEN?
YOU WERE THINKING OF HER JUST NOW, WEREN'T YOU?
......

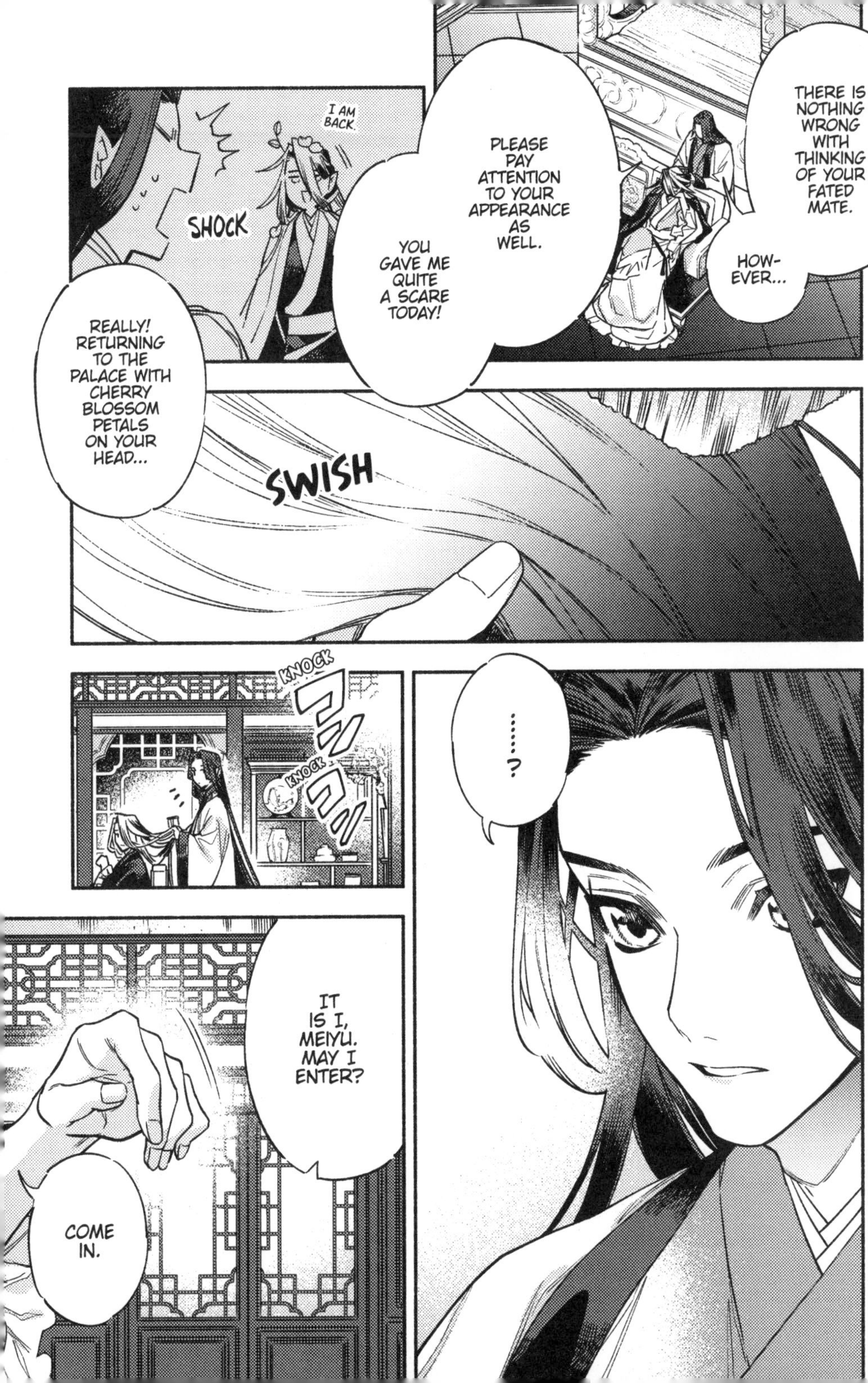
THERE IS NOTHING WRONG WITH THINKING OF YOUR FATED MATE.
HOW-EVER...
PLEASE PAY ATTENTION TO YOUR APPEARANCE AS WELL.
YOU GAVE ME QUITE A SCARE TODAY!
I AM BACK.
SHOCK
REALLY! RETURNING TO THE PALACE WITH CHERRY BLOSSOM PETALS ON YOUR HEAD...
SWISH
......?
KNOCK
KNOCK
IT IS I, MEIYU. MAY I ENTER?
COME IN.

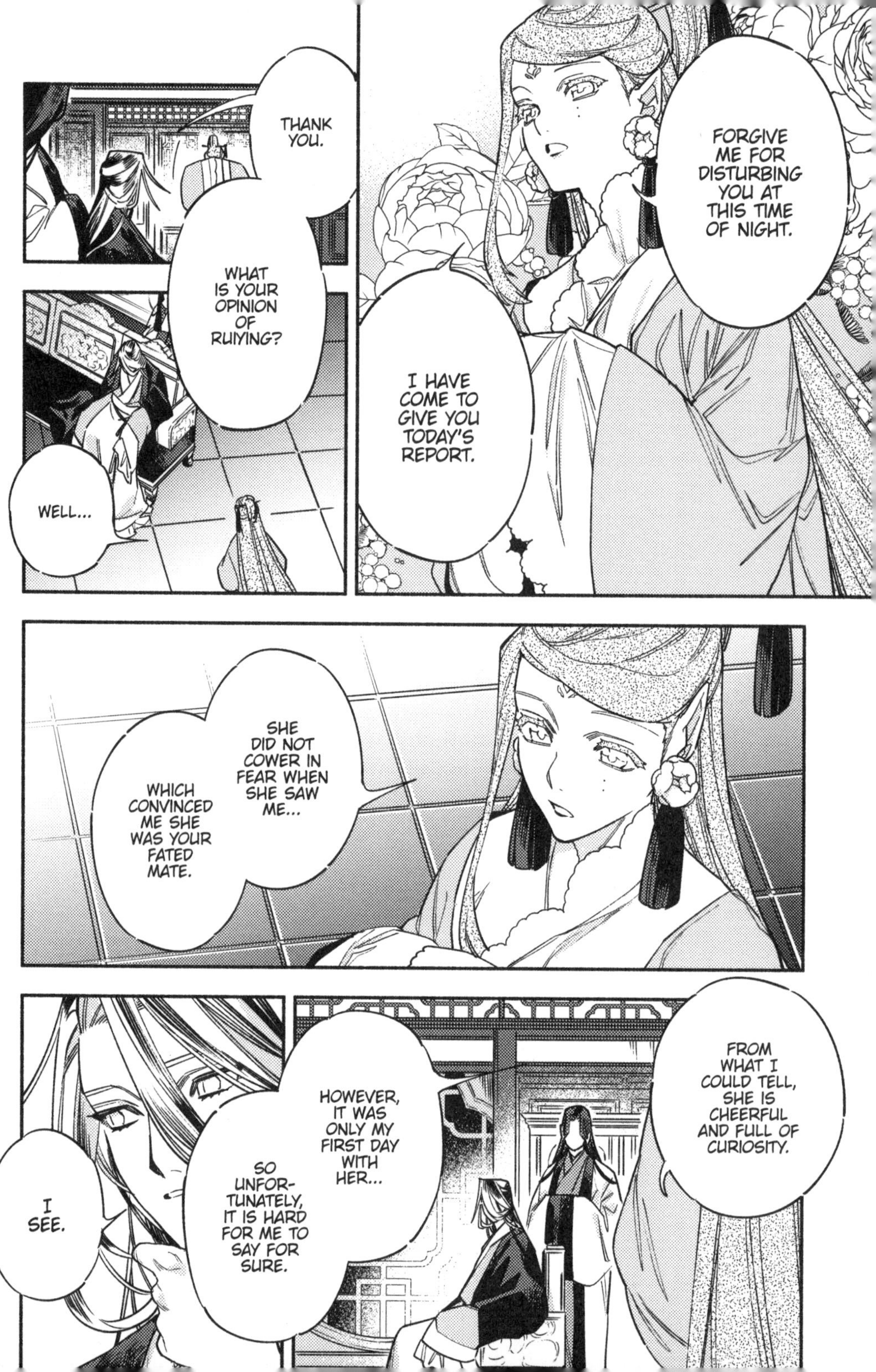
FORGIVE ME FOR DISTURBING YOU AT THIS TIME OF NIGHT.
I HAVE COME TO GIVE YOU TODAY'S REPORT.
THANK YOU.
WHAT IS YOUR OPINION OF RUIYING?
WELL...
SHE DID NOT COWER IN FEAR WHEN SHE SAW ME...
WHICH CONVINCED ME SHE WAS YOUR FATED MATE.
FROM WHAT I COULD TELL, SHE IS CHEERFUL AND FULL OF CURIOSITY.
HOWEVER, IT WAS ONLY MY FIRST DAY WITH HER...
SO UNFOR-TUNATELY, IT IS HARD FOR ME TO SAY FOR SURE.
I SEE.

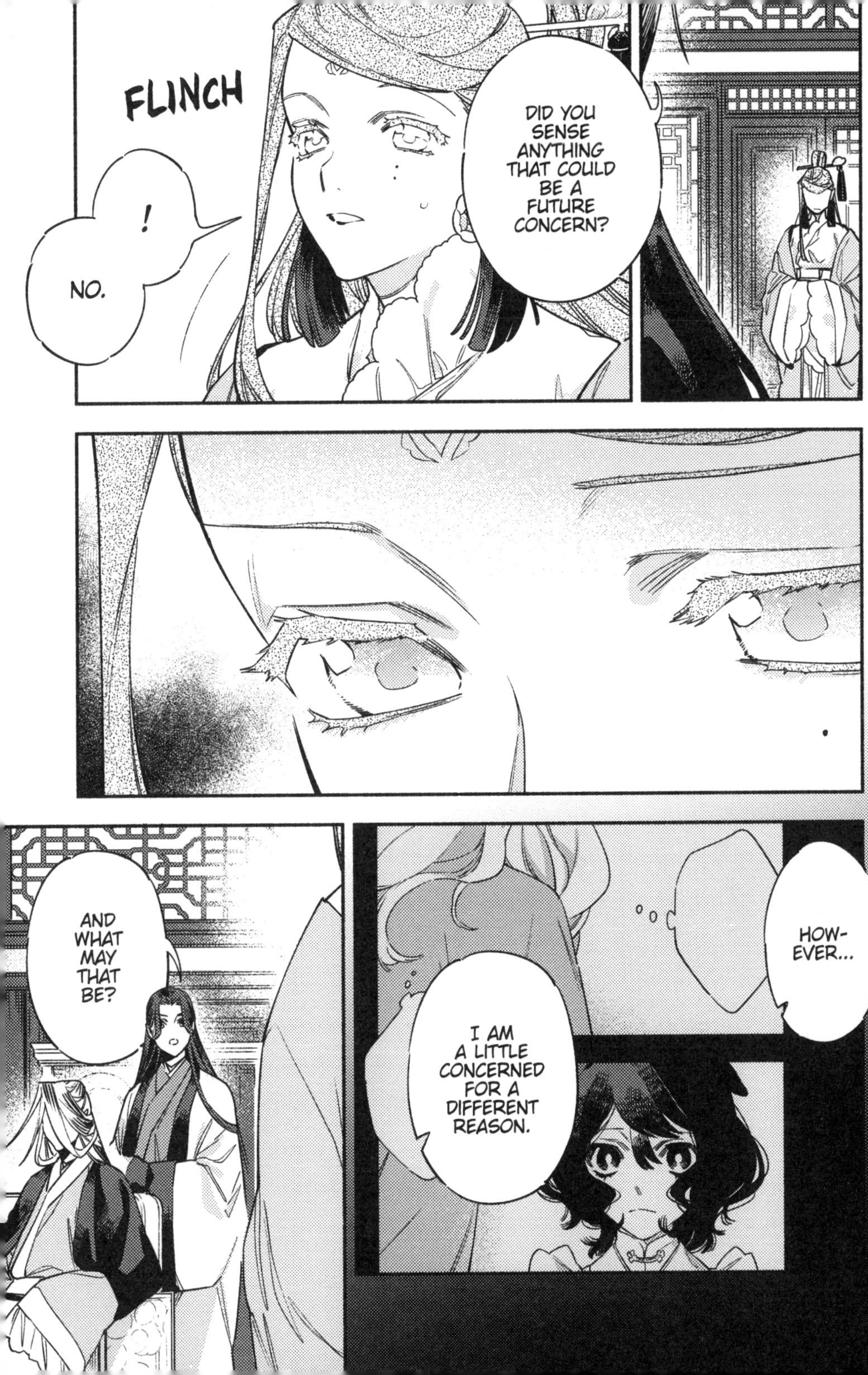
DID YOU SENSE ANYTHING THAT COULD BE A FUTURE CONCERN?
FLINCH
!
NO.
HOW-EVER...
I AM A LITTLE CONCERNED FOR A DIFFERENT REASON.
AND WHAT MAY THAT BE?

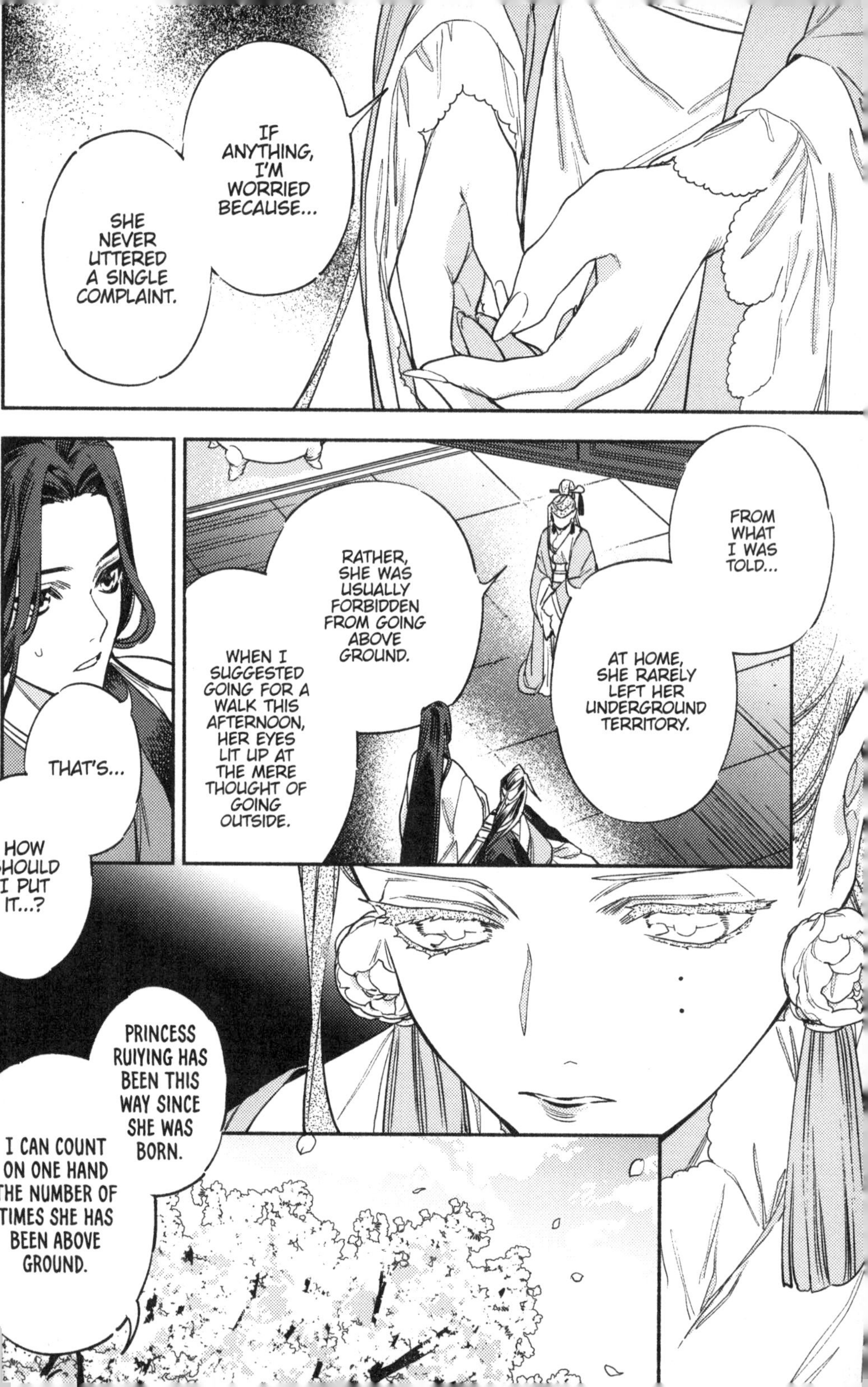
IF ANYTHING, I'M WORRIED BECAUSE...
SHE NEVER UTTERED A SINGLE COMPLAINT.
FROM WHAT I WAS TOLD...
AT HOME, SHE RARELY LEFT HER UNDERGROUND TERRITORY.
RATHER, SHE WAS USUALLY FORBIDDEN FROM GOING ABOVE GROUND.
WHEN I SUGGESTED GOING FOR A WALK THIS AFTERNOON, HER EYES LIT UP AT THE MERE THOUGHT OF GOING OUTSIDE.
THAT'S...
HOW SHOULD I PUT IT...?
PRINCESS RUIYING HAS BEEN THIS WAY SINCE SHE WAS BORN.
I CAN COUNT ON ONE HAND THE NUMBER OF TIMES SHE HAS BEEN ABOVE GROUND.

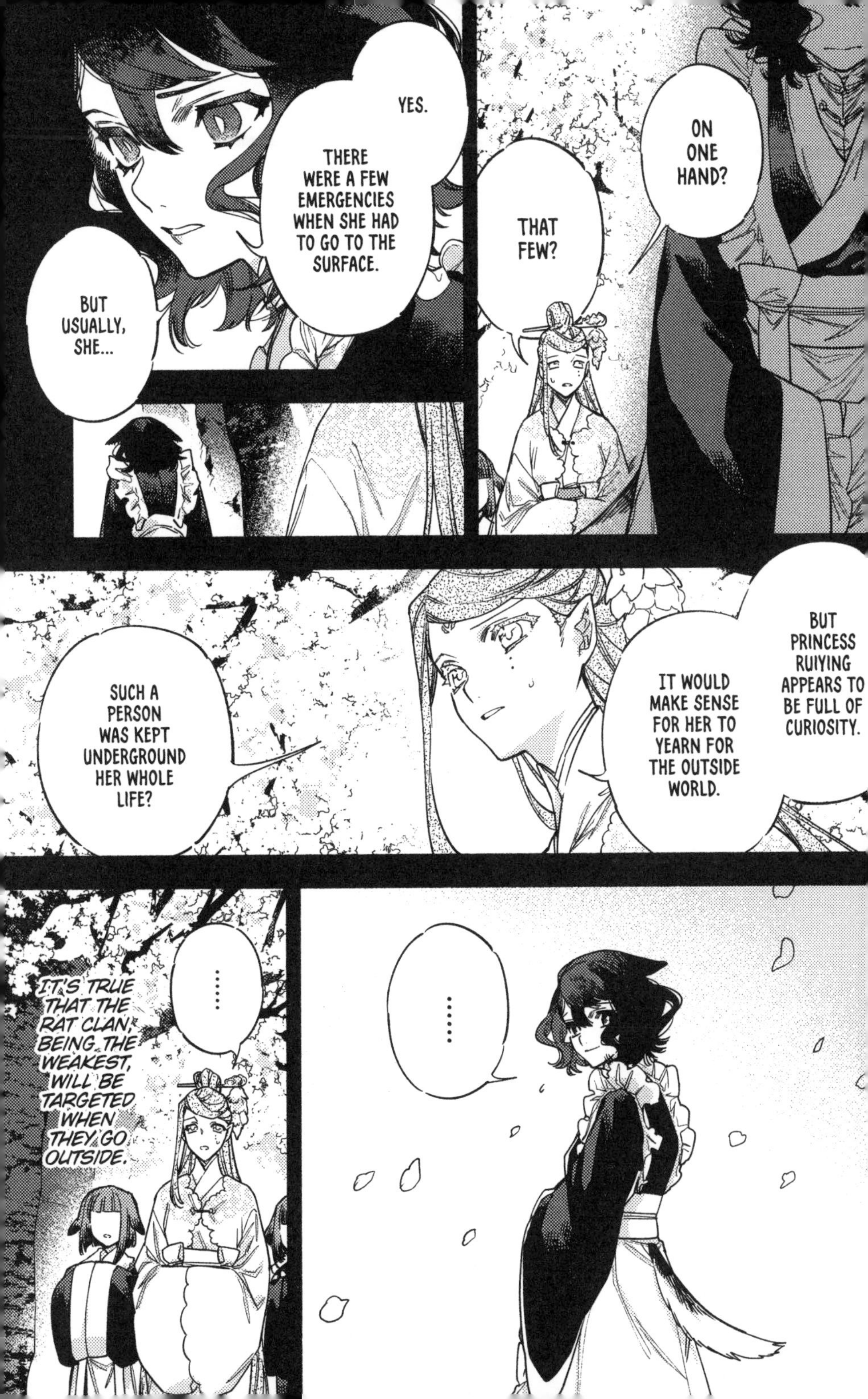
ON ONE HAND?
THAT FEW?
YES.
THERE WERE A FEW EMERGENCIES WHEN SHE HAD TO GO TO THE SURFACE.
BUT USUALLY, SHE...
BUT PRINCESS RUIYING APPEARS TO BE FULL OF CURIOSITY.
IT WOULD MAKE SENSE FOR HER TO YEARN FOR THE OUTSIDE WORLD.
SUCH A PERSON WAS KEPT UNDERGROUND HER WHOLE LIFE?
......
......
IT'S TRUE THAT THE RAT CLAN, BEING THE WEAKEST, WILL BE TARGETED WHEN THEY GO OUTSIDE.

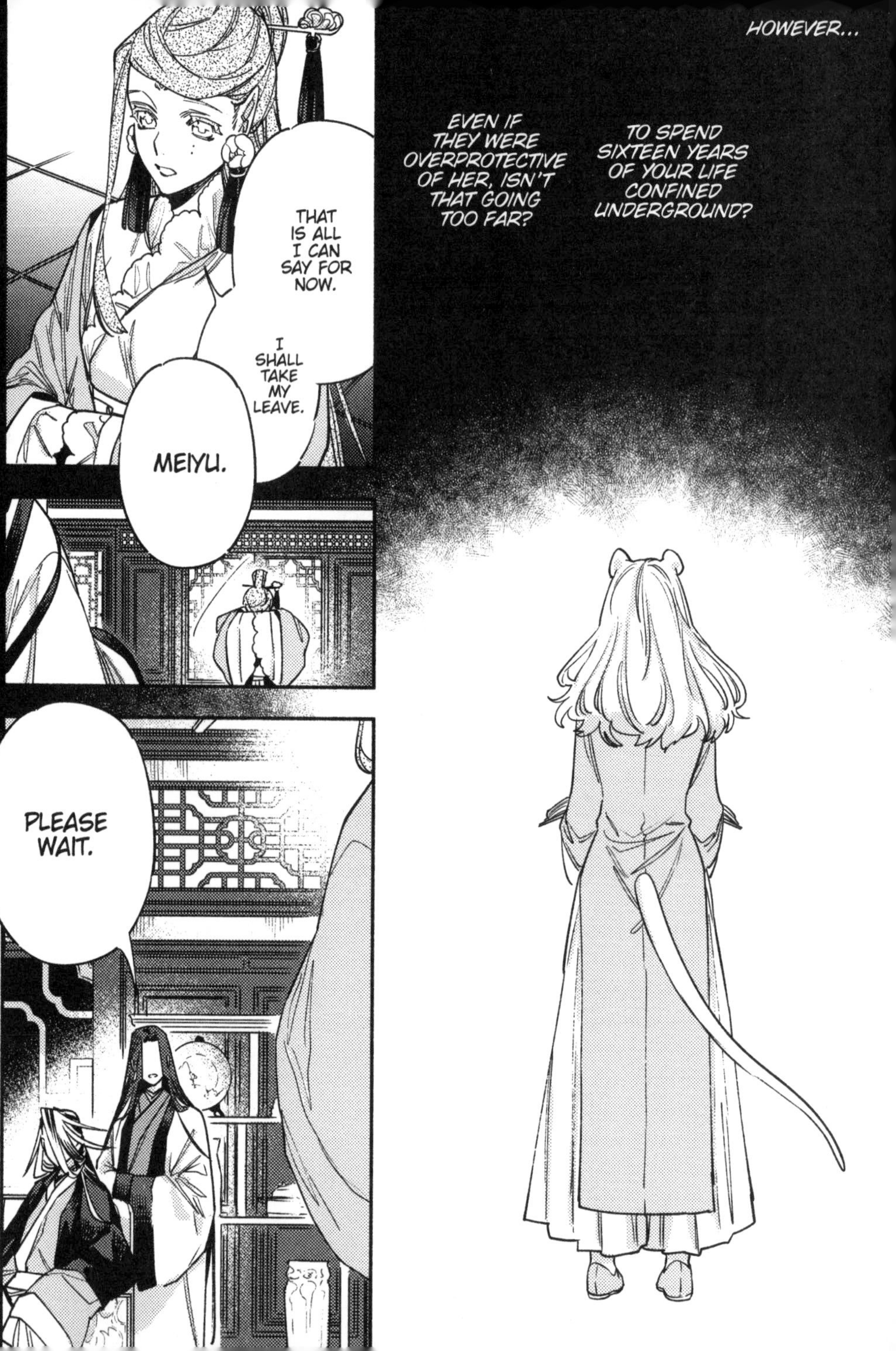
HOWEVER...
TO SPEND SIXTEEN YEARS OF YOUR LIFE CONFINED UNDERGROUND?
EVEN IF THEY WERE OVERPROTECTIVE OF HER, ISN'T THAT GOING TOO FAR?
THAT IS ALL I CAN SAY FOR NOW.
I SHALL TAKE MY LEAVE.
MEIYU.
PLEASE WAIT.

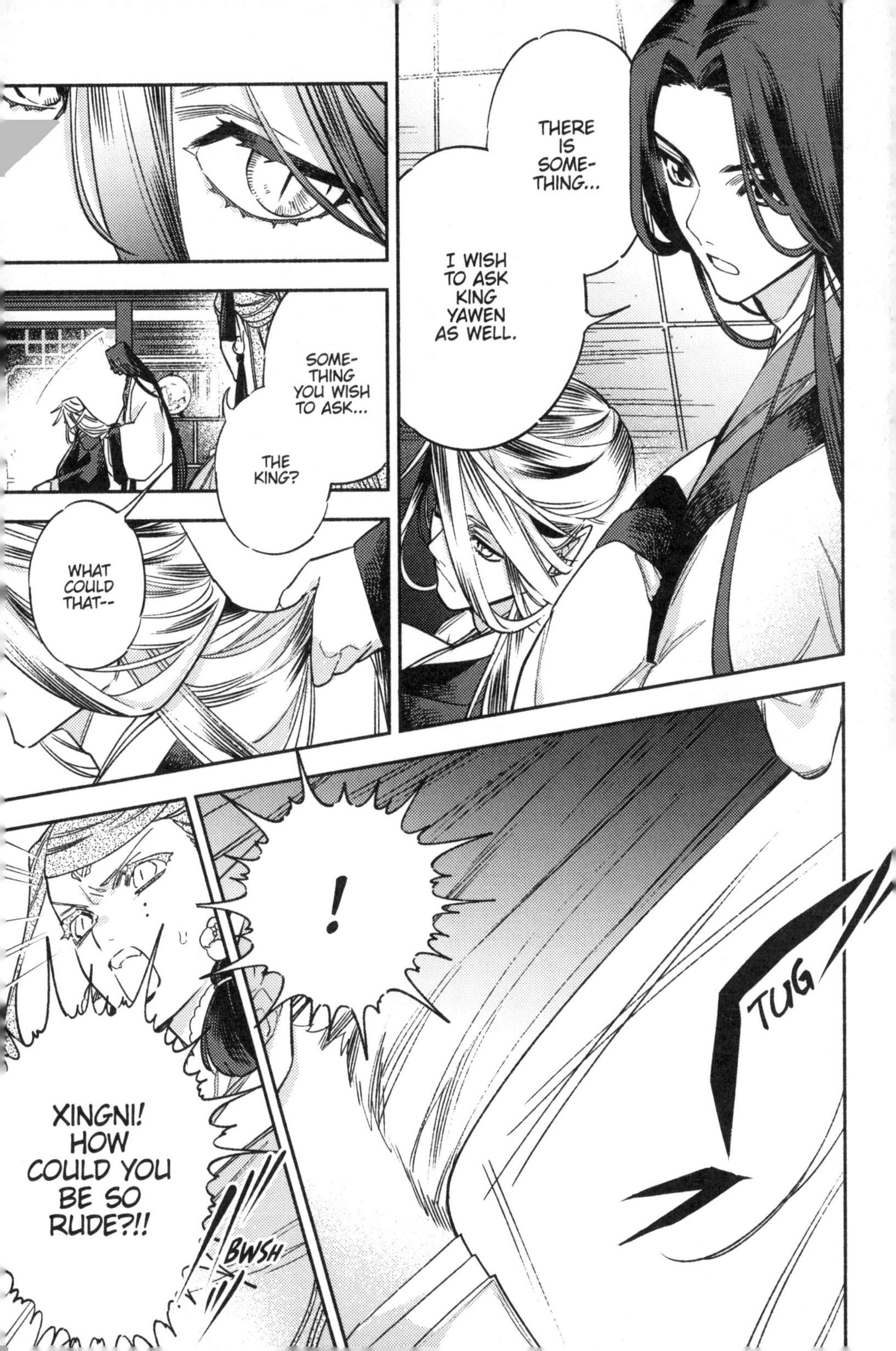
THERE IS SOME-THING...
I WISH TO ASK KING YAWEN AS WELL.
SOME-THING YOU WISH TO ASK...
THE KING?
WHAT COULD THAT--
TUG
!
XINGNI! HOW COULD YOU BE SO RUDE?!!
BWSH

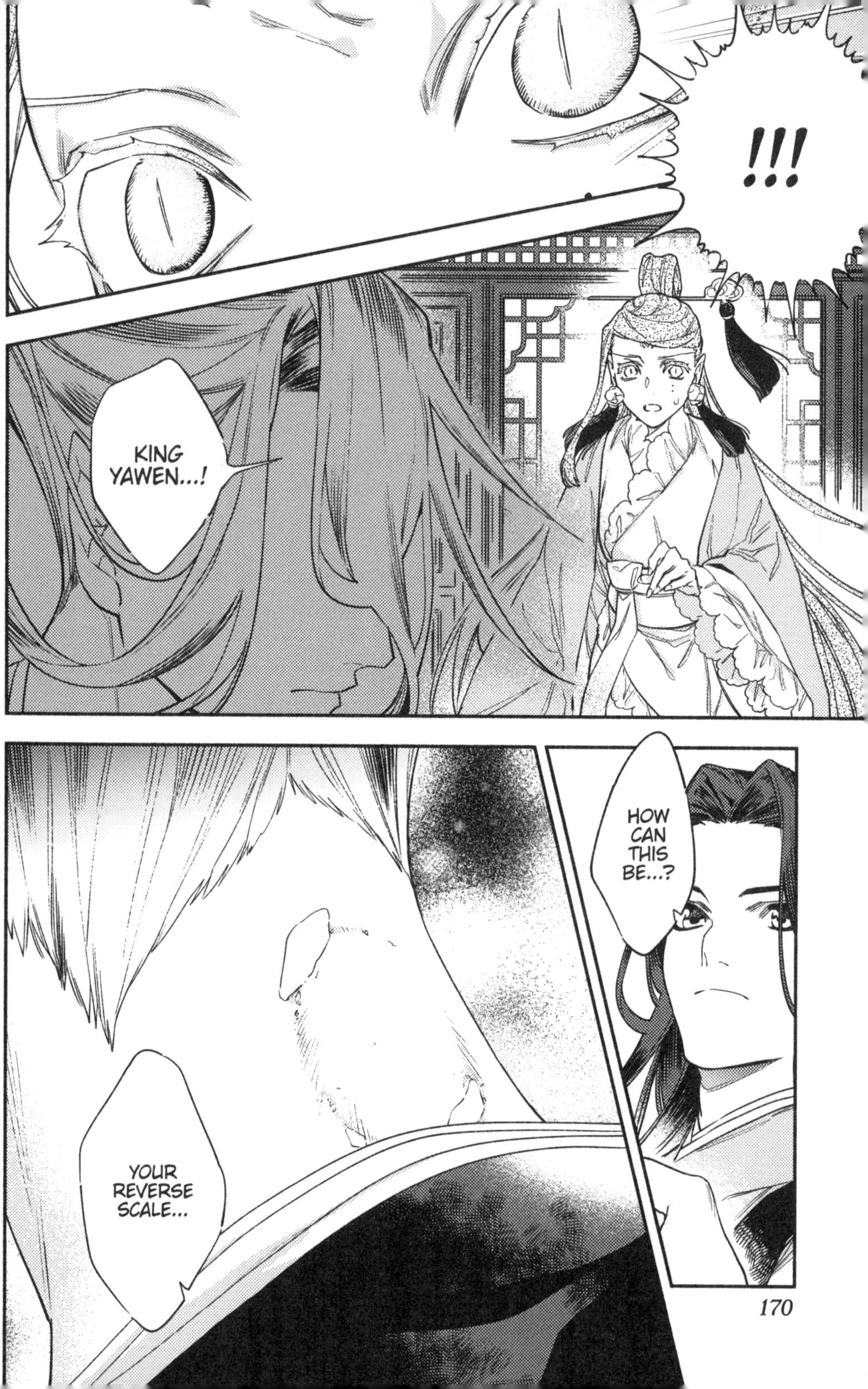
!!!
KING YAWEN...!
HOW CAN THIS BE...?
YOUR REVERSE SCALE...

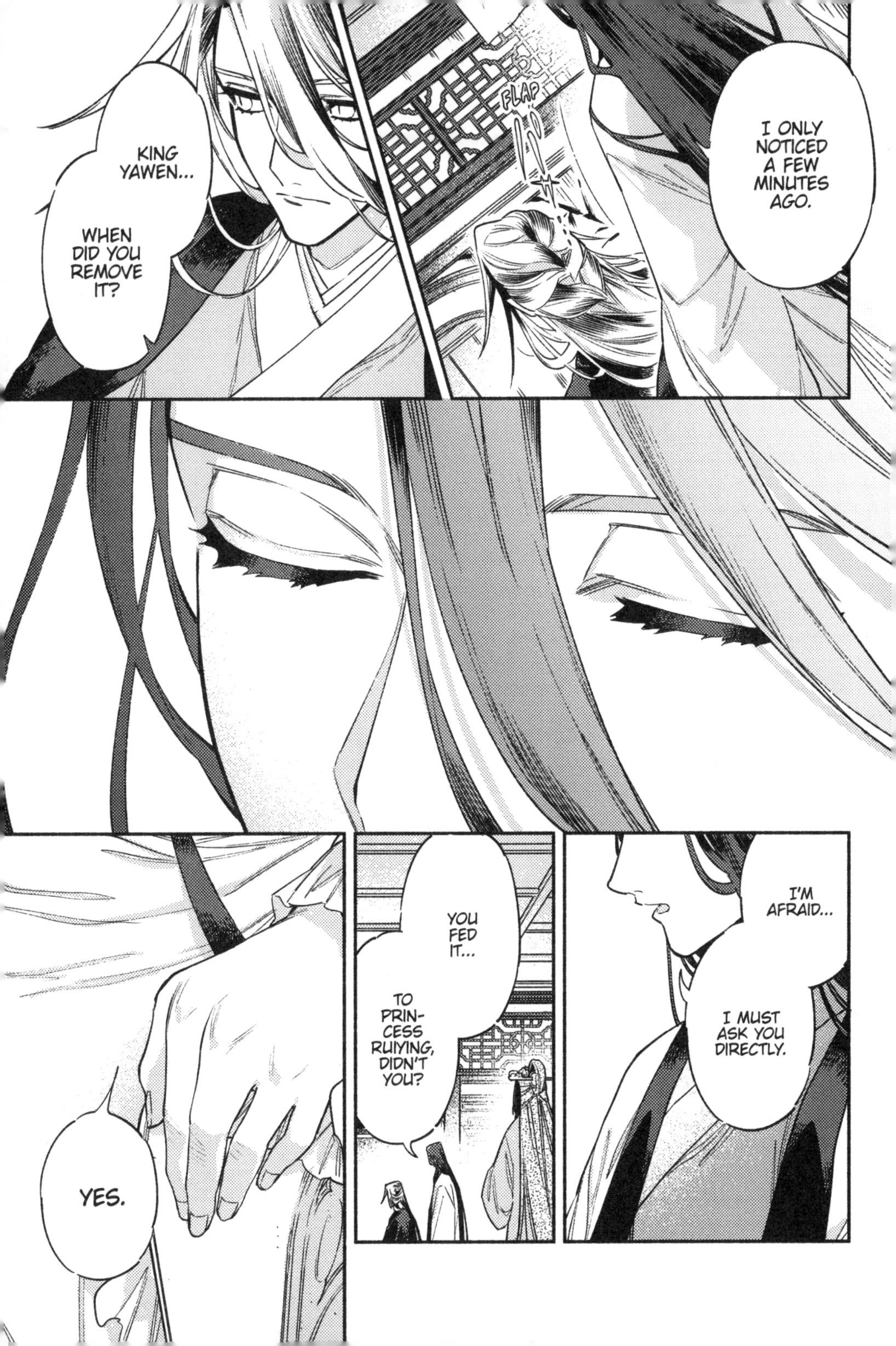
FLAP
I ONLY NOTICED A FEW MINUTES AGO.
KING YAWEN...
WHEN DID YOU REMOVE IT?
I'M AFRAID...
I MUST ASK YOU DIRECTLY.
YOU FED IT...
TO PRINCESS RUIYING, DIDN'T YOU?
YES.

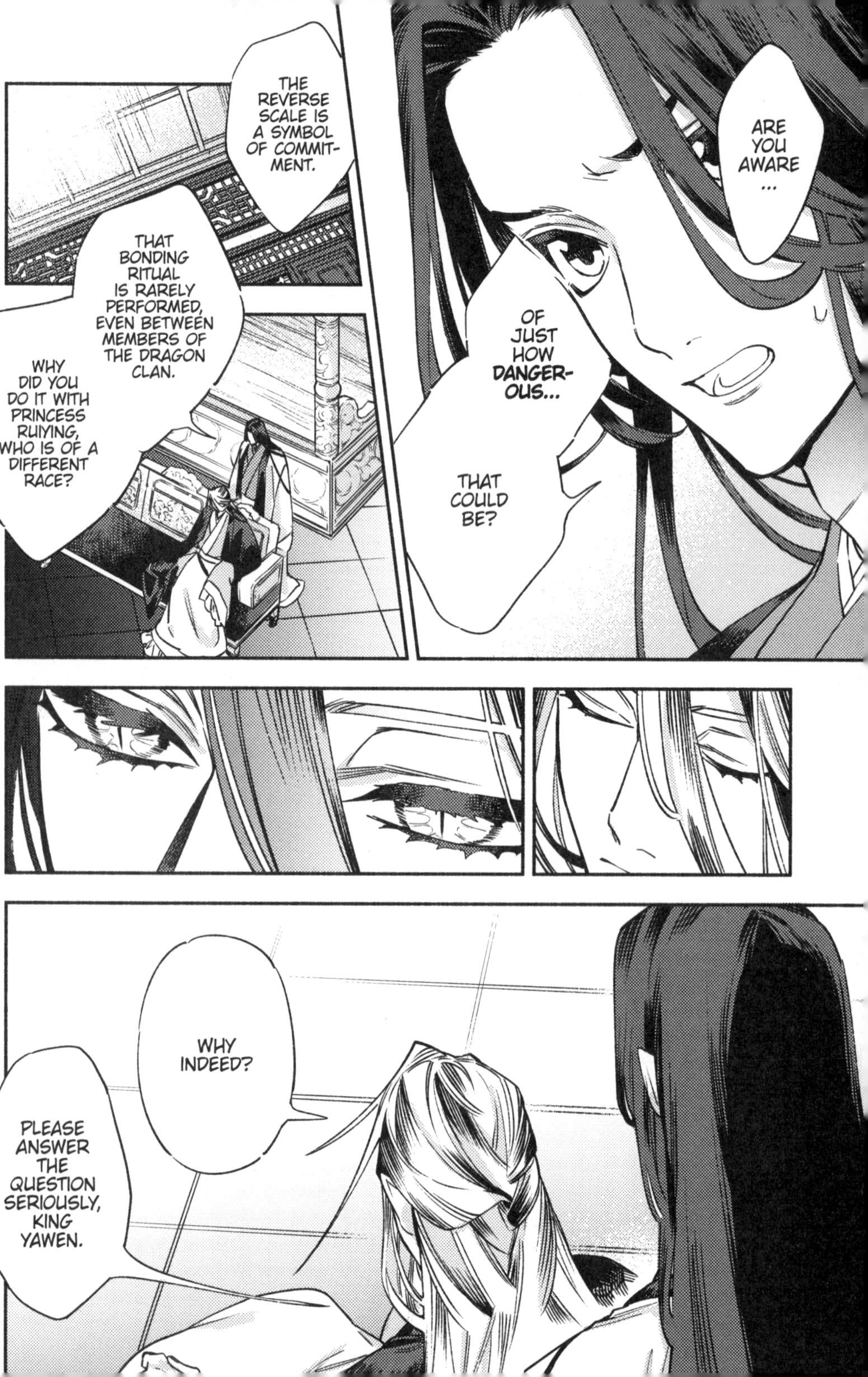
ARE YOU AWARE ...
OF JUST HOW DANGEROUS...
THAT COULD BE?
THE REVERSE SCALE IS A SYMBOL OF COMMITMENT.
THAT BONDING RITUAL IS RARELY PERFORMED, EVEN BETWEEN MEMBERS OF THE DRAGON CLAN.
WHY DID YOU DO IT WITH PRINCESS RUIYING, WHO IS OF A DIFFERENT RACE?
WHY INDEED?
PLEASE ANSWER THE QUESTION SERIOUSLY, KING YAWEN.

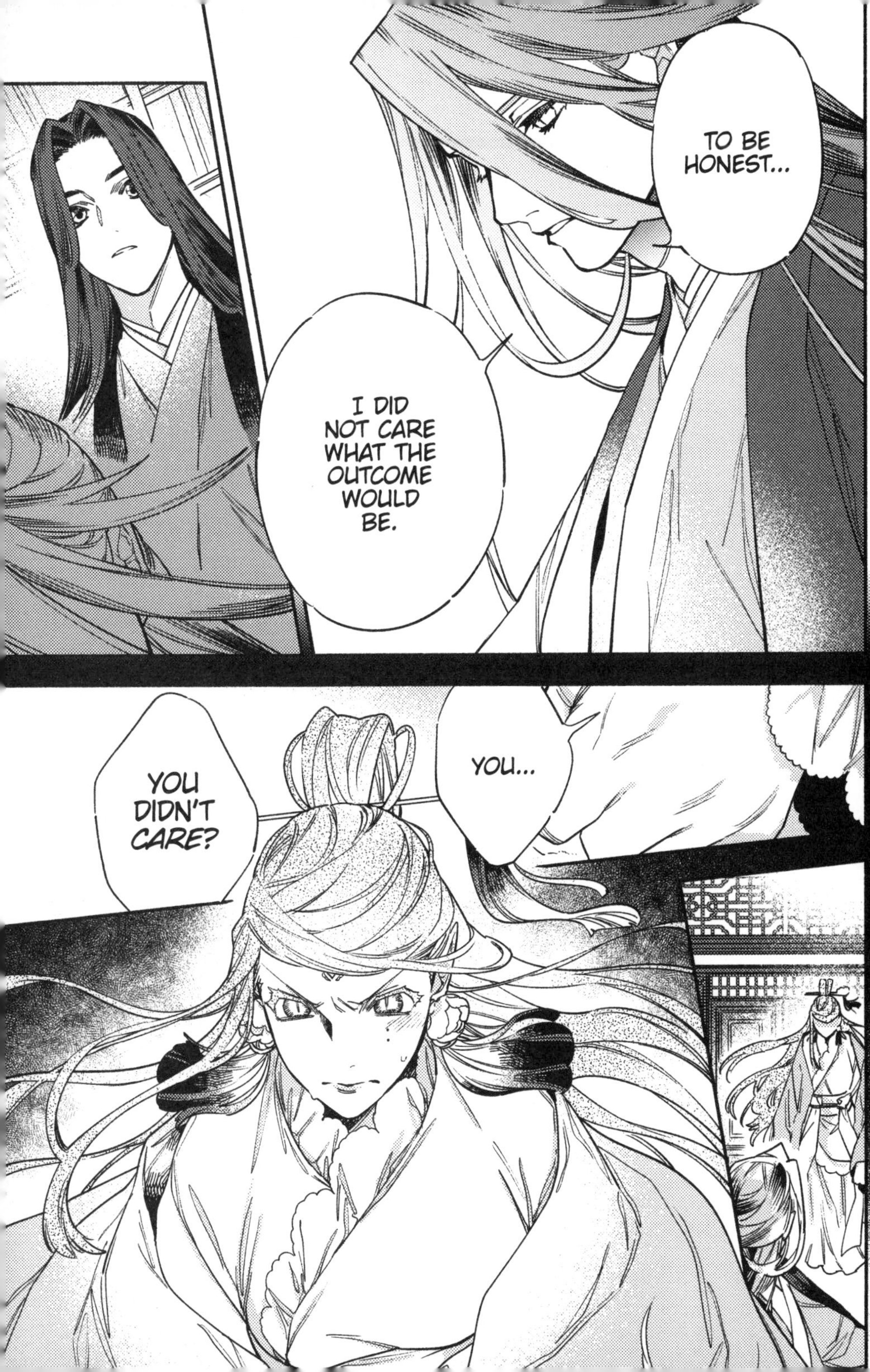
TO BE HONEST...
I DID NOT CARE WHAT THE OUTCOME WOULD BE.
YOU...
YOU DIDN'T CARE?

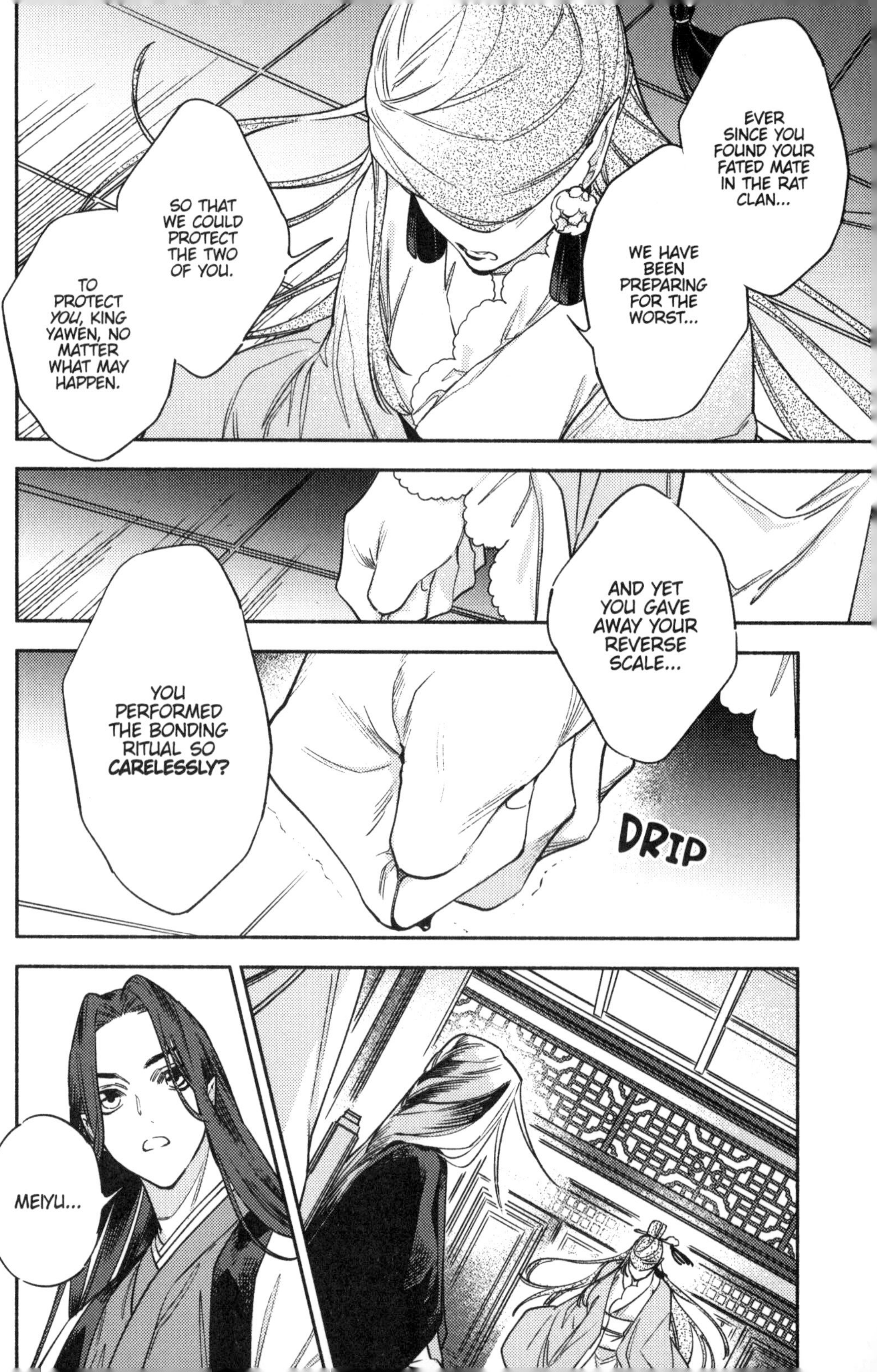
EVER SINCE YOU FOUND YOUR FATED MATE IN THE RAT CLAN...
WE HAVE BEEN PREPARING FOR THE WORST...
SO THAT WE COULD PROTECT THE TWO OF YOU.
TO PROTECT *YOU*, KING YAWEN, NO MATTER WHAT MAY HAPPEN.
AND YET YOU GAVE AWAY YOUR REVERSE SCALE...
YOU PERFORMED THE BONDING RITUAL SO **CARELESSLY?**
DRIP
MEIYU...

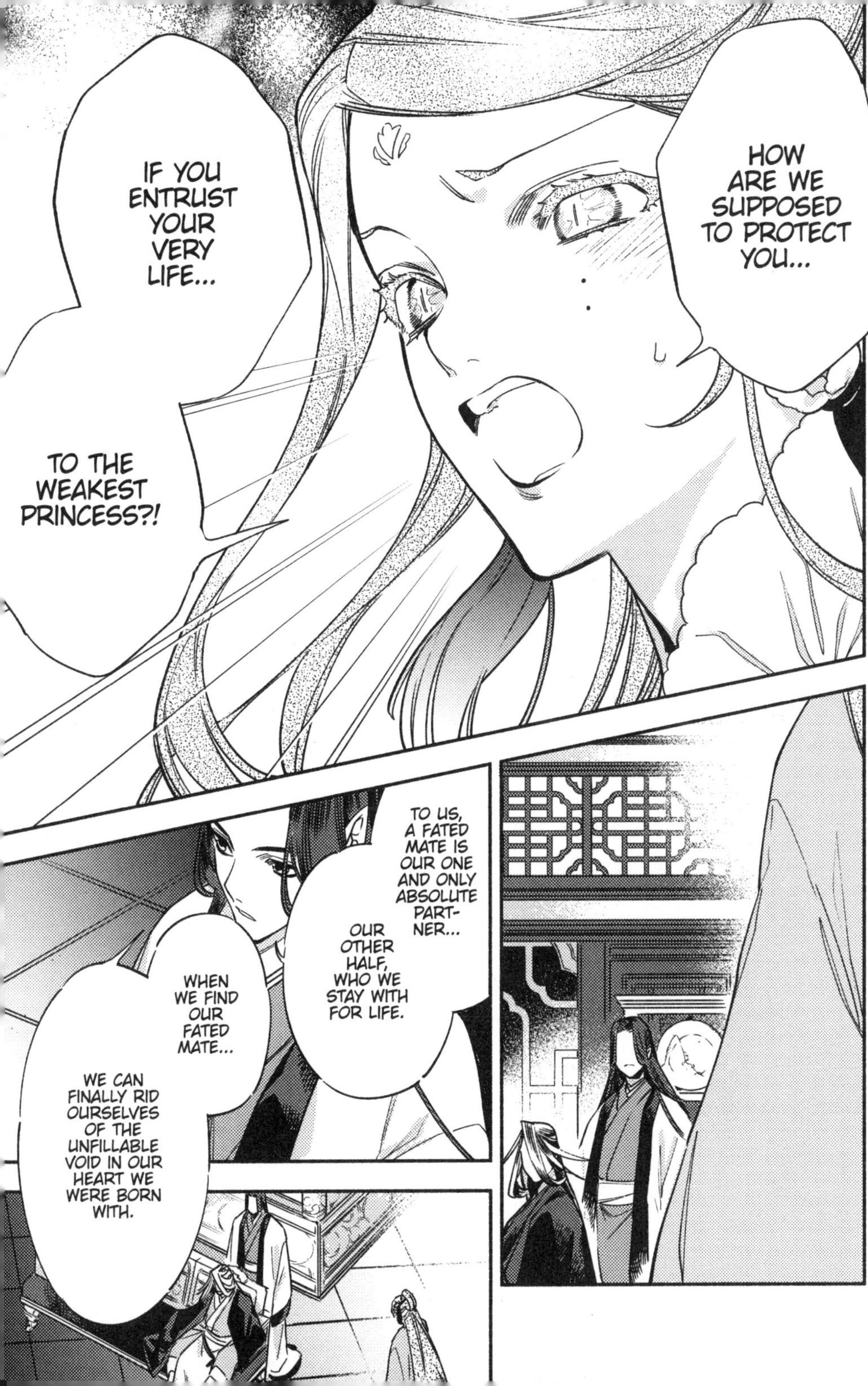
HOW ARE WE SUPPOSED TO PROTECT YOU...
IF YOU ENTRUST YOUR VERY LIFE...
TO THE WEAKEST PRINCESS?!
TO US, A FATED MATE IS OUR ONE AND ONLY ABSOLUTE PART-NER...
OUR OTHER HALF, WHO WE STAY WITH FOR LIFE.
WHEN WE FIND OUR FATED MATE...
WE CAN FINALLY RID OURSELVES OF THE UNFILLABLE VOID IN OUR HEART WE WERE BORN WITH.

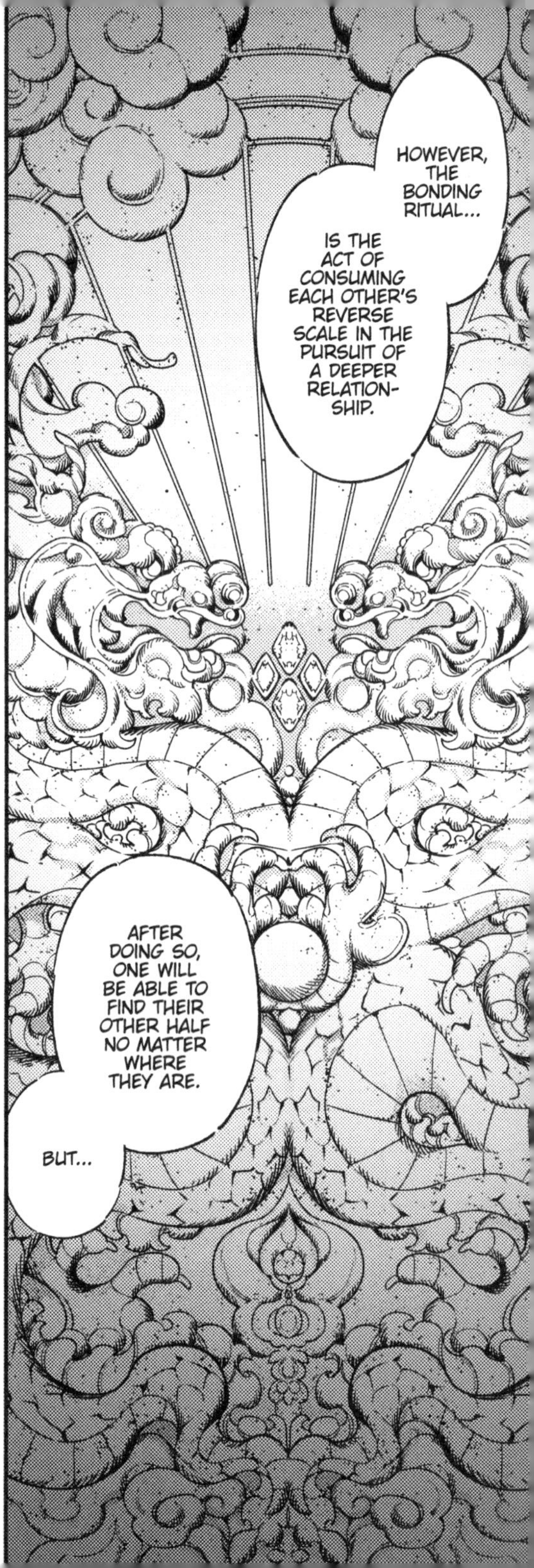
HOWEVER, THE BONDING RITUAL...
IS THE ACT OF CONSUMING EACH OTHER'S REVERSE SCALE IN THE PURSUIT OF A DEEPER RELATIONSHIP.
AFTER DOING SO, ONE WILL BE ABLE TO FIND THEIR OTHER HALF NO MATTER WHERE THEY ARE.
BUT...

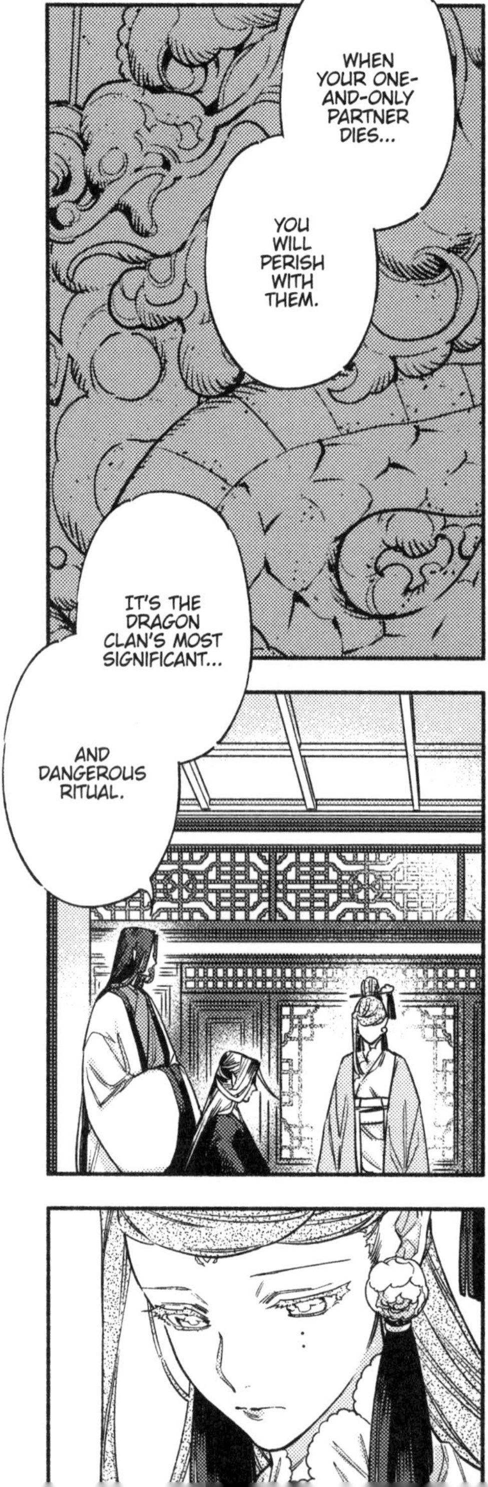
WHEN YOUR ONE-AND-ONLY PARTNER DIES...
YOU WILL PERISH WITH THEM.
IT'S THE DRAGON CLAN'S MOST SIGNIFICANT...
AND DANGEROUS RITUAL.

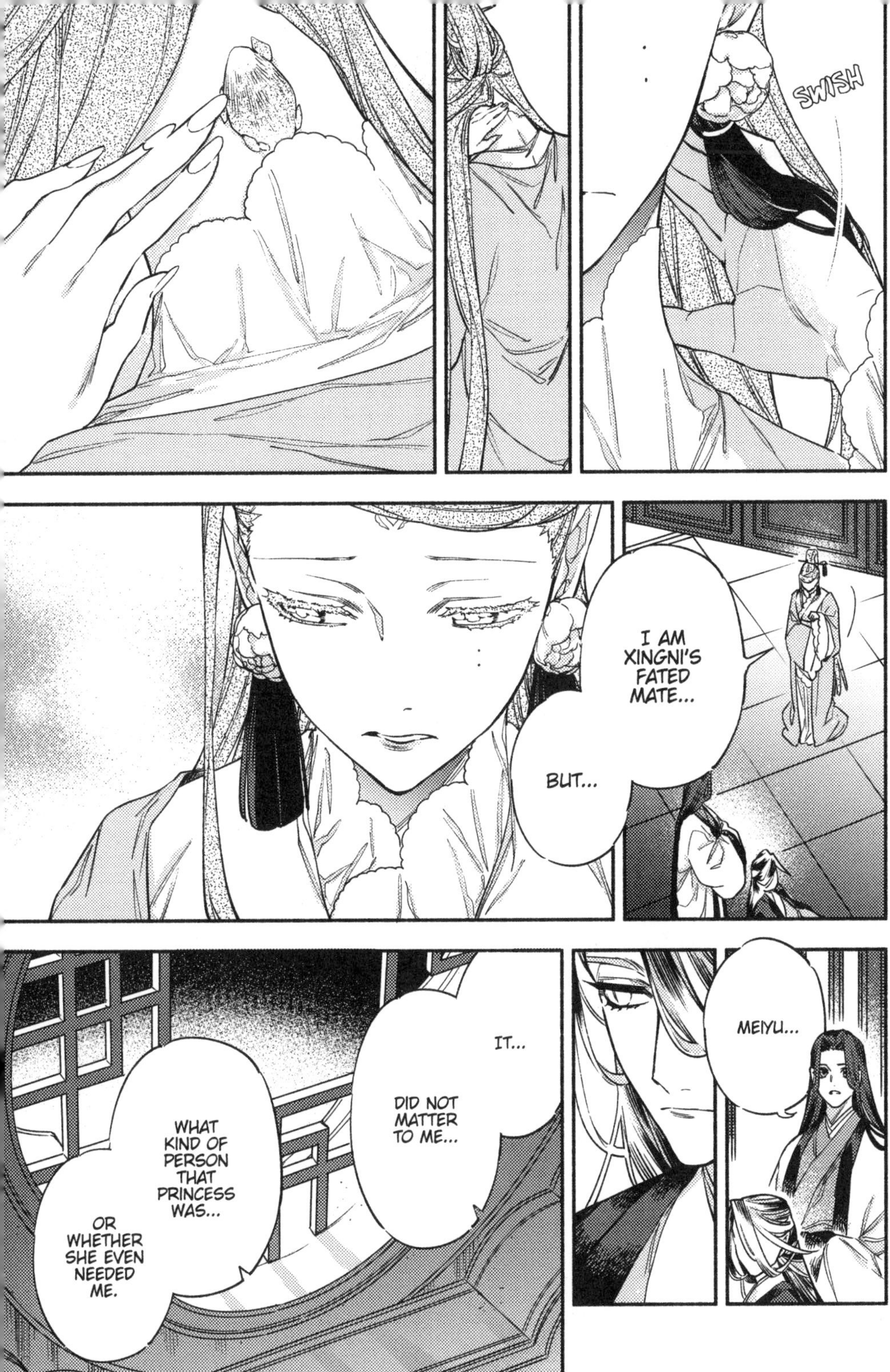
SWISH
I AM XINGNI'S FATED MATE...
BUT...
MEIYU...
IT...
DID NOT MATTER TO ME...
WHAT KIND OF PERSON THAT PRINCESS WAS...
OR WHETHER SHE EVEN NEEDED ME.

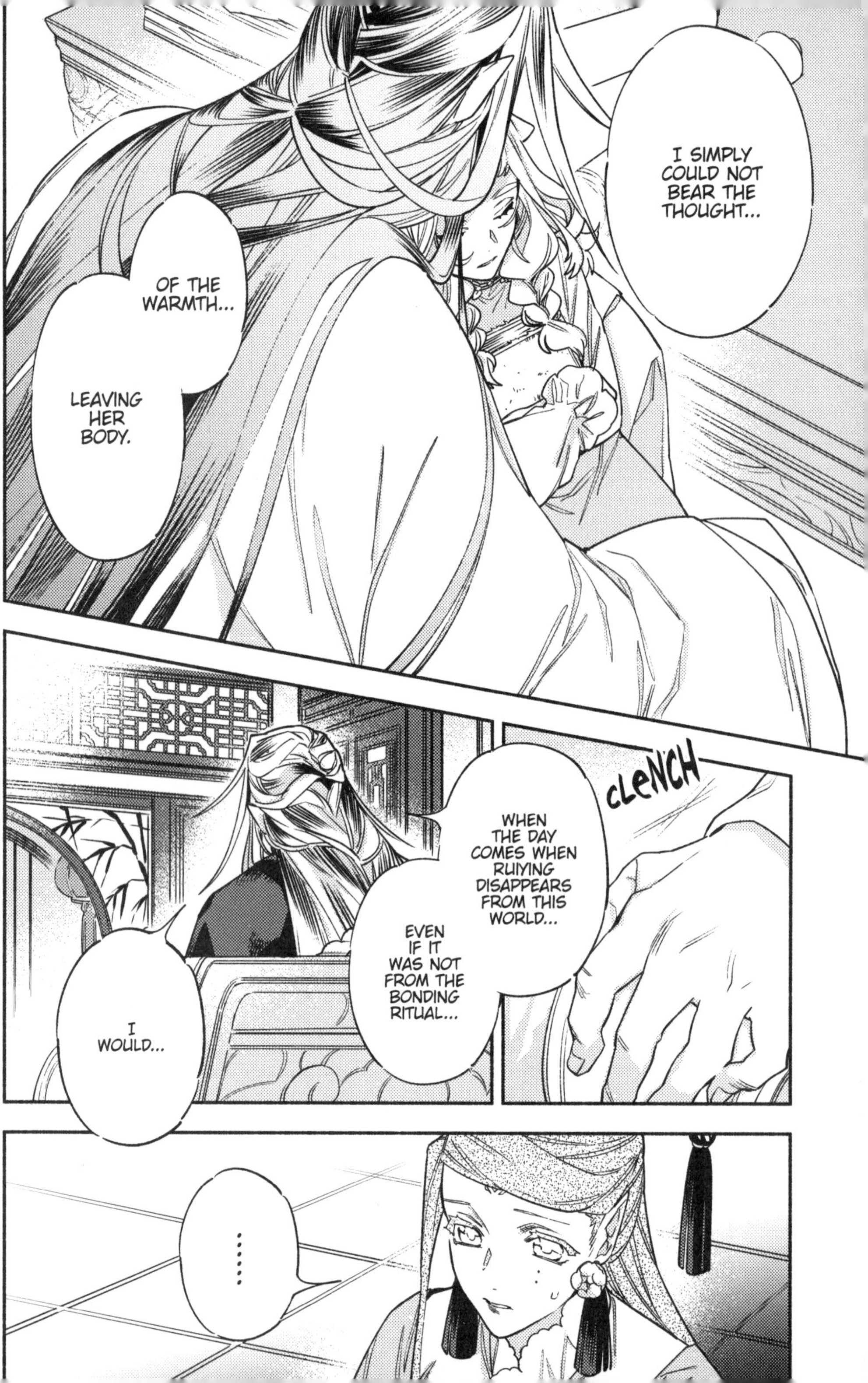
I SIMPLY COULD NOT BEAR THE THOUGHT...
OF THE WARMTH...
LEAVING HER BODY.
CLENCH
WHEN THE DAY COMES WHEN RUIYING DISAPPEARS FROM THIS WORLD...
EVEN IF IT WAS NOT FROM THE BONDING RITUAL...
I WOULD...
......

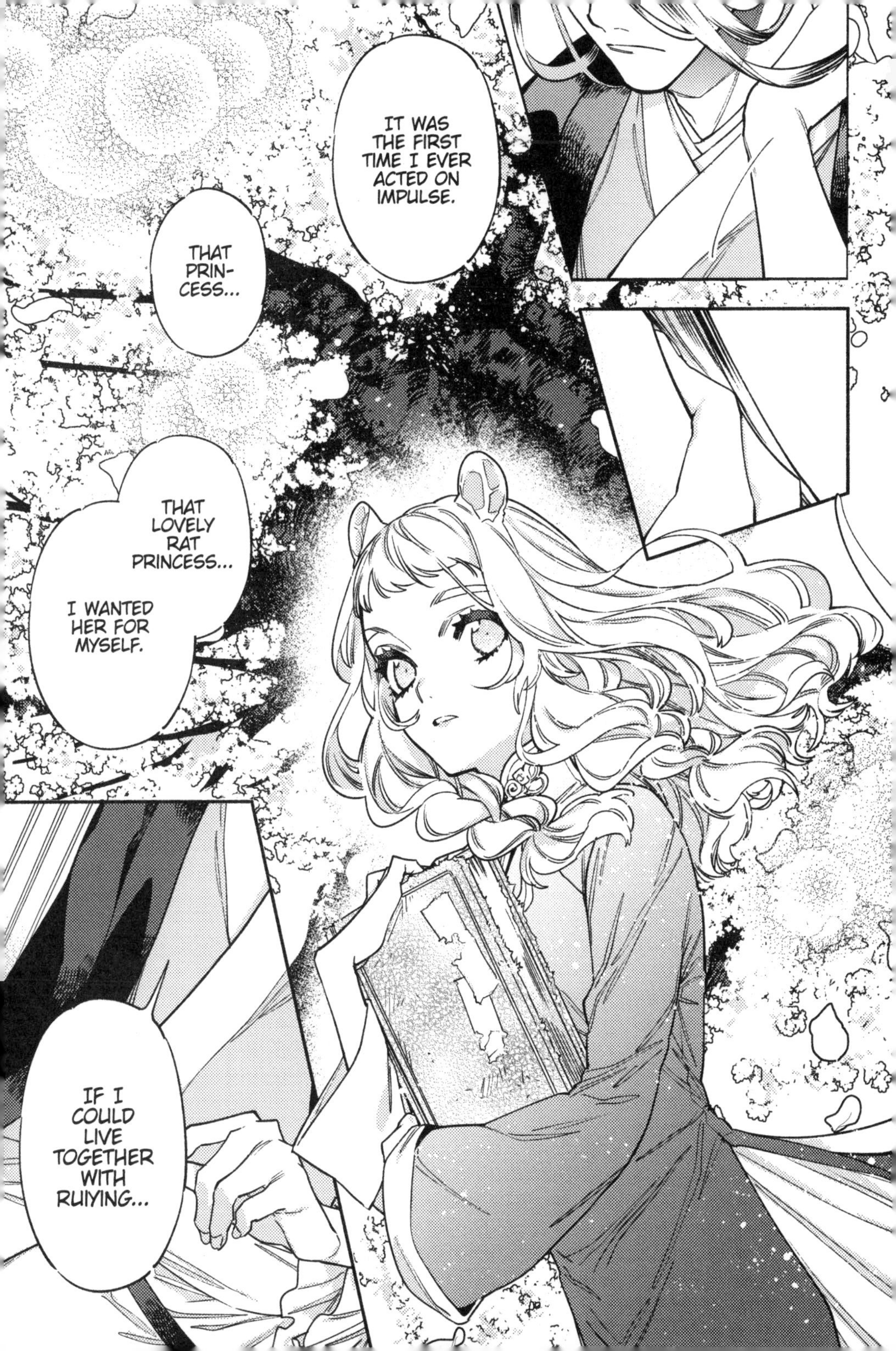
IT WAS THE FIRST TIME I EVER ACTED ON IMPULSE.
THAT PRIN-CESS...
THAT LOVELY RAT PRINCESS... I WANTED HER FOR MYSELF.
IF I COULD LIVE TOGETHER WITH RUIYING...

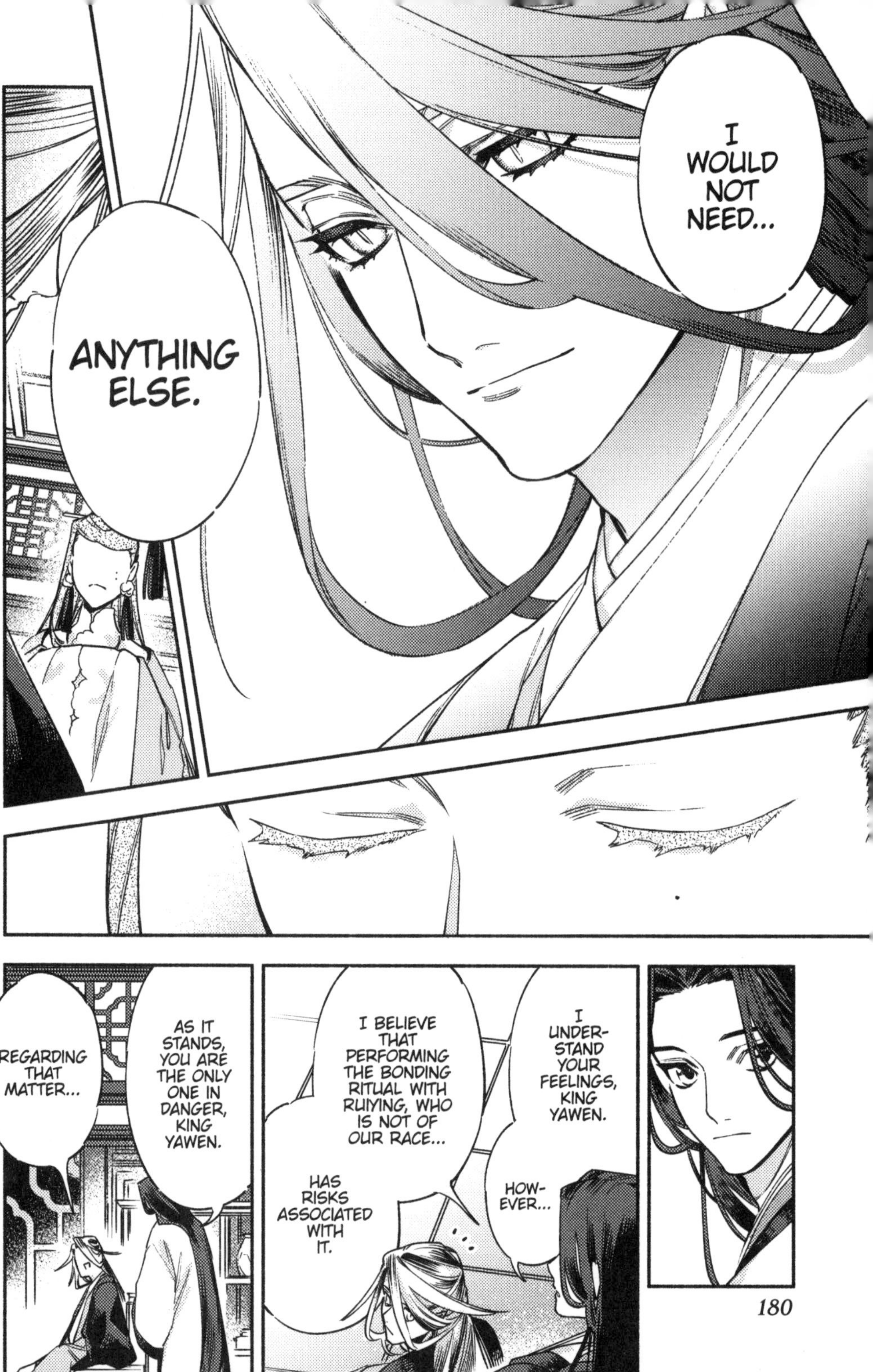
I WOULD NOT NEED...
ANYTHING ELSE.
I UNDER-STAND YOUR FEELINGS, KING YAWEN.
HOW-EVER...
I BELIEVE THAT PERFORMING THE BONDING RITUAL WITH RUIYING, WHO IS NOT OF OUR RACE...
HAS RISKS ASSOCIATED WITH IT.
...
AS IT STANDS, YOU ARE THE ONLY ONE IN DANGER, KING YAWEN.
REGARDING THAT MATTER...

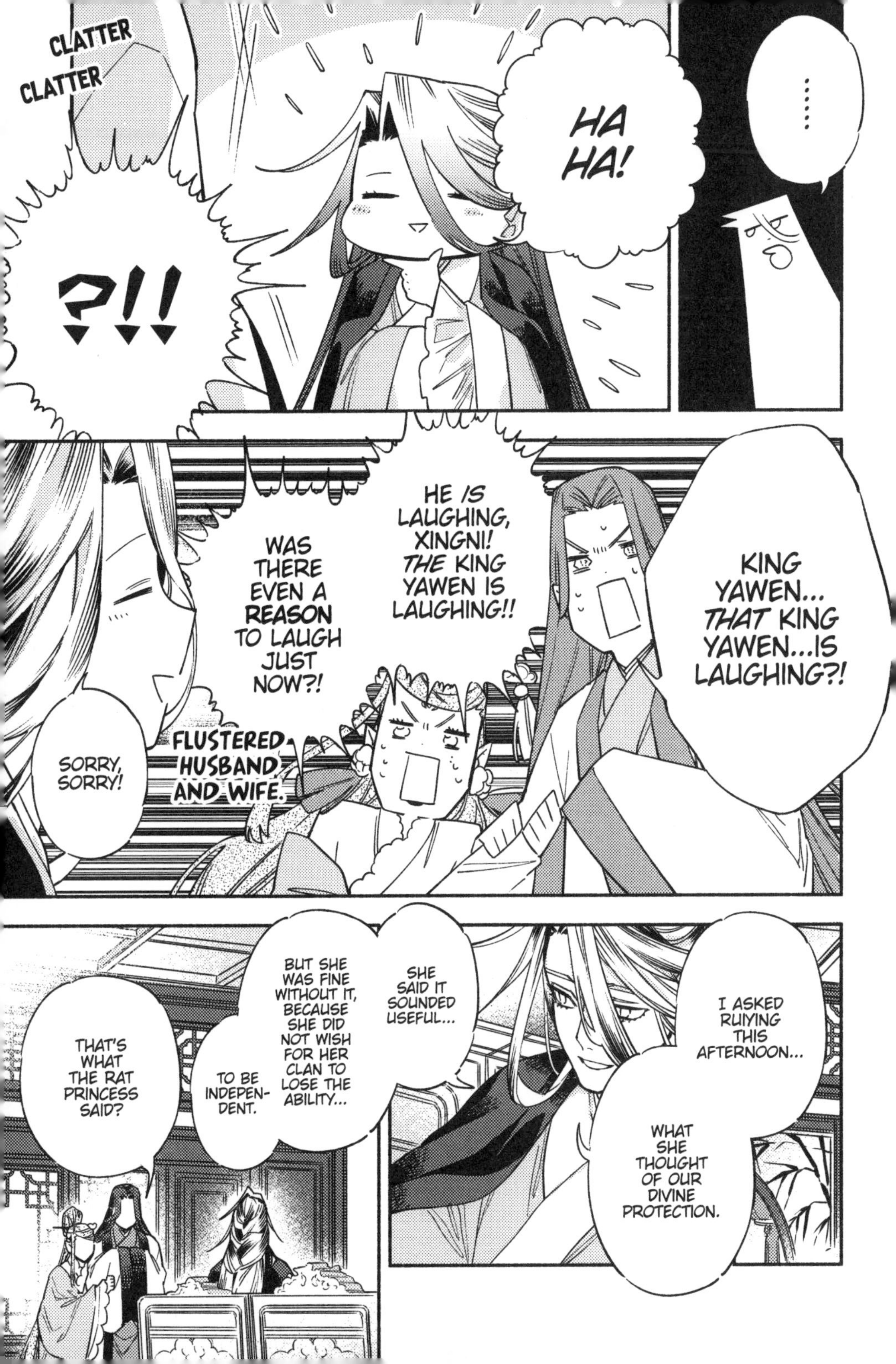
......
HA HA!
CLATTER CLATTER
?!!
KING YAWEN... *THAT* KING YAWEN...IS LAUGHING?!
HE *IS* LAUGHING, XINGNI! *THE* KING YAWEN IS LAUGHING!!
WAS THERE EVEN A **REASON** TO LAUGH JUST NOW?!
FLUSTERED HUSBAND AND WIFE.
SORRY, SORRY!
I ASKED RUIYING THIS AFTERNOON...
WHAT SHE THOUGHT OF OUR DIVINE PROTECTION.
SHE SAID IT SOUNDED USEFUL...
BUT SHE WAS FINE WITHOUT IT, BECAUSE SHE DID NOT WISH FOR HER CLAN TO LOSE THE ABILITY...
TO BE INDEPEN-DENT.
THAT'S WHAT THE RAT PRINCESS SAID?

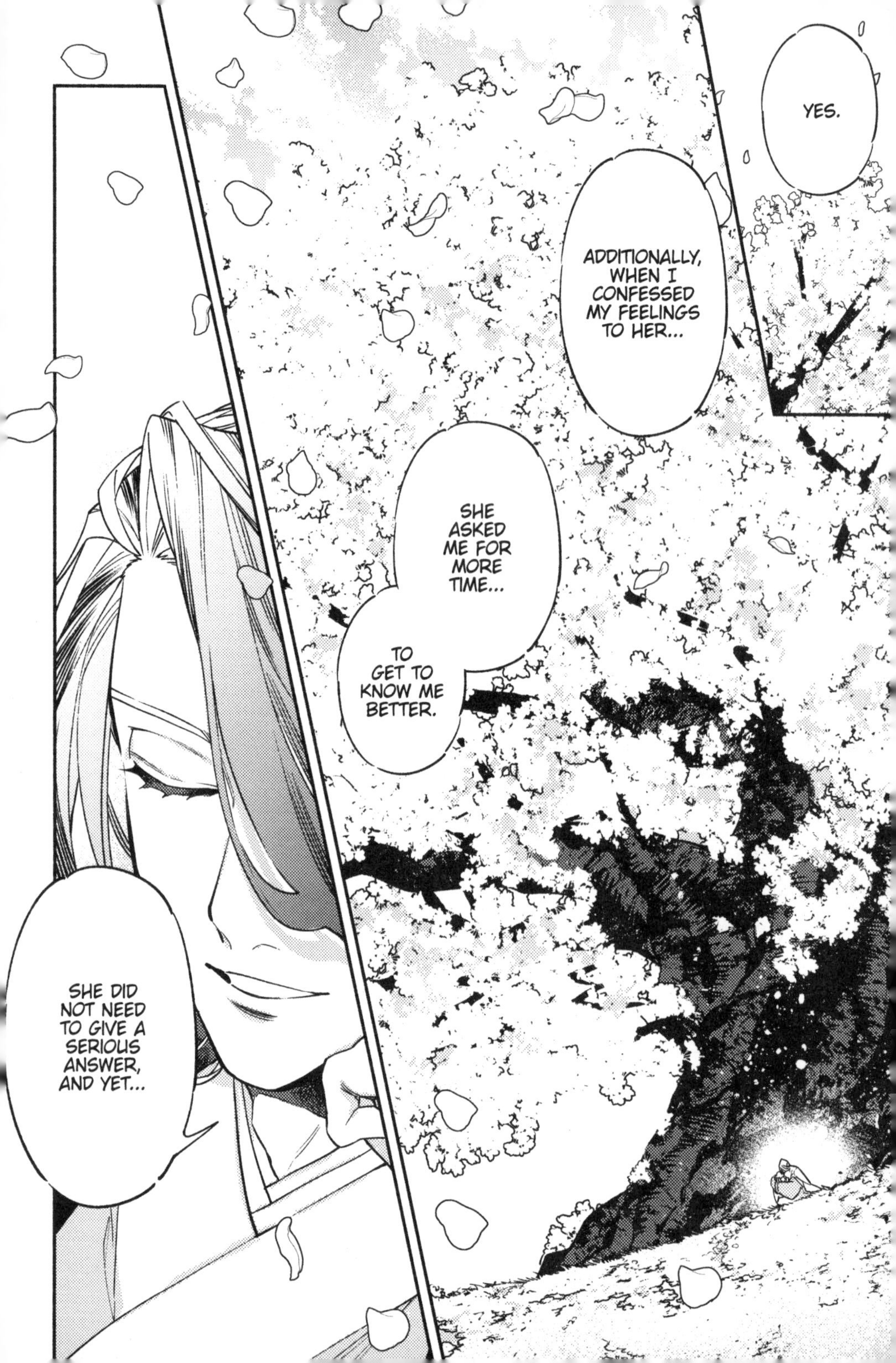
YES.
ADDITIONALLY, WHEN I CONFESSED MY FEELINGS TO HER...
SHE ASKED ME FOR MORE TIME...
TO GET TO KNOW ME BETTER.
SHE DID NOT NEED TO GIVE A SERIOUS ANSWER, AND YET...

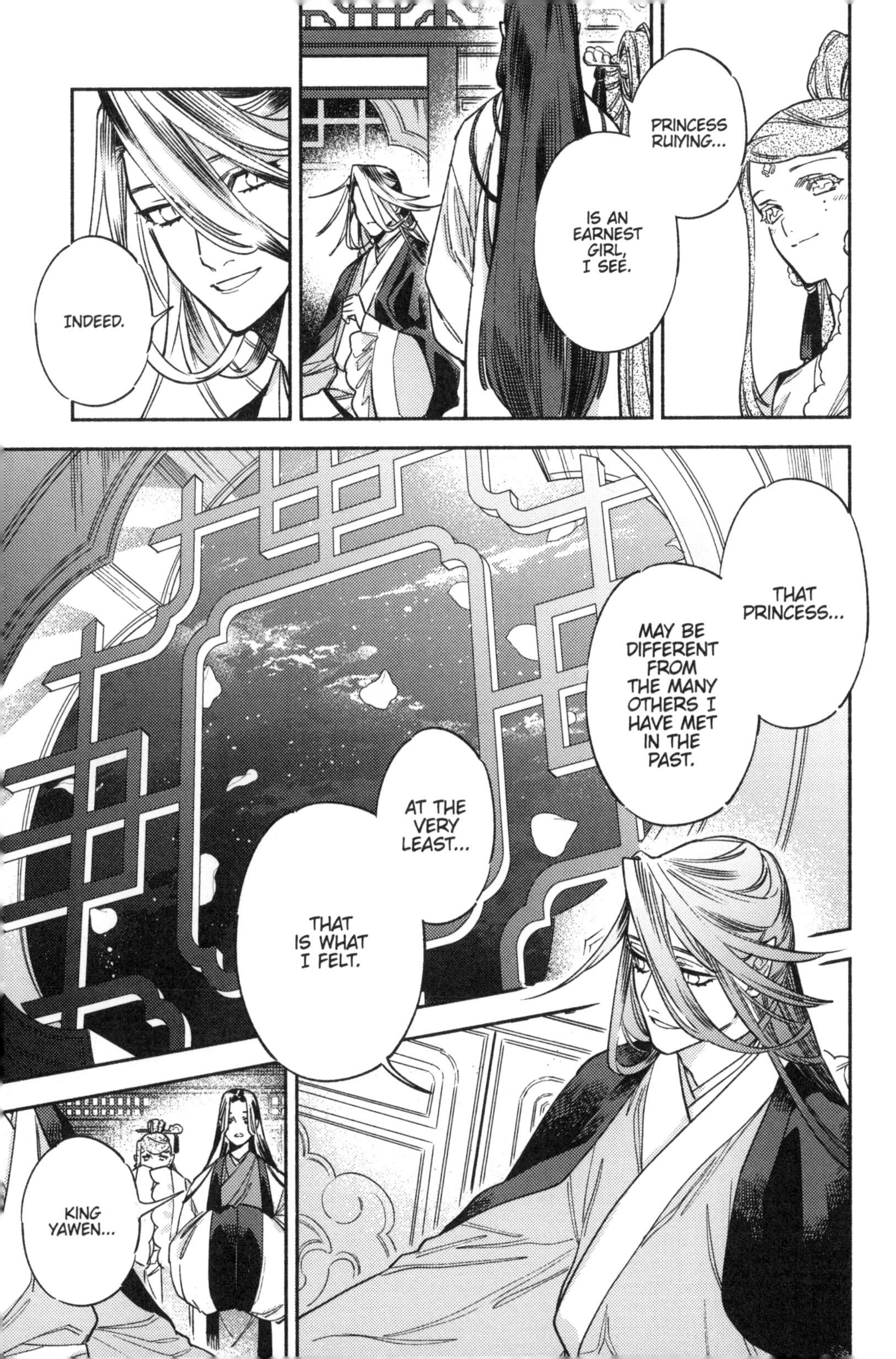
PRINCESS RUIYING...
IS AN EARNEST GIRL, I SEE.
INDEED.
THAT PRINCESS...
MAY BE DIFFERENT FROM THE MANY OTHERS I HAVE MET IN THE PAST.
AT THE VERY LEAST...
THAT IS WHAT I FELT.
KING YAWEN...

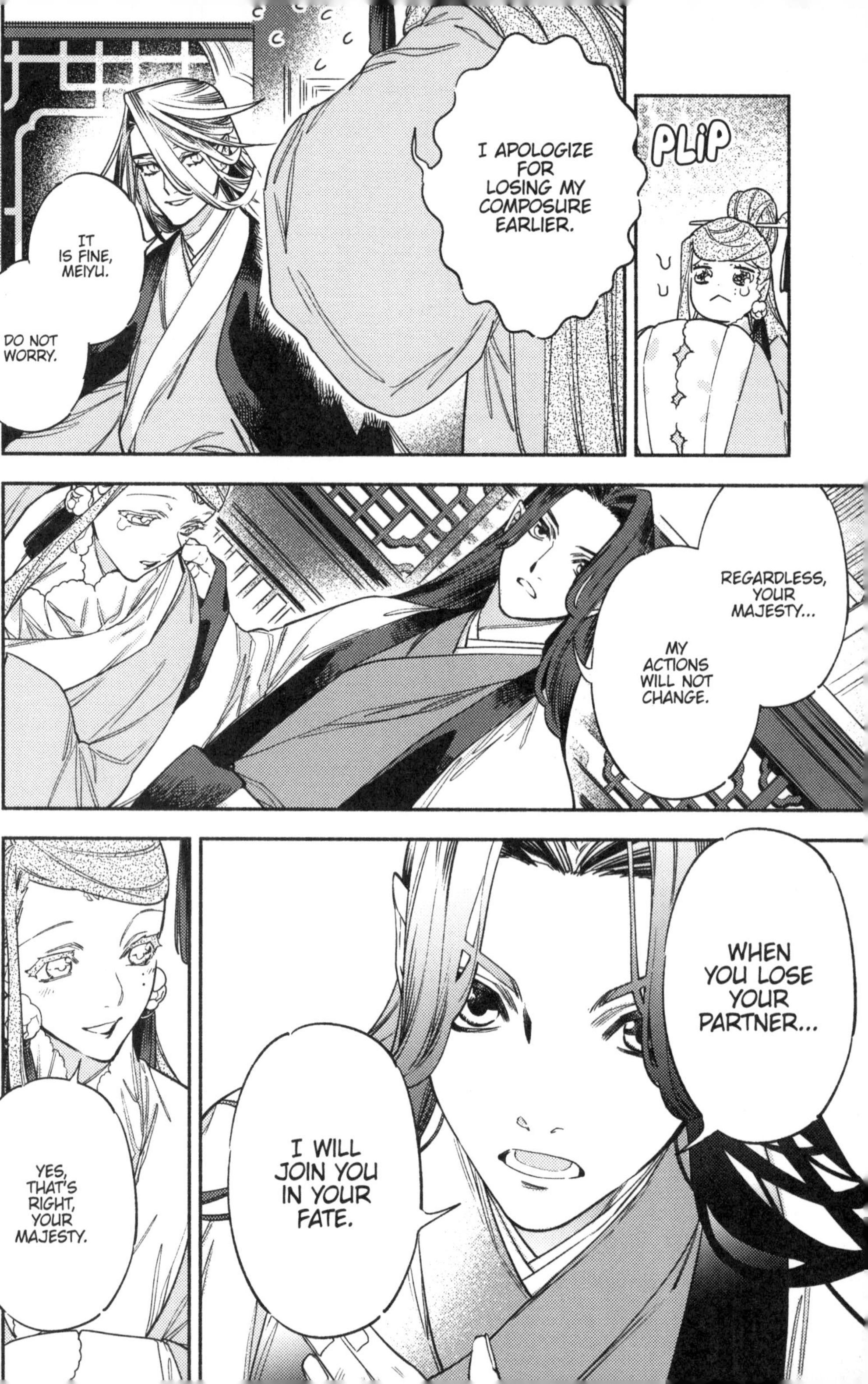
PLIP
I APOLOGIZE FOR LOSING MY COMPOSURE EARLIER.
IT IS FINE, MEIYU.
DO NOT WORRY.
REGARDLESS, YOUR MAJESTY...
MY ACTIONS WILL NOT CHANGE.
WHEN YOU LOSE YOUR PARTNER...
I WILL JOIN YOU IN YOUR FATE.
YES, THAT'S RIGHT, YOUR MAJESTY.

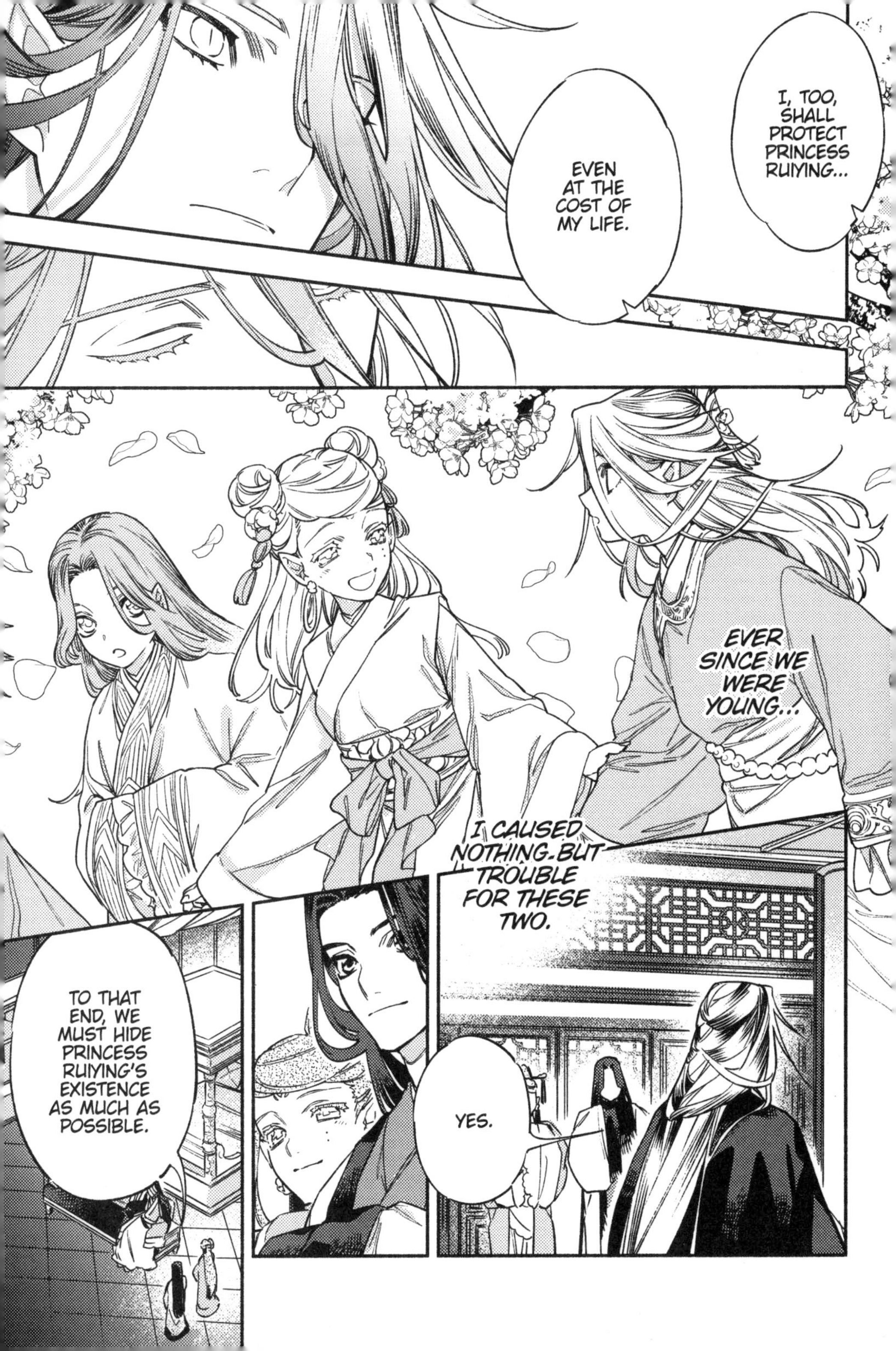
I, TOO, SHALL PROTECT PRINCESS RUIYING...
EVEN AT THE COST OF MY LIFE.
EVER SINCE WE WERE YOUNG...
I CAUSED NOTHING BUT TROUBLE FOR THESE TWO.
YES.
TO THAT END, WE MUST HIDE PRINCESS RUIYING'S EXISTENCE AS MUCH AS POSSIBLE.

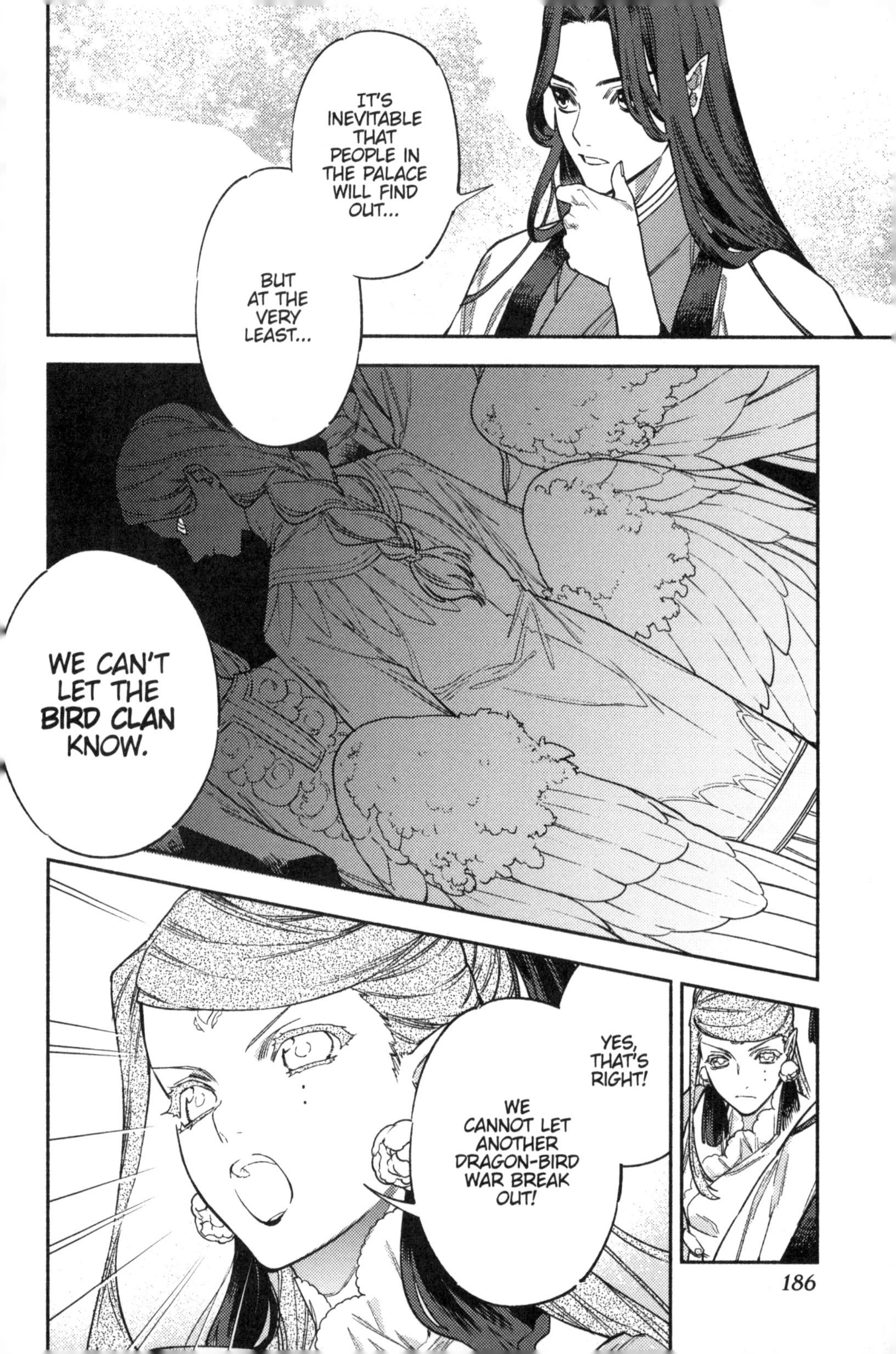
IT'S INEVITABLE THAT PEOPLE IN THE PALACE WILL FIND OUT...
BUT AT THE VERY LEAST...
WE CAN'T LET THE BIRD CLAN KNOW.
YES, THAT'S RIGHT!
WE CANNOT LET ANOTHER DRAGON-BIRD WAR BREAK OUT!

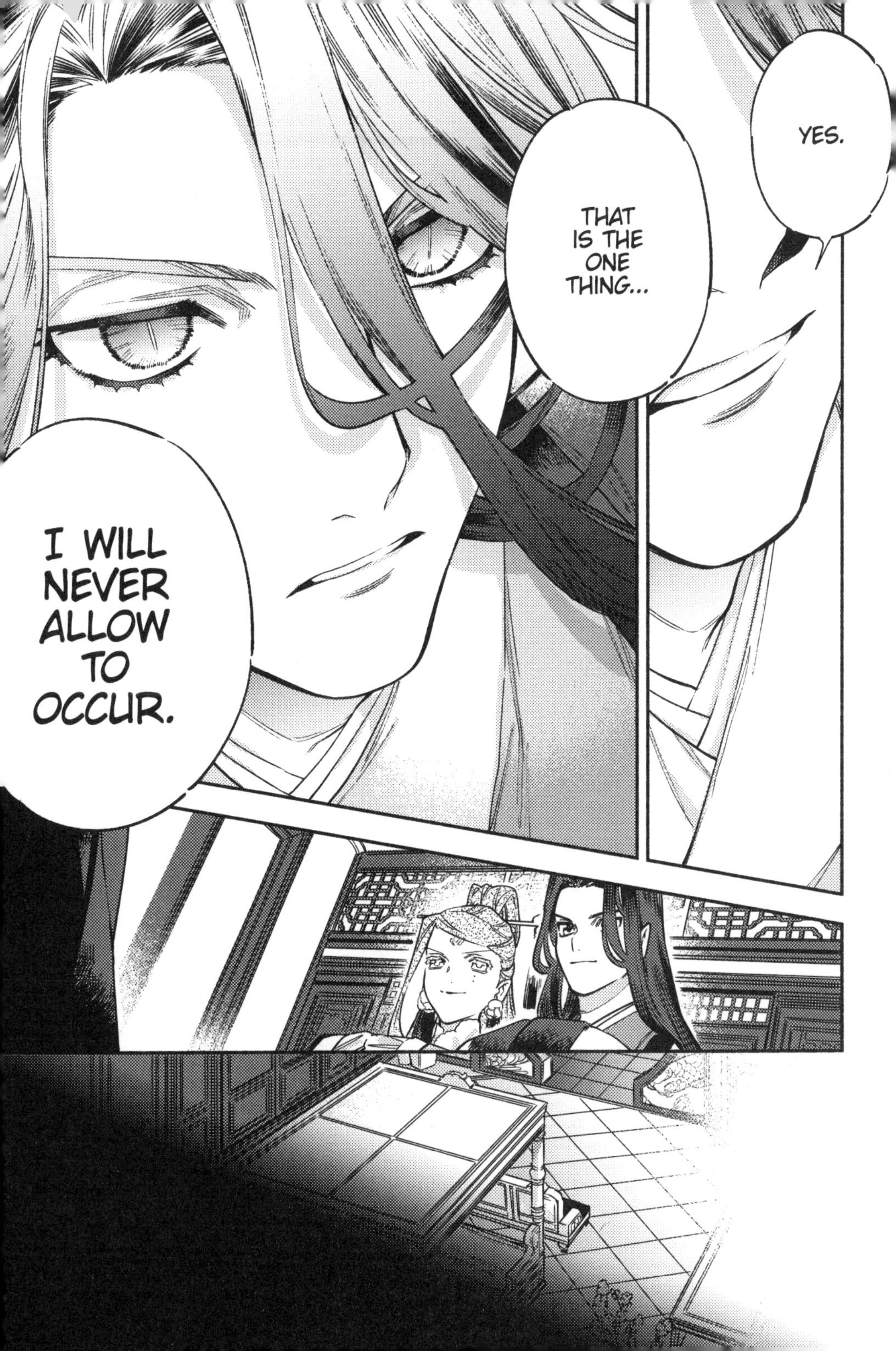
YES.
THAT IS THE ONE THING...
I WILL NEVER ALLOW TO OCCUR.

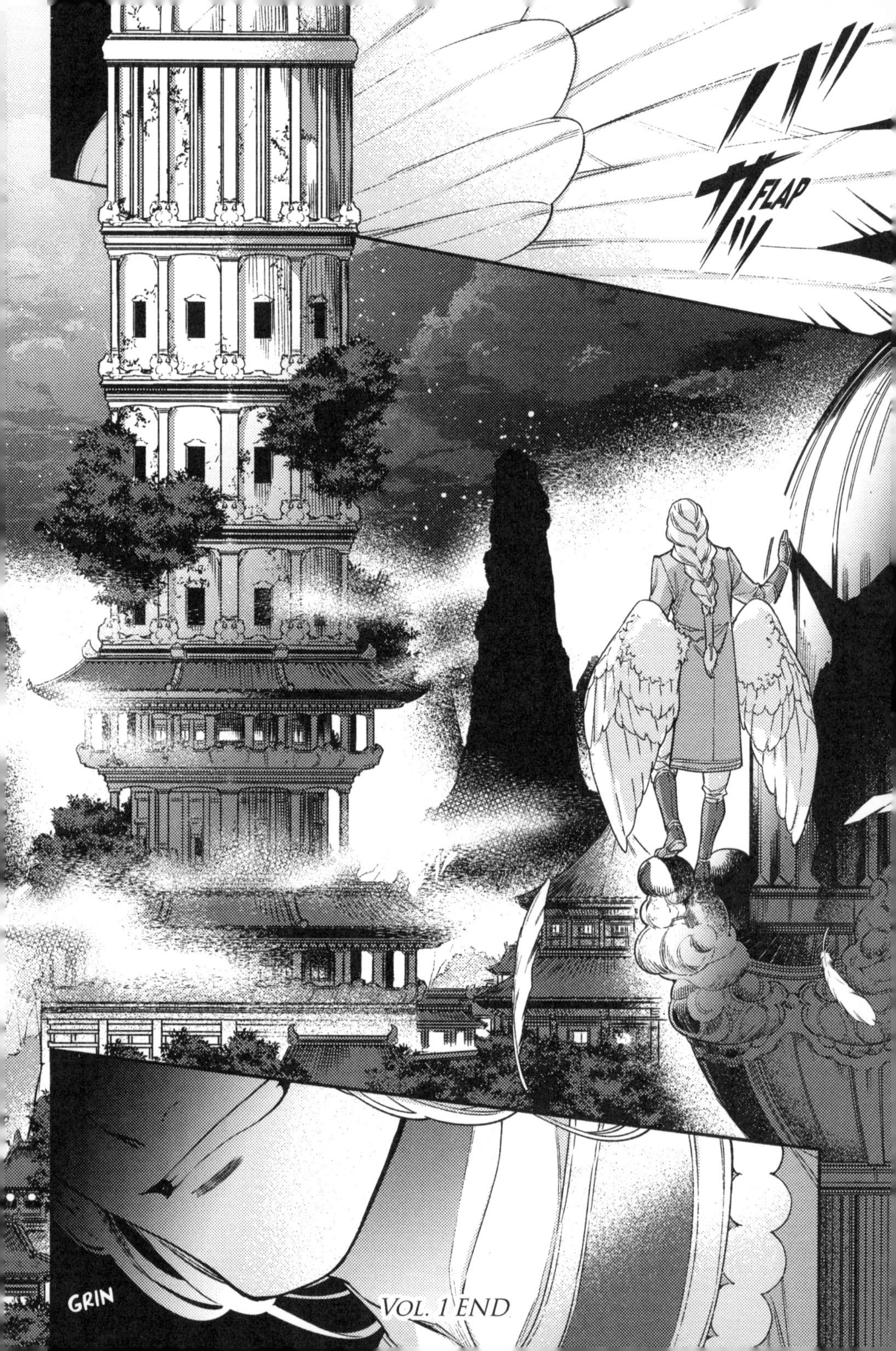
FLAP
GRIN
VOL. 1 END

Next Volume Preview

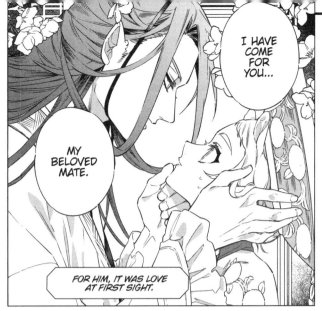

I HAVE COME FOR YOU...
MY BELOVED MATE.
FOR HIM, IT WAS LOVE AT FIRST SIGHT.
IN CONSUMING HIS REVERSE SCALE, THE RAT PRINCESS WAS ENTRUSTED WITH THE DRAGON KING'S LIFE.
THROUGH A PEACEFUL LIFE IN THE REAR PALACE, THE TWO GRADUALLY GROW CLOSER...
I AM GLAD TO HAVE YOU AS MY SOULMATE.
FLAP
BUT THE BIRD CLAN DRAWS NEAR!

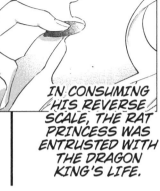

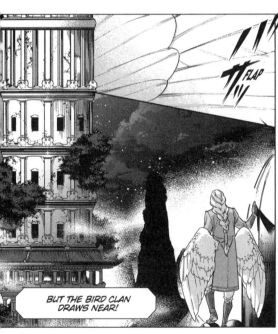

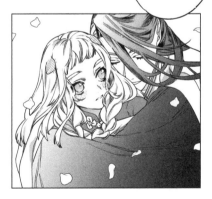

The Dragon King's Imperial Wrath

Falling in Love with the Bookish Princess of the Rat Clan

2

Coming Soon

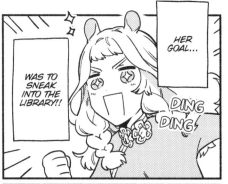

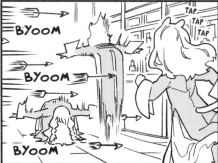

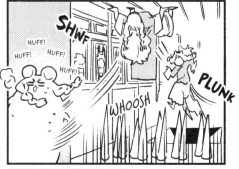

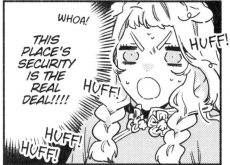

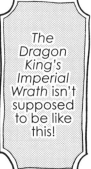

The Dragon King's Imperial Wrath isn't supposed to be like this!

INCREDIBLE AT GIVING STRONGER PEOPLE THE EVIL EYE.

WHICH TERRITORY DO YA COME FROM?!!

HER GOAL...
WAS TO SNEAK INTO THE LIBRARY!!
DING DING
TAP TAP TAP
BYOOM
BYOOM
BYOOM
SHWF
HUFF! HUFF! HUFF! HUFF!
PLUNK
WHOOSH
WHOA!
THIS PLACE'S SECURITY IS THE REAL DEAL!!!!
HUFF!
HUFF!
HUFF!
HUFF!

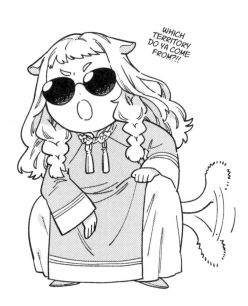

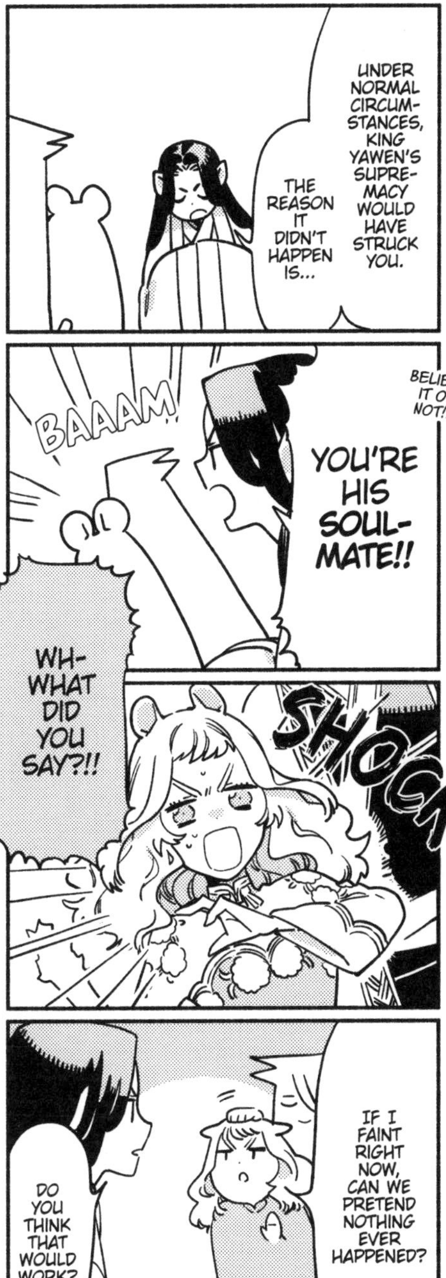
UNDER NORMAL CIRCUM-STANCES, KING YAWEN'S SUPREMACY WOULD HAVE STRUCK YOU.
THE REASON IT DIDN'T HAPPEN IS...
BAAAM
BELIEVE IT OR NOT!!!
YOU'RE HIS SOUL-MATE!!
SHOCK
WH-WHAT DID YOU SAY?!!
IF I FAINT RIGHT NOW, CAN WE PRETEND NOTHING EVER HAPPENED?
DO YOU THINK THAT WOULD WORK?

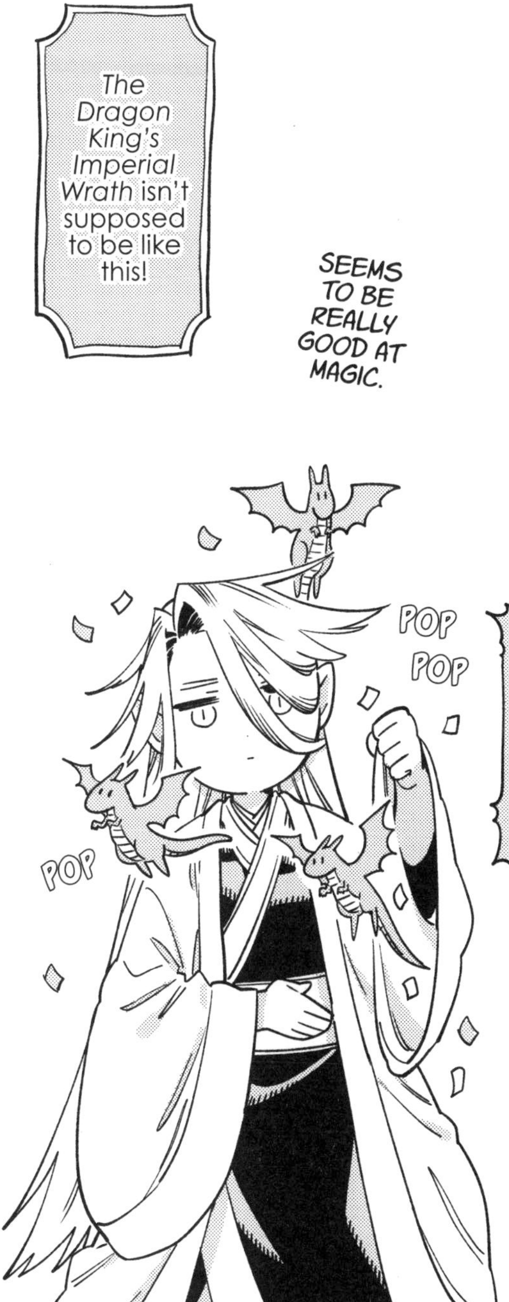
The Dragon King's Imperial Wrath isn't supposed to be like this!
SEEMS TO BE REALLY GOOD AT MAGIC.
POP
POP
POP

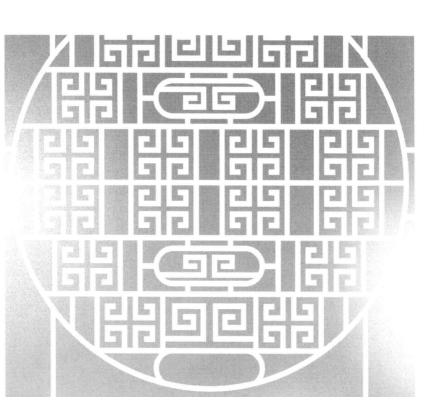

THE DRAGON KING'S IMPERIAL WRATH

FALLING IN LOVE
WITH THE BOOKISH PRINCESS
OF THE RAT CLAN

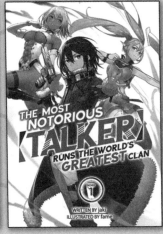

SEVEN SEAS ENTERTAINMENT PRESENTS

THE DRAGON KING'S IMPERIAL WRATH

FALLING IN LOVE WITH THE BOOKISH PRINCESS OF THE RAT CLAN

story by AKIRA SHIKIMI   art by AKIKO KAWANO   VOL. 1

TRANSLATION
Minna Lin

LETTERING
Danya Shevchenko

LOGO DESIGN
George Panella

COVER DESIGN
H. Qi

PROOFREADER
Kurestin Armada

SENIOR EDITOR
Shannon Fay

PRODUCTION DESIGNER
Eve Grandt

PRODUCTION MANAGER
Lissa Pattillo

PREPRESS TECHNICIAN
Melanie Ujimori
Jules Valera

EDITOR-IN-CHIEF
Julie Davis

ASSOCIATE PUBLISHER
Adam Arnold

PUBLISHER
Jason DeAngelis

Ryuoheikano Gekirinsama ～Honzukinezumihimedesuga, Nazeka Ryuono Saiaininarimashita～Vol. 1
© 2021 Akiko Kawano, Akira Shikimi. All rights reserved.
First published in Japan in 2021 by Ichijinsha Inc., Tokyo.
Publication rights for this English edition arranged through Kodansha Ltd., Tokyo.

Seven Seas press and purchase enquiries can be sent to Marketing Manager Lianne Sentar at press@gomanga.com. Information regarding the distribution and purchase of digital editions is available from Digital Manager CK Russell at digital@gomanga.com.

Seven Seas and the Seven Seas logo are trademarks of Seven Seas Entertainment. All rights reserved.

ISBN: 978-1-68579-703-4
Printed in Canada
First Printing: May 2023
10 9 8 7 6 5 4 3 2 1

READING DIRECTIONS

This book reads from *right to left*, Japanese style. If this is your first time reading manga, you start reading from the top right panel on each page and take it from there. If you get lost, just follow the numbered diagram here. It may seem backwards at first, but you'll get the hang of it! Have fun!!

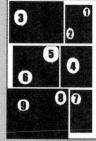

Follow us online: www.SevenSeasEntertainment.com